War Crimes and Trials

War Crimes and Trials

A Primary Source Guide

James Larry Taulbee

BLOOMSBURY ACADEMIC
NEW YORK • LONDON • OXFORD • NEW DELHI • SYDNEY

BLOOMSBURY ACADEMIC
Bloomsbury Publishing Inc
1385 Broadway, New York, NY 10018, USA
50 Bedford Square, London, WC1B 3DP, UK
29 Earlsfort Terrace, Dublin 2, Ireland

BLOOMSBURY, BLOOMSBURY ACADEMIC and the Diana logo
are trademarks of Bloomsbury Publishing Plc

First published in the United States of America by ABC-CLIO 2018
Paperback edition published by Bloomsbury Academic 2024

Copyright © Bloomsbury Publishing Inc, 2024

Cover design: Silverander Communications
Cover photo: German Nazi party leader Hermann Göring in the witness stand at the International
Military Tribunal at Nuremberg. Photograph taken by Ray d'Addario, 1946.
(LEONE-ullstein bild/Granger, NYC)

All rights reserved. No part of this publication may be reproduced or
transmitted in any form or by any means, electronic or mechanical,
including photocopying, recording, or any information storage or retrieval
system, without prior permission in writing from the publishers.

Bloomsbury Publishing Inc does not have any control over, or responsibility for,
any third-party websites referred to or in this book. All internet addresses given
in this book were correct at the time of going to press. The author and publisher
regret any inconvenience caused if addresses have changed or sites have
ceased to exist, but can accept no responsibility for any such changes.

Library of Congress Cataloging-in-Publication Data
Names: Taulbee, James Larry, 1942– author, compiler.
Title: War crimes and trials : a primary source guide / James Larry Taulbee.
Description: Santa Barbara, California : ABC-CLIO, 2018. |
Includes bibliographical references and index.
Identifiers: LCCN 2018017956 (print) | LCCN 2018019257 (ebook) |
ISBN 9781440838019 (eBook) | ISBN 9781440838002 (hardcopy : alk. paper)
Subjects: LCSH: War crime trials—History. | War crime
trials—History—Sources. | LCGFT: Trial and arbitral proceedings.
Classification: LCC KZ1168.5 (ebook) |
LCC KZ1168.5.T38 2018 (print) | DDC 341.6/9—dc23
LC record available at https://lccn.loc.gov/2018017956

ISBN: HB: 978-1-4408-3800-2
PB: 979-8-7651-3280-7
ePDF: 978-1-4408-3801-9
eBook: 979-8-2161-6320-6

To find out more about our authors and books visit www.bloomsbury.com
and sign up for our newsletters.

Contents

Preface   xv

Prelude: Purposes and Plan of the Book   xix

Abbreviations and Legal Terms   xxi

1 What Is a War Crime?   1
  War and Armed Conflict   1
  Law and War   2
  Pre–World War I: Evolution of Contemporary Law   2
   DOCUMENT: GENEVA CONVENTION   4
  The Lieber Code and the American Civil War   5
   DOCUMENT: THE LIEBER CODE (GENERAL ORDERS NO. 100)   5
  The 1899 and 1907 Hague Conventions   8
   DOCUMENT: LIST OF 1907 HAGUE CONVENTIONS   9
   DOCUMENT: 1907 HAGUE CONVENTION IV: ANNEX   10
   DOCUMENT: 1907 HAGUE CONVENTION X   12
  Naval Warfare   13
   DOCUMENT: MANUAL OF THE LAWS OF NAVAL WAR   13
  References   16

2 World War I: Leipzig   17
   DOCUMENT: REPORT, COMMISSION ON THE RESPONSIBILITY OF THE AUTHORS OF THE WAR AND ON ENFORCEMENT OF PENALTIES   17
   DOCUMENT: TREATY OF VERSAILLES   19
  Trials   20
  Trial Summaries #1: The *Dover Castle* and the *Llandovery Castle*   21
   DOCUMENT: *DOVER CASTLE*   21
   DOCUMENT: *LLANDOVERY CASTLE*   23
  Superior Orders as a Defense   26
  References   27

3 Between World War I and World War II   28
    The League of Nations   28
        DOCUMENT: COVENANT OF THE LEAGUE OF NATIONS   28
    Why Did the League Fail?   31
    The Kellogg-Briand Pact: Regulating the *jus ad bellum*   32
        DOCUMENT: KELLOGG-BRIAND PACT—TREATY BETWEEN THE UNITED STATES AND OTHER POWERS PROVIDING FOR THE RENUNCIATION OF WAR AS AN INSTRUMENT OF NATIONAL POLICY   32
    What Did Kellogg-Briand Accomplish?   33
    Extending the Scope of the *jus in bello*   33
    Chemical and Biological Weapons   33
        DOCUMENT: PROTOCOL FOR THE PROHIBITION OF THE USE IN WAR OF ASPHYXIATING GAS AND OF BACTERIOLOGICAL METHODS OF WARFARE   34
    Prisoners of War (POWs)   35
        DOCUMENT: CONVENTION OF JULY 27, 1929, RELATIVE TO THE TREATMENT OF PRISONERS OF WAR   35
    References   38

4 World War II   39
    What Caused World War II?   39
    Germany   39
    War Crimes   40
    Nazi Party Organizations   41
    Trials   42
    References   42

5 Anton Dostler Case   44
        DOCUMENT: THE FÜHRERBEFEHL OF 18 OCTOBER, 1942   44
    Trial Summary #2: The *Dostler* Case   46
        DOCUMENT: THE ANTON DOSTLER CASE   47
    The Importance of the Ruling on Jurisdiction   51
    Reprisals   52
    Superior Orders as a Defense   53
    Reference   53

6 German Concentration and Extermination Camps   54
    The "Final Solution"   56
    References   57

7 Zyklon B Trial   58
    Fritz Haber   58
    What Is Zyklon B?   59
    Fritz Haber and the Nazis   59

Preparing for the "Final Solution"   60
Trial Summary #3: The Zyklon B Case   61
>   DOCUMENT: THE ZYKLON B CASE   62
Setting the Stage for the Defense   64
Some Additional Notes for Future Reference   65
References   67

8 Belsen Trial   68
Charges   70
Trial Summary #4: Belsen Trial   71
>   DOCUMENT: BELSEN TRIAL: JOSEF KRAMER AND 44 OTHERS   71
Some Observations about the Testimony   76
A Note on Camp Organization   76
References   77

9 Buchenwald Trial   78
Defendants   79
Trial Summary #5: Buchenwald Trial   80
>   DOCUMENT: BUCHENWALD TRIAL (*UNITED STATES OF AMERICA V. JOSIAS PRINCE ZU WALDECK ET AL.*)   80
Some Additional Findings of the Court   83
References   84

10 The Malmedy Massacre Trial   85
Malmedy   85
Trial Summary #6: Malmedy Massacre   86
>   DOCUMENT: MALMEDY MASSACRE (*UNITED STATES V. VALENTIN BERSIN, ET AL.*)   86
The Rest of the Story   90
References   91

11 The Nuremberg Trial   92
>   DOCUMENT: INTERNATIONAL CONFERENCE ON MILITARY TRIALS (LONDON CHARTER)   92
A Note on the Tokyo Trials   94
Nuremberg: Jurisdiction and Procedure   94
Nuremberg   95
Hermann Göring   96
Rudolf Höss (Hoess)   97
Trial Summary #7: Trial of the Major War Criminals   97
Was the Nuremberg Trial an Exercise in Victor's Justice?   101
Significance   102
References   103

Contents

12 Allied Control Council Law No. 10 104
    DOCUMENT: ALLIED CONTROL COUNCIL LAW NO. 10 (CCL NO. 10)—
    PUNISHMENT OF PERSONS GUILTY OF WAR CRIMES, CRIMES
    AGAINST PEACE AND AGAINST HUMANITY 105
  References 108

13 The Medical Case (Doctors' Trial): *United States v. Karl Brandt, et al.* 109
  Trial Summary #8: The Medical Case 111
    DOCUMENT: *UNITED STATES V. KARL BRANDT, ET AL.* 111
  Why? 113
  References 114

14 Einsatzgruppen Case: *United States of America v. Otto Ohlendorf, et al.* 115
  Otto Ohlendorf 116
  Trial Summary #9: Einsatzgruppen Case 116
    DOCUMENT: *UNITED STATES V. OTTO OHLENDORF, ET AL.* 117
  Discussion 120
  A Curious Defense 120
  References 121

15 Tokyo War Crimes Trial 122
  International Military Tribunal for the Far East 122
    DOCUMENT: CHARTER OF THE INTERNATIONAL MILITARY
    TRIBUNAL FOR THE FAR EAST 122
  Alliance with Germany 123
  The War in the Pacific 124
  Emperor Hirohito 125
  General Hideki Tōjō 127
  Composition of the Court 127
  Trial Summary #10: Trial of Major Japanese War Criminals 127
    DOCUMENT: TRIAL OF MAJOR JAPANESE WAR CRIMINALS 128
  The Tokyo Trials and Victor's Justice 132
  References 133

16 General Tomoyuki Yamashita 134
  The *Yamashita* Case: Command Responsibility 134
  Trial Summary #11: Trial of General Tomoyuki Yamashita 135
    DOCUMENT: *IN RE YAMASHITA* 327 U.S. 1 (1946) 135
  The Rest of the Story 138
  References 140

17 Khabarovsk War Crime Trial 141
  Japanese Bacteriological Weapons Program 141
  Shirō Ishii and Unit 731 142

General Otozō Yamada   143
Trial Summary #12: General Otozō Yamada and Eleven Others   143
  DOCUMENT: GENERAL OTOZŌ YAMADA AND ELEVEN OTHERS   144
Testimony   144
War Crimes and the Politics of Self-Interest   147
References   147

18 The Eichmann Trial   148
The Eichmann Saga   149
The Wannsee Conference   151
Implementing the "Final Solution"   152
Trial Summary #13: Karl Adolf Eichmann   152
  DOCUMENT: *THE ATTORNEY GENERAL V. ADOLF EICHMANN*   152
Testimony   153
Some Questions without Good Answers   157
References   159

19 My Lai Massacre: Vietnam War   160
Conscription (The Draft)   160
The Defendant   161
Army Operations in Vietnam   161
The My Lai Operation   162
The Investigation   162
The Uniform Code of Military Justice   163
  DOCUMENT: THE UNIFORM CODE OF MILITARY JUSTICE   163
Trial Summary #14: *United States v. Calley*   165
  DOCUMENT: *UNITED STATES V. WILLIAM LAWS CALLEY JR.*   165
Aftermath   170
Changes   171
References   172

20 Updating the Rules of War after World War II   173
What Changed?   173
The United Nations Charter   173
  DOCUMENT: THE CHARTER OF THE UNITED NATIONS   174
The Geneva Conventions   176
  DOCUMENT: THE 1949 GENEVA CONVENTIONS   177
Geneva Convention for the Amelioration of the Conditions of the Wounded and Sick in Armed Forces in the Field of August 12, 1949 (Geneva I)   177
Geneva Convention for the Amelioration of the Conditions of Wounded, Sick, and Shipwrecked Members of Armed Forces at Sea of August 12, 1949 (Geneva II)   178
Geneva Convention Relative to the Treatment of Prisoners of War of August 12, 1949 (Geneva III)   179

Geneva Convention for the Protection of Civilian Persons in Time of War of August 12, 1949 (Geneva IV) 181
The Common Articles 182
The Additional Protocols 183
  DOCUMENT: GENEVA PROTOCOL ADDITIONAL I 184
  DOCUMENT: GENEVA PROTOCOL ADDITIONAL II 187
  DOCUMENT: PROTOCOL ADDITIONAL III (2005) 191
Grave Breaches and War Crimes 193
Moving from the Law on the Books to Making the Law Work in Action 193
References 194

21 The Genocide Convention 195
The Genocide Convention: The Politics of Definition 195
  DOCUMENT: CONVENTION ON THE PREVENTION AND PUNISHMENT OF THE CRIME OF GENOCIDE 196
Innovations and Problems 199
References 200

22 The International Criminal Tribunal for the Former Yugoslavia 201
Yugoslavia 201
Mandate 204
  DOCUMENT: THE STATUTE OF THE INTERNATIONAL TRIBUNAL FOR THE PROSECUTION OF THE PERSONS RESPONSIBLE FOR SERIOUS VIOLATIONS OF INTERNATIONAL HUMANITARIAN LAW COMMITTED IN THE TERRITORY OF THE FORMER YUGOSLAVIA SINCE 1991 204
Structure 206
The Appeals Chamber 207
Office of the Prosecutor and the Registry 208
Mechanism for International Tribunals 208
Guilty Pleas 209
Problems 209
References 211

23 Duško Tadić Trial 212
Introduction: The Bosnian Wars 212
Duško Tadić 213
International Tribunal for the Prosecution of Persons Responsible for Serious Violations of International Humanitarian Law Committed in the Territory of the Former Yugoslavia since 1991 214
  DOCUMENT: RULES OF PROCEDURE AND EVIDENCE 214
What Is the Purpose of a Trial? 217
Trial Summary #15: *Prosecutor v. Duško Tadić* (aka "Dule") 218
DOCUMENT: Opening Statement by Presiding Judge Gabrielle Kirk McDonald 218

Testimony   219
Why Tadić?   225
References   226

24   Slobodan Milošević   227
The Dayton Agreement   228
Kosovo and "The Turks"   229
Indictment and Transfer   231
Trial Summary #16: *Prosecutor v. Slobodan Milošević*   231
Testimony   232
    DOCUMENT: EVIDENCE THAT THE YUGOSLAV MILITARY HAD INVESTIGATED AND PROSECUTED WAR CRIMES   233
A Mixed Legacy   238
References   239

25   Radovan Karadžić   240
The Tribulations of Trials   242
Trial Summary #17: *Prosecutor v. Radovan Karadžić*   242
    DOCUMENT: PROSECUTOR V. RADOVAN KARADŽIĆ   243
Testimony   244
Second Witness   246
Timely Justice and the Requirement of "Fair" Trials   249
The Appeals Process   250
    DOCUMENT: RADOVAN KARADŽIĆ'S APPEAL BRIEF   251
References   253

26   Trial of Radislav Krstić   254
Bosnian Serb Army   254
Radislav Krstić   254
Srebrenica   255
Trial Summary #18: *Prosecutor v. Radislav Krstić*   256
    DOCUMENT: PROSECUTOR V. RADISLAV KRSTIĆ   256
Testimony   257
The Appeal   260
References   262

27   Croatia, Operation Storm, and Ante Gotovina   263
Croatia   263
    DOCUMENT: OPERATION STORM: CROATIA'S TRIUMPH, SERBIA'S GRIEF   263
Balkan Transitional Justice   264
Croatia and the ICTY   264
Ante Gotovina, Ivan Čermak, and Mladen Markač   266
Trial Summary #19: Appeal of Ante Gotovina and Mladen Markač   268
    DOCUMENT: SUMMARY OF APPEALS JUDGMENT   269
Issues for the Future   272

Politics and the Law 273
References 273

28 Rwanda: The Genocide 274
Setting the Stage: The Colonial Legacy 274
Prelude to Genocide 276
Refugees and the Rwandan Patriotic Front 276
The Situation in Rwanda 277
   DOCUMENT: HUTU TEN COMMANDMENTS 278
Preparation 279
The Spark 280
The Genocide Begins 281
The RPF Advance 282
The Whims of International Response 283
The International Criminal Tribunal for Rwanda 283
References 284

29 The International Criminal Tribunal for Rwanda: Jean-Paul Akayesu 285
The Politics of Places 286
Establishing Genocide 287
   DOCUMENT: ANALYSIS FRAMEWORK TO DETERMINE IF GENOCIDE HAS OCCURRED 288
Trial Summary #20: *Prosecutor v. Jean-Paul Akayesu* 290
   DOCUMENT: *PROSECUTOR V. JEAN-PAUL AKAYESU* 290
Testimony 290
Notable Firsts 294
Defending Accusations of Genocide 294
Decision 295
References 295

30 *Prosecutor v. Théoneste Bagosora, et al.* (The Military Trial 1) 296
Théoneste Bagosora 296
Gratien Kabiligi 297
Aloys Ntabakuze 297
Anatole Nsengiyumva 298
Trial Summary #21: *Prosecutor v. Théoneste Bagosora, Gratien Kabiligi, Aloys Ntabakuze, and Anatole Nsengiyumva* 298
   DOCUMENT: ICTR-98-41-T 298
Testimony 299
The Problem of Punishment 302
Nature of Sentences 304
References 304

31 *Prosecutor v. Jean-Bosco Barayagwiza, Ferdinand Nahimana, and Hassan Ngeze* 305
The Media Trial   305
Jean-Bosco Barayagwiza   307
A Lesson in Legal Procedure   307
Ferdinand Nahimana   308
Hassan Ngeze   309
Trial Summary #22: *Prosecutor v. Jean-Bosco Barayagwiza, Ferdinand Nahimana, and Hassan Ngeze*   309
   DOCUMENT: "JUDGEMENT AND SENTENCE," DECEMBER 3, 2003 (PARAS. 392–398; 408–409)   309
Testimony   310
The Power of the Media in a Closed Environment   312
A Final Note on the ICTR   313
References   314

32 The Special Court for Sierra Leone: The Charles Taylor Trial   315
Background: Liberia and Sierra Leone   315
Liberia   315
Sierra Leone and Liberia   316
   DOCUMENT: STATUTE OF THE SPECIAL COURT FOR SIERRA LEONE   317
The Statute   320
Charles Taylor Indictment   321
Trial Summary #23: *Prosecutor v. Charles Ghankay Taylor*   321
   DOCUMENT: *PROSECUTOR V. CHARLES GHANKAY TAYLOR*   321
Testimony   322
Appeal   325
The Residual Special Court   326
References   326

33 The International Criminal Court   328
Politics and Promise   328
   DOCUMENT: ROME STATUTE OF THE INTERNATIONAL CRIMINAL COURT   330
A Note on Other Courts   332
Structure and Jurisdiction   332
How Do Cases Come to the Court?   334
Article 16: Deferral of Investigation and Prosecution   334
Article 9: Elements of Crimes   335
   DOCUMENT: ELEMENTS OF CRIMES: CRIMES AGAINST HUMANITY   335
Article 7: Crimes against Humanity   336
The United States and the ICC   338
Other Crises: The Politics of Prosecution   340

Deferred Issue: The Crime of Aggression   340
  DOCUMENT: JURISDICTION OVER THE CRIME OF AGGRESSION   341
Activation   344
  DOCUMENT: ELEMENTS OF CRIMES: AGGRESSION   345
References   346

34 *Prosecutor v. Thomas Lubanga Dyilo*   347
Democratic Republic of the Congo   347
Referral and Arrest   348
Warrant of Arrest   349
Warrant for Thomas Lubanga Dyilo   350
  DOCUMENT: WARRANT OF ARREST, SITUATION IN THE DEMOCRATIC REPUBLIC OF THE CONGO IN THE CASE OF THE *PROSECUTOR V. THOMAS LUBANGA DYILO*   350
Legal Issues Prior to the Trial   352
The First Stay of Trial Proceedings   353
The Second Stay of Trial Proceedings   354
Trial Summary #24: *Prosecutor v. Thomas Lubanga Dyilo*   355
  DOCUMENT: XI. INDIVIDUAL CRIMINAL RESPONSIBILITY OF THOMAS LUBANGA (ARTICLE 25(3)(A) OF THE STATUTE   355
Testimony   356
Controversy   358
References   359

35 *Prosecutor v. Jean-Pierre Bemba Gombo*   360
Bemba and the First Congo War (1996)   360
The Second Congo War   360
Movement toward Peace   361
Bemba and the 2006 Presidential Election   362
Indictment and Arrest   362
Role of the LAC   363
The Plot to Prevent the Trial   364
Trial Summary #25: *Prosecutor v. Jean-Pierre Bemba Gombo*   364
  DOCUMENT: DEFINITION OF COMMAND RESPONSIBILITY   364
A Crime Not Punished   368
Appeals Chamber Decision   368
References   371

Index   373

Preface

Prepare yourself to enter a very different reality. The rules regulating armed conflict (war) turn one of the fundamental rules of domestic society on its head. The rules of war define who can kill and who can be killed. Armed conflict often results in incidents that horrify most people. The rules of war attempt to avoid atrocities by incorporating pragmatic humanitarian considerations into a brutal endeavor. Legal decisions involving war and other armed conflicts may perplex readers because the results may not always correspond to a common-sense idea of "justice." The cases in this book deal with the darkest side of combat.

Writing this book presented many challenges. First and most difficult, all war crime trials take place in a specific historical context. During the time frame covered in this book, the attitudes toward war and acceptable tactics changed dramatically. Because trials reflect the legal standards and attitudes toward war and other uses of armed force during a specific period, the task required making many decisions about what the reader needed to know about the context in which the trial occurred. The Nazi era presented a special challenge. Many people know the popular names of organizations such as the Gestapo without understanding their mission or where they fit into the complex hierarchy of Nazi Party organization. For this reason, a table in chapter 4 summarizes the important organizations and their relationship to one another.

Second, the book could have been written using just World War II. The trials under Allied Control Council #10 alone would have provided twelve interesting trials. Equally, it could have been done with just the International Criminal Tribunals for the former Yugoslavia and Rwanda. The cases chosen illustrate many different situations and legal principles. In this sense, the book covers the evolution of new legal principles in very broad strokes.

Third, in analyzing trials for war crimes, inevitably the question of "victor's justice" is raised. Very simply defined, victor's justice means the winner of a war can try anyone it wishes for real or imagined offenses. Yet, similar acts by its own military will go unpunished. Complaints of victor's justice will always be part of international war crime trials. The issue is, however, the quality of the procedures that produce the verdicts. The Nuremberg Trial(s) did not adhere strictly to the American ideal standard for a "fair" trial. Yet, the trials did not result in unfair verdicts. Short as they were, the accused had their days in court to tell their stories and defend their actions. No one can challenge the verdicts as not supported by the evidence. Some of the accused were acquitted. There is a very great difference between the Nuremberg and Tokyo trials and what became known as "show" trials where the defendant has already been deemed guilty and the only purpose of the trial is a public confession by the accused.

Accusations of victor's justice assume many different guises. The Khabarovsk trial actually raised the issue of victor's justice in another way—the question of who was prosecuted and who was not prosecuted. This question lurks in the wings of every set of trials. In his book *I Owe Russia $1200* (1963), Bob Hope recounts a joke he told about the 1957 launch of Sputnik. The Soviet accomplishment had sent shockwaves throughout the United States and Western Europe. Most people in the West believed that the Soviet Union had lagged far behind the United States and Europe in scientific and technological capabilities. Yet the Soviets had solved the problem of placing a satellite in orbit, while Western scientists still struggled with the challenge. To reduce the joke to the punchline, Hope observed that the launch meant that the German "war criminal" scientists the Soviet Union had captured were more accomplished than the German "war criminal" scientists that the United States had captured. That "joke" hit very close to home and was not well received. Chapter 17 discusses the issue with respect to chemical and bacteriological weapons. Ordinarily the Soviet Union did not publish or otherwise publicize the results of their war crime trials unless they had propaganda value in terms of raising some difficult questions for the Western powers, and in particular, the United States. The Soviet trial raised serious questions about why the United States did not prosecute the Japanese biological scientists they had captured.

Accusations of victor's justice come into play in other ways as well. As I finished the final chapter of this book, two dramatic events occurred in The Hague (Netherlands). Ratko Mladić, a general in the Bosnian Serb Army, and Slobodan Praljak, a general in the Croatian Army, were defendants before the International Criminal Tribunal for the former Yugoslavia (ICTY) at The Hague. In their countries, popular opinion regarded both as national heroes, not as war criminals. In late November 2017, after a five-year trial, an ICTY Trial Chamber found Mladić, guilty on eleven counts of the indictment and sentenced him to life imprisonment for his role in the July 1995 genocide committed at Srebrenica in Bosnia. In early December, Praljak committed suicide by drinking poison after the Appeals Chamber upheld the guilty verdict and confirmed the twenty-year sentence for war crimes and crimes against humanity he received from the Trial Chamber. Serbs and Croats were totally outraged while the Bosnians felt that justice, although considerably delayed, had finally been done. Welcome to the contemporary world of increasing tribalism.

Fourth, we live in a time when a large number of internal conflicts have raised the question of why should one side follow the rules, when the other side clearly does not. Does following the rules expose soldiers to excessive and unnecessary risk? The short answer is not necessarily. Becoming a soldier does not mean signing a suicide pact. The rules of armed conflict are dependent upon context and the standard of "reasonableness." Phrases such as "incidental civilian damage" and "as much as possible" take into account the "fog" of war, the chaos, confusion, and uncertainty that is inherent in violent engagements. *Military necessity*, although not defined in any international convention, still forms an integral part of the laws and customs of war. As such, it also is governed by reasonableness in context and is not a license to violate the rule as a matter of convenience.

Moreover, there are pragmatic reasons to follow the rules. For many in today's world, the unwillingness and lack of political will to enforce the rules limiting the damage to population and infrastructures will be a long-lasting burden. Conflicts end, but the deep scars left by the conflicts will endure. Rebuilding infrastructure may drag on because of lack of available resources, but repairing the damage wreaked on people may take generations. Once fractured, re-establishing the bonds essential for a peaceful, functioning society may be problematic at best considering the role that the narrow politics of ethnicity and religion has played in fueling and sustaining the struggles.

Finally, I owe debts to many people. The always helpful staff of Emory University libraries deserves great thanks for locating a number of hard to find materials quickly. My editors at ABC-CLIO have been understanding and supportive. My wife Diane, patiently, and with good humor, read and copyedited much of the manuscript while also providing encouragement and support for the project. Those anonymous folks tasked with copyediting duties deserve the highest praise. Their attention to detail also caught many things that needed clarification and amendment. Needless to say, any errors of commission or omission are mine.

J.L.T.
Canton, GA
January 2018

Prelude: Purposes and Plan of the Book

This book presents and analyzes twenty-five trials for war crimes. Narrowing the number to only twenty-five proved a daunting task. The trials selected illustrate what the author considers the most important ideas that underlie the *laws and customs of war* that have developed over the last 150 years. Mark the phrase, the *laws and customs of war* because it will occur over and over again in discussions of the trials.

Note that some prominent trials such as the leadership of the Khmer Rouge government in Cambodia have not been included because they do not involve war crimes. Those crimes occurred during a period when Cambodia (1974–1979) was not at war. For ideological reasons, the Cambodian government systematically murdered its own citizens during a time of peace. In contrast, the Armenian genocide (Turkey, 1915–1918) took place as part of a deliberate strategy by the Turkish government during a war (World War I). Some other trials of interest that might have been included in this book, such as those in Guatemala (2016) that had just begun during the preparation and writing of this book, did not have verdicts or other important materials available for analysis.

Abbreviations and Legal Terms

AFDL	Alliance des Forces Démocratiques pour la Libération du Congo-Zaïre (Alliance of Democratic Forces for the Liberation of Congo-Zaire)
ALiR	Armée de Libération du Rwanda
CAAF	Court of Appeals for the Armed Forces
CAR	Central African Republic
CBW	chemical and bacteriological weapons
CCL 10	Allied Control Council Law Number 10
CDR	Coalition pour la Défense de la République
DRC	Democratic Republic of the Congo
ECOWAS	Economic Community of West African States
HVO	Hrvatsko vijeće obrane (Croatian Council of Defense)
ICC	International Criminal Court
ICL	International Criminal Law
ICTR	International Criminal Tribunal for Rwanda
ICTY	International Criminal Tribunal for the Former Yugoslavia
IHL	International Humanitarian Law
ILC	International Law Commission
IMT	International Military Tribunal (Nuremberg)
IMTFE	International Military Tribunal for the Far East (Tokyo)
JNA	Jugoslovenska narodna armija (Yugoslav national army)
MICT	Mechanism for International Criminal Tribunals
MLC	Mouvement de Liberation du Congo
MONUC	Mission de l'Organisation des Nations Unies en République démocratique du Congo (UN Mission in the Congo; now MONUSCO)
MRND	Mouvement révolutionaire national pour le développement (National Republican Movement for Development)
NATO	North Atlantic Treaty Organization

NPFL	National Patriotic Front of Liberia
NSDAP	Nationalsozialistische Deutsche Arbeiterpartei (National Socialist German Workers Party, or Nazi Party)
OKW	Oberkommando der Wehrmacht (The High Military Command in Nazi Germany)
ONUC	Organisation des Nations Unies au Congo (Peacekeeping force deployed to the Congo in 1960)
OSAPG	Office of the UN Special Adviser on the Prevention of Genocide
OTP	Office of the Prosecutor
RCD-G	Rassemblement congolais pour la démocratie-Goma (Congolese Rally for Democracy-Goma)
RCD-ML	Rassemblement congolais pour la démocratie-Mouvement de libération (Congolese Rally for the Democratic Revolutionary Movement)
RPF	Rwandan Patriotic Front
RSHA	Reichssicherheitshauptamt (Reich Main Security Office (Nazi Germany)
RTLM	Radio-Télévision Libre des Mille Collines
RUF	Revolutionary United Front (Sierra Leone)
RuSHA	Rasse-und Siedlungshauptamt (Race and Resettlement, the Central Office for Jewish Affairs and Evacuation)
SC	United Nations Security Council
SCSL	Special Court for Sierra Leone
SDS	Srpska Demokratska Stranka (Serbian Democratic Party)
SFOR	Stabilisation Force in Bosnia and Herzegovina
UCMJ	Uniform Code of Military Justice
UNAMISL	United Nations Mission in Sierra Leone
UNEF	United Nations Emergency Force (first UN peacekeeping effort)
UNPROFOR	United Nations Protection Force (Croatia)
UNSFOR	United Nations Stabilization Force for Bosnia-Herzegovina
UPC	Union des Patriotes Congolais (Union of Congolese Patriots)
USSR	Union of Soviet Socialist Republics
VJ	Vojska Jugoslavije (armed force of the Federal Republic of Yugoslavia)
VRS	Vojska Republike Srpske (Bosnian Serb Army)

Legal Terms

ad hoc	a temporary arrangement set up to accomplish a particular purpose
bis	two (2), so 15*bis* should be read as 15.2

de novo	from the beginning
ex parte	with respect to, or in the interests of, one side only or that of an interested outside party
ex post facto	literally "after the fact"; pertains to legislation that would criminalize an act after the action occurred
in personam	pertaining to individuals, such as *in personam* jurisdiction
in rem	pertaining to "things"; legal action directed toward property
jus (ius) ad bellum	the law governing the initiation of armed conflict
jus (ius) in bello	the law governing individual behavior in armed conflict
mens rea	the personal knowledge of wrongdoing; i.e., did the person know that the actions were a crime when they committed the offense
ne bis in idem	literally nothing twice; legal definition of double jeopardy
nulla poena sine lege	no penalty without a prior law
nullum crimen sine lege	no crime without a prior law; the legal definition of ex post facto (after the fact) prosecutions
prima facie	valid on first inspection or presentation; meaning that enough evidence exists to initiate or continue a prosecution
proprio motu	on their own initiative; the prosecutor of the ICC has the power to initiate an investigation on his or her own judgement
quater	four (4), so 15*quater* should be read as 15.4
quinquies	five (5), so 15*quiquies* should be read as 15.5
ter	three (3), so 15*ter* should be read as 15.3
tu quoque	a legal defense that claims "you did the same thing"
writ of certiorari	a *writ of certiorari* is an order a higher court issues in order to review the decision and proceedings in a lower court

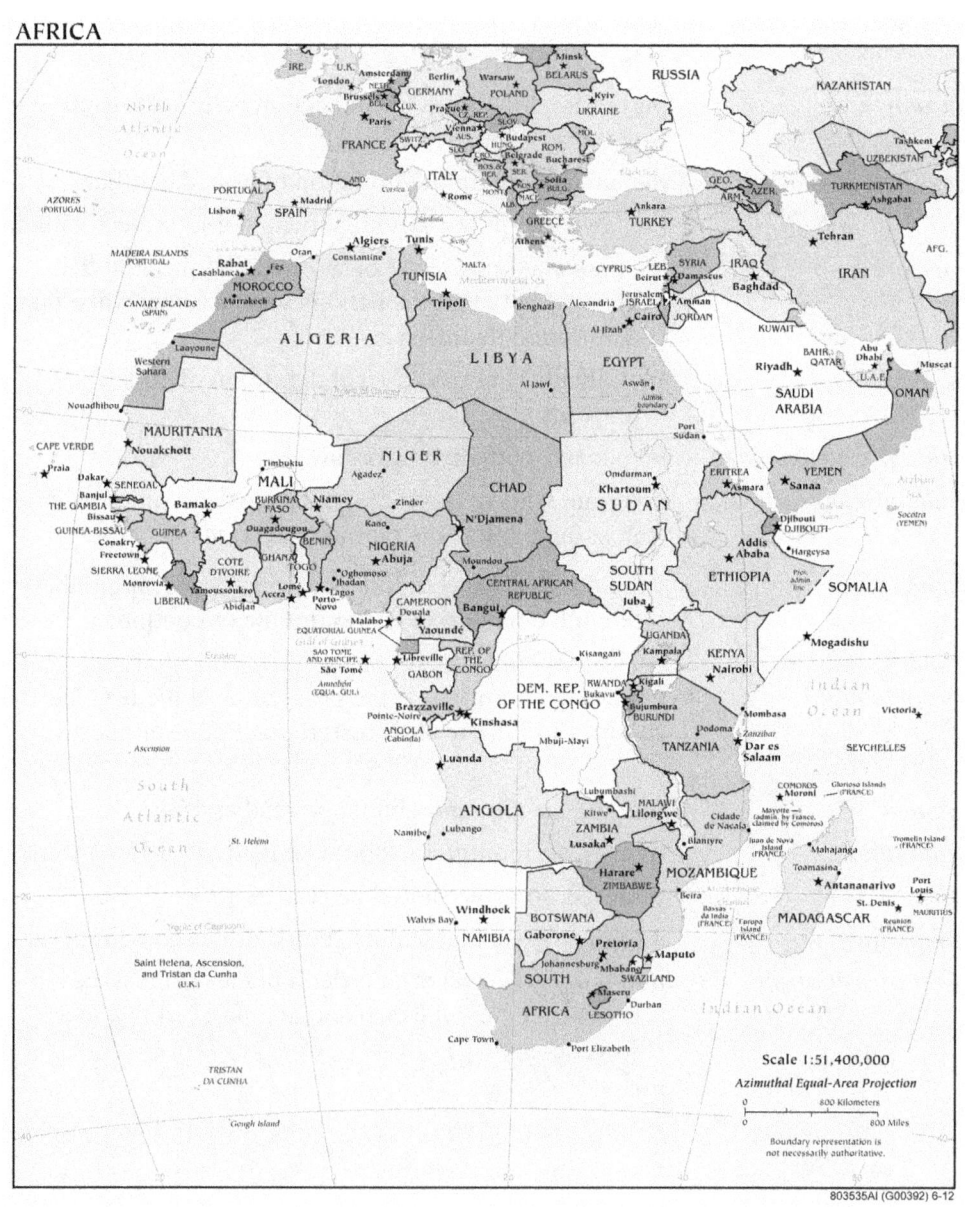
(CIA Factbook)

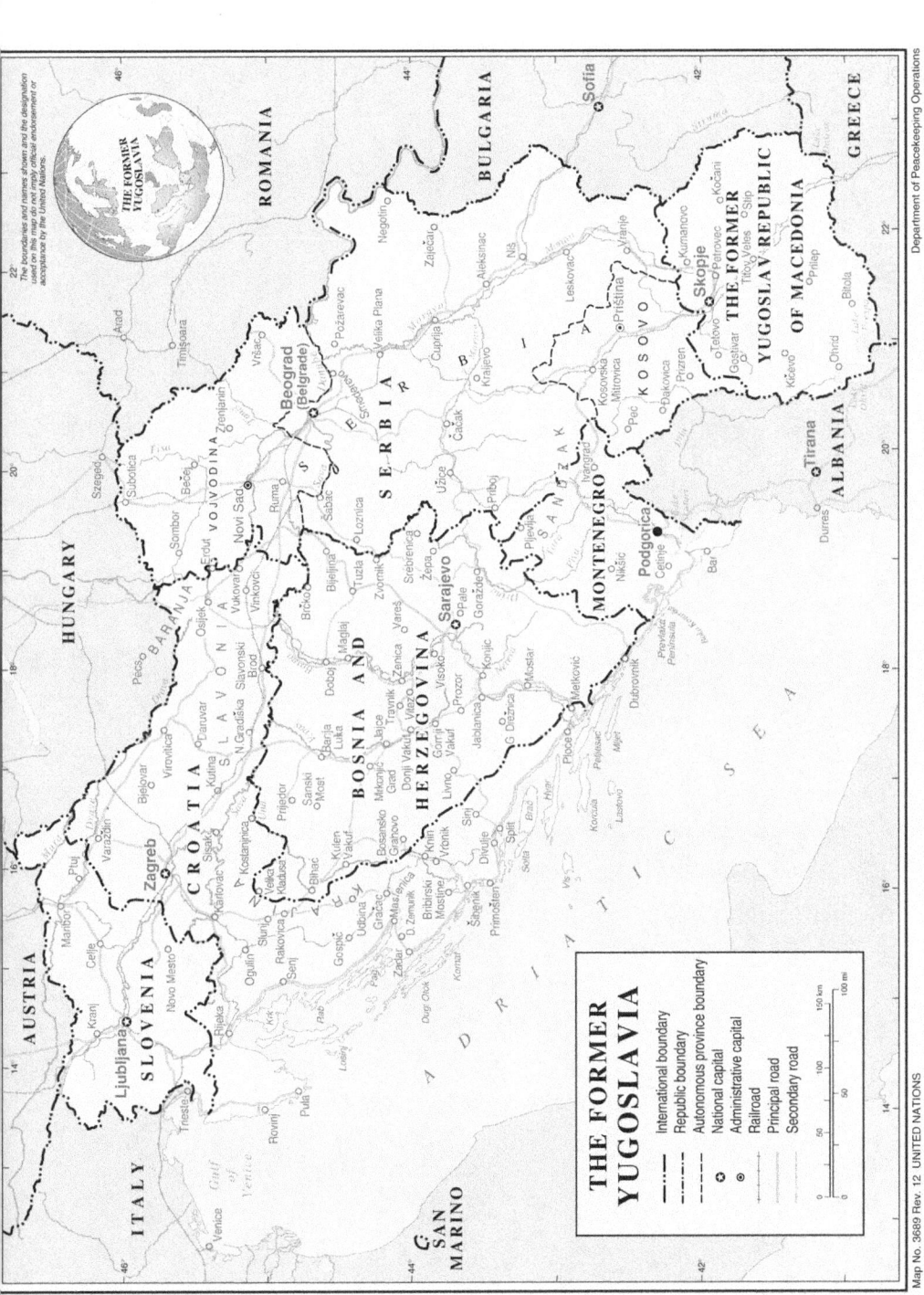

The Former Yugoslavia, Map No. 3689 Rev.12, June 2007, UNITED NATIONS (http://www.un.org/Depts/Cartographic/map/profile/frmryugo.pdf)

1

What Is a War Crime?

A war crime occurs when a person or a group commits an act or acts that violate formal and widely accepted laws that define the standards of permissible behavior in an armed conflict. War crimes comprise two different classes of actions. First, the illegal resort to war would violate the *jus ad bellum* or law governing the initiation of armed force. Under contemporary international law, the resort to armed force is illegal. Second, the *jus in bello,* the law governing appropriate weapons, tactics, and targets, comprises crimes that occur during hostilities. The discussions in this book will primarily focus on crimes involving the *jus in bello* because no one has ever been arrested and tried solely for violation of the *jus ad bellum*.

WAR AND ARMED CONFLICT

Armed conflict and war involve acts considered unacceptable in everyday life. War requires that participants deliberately kill and wound others and intentionally destroy property. Everyone intuitively understands that nothing like war exists as part of a well-ordered domestic society. In fact, the idea that war should be conducted within rules that limit the nature of the conflict runs counter to our basic instincts. Should not all means available be allowed in war because, in war, winning is everything? Losing as the outcome has little to recommend it. Modern warfare is not a game that values "good sportsmanship" as a virtue. The idea that combatants should have to conform to a set of guidelines when their lives may depend on the weapons and tactics selected seems naive at best. Instincts tell us that the only rule ought to be "anything goes." Carl von Clausewitz, in his classic work *On War*, described war as having no limits. Because both sides want to win, the inherent logic of war does not encourage restraint in the methods one may use. This logic suggests that the utmost exertion of force against the enemy would be the best. Clausewitz argued that the "ruthless user of force who shrinks from no amount of bloodshed must gain an advantage if his opponent does not do the same" (1976, 75–76).

LAW AND WAR

Considering the observation by Clausewitz, who had experienced war firsthand many times, strongly suggests that advocating the equivalent of American football rules for wars—conflicts that clearly have no impartial referees—would seem to mark the writer or speaker as not in complete touch with reality. Nonetheless, as weapons have become more powerful and destructive, rules that define appropriate targets and rules that minimize unnecessary suffering have been adopted by governments. In studying the materials in this book, keep in mind that these two ideas underlie most of the legal regimes that govern war. The rules concerning targets actually derive from the idea of military efficiency—one should not use scarce military resources to target individuals, buildings, and other facilities that do not directly contribute to the enemy's war effort. The rule regarding suffering stems from a humanitarian concern that presumes that both sides have an interest in the welfare of their own sick and wounded. Historical evidence suggests that apart from limitations that flow from the state of technology and capacity for organization that constrain what each side can do to the other, restraints have derived more from considerations of expediency and utility than from any sense of sympathy for the suffering.

Rules governing conduct in warfare obviously have a very different purpose from those that regulate individual interactions within a state. These rules turn the moral universe upside down because they authorize killing as ordinary actions while specifying exceptions to the right to kill. The laws of war define who can legitimately kill and be killed. In contrast, rules in domestic law prohibit killing except in extraordinary circumstances (such as self-defense). Domestically, those who kill repeatedly are anathematized as serial killers. In war, killing frequently makes individuals excellent soldiers and heroes.

A war crime occurs when a party subject to the rules violates a rule in the accepted codes. Thus, on the one hand, given the legal reasoning that applies to war, the Japanese pilots who participated in the Battle of Midway (June 1942) did not bear individual liability for their actions nor did their commanders who issued orders to find and destroy the American aircraft carriers. With the initiation of war, the pilots and their commanders had become combatants who now had the right to kill enemy combatants. The American carrier fleet and personnel were legitimate targets for destruction. If captured, the Japanese pilots and commanders would not be not subject to arrest and trial for murder or other crimes unless they had violated some specific provisions of the laws and customs of war. They would become prisoners of war. On the other hand, Japanese commanders and soldiers who organized the Bataan Death March (1942) committed numerous crimes. They were held accountable for deliberately and repeatedly violating explicit rules that mandated humane treatment of prisoners of war (POWs).

PRE-WORLD WAR I: EVOLUTION OF CONTEMPORARY LAW

Historically, different societies have had very different ideas about the nature of wars, and the roles and obligations of those who fight them. Rules about the waging of war have evolved from the circumstances that come from shared conceptions about the nature and role of war among or between participants. The past provides examples where rules have evolved, but the examples do not necessarily provide guidelines for current practice because the nature of warfare has changed significantly. For example, in the Middle Ages, the provisions of the *chivalric code* (literally, the "law of the horse soldier") defined rights and obligations for nobles and knights but had nothing to say about the conduct of ordinary soldiers in battle. The code has very little relevance for armed conflicts in the twenty-first century.

A Note on the *Jus ad Bellum*

Until the United Nations Charter entered into force in 1945, the resort to war and the use of force as a method of retaliation or reprisal for an alleged wrong had few legal restrictions. Textbooks on international law were divided into two sections: the law of peaceful relations and the laws of war and neutrality (*jus in bello*). International law had nothing to say about the transition (*jus ad bellum*)—the decision to go to war. In fact, the use of force to acquire territory (conquest) formed a perfectly legitimate exercise of sovereign rights. Note that the consolidation of France, Germany, and Italy prior to World War I, as well as that of the Russian and Austro-Hungarian Empires depended upon the successful use of force.

Origins of the Contemporary *Jus in Bello*

Up until the middle of the nineteenth century, armies did not have any organized battlefield facilities to treat those who were wounded. The work of Henry Dunant heightened concern over the sick and wounded, resulting in the first Geneva Convention (1864) that led to the creation of the International Committee of the Red Cross. In his quest for a meeting with Emperor Napoleon III concerning his failing business enterprise in Algeria, Henry Dunant witnessed the Battle of Solferino (1859). The single-day encounter produced approximately 40,000 dead and wounded, many of whom were left on the battlefield without any medical attention. Appalled, Dunant set about organizing an effort to deal with the situation. Upon his return to Geneva, he wrote and published a book at his own expense, *A Memory of Solferino*, in which he proposed that private national organizations should care for the wounded in wartime. He also advocated a novel approach—the activities of such organizations should be recognized by international agreement. He became an active advocate. His efforts resulted in a conference at Geneva in October 1863 to consider a draft convention produced by a committee, the International Committee to Aid the Militarily Wounded. This evolved into the International Committee of the Red Cross. The main principles laid down in the Convention and maintained by later Geneva Conventions were:

- relief to the wounded without any distinction as to nationality;
- neutrality (inviolability) of medical personnel and medical establishments and units; and
- the distinctive sign of the red cross on a white ground.

Another conference in August 1864 adopted the Convention without major alterations. These principles still form the basis of contemporary international humanitarian law.

DOCUMENT: GENEVA CONVENTION

When: Adopted August 22, 1864
Where: Geneva, Switzerland
Source: "Convention for the Amelioration of the Condition of the Wounded in Armies in the Field. Geneva, 22 August 1864, Entered into Force June 22, 1865," Online at https://www.icrc.org/ihl/INTRO/120?OpenDocument.
Significance: Dunant's efforts generated the first Geneva Convention (1864) that led to the creation of the International Committee of the Red Cross (ICRC). The 1864 Geneva Convention marks the first modern international treaty dealing with mitigating the circumstances of war.

Article 1. Ambulances and military hospitals shall be recognized as neutral, and as such, protected and respected by the belligerents as long as they accommodate wounded and sick.

Neutrality shall end if the said ambulances or hospitals should be held by a military force.

Art. 2. Hospital and ambulance personnel, including the quarter-master's staff, the medical, administrative and transport services, and the chaplains, shall have the benefit of the same neutrality when on duty, and while there remain any wounded to be brought in or assisted.

Art. 3. The persons designated in the preceding Article may, even after enemy occupation, continue to discharge their functions in the hospital or ambulance with which they serve, or may withdraw to rejoin the units to which they belong.

When in these circumstances they cease from their functions, such persons shall be delivered to the enemy outposts by the occupying forces.

Art. 4. The material of military hospitals being subject to the laws of war, the persons attached to such hospitals may take with them, on withdrawing, only the articles which are their own personal property. Ambulances, on the contrary, under similar circumstances, shall retain their equipment.

Art. 5. Inhabitants of the country who bring help to the wounded shall be respected and shall remain free. Generals of the belligerent Powers shall make it their duty to notify the inhabitants of the appeal made to their humanity, and of the neutrality which humane conduct will confer.

The presence of any wounded combatant receiving shelter and care in a house shall ensure its protection. An inhabitant who has given shelter to the wounded shall be exempted from billeting and from a portion of such war contributions as may be levied.

Art. 6. Wounded or sick combatants, to whatever nation they may belong, shall be collected and cared for.

Commanders-in-Chief may hand over immediately to the enemy outposts enemy combatants wounded during an engagement, when circumstances allow and subject to the agreement of both parties

Those who, after their recovery, are recognized as being unfit for further service, shall be repatriated.

The others may likewise be sent back, on condition that they shall not again, for the duration of hostilities, take up arms.

Evacuation parties, and the personnel conducting them, shall be considered as being absolutely neutral.

Art. 7. A distinctive and uniform flag shall be adopted for hospitals, ambulances and evacuation parties.

It should in all circumstances be accompanied by the national flag.

An armlet may also be worn by personnel enjoying neutrality but its issue shall be left to the military authorities.

Both flag and armlet shall bear a red cross on a white ground.

Art. 8. The implementing of the present Convention shall be arranged by the Commanders-in-Chief of the belligerent armies following the instructions of their respective Governments and in accordance with the general principles set forth in this Convention.

[Articles 9–10 omitted]

THE LIEBER CODE AND THE AMERICAN CIVIL WAR

The second notable origin of present-day rules applicable to warfare occurred in 1863 when General-in-Chief for the Union Army, Major General Henry Halleck, commissioned a Columbia Law School professor, Francis Lieber, to write a code of conduct for the Union Army.

Document: The Lieber Code (General Orders No. 100)

When: April 24, 1863
Where: Washington, D.C.
Source: Francis Lieber, *Instructions for the Government of Armies of the United States in the Field* (Washington, DC: Government Printing Office, 1898). Online at http://avalon.law.yale.edu/19th_century/lieber.asp.

Significance: Lieber's *Instructions for the Government of the Armies of the United States in the Field* was issued to the Union Army during the American Civil War on April 24, 1863. The Lieber Code impressed military men and governments elsewhere. The *Instructions* became the model for numerous national manuals (Italy, 1896 and 1900; Russia, 1904; and France, 1901 and 1912). It also influenced two private attempts at codification—the 1880 Institute of International Law prepared the so-called *Oxford Manual* (*Manuel de Lois de la Guerre sur Terre*) sponsored by the Institute of International Law and the 1894 work by Friedrich Geffcken that also anticipated several important aspects of the 1899 and 1907 Hague Conventions. The *Oxford Manual* is still cited with approval by European writers. The Lieber Code contained many provisions that have become part of the rules applicable to contemporary war.

The Lieber Code highlights the inherent tension between humanitarian concerns and the pressures generated by the goal of winning. In particular, pay special attention to Articles 22–25 and Articles 29–30. Articles 22–25 identify a rudimentary statement of noncombatant immunity, which is discussed in more detail later in the document. But, then note also the statement in Article 29 that parallels that of Clausewitz concerning permissible means.

Art. 11. The law of war does not only disclaim all cruelty and bad faith concerning engagements concluded with the enemy during the war, but also the breaking of stipulations solemnly contracted by the belligerents in time of peace, and avowedly intended to remain in force in case of war between the contracting powers.

It disclaims all extortions and other transactions for individual gain; all acts of private revenge, or connivance at such acts [all emphases in document have been added].

Offenses to the contrary shall be severely punished, and especially so if committed by officers.

[Articles 12, 13 omitted]

Art. 14. *Military necessity*, as understood by modern civilized nations, consists in the necessity of those measures which are indispensable for securing the ends of the war, and which are lawful according to the modern law and usages of war.

Art. 15. Military necessity admits of all direct destruction of life or limb of armed enemies, and of other persons whose destruction is incidentally unavoidable in the armed contests of the war; it allows of the capturing of every armed enemy, and every enemy of importance to the hostile government, or of peculiar danger to the captor; it allows of all destruction of property, and obstruction of the ways and channels of traffic, travel, or communication, and of all withholding of sustenance or means of life from the enemy; of the appropriation of whatever an enemy's country affords necessary for the subsistence and safety of the army, and of such deception as does not involve the breaking of good faith either positively pledged, regarding agreements entered into during the war, or supposed by the modern law of war to exist. Men who take up arms against one another in public war do not cease on this account to be moral beings, responsible to one another and to God.

Art. 16. Military necessity does not admit of cruelty—that is, the infliction of suffering for the sake of suffering or for revenge, nor of maiming or wounding except in fight, nor of torture to extort confessions. It does not admit of the use of poison in any way, nor of the wanton devastation of a district. It admits of deception, but disclaims acts of *perfidy*; and, in general, military necessity does not include any act of hostility which makes the return to peace unnecessarily difficult.

Art. 17. War is not carried on by arms alone. It is lawful to starve the hostile belligerent, armed or unarmed, so that it leads to the speedier subjection of the enemy.

Art. 18. When a commander of a besieged place expels the noncombatants, in order to lessen the number of those who consume his stock of provisions, it is lawful, though an extreme measure, to drive them back, so as to hasten on the surrender.

Art. 19. Commanders, whenever admissible, inform the enemy of their intention to bombard a place, so that the noncombatants, and especially the women and children, may be removed before the bombardment commences. But it is no infraction of the common law of war to omit thus to inform the enemy. Surprise may be a necessity.

Art. 20. Public war is a state of armed hostility between sovereign nations or governments. It is a law and requisite of civilized existence that men live in political, continuous societies, forming organized units, called states or nations, whose constituents bear, enjoy, suffer, advance and retrograde together, in peace and in war.

Art. 21. The citizen or native of a hostile country is thus an enemy, as one of the constituents of the hostile state or nation, and as such is subjected to the hardships of the war.

Art. 22. Nevertheless, as civilization has advanced during the last centuries, so has likewise steadily advanced, especially in war on land, the *distinction between the private individual belonging to a hostile country and the hostile country itself, with its men in arms.* The principle has been more and more acknowledged that the unarmed citizen is to be spared in person, property, and honor as much as the exigencies of war will admit.

Art. 23. *Private citizens are no longer murdered, enslaved, or carried off to distant parts,* and the inoffensive individual is as little disturbed in his private relations as the commander of the hostile troops can afford to grant in the overruling demands of a vigorous war.

Art. 24. The almost universal rule in remote times was, and continues to be with barbarous armies, that the private individual of the hostile country is destined to suffer every privation of liberty and protection, and every disruption of family ties. Protection was, and still is with uncivilized people, the exception.

Art. 25. In modern regular wars of the Europeans, and their descendants in other portions of the globe, protection of the inoffensive citizen of the hostile country is the rule; privation and disturbance of private relations are the exceptions.

[Article 26 omitted]

Art. 27. The law of war can no more wholly dispense with retaliation than can the law of nations, of which it is a branch. Yet civilized nations acknowledge retaliation as the sternest feature of war. A reckless enemy often leaves to his opponent no other means of securing himself against the repetition of barbarous outrage

Art. 28. Retaliation will, therefore, never be resorted to as a measure of mere revenge, but only as a means of protective retribution, and moreover, cautiously and unavoidably; that is to say, retaliation shall only be resorted to after careful inquiry into the real occurrence, and the character of the misdeeds that may demand retribution.

Unjust or inconsiderate retaliation removes the belligerents farther and farther from the mitigating rules of regular war, and by rapid steps leads them nearer to the internecine wars of savages.

Art. 29. Modern times are distinguished from earlier ages by the existence, at one and the same time, of many nations and great governments related to one another in close intercourse.

Peace is their normal condition; war is the exception. The ultimate object of all modern war is a renewed state of peace.

The more vigorously wars are pursued, the better it is for humanity. Sharp wars are brief.

Art. 30. Ever since the formation and coexistence of modern nations, and ever since *wars have become great national wars, war has come to be acknowledged not to be its own end, but the means to obtain great ends of state*, or to consist in defense against wrong; and *no conventional restriction of the modes adopted to injure the enemy is any longer admitted*; but the law of war imposes many limitations and restrictions on principles of justice, faith, and honor.

THE 1899 AND 1907 HAGUE CONVENTIONS

In 1899, the major states met to consider a proposal from Tsar Nicholas II for an arms control agreement. The First Hague Peace Conference met from May 18 to July 29, 1899, with twenty-six nations in attendance. Although the conference of 1899 failed to achieve its primary objective, a limitation on armaments, it did produce conventions (treaties) that more precisely defined the conditions for declaring a state of war, as well as codifying the customary law of war on land and sea in an international agreement. The 1907 Conference modified and expanded the work of the 1899 Conference. The Second Hague Conference in 1907 generally receives more attention because of its extensive efforts to codify the law of war.

Although the 1907 Conference produced fourteen separate multilateral treaties (conventions), Hague IV, Respecting the Laws and Customs of War on Land receives by far the most attention. Hague IV drew heavily on the Lieber Code. While a hundred years or so has diminished the importance of some, this effort still continues today to form the basic structure of rules governing contemporary warfare. A third Hague conference was scheduled for 1914, but unfortunately had to be cancelled because of World War I.

DOCUMENT: LIST OF 1907 HAGUE CONVENTIONS

When: 1907
Where: The Hague, Netherlands
Source: The Avalon Project, Yale University Lilian Goldman Law Library, http://avalon.law.yale.edu/subject_menus/lawwar.asp.
Significance: The Hague Conferences left a deep and lasting imprint on international law and procedure. Many subsequent multilateral treaties dealing with armed conflict drew on the principles and concepts in these treaties. Nonetheless, a number of these, particularly those dealing with the rights and duties of neutrals, have been either rendered irrelevant or severely modified by provisions in the United Nations Charter and other subsequent multilateral treaties. All are available in full text from The Avalon Project or the website of the International Committee of the Red Cross.

- **[I]** Convention for the Pacific Settlement of International Disputes
  [Author comment: As of February 2018, this convention is still in force for 102 states. Together with the 1899 Convention the two treaties provide the statute for the Permanent Court of Arbitration (PCA). It is headquartered in The Hague, Netherlands.]
- **[II]** Convention Respecting the Limitation of the Employment of Force for Recovery of Contract Debts
  [Author comment: The Contracting Powers agreed not to use armed force for the recovery of contract debts owed to its nationals by the Government of another country.]
- **[III]** Convention Relative to the Opening of Hostilities
  [Author comment: This convention sets out the formal procedure for making a declaration of war.
  The adoption of the Charter of the United Nations made it irrelevant.]
- **[IV]** Convention Respecting the Laws and Customs of War on Land
  [Author comment: This confirms, with minor modifications, the provisions of Hague Convention II of 1899. All major powers ratified it. See later discussion.]
- **[V]** Convention Relative to the Rights and Duties of Neutral Powers and Persons in Case of War on Land
- **[VI]** Convention Relative to the Legal Position of Enemy Merchant Ships at the Start of Hostilities

- **[VII]** Convention Relative to the Conversion of Merchant Ships into Warships
- **[VIII]** Convention Relative to the Laying of Automatic Submarine Contact Mines
- **[IX]** Convention Concerning Bombardment by Naval Forces in Time of War
  [Author comment: Forbids the bombardment by naval forces of undefended ports, towns, villages, dwellings, or buildings.]
- **[X]** Convention for the Adaptation to Maritime Warfare of the Principles of the Geneva Convention (of 6 July 1906)
  [Author comment: See discussion later in the chapter.]
- **[XI]** Convention Relative to Certain Restrictions with Regard to the Exercise of the Right of Capture in Naval War
  [Author comment: Codified what had been a rule of customary international law by exempting small vessels such as coastal fishing boats from capture.]
- **[XII]** Convention Relative to the Establishment of an International Prize Court
  [Author comment: This convention would have established an International Prize Court for the resolution of conflicting claims relating to captured ships during wartime. It never received enough ratifications to enter into force. Only one state ratified it. The submarine changed the nature of naval warfare. Instead of capturing enemy merchant ships as "prizes of war" and then selling them and their goods, the goal became to sink as many as possible.]
- **[XIII]** Convention Concerning the Rights and Duties of Neutral Powers in Naval War
- **[XIV]** Declaration Prohibiting the Discharge of Projectiles and Explosives from Balloons

DOCUMENT: 1907 HAGUE CONVENTION IV: ANNEX

When: October 18, 1907
Where: The Hague, Netherlands
Source: "Convention (IV) Respecting the Laws and Customs of War on Land and Its Annex: Regulations Concerning the Laws and Customs of War on Land. The Hague, 18 October 1907," Online at https://www.icrc.org/ihl/INTRO/195.
Significance: Article 1 of Section I, Chapter I of the Annex still forms the definition of a lawful combatant today. Article 2 also sets basic requirements for treatment of Prisoners of War (POWs) that have become part of contemporary international humanitarian law (IHL).

CHAPTER I
The Qualifications of Belligerents

Article 1. The laws, rights, and duties of war apply not only to armies, but also to militia and volunteer corps fulfilling the following conditions:

1. To be commanded by a person responsible for his subordinates;
2. To have a fixed distinctive emblem recognizable at a distance;
3. To carry arms openly; and
4. To conduct their operations in accordance with the laws and customs of war.

In countries where militia or volunteer corps constitute the army, or form part of it, they are included under the denomination "army."

Art 2. The inhabitants of a territory which has not been occupied, who, on the approach of the enemy, spontaneously take up arms to resist the invading troops without having had time to organize themselves in accordance with Article 1, shall be regarded as belligerents if they carry arms openly and if they respect the laws and customs of war.

Art 3. The armed forces of the belligerent parties may consist of combatants and non-combatants. In the case of capture by the enemy, both have a right to be treated as prisoners of war.

CHAPTER II
Prisoners of War

Art 4. Prisoners of war are in the power of the hostile Government, but not of the individuals or corps who capture them.

They must be humanely treated.

All their personal belongings, except arms, horses, and military papers, remain their property.

Art. 5. Prisoners of war may be interned in a town, fortress, camp, or other place, and bound not to go beyond certain fixed limits, but they cannot be confined except as in indispensable measure of safety and only while the circumstances which necessitate the measure continue to exist.

Art. 6. The State may utilize the labour of prisoners of war according to their rank and aptitude, officers excepted. The tasks shall not be excessive and shall have no connection with the operations of the war.

Prisoners may be authorized to work for the public service, for private persons, or on their own account.

Work done for the State is paid for at the rates in force for work of a similar kind done by soldiers of the national army, or, if there are none in force, at a rate according to the work executed.

When the work is for other branches of the public service or for private persons the conditions are settled in agreement with the military authorities.

The wages of the prisoners shall go towards improving their position, and the balance shall be paid them on their release, after deducting the cost of their maintenance.

Art. 7. The Government into whose hands prisoners of war have fallen is charged with their maintenance.

In the absence of a special agreement between the belligerents, prisoners of war shall be treated as regards board, lodging, and clothing on the same footing as the troops of the Government who captured them.

DOCUMENT: 1907 HAGUE CONVENTION X

When: October 18, 1907
Where: The Hague, Netherlands
Source: "Convention for the Adaptation to Maritime Warfare of the Principles of the Geneva Convention (of 6 July 1906),"Online at http://avalon.law.yale.edu/20th_century/hague10.asp.
Significance: The convention exempts hospital ships from attack, giving them the same protection enjoyed by medical personnel and facilities on land. This convention will be important in the later discussion of trials after World War I.

Art. 1. Military hospital ships, that is to say, ships constructed or assigned by States specially and solely with a view to assisting the wounded, sick and shipwrecked, the names of which have been communicated to the belligerent Powers at the commencement or during the course of hostilities, and in any case before they are employed, shall be respected, and cannot be captured while hostilities last.

These ships, moreover, are not on the same footing as war-ships as regards their stay in a neutral port.

Art. 2. Hospital ships, equipped wholly or in part at the expense of private individuals or officially recognized relief societies, shall likewise be respected and exempt from capture, if the belligerent Power to whom they belong has given them an official commission and has notified their names to the hostile Power at the commencement of or during hostilities, and in any case before they are employed.

These ships must be provided with a certificate from the competent authorities declaring that the vessels have been under their control while fitting out and on final departure.

Art. 3. Hospital ships, equipped wholly or in part at the expense of private individuals or officially recognized societies of neutral countries shall be respected and exempt from capture, on condition that they are placed under the control of one of the belligerents, with the previous consent of their own Government and with the authorization of the belligerent himself, and that the latter has notified their names to his adversary at the commencement of or during hostilities, and in any case, before they are employed.

Art. 4. The ships mentioned in Articles 1, 2, and 3 shall afford relief and assistance to the wounded, sick, and shipwrecked of the belligerents without distinction of nationality.

The Governments undertake not to use these ships for any military purpose.

These vessels must in no wise hamper the movements of the combatants.

During and after an engagement they will act at their own risk and peril.

The belligerents shall have the right to control and search them; they can refuse to help them, order them off, make them take a certain course, and put a commissioner on board; they can even detain them, if important circumstances require it.

As far as possible, the belligerents shall enter in the log of the hospital ships the orders which they give them.

NAVAL WARFARE

On inspection, the 1907 Hague Conventions did address several issues with respect to naval warfare. What the conference did not do is address questions related to the *guerre de course* (literally, the "war of the chase") at sea in the same manner as the Annex to Hague IV did for war on land. This part of naval warfare continued to be governed by customary international law. Several treaties had attempted to codify the rules, but in essence the last major alteration by multilateral treaty was the 1856 prohibition on privateers in the Treaty of Paris. The following is an excerpt from the 1913 *Manual of the Laws of Naval War* (Oxford, 1913) that is often cited as a statement of the customary law as embodied in practice.

If you read either the Patrick O'Brien series (or saw the movie *Master and Commander* [2002] based on them) or any of the C. S. Forester Horatio Hornblower series, an important activity for the crews of French and British warships was the capture of prizes—enemy merchant vessels. The captured vessels would then be taken to port where a Prize Court would condemn them (confirm as enemy property) and authorize the auction of ship and goods. The Captain and the crew would share in the proceeds. Given the pay and conditions in the Royal Navy, every seaman dreamed of surviving service with a commanding officer who had an "eye for the prize." Sufficient prize money would permit retirement and perhaps purchase of a pub in a village someplace to enjoy their return to civilian life. The realities of modern warfare effectively ended this customary practice.

DOCUMENT: MANUAL OF THE LAWS OF NAVAL WAR

When:	August 9, 1913
Where:	Oxford, England
Source:	International Committee of the Red Cross. Online at https://ihl-databases.icrc.org/ihl/INTRO/265?OpenDocument.
Significance:	The following excerpt deals with the capture of merchant ships, which presumably also applied to all warships including submarines. Early in World War I, the German Navy complied, but the submarine proved too slow and vulnerable to be an effective weapon against the surface warships of the period. Submarine commanders instead concentrated on merchant shipping. Late in

the war, Germany resorted to unrestricted submarine warfare against British shipping in an effort to cut off vital supplies. Beginning in February 1917, over the next six months, German submarines destroyed over 3.8 million tons of British shipping. If not for the entry of the United States into the war and its assistance, the German tactic may well have worked.

Preamble

(1) Definitions.

"Capture" is the act by which the commander of a war-ship substitutes his authority for that of the captain of the enemy ship, subject to the subsequent judgment of the prize court as to the ultimate fate of the ship and its cargo.

"Seizure," when applied to a ship, is the act by which a war-ship takes possession of the vessel detained, with or without the consent of the captain of the latter. Seizure differs from capture in that the ultimate fate of the vessel may not be involved as a result of its condemnation.

Applied to goods alone, seizure is the act by which the war-ship, with or without the consent of the captain of the vessel detained, takes possession of the goods and holds them or disposes of them subject to the subsequent judgment of the prize court.

"Confiscation" is the act by which the prize court renders valid the capture of a vessel or the seizure of its goods.

The word "prize" is a general expression applying to a captured ship or to seized goods.

By "public ships" are meant all ships other than war-ships which, belonging to the State or to individuals, are set apart for public service and are under the orders of an officer duly commissioned by the State.

SECTION I
On Localities Where Hostilities May Take Place

Article 1. Rules peculiar to naval warfare are applicable only on the high seas and in the territorial waters of the belligerents, exclusive of those waters which, from the standpoint of navigation, ought not to be considered as maritime.

. . .

SECTION III
On Means of Injuring the Enemy

Art. 14
Principle. The right of belligerents to adopt means of injuring the enemy is not unlimited.

[**Author comment:** *The forbidden means set out in Articles 15–17 reprise those forbidden on land with one important addition in Article 17(2). In the following 17.1 and 17.3 are omitted.*]

Art. 17
It is also forbidden…

(2) To sink a ship which has surrendered before having taken off the crew

. . .

Art. 33. Principle of capture. Public and private vessels of enemy nationality are subject to capture, and enemy goods on board, public or private, are liable to seizure

. . .

SECTION VIII
On the Formalities of Seizure and on Prize Procedure

Art. 100. Formalities of seizure. When, after the search has been conducted, the vessel is considered subject to capture, the officer who seizes the ship must:

(1) Seal all the ship's papers after having inventoried them;
(2) Draw up a report of the seizure, as well as a short inventory of the vessel stating its condition;
(3) State the condition of the cargo which he has inventoried, then close the hatchways of the hold, the chests and the store-room and, as far as circumstances will permit, seal them;
(4) Draw up a list of the persons found on board;
(5) Put on board the seized vessel a crew sufficient to retain possession of it, maintain order upon it, and conduct it to such port as he may see fit.

. . .

Art. 102. The seized ship must be taken to the nearest possible port belonging either to the captor State or to an allied belligerent Power, which offers safe refuge, and has means of easy communication with the prize court charged with deciding upon the capture. During the voyage, the prize shall sail under the flag and the pendant carried by the war-ships of the State.

. . .

Art. 104. Destruction of vessels and goods liable to confiscation. Belligerents are not permitted to destroy seized enemy ships, except in so far as they are subject to confiscation and because of exceptional necessity, that is, when the safety of the captor ship or the success of the war operations in which it is at that time engaged, demands it. Before the vessel is destroyed all persons on board must be placed in safety, and all the ship's papers and other documents which the parties interested consider relevant for the purpose of deciding on the validity of the capture must be taken on board the war-ship. The same rule shall hold, as far as possible, for the goods. A "procès-verbal" of the destruction of the captured ship and of the reasons which led to it must be drawn up.

References

Aldrich, George H., and Christine M. Chinkin. 2000. "A Century of Achievement and Unfinished Work." *American Journal of International Law* 94(1): 90–98.

Bloch, Ivan Stanislavovich. *The Future of War in Its Technical, Economic and Political Relations*. Lenox, MA: HardPress Publishing. Reissue of 1898 edition.

Caron, David D. 2000. "War and International Adjudication: Reflections on the 1899 Peace Conference." *American Journal of International Law* 94(1): 4–30.

Clausewitz, Carl von. 1976. *On War*. Edited and translated by Michael Howard and Peter Paret. Princeton, NJ: Princeton University Press.

Neff, Stephen C. 2005. *War and the Law of Nations: A General History*. Cambridge: Cambridge University Press.

Neff, Stephen C. 2010. *Justice in Blue and Gray: A Legal History of the Civil War*. Cambridge, MA: Harvard University Press.

Paust, Jordan J. 2001. "Dr. Francis Lieber and the Lieber Code." *American Society of International Law Proceedings* 95: 111–115.

Witt, John Fabian. 2012. *Lincoln's Code: The Laws of War in American History*. New York: Free Press.

2

World War I: Leipzig

After World War I, diplomatic efforts centered on preventing war, not making it more humane. Because of the huge cost in human life and monetary outlay, public opinion in the victorious countries demanded that Germany should be severely punished for its actions in initiating the war. Crimes formed the first item on the agenda of the Paris Peace Conference. At the preliminary peace conference in January 1919, the delegates voted to form a committee to deal with the issues of establishing a war crimes tribunal.

DOCUMENT: REPORT, COMMISSION ON THE RESPONSIBILITY OF THE AUTHORS OF THE WAR AND ON ENFORCEMENT OF PENALTIES

When:	March 29, 1919
Where:	Paris (Versailles), France
Source:	Online at: LTD, Legal Tools Database, https://www.legal-tools.org/en/browse/record/63159c/
Significance:	The Commission struggled with several important issues. As noted in earlier discussions, before World War I no provision of international law prohibited the resort to war. Committing a state to fight a war did not constitute an illegal act. The devastation of property and massive loss of life in World War I now made everyone think about the negative consequences of war, rather than taking war as an acceptable tool of foreign policy. War now became something to be prevented and avoided. The difficulty for the Commission came from a simple conclusion. They realized that, despite the devastation, no clear formal law existed that would have permitted the prosecution of Kaiser Wilhelm. Traditional international law was based upon the idea of *collective responsibility*: this meant that individuals who may have ordered the initiation of a war bore no personal responsibility for what they did because they were acting on behalf of the state. Note in the discussion the proposal for an international criminal tribunal.

[T]he Commission was of the opinion that the graver charges and those involving more than one country should be tried before an international body, to be called the High Tribunal, which "shall be composed of three persons appointed by each of the following governments: The United States of America, the British Empire, France, Italy, and Japan, and one person appointed by each of the following governments: Belgium, Greece, Poland, Portugal, Roumania, Serbia, and Czecho-Slovakia"; the members of this tribunal to be selected by each country "from among the members of their national courts or tribunals, civil or military, and now in existence or erected as indicated above." (p. 145) . . . The cases selected for trial are to be determined and the prosecutions directed by "a prosecuting commission" composed of a representative of the United States of America, the British Empire, France, Italy, and Japan, to be assisted by a representative of one of the other governments, presumably a party to the creation of the court or represented in it.

. . .

The American representatives felt very strongly that too great attention could not be devoted to the creation of an *international criminal court* for the trial of individuals, for which a precedent is lacking, and which appears to be unknown in the practice of nations. They were of the opinion that an act could not be a crime in the legal sense of the word, unless it were made so by law, and that the commission of an act declared to be a crime by law could not be punished unless the law prescribed the penalty to be inflicted. [**Author comment:** *The issue is* ex post facto *law.*]

. . .

The American representatives therefore proposed that acts affecting the persons or property of one of the Allied or Associated Governments should be tried by a military tribunal of that country; that acts involving more than one country, such as treatment by Germany of prisoners contrary to the usages and customs of war, could be tried by a tribunal either made up of the competent tribunals of the countries affected or of a commission thereof possessing their authority. In this way existing national tribunals or national commissions which could legally be called into being would be utilized, and not only the law and the penalty would be already declared, but the procedure would be settled.

. . .

The majority of the Commission, however, was not influenced by the legal argument. They appeared to be fixed in their determination to try and punish by judicial process the "ex-Kaiser" of Germany. That there might be no doubt about their meaning, they insisted that the jurisdiction of the high tribunal whose constitution they recommended should include the heads of states, and they therefore inserted a provision to this effect in express words in the clause dealing with the jurisdiction of the tribunal. (p. 148)

DOCUMENT: TREATY OF VERSAILLES

When:	June 28, 1919
Where:	Paris (Versailles), France
Source:	The Avalon Project, Yale Law School. Online at http://avalon.law.yale.edu/imt/partvii.asp.
Significance:	The Treaty of Versailles embodied the settlement imposed upon Germany by the major allies. The body of the treaty contained the Covenant of the League of Nations, the document that officially established the organization. Germany felt the settlement terms were very harsh. During his rise to power, Hitler very effectively used this dissatisfaction to bring the National Socialist (Nazi) Party to prominence and eventual control of the government. Article 227 provided for a special tribunal to try the Kaiser even though both the United States and Japan had argued that the charges would be unprecedented because no law prior to World War I prohibited the resort to war. Article 228 gave the Allies the right to try those accused of violations of the "laws and customs of war" before military tribunals.

Article 227

The Allied and Associated Powers publicly arraign William II of Hohenzollern, formerly German Emperor, for a supreme offence against international morality and the sanctity of treaties. A special tribunal will be constituted to try the accused, thereby assuring him the guarantees essential to the right of defence. It will be composed of five judges, one appointed by each of the following Powers: namely, the United States of America, Great Britain, France, Italy and Japan.

In its decision the tribunal will be guided by the highest motives of international policy, with a view to vindicating the solemn obligations of international undertakings and the validity of international morality. It will be its duty to fix the punishment which it considers should be imposed. The Allied and Associated Powers will address a request to the Government of the Netherlands for the surrender to them of the ex-Emperor in order that he may be put on trial.

Article 228

The German Government recognises the right of the Allied and Associated Powers to bring before military tribunals persons accused of having committed acts in violation of the laws and customs of war. Such persons shall, if found guilty, be sentenced to punishments laid down by law. This provision will apply notwithstanding any proceedings or prosecution before a tribunal in Germany or in the territory of her allies.

The German Government shall hand over to the Allied and Associated Powers, or to such one of them as shall so request, all persons accused of having committed an act in violation of the laws and customs of war, who are specified either by name or by the rank, office or employment which they held under the German authorities.

TRIALS

After the war, the Allied Powers submitted to the German government a list of 854 names of individuals alleged to have committed prosecutable war crime offenses. The list included Germany's most prominent statesmen and military leaders during World War I: Paul von Hindenburg, Theobald von Bethmann-Hollweg, Bernhard von Bülow, Generals Helmuth von Moltke and Erich Ludendorff, and Admirals Reinhold Scheer and Alfred von Tirpitz. The Allies faced a problem. Unlike the situation after World War II when they occupied a defeated Germany, the surrender in World War I did not include occupation of Germany. Even as a defeated power, the German government vigorously resisted the demand that these individuals either be tried as war criminals or handed over to the Allied Powers for trial. The list of 854 was eventually reduced to 45. Only twelve of these actually went to trial before the German Supreme Court with charges very narrowly based upon the law of war contained in Hague Convention IV. Kaiser Wilhelm was never tried because The Netherlands granted him political asylum and refused to hand him over for prosecution. Table 2.1 provides a quick summary of trials, verdicts, and sentences for trials held in Leipzig.

Table 2.1 World War I: Leipzig Trials: Defendants and Verdicts

Defendant	Charge	Verdict	Sentence
Sergeant Karl Heynen	Mistreatment POWs	Guilty	10 months
Captain Emil Müller	Mistreatment POWs	Guilty	6 months
Private Robert Neumann	Mistreatment POWs	Guilty	6 months
Lieutenant Captain Karl Neumann	Torpedoing the hospital ship *Dover Castle*	Not Guilty	
First-Lieutenant Ludwig Dithmar	Torpedoing the hospital ship *Llandovery Castle* and firing on survivors in lifeboats	Guilty	4 years
First-Lieutenant John Boldt	Torpedoing the hospital ship *Llandovery Castle* and firing on survivors in lifeboats	Guilty	4 years
Max Ramdohr	Mistreatment of Belgian children	Not Guilty	
Major Benno Crucius	Passing on alleged order of Lieutenant-General Karl Stenger	Guilty	2 years
First-Lieutenant Adolph Laule	Killing a POW	Not Guilty	
Lieutenant-General Hans von Schack	Mistreatment of POWs	Not Guilty	
Major-General Benno Kruska	Mistreatment of POWs	Not Guilty	
Lieutenant-General Karl Stenger	Ordering the killing of POWs	Not Guilty	

The position the German courts took with the respect to the defense of superior orders is the reason for highlighting the two trials that follow. Note the reasoning in these two trials because superior orders will play a major role in the defense strategies of individuals placed on trial by courts and military commissions in the aftermath of World War II. The *Llandovery Castle* case differs from the *Dover Castle* case with respect to two important factors. First, the commander of the submarine targeted a ship that was sailing outside the zone specified in the standing orders from the High Command. Second, the orders of the commander and the subsequent actions of the accused crew members in firing on unarmed survivors in the lifeboats were clear violations of the laws and customs of war.

TRIAL SUMMARIES #1: THE *DOVER CASTLE* AND THE *LLANDOVERY CASTLE*

The *Dover Castle* and the *Llandovery Castle* cases are discussed together because they both involve submarine commanders deliberately sinking a hospital ship. Both cases involve a defense plea of "acting under superior orders," but they have very different outcomes.

Document: *Dover Castle*

When:	June 4, 1921
Where:	Leipzig, Germany
Court:	German Supreme Court
Defendant:	Lieutenant-Captain (First Lieutenant) Karl Neumann
Source:	Claud Mullins, *The Leipzig [sic] Trials: An Account of the War Criminals' Trials and a Study of German Mentality*. London: H. F. & G. Witherby, 1921, 102–107. Online at: https://archive.org/details/leipzigtrialsac00mull.
Charge:	Destroying a hospital ship in violation of the laws and customs of war
Facts:	The accused readily admitted that he torpedoed the hospital ship.
Defense:	Superior orders; all on board survived
Verdict:	Not Guilty
Significance:	The court found the defendant Not Guilty, although he "frankly" admitted to sinking the *Dover Castle* deliberately.

Court Summary of Facts

During the war the accused, as First Lieutenant *[**Author comment**: Lieutenant Captain]* in the Navy, was Commander of the Submarine U.C. 67. In the list communicated by the Allied Powers to the Government by virtue of Art. 228, par. 2, of the Treaty of Peace he was charged with having, on 26th May, 1917, torpedoed the English hospital ship *Dover Castle* without warning and with having sunk her with exceptional brutality.

...

During the day he sighted two steamers, escorted by two destroyers. The weather was clear and sunny. The accused was therefore soon able to see that the two steamers carried the distinctive outward signs laid down for military hospital ships by the 10th Hague Convention . . . of 18th October, 1907. He then approached nearer to the convoy, which was pursuing a zig-zag course, and about 6.0 p.m. he fired a torpedo at the steamer nearest to him. The steamer was hit; it remained stationary, but did not sink. One of the destroyers, which were accompanying it, came alongside its starboard side and took off its crew, as well as all the sick and wounded on board. Only after this had taken place, about 1½ hours after the first torpedo, did the accused sink the vessel by firing a second torpedo. He then rose to the surface and found out from the markings on the unmanned life-boats which were drifting about that the sunken steamer was the *Dover Castle*.

...

[Author comment: *Summary of reasoning for the Germany Admiralty issuing an order restricting the movement of hospital ships in violation of the 19th Hague Convention.]*

It [the German Admiralty] stated that it would not entirely repudiate the convention, but was compelled to restrict the navigation of enemy hospital ships. . . . The hospital ships had to be reported at least six weeks previously and were to keep to a given course on leaving Greece. After a reasonable period of grace, it was announced, all other enemy hospital ships in the Mediterranean would be regarded as vessels of war and forthwith attacked. The . . . memorandum reached the enemy governments in the early part of April, 1917.

It corresponds with the order of the Admiralty issued on 29th March, 1917, to the German Flotilla in the Mediterranean.

> As from 8 April hospital ships generally are no longer to be permitted in the blockaded area of the Mediterranean, including the route to Greece. Only a few special hospital ships, which have been notified by name at least six weeks previously, may use the channel up to the Port of Kalamata. Advise submarines that as from 8 April every hospital ship on the routes named is to be attacked forthwith, excepting such only as have been expressly notified from here, in which cases speed, times of arrival and departure will be exactly stated.

This order was communicated to the accused before his departure from Cattaro.

...

[Author comment: *Unlike the following trial, the trial summary proceeds directly to the reasoning in acquittal.]*

Court Reasoning

It is a military principle that the subordinate is bound to obey the orders of his superiors. This duty of obedience is of considerable importance from the point of view of the criminal law. Its consequence is that, when the execution of a service order involves an offence against the criminal law, the superior giving the order is alone responsible This is in accordance with the terms of the German law, §47, para. 1 of the Military Penal Code. It also accords with the legal principles of all other civilized states (see, for example, as regards England, the Manual of Military Law (1914), chapter XIV, Art. 443 quoted in Verdross . . . "Breaches of International Law in the Conduct of War and National claims for punishment," page 95).

The Admiralty Staff was the highest service authority over the accused. He was in duty bound to obey their orders in service matters. So far as he did that, he was free from criminal responsibility. Therefore he cannot be held responsible for sinking the hospital ship *Dover Castle* according to orders. Under §47 of the Military Penal Code quoted above, there are two exceptional cases in which the question of the punishment of a subordinate who has acted in conformity with his orders can arise. He can in the first place be held responsible, if he has gone beyond the orders given him. In the present case the accused has not gone beyond his orders. It was impossible to give a warning to the *Dover Castle* before the torpedo was fired, because she was escorted by two warships. The accused is not charged with any peculiar brutality in sinking the ship. On the contrary he made it possible to save all the sick and wounded on board the Dover Castle by allowing about 14 hours to elapse between the firing of the first and second torpedoes.

According to §47 of the Military Penal Code No. 2, a subordinate who acts in conformity with orders is also liable to punishment as an accomplice, when he knows that his superiors have ordered him to do acts which involve a civil or military crime or misdemeanor. There has been no case of this here.

DOCUMENT: *LLANDOVERY CASTLE*

When:	July 16, 1921
Where:	Leipzig, Germany
Court:	German Supreme Court
Defendants:	First-Lieutenant Ludwig Dithmar and First-Lieutenant John Boldt
Source:	Claud Mullins, *The Leipzeig [sic] Trials: An Account of the War Criminals' Trials and a Study of German Mentality.* London: H. F. & G. Witherby, 1921, pp. 108–121, 122–123, 127–129, 130–133. Online at: https://archive.org/details/leipzeigtrialsac00mull.
Charges:	Destroying a hospital ship in violation of the laws and customs of war; firing on survivors in lifeboats of the hospital ship *Llandovery Castle*
Defense:	Superior orders
Verdict:	Guilty (4-year sentences) for both Dithmar and Boldt
Significance:	Unlike Karl Neumann in the *Dover Castle* case, the commander of U-boat 86 was not operating in the forbidden zone. The actions of Lieutenant Helmut Patzig did not fall within the guidelines of the standing order from his superiors. His and the subsequent

actions of the crew violated fundamental provisions of the Hague Conventions as well as customary international law.

Court Summary of Facts

At the end of the month of June, 1918, the *Llandovery Castle* was on her way back to England from Halifax, after having carried sick and wounded there. She had on board ... a total of two hundred and fifty eight persons.... A witness testified that there were no combatants or munitions on board. On the evening of June 27, 1918 the *Llandovery Castle* was sunk in the Atlantic Ocean, about 116 miles southwest of Fastnet (Ireland), by a torpedo from the German U-boat 86. Of those on board only 24 persons were saved. The commander of U-boat, First-Lieutenant Patzig, was subsequently promoted to captain. His present whereabouts are unknown. The accused Dithmar was the first officer of the watch, and the accused Boldt the second. Patzig recognized the character of the ship, which he had been pursuing for a long time, at the latest when she exhibited at dusk the lights prescribed for hospital ships by the Tenth Hague Convention.

In accordance with international law, the German U-boats were forbidden to torpedo hospital ships. According both to the German and the British Governments' interpretation of the said Hague Convention, ships, which were used for the transport of military persons wounded and fallen ill in war on land, belonged to this category. The German Naval Command had given orders that hospital ships were only to be sunk within the limits of a certain barred area. However, the attack on the *Llandovery Castle* occurred a long way from the prohibited area. Patzig knew this and was aware that by torpedoing the *Llandovery Castle* he was acting against orders.

[Author comment: *The Court at this point engaged in an extensive discussion of how many lifeboats were launched as the* Llandovery Castle *sunk and the actions of the U-boat afterwards. It concluded that "Thus, after the sinking of the* Llandovery Castle, *there were still left three of her boats with people on board." After sinking the ship, the submarine surfaced and conducted an interrogation of survivors on the Captain's lifeboat. It then left, but returned a second time.]*

Court Summary of Testimony

The U-boat soon returned, and made straight for the captain's boat. Its occupants feared ... they might be run down. ... After passing by the second time, the U-boat once more went away. The lifeboat, which had hoisted a sail in the meantime, endeavored to get away. But after a brief period, the occupants of the boat noticed firing from the U-boat. ... After firing had ceased, the occupants of the lifeboat saw nothing more of the U-boat. The captain's boat cruised about for some 36 hours altogether. ... On the 29th June, in the morning, it was found by the English destroyer *Lysander*. The crew were taken on board and the boat left to its fate. During the 29th June, the commander of the English Fleet caused a search to be made for the other lifeboats of the *Llandovery Castle*. The English sloop *Snowdrop* and four American destroyers systematically searched the area, where the boats from the sunken ship might be drifting about. The *Snowdrop* found an undamaged boat of the Llandovery Castle 9 miles from the spot on which the *Lysander* had found the captain's boat. The boat was empty, but had been occupied, as was shown by the position of the sail. . . . No other boat from the *Llandovery Castle* and no more survivors were found. The firing from the U-boat was not only noticed by the occupants of the captain's boat. It was also heard by the witnesses Popitz, Knoche, Ney, Tegtmeier and Kass, who were members of the crew of the U-boat.

. . .

After the [second] examination was completed . . . the whole of the crew went below deck, as is the case when the order to be ready for diving is given. There only remained on deck Commander Patzig, the accused, his officers of the watch and, by special order, the first boatswain's mate, Meissner, who has since died. It is doubtful whether the latter first went below and was then called on deck again, or whether he remained on deck. . . . Firing commenced sometime after the crew had gone below. The witnesses heard distinctly that only the stern gun, a 8.8 c/m gun was in action. While firing, the U-boat moved about. It did not submerge even after the firing had ceased, but continued on the surface.

Court Reasoning

The prosecution assumes that the firing of the U-boat was directed against the lifeboats of the *Llandovery Castle*. The court has arrived at the same conclusion as the result of the evidence given at this time. . . . In this connection we must refer to the opinion of the actual witnesses, both English and German. With the exception of a few German witnesses, who adduce nothing to the contrary, but simply abstain from expressing any opinion at all, they all, from their own impressions, describe the firing as being directed against the lifeboats. . . . The crew of the U-boat have the same conviction. . . . The firing on the boats was an offence against the law of nations. In war on land the killing of unarmed enemies is not allowed (compare the Hague regulations as to war on land, para. 23(c)), similarly in war at sea, the killing of shipwrecked people, who have taken refuge in life-boats, is forbidden.

. . .

The rule of international law, which is here involved, is simple and is universally known. No possible doubt can exist with regard to the question of its applicability. The court must in this instance affirm Patzig's guilt of killing contrary to international law. . . . The two accused knowingly assisted Patzig in this killing, by the very fact of their having accorded him their support in the manner, which has already been set out. It is not proved that they were in agreement with his intentions. . . . They are, therefore, only liable to punishment as accessories. (Para. 49 of the Penal Code.)

Patzig's order does not free the accused from guilt. It is true that according to para. 47 of the Military Penal Code, if the execution of an order in the ordinary course of duty involves such a violation of the law as is punishable, the superior officer issuing such an order is alone responsible. According to No. 2, however, the subordinate obeying such an order is liable to punishment, if it was known to him that the order of the superior involved the infringement of civil or military law. This applies in the case of the accused. It is certainly to be urged in favor of the military subordinates, that they are under no obligation to question the order of their superior officer, and they can count upon its legality. *But no such confidence can be held to exist, if such an order is universally known to everybody, including also the accused, to be without any doubt whatever against the law* [emphasis added]. This happens only in rare and exceptional cases. But this case was precisely one of them, for in the present instance, it was perfectly clear to the accused that killing defenceless people in the life-boats could be nothing else but a breach of the law. . . . They should . . . have refused to obey. . . .

SUPERIOR ORDERS AS A DEFENSE

Comparing the facts and reasoning in the *Llandovery Castle* case with that of the court in the *Dover Castle* case illustrates the struggle courts had in coming to grips with actions that violated well-established rules, but resulted from an order or policy that came from a superior. In the *Dover Castle* case, the judges went to great lengths to justify the legitimacy of the standing order. This exercise evaded the core issue and permitted the judges to focus on the fact that the ship was sunk within the parameters of the order with no loss of life. The Court then reasoned that all military organizations operate on a fundamental military principle: *subordinates must obey the orders of their superiors*. The duty of obedience is of considerable importance from the point of view of the criminal law of war, because in consequence, when the execution of a service order involves an offence against the criminal law, *the superior giving the order is alone responsible*. The accused accordingly sank the *Dover Castle* in obedience to, and within the guidelines established in the service order of his highest superiors. He considered the order to be lawful and binding. He could not, therefore, be punished for his conduct.

The difficulty in the Neumann verdict comes from the fact that in German practice, one cannot normally use a domestic law in defense of a violation of a clear rule of international law, nor does the fact that similar rules exist in other militaries justify its use other than in mitigation. In this case, the German Admiralty had invoked the principle of "military necessity" as a justification for issuing orders that contravened the Convention. Discussion of the ramifications of that defense lies considerably outside the scope of this book.

The judges in the two trials did discuss instances where a subordinate may still face charges even though he or she claimed to be "just following orders." The Court had to face a situation where clearly a very serious war crime had occurred—deliberate firing on defenseless individuals. The narrative in the decision reflects that the judges found the testimony of survivors and others credible and the actions shocking. The Court recognized the difficulty of disobeying an order (particularly on a submarine) and the possible repercussions for individuals who disobey. The transcript says: "The defence finally points out that the accused must have considered that Patzig would have enforced his orders, weapon in hand, if they had not obeyed them." The Court took these circumstances into account in the sentences given the two. Seemingly no one ever searched very hard for Patzig. He never showed up for trial. Lieutenant Boldt escaped prison in November, four months after his incarceration. Dithmar followed his lead two months later escaping in January 1922.

In the cases in this book, many defendants will raise the issue of superior orders as justification for their actions. In the trials at the end of World War II, attitudes toward the defense of "superior orders" had evolved. *The Oxford Handbook of International Law in Armed Conflict* states:

> Being ordered by a superior officer to violate IHL [international humanitarian law] does not absolve the person who commits the violation of responsibility for the action. . . . [A]n assessment must be made, from the penal point of view, of the ability of the person to understand that the action taken was a violation, the seriousness of the act, and *the degree of pressure* to which he or she was subjected. Account should be duly taken of all such factors in cases, for example, that involve very young or uneducated soldiers who were compelled under threat of death to kill a civilian or an enemy soldier. (Clapham and Gaeta 2014, 107–108, emphasis added)

The quote makes two important points that apply to Lieutenants Dithmar and Boldt and to every other case in this book. Actions always happen within a *distinctive context*, that is, a specific set of circumstances that define the incident. Basically, the point of a trial is to determine the *facts* of a case that will then set the stage for an appropriate decision on guilt or innocence. If guilty, the facts will determine the severity of the sentence. To give a domestic analogy, the facts as determined by a trial that involves a death will determine if the action that caused the death was a legitimate exercise of self-defense, manslaughter, second-degree murder, or first-degree murder. In the *Llandovery Castle* case, the Court did not take superior orders as a defense that would totally excuse their actions; but, it did take it into account in the sentences given.

References

Bass, Gary Jonathan. 2000. *Stay the Hand of Vengeance: The Politics of War Crimes Tribunals*. Princeton, NJ: Princeton University Press.

Clapham, Andrew, and Paola Gaeta, eds. 2014. *The Oxford Handbook of International Law in Armed Conflict*. Oxford: Oxford University Press.

Willis, James F. 1982. *Prologue to Nuremberg: The Politics and Diplomacy of Punishing War Criminals of the First World War*. Westport, CT: Greenwood.

3

Between World War I and World War II

THE LEAGUE OF NATIONS

Because of the great devastation caused by World War I, efforts after the war centered on measures designed to avoid war rather than preparations for war. The post–World War I era saw an innovation in the League of Nations, an international organization designed to provide a *collective security* regime (a pledge of joint action against states that violated the provisions of the Covenant) for member states. The Covenant did not make the resort to force illegal. Instead, it laid out procedures to promote peaceful settlements of disputes. Unfortunately, the League was seen by many of the victors as the means of preserving the status quo established in the treaties ending the war. The United States did not ratify the Treaty of Versailles, so it never became a member of the League, even though it was in large part the brainchild of President Woodrow Wilson. The League had some initial successes, but member states failed to take decisive action when the organization faced major challenges in the 1930s from the activities of Japan in Korea and China, of Italy in Abyssinia (Ethiopia), and of Germany in repudiating the Versailles settlement and rebuilding its military. War-weary member states, which saw the organization as a tool to prevent war, were reluctant to take action that might lead to the use of force and another costly war. After expelling the Soviet Union (USSR) for its invasion of Finland in December 1939, the League ceased operations, although it remained legally in existence until April 1946.

DOCUMENT: COVENANT OF THE LEAGUE OF NATIONS

When:	January 10, 1920
Where:	Geneva, Switzerland
Source:	The Avalon Project. Online at http://avalon.law.yale.edu/20th_century/leagcov.asp.
Significance:	As the first attempt to set up an international collective security regime, the League signaled that a sea change had occurred concerning the feasibility and utility of the use of force as a response to crises. The Covenant did not outlaw war. It sought to provide formal

procedures for states to settle their differences through peaceful means. Despite the fact that the League was the brainchild of President Woodrow Wilson, the U.S. Senate refused to ratify the treaty. The United States did not join the League and remained a non-member throughout its existence. While the League ultimately failed, it set the stage for a successor organization—the United Nations.

Article 10.
The Members of the League undertake to respect and preserve as against external aggression the territorial integrity and existing political independence of all Members of the League. In case of any such aggression or in case of any threat or danger of such aggression the Council shall advise upon the means by which this obligation shall be fulfilled.

Article 11.
Any war or threat of war, whether immediately affecting any of the Members of the League or not, is hereby declared a matter of concern to the whole League, and the League shall take any action that may be deemed wise and effectual to safeguard the peace of nations. In case any such emergency should arise the Secretary General shall on the request of any Member of the League forthwith summon a meeting of the Council.

It is also declared to be the friendly right of each Member of the League to bring to the attention of the Assembly or of the Council any circumstance whatever affecting international relations which threatens to disturb international peace or the good understanding between nations upon which peace depends.

Article 12.
The Members of the League agree that, *if there should arise between them any dispute likely to lead to a rupture they will submit the matter either to arbitration or judicial settlement or to enquiry by the Council, and they agree in no case to resort to war until three months after the award* [all emphases in document have been added] by the arbitrators or the judicial decision, or the report by the Council. In any case under this Article the award of the arbitrators or the judicial decision shall be made within a reasonable time, and the report of the Council shall be made within six months after the submission of the dispute.

Article 13.
The Members of the League agree that whenever any dispute shall arise between them which they recognise to be suitable for submission to arbitration or judicial settlement and which cannot be satisfactorily settled by diplomacy, they will submit the whole subject-matter to arbitration or judicial settlement.

Disputes as to the interpretation of a treaty, as to any question of international law, as to the existence of any fact which if established would constitute a breach of any international obligation, or as to the extent and nature of the reparation to be made for any such breach, are declared to be among those which are generally suitable for submission to arbitration or judicial settlement.

For the consideration of any such dispute, the court to which the case is referred shall be the Permanent Court of International Justice, established in accordance with Article 14, or any tribunal agreed on by the parties to the dispute or stipulated in any convention existing between them.

The Members of the League agree that they will carry out in full good faith any award or decision that may be rendered, and that they will not resort to war against a Member of the League which complies therewith. In the event of any failure to carry out such an award or decision, the Council shall propose what steps should be taken to give effect thereto.

[Article 14 omitted]

Article 15.

If there should arise between Members of the League any dispute likely to lead to a rupture, which is not submitted to arbitration or judicial settlement in accordance with Article 13, the Members of the League agree that they will submit the matter to the Council. Any party to the dispute may effect such submission by giving notice of the existence of the dispute to the Secretary General, who will make all necessary arrangements for a full investigation and consideration thereof.

For this purpose the parties to the dispute will communicate to the Secretary General, as promptly as possible, statements of their case with all the relevant facts and papers, and the Council may forthwith direct the publication thereof.

The Council shall endeavour to effect a settlement of the dispute, and if such efforts are successful, a statement shall be made public giving such facts and explanations regarding the dispute and the terms of settlement thereof as the Council may deem appropriate.

If the dispute is not thus settled, the Council either unanimously or by a majority vote shall make and publish a report containing a statement of the facts of the dispute and the recommendations which are deemed just and proper in regard thereto.

Any Member of the League represented on the Council may make public a statement of the facts of the dispute and of its conclusions regarding the same.

If a report by the Council is unanimously agreed to by the members thereof other than the Representatives of one or more of the parties to the dispute, the Members of the League agree that they will not go to war with any party to the dispute which complies with the recommendations of the report.

If the Council fails to reach a report which is unanimously agreed to by the members thereof, other than the Representatives of one or more of the parties to the dispute, the Members of the League reserve to themselves the right to take such action as they shall consider necessary for the maintenance of right and justice.

If the dispute between the parties is claimed by one of them, and is found by the Council, to arise out of a matter which by international law is solely within the domestic jurisdiction of that party, the Council shall so report, and shall make no recommendation as to its settlement.

The Council may in any case under this Article refer the dispute to the Assembly. The dispute shall be so referred at the request of either party to the dispute, provided that such request be made within fourteen days after the submission of the dispute to the Council.

In any case referred to the Assembly, all the provisions of this Article and of Article 12 relating to the action and powers of the Council shall apply to the action and powers of the Assembly, provided that a report made by the Assembly, if concurred in by the Representatives of those Members of the League represented on the Council and of a majority of the other Members of the League, exclusive in each case of the Representatives of the parties to the dispute, shall have the same force as a report by the Council concurred in by all the members thereof other than the Representatives of one or more of the parties to the dispute.

Article 16.
Should any Member of the League resort to war in disregard of its covenants under Articles 12, 13 or 15, it shall ipso facto be deemed to have committed an act of war against all other Members of the League, which hereby undertake immediately to subject it to the severance of all trade or financial relations, the prohibition of all intercourse between their nationals and the nationals of the covenant-breaking State, and the prevention of all financial, commercial or personal intercourse between the nationals of the covenant-breaking State and the nationals of any other State, whether a Member of the League or not.

It shall be the duty of the Council in such case to recommend to the several Governments concerned what effective military, naval or air force the Members of the League shall severally contribute to the armed forces to be used to protect the covenants of the League.

The Members of the League agree, further, that they will mutually support one another in the financial and economic measures which are taken under this Article, in order to minimise the loss and inconvenience resulting from the above measures, and that they will mutually support one another in resisting any special measures aimed at one of their number by the covenant-breaking State, and that they will take the necessary steps to afford passage through their territory to the forces of any of the Members of the League which are co-operating to protect the covenants of the League.

Any Member of the League which has violated any covenant of the League may be declared to be no longer a Member of the League by a vote of the Council concurred in by the Representatives of all the other Members of the League represented thereon.

WHY DID THE LEAGUE FAIL?

The Charter of the League was contained within the Treaty of Versailles that ended World War I. The League Covenant did not outlaw war. It obligated member states to attempt a settlement of any dispute by peaceful means before resorting to the use of force. Note, in particular, the language of Article 12, which permits a state dissatisfied with a settlement produced through peaceful means to initiate the resort to force after a mandatory "cooling off" period.

The League never lived up to its promise. Its failure had many roots. Even though the League was the brainchild of U.S. president Woodrow Wilson, the United States failed to ratify the Treaty of Versailles and never joined. The United States instead retreated back into an isolationist foreign policy. The onset of the economic disaster of the Great Depression that began in October 1929 reinforced the reluctance of the United States to be more than marginally engaged in areas where it felt that it had little interest.

The League did attempt a rudimentary collective security arrangement. Article 16 declared that a resort to force in violation of the procedures outlined in the Covenant would theoretically be viewed as an attack on all members. The problem lay in the lack of any mandatory requirement to do more than consult about future action in such a case. The League did not have its own armed forces. It had to depend on members to act. States exhausted by the devastation of World War I had little interest in assuming an obligation to go to war against an unspecified future enemy. The memory of the large loss of life in World War I reinforced this attitude. The onset of the Great Depression provided a further excuse not to take action. In the end, the League failed because of the lack of political will among member states to impose more than token sanctions on states like Japan, Italy, and Germany, which openly violated the obligations laid out in the Covenant.

THE KELLOGG-BRIAND PACT: REGULATING THE *JUS AD BELLUM*

Dissatisfaction with the League led states to seek other means to place limits on the resort to force. The Kellogg-Briand Pact is perhaps the most well-known of the efforts to get states to renounce the use of force in their foreign relations.

DOCUMENT: KELLOGG-BRIAND PACT—TREATY BETWEEN THE UNITED STATES AND OTHER POWERS PROVIDING FOR THE RENUNCIATION OF WAR AS AN INSTRUMENT OF NATIONAL POLICY

When: August 27, 1928
Where: Paris, France
Source: *United States Statutes at Large*, Vol. 46, part 2, p. 2343. Washington, DC: Government Printing Office. Online at http://avalon.law.yale.edu/20th_century/kbpact.asp.
Significance: This treaty has only two provisions but stands as the prime example of attempts to have states formally commit to peaceful resolution of disputes. It will play a major role in the justifications for a charge of "crimes against peace" in the London Charter that authorized the Nuremberg war crime trials after World War II.

Article I
The High Contracting Parties solemnly declare in the names of their respective peoples that they condemn recourse to war for the solution of international

controversies, and renounce it, as an instrument of national policy in their relations with one another.

Article II
The High Contracting Parties agree that the settlement or solution of all disputes or conflicts of whatever nature or of whatever origin they may be, which may arise among them, shall never be sought except by pacific means [emphasis added].

WHAT DID KELLOGG-BRIAND ACCOMPLISH?

The treaty eventually had 62 States Parties, but it lacked any provision that would have obligated member countries to take action in case of a violation. The first major test of the pact came with the Japanese invasion of Manchuria (China) in 1931. Japan had ratified the treaty. Other parties to the pact took no action beyond verbal disapproval. The onset of the worldwide depression coupled with a reluctance to see the integrity of China as of sufficient importance to warrant war inhibited either the League of Nations or the United States from taking any action. States concerned with their own internal economic woes had little interest in undertaking expensive international ventures to defend abstract principles. Given the unwillingness of states parties to enforce the pact through effective sanctions against those countries that violated its provisions, the treaty had little impact on events that led to World War II. As an interesting note, Secretary of State Frank Kellogg earned the Nobel Peace Prize in 1929 for his work on the Peace Pact.

EXTENDING THE SCOPE OF THE *JUS IN BELLO*

Although countermining smoke was used by the South during the American Civil War (1860–1865), historians agree that the first modern use of chemical weapons occurred in World War I. As noted previously, the primary focus in the period between World War I and World War II was on enhancing restrictions on the resort to war. Yet two other concerns, issuing from events in World War I, became priorities as well: the use of poison gas and the treatment of prisoners of war (POWs).

CHEMICAL AND BIOLOGICAL WEAPONS

The conviction that even in the heat of battle certain tactics are not permissible runs through both the Lieber Code and Hague IV. Both explicitly forbade the use of poison. The introduction of poisonous gas as a weapon in World War I resulted in a widespread condemnation of the tactic. Around 1.3 million casualties were attributed to the use of gas. It clearly also escalated material costs because equipping all soldiers with protective equipment proved very expensive. Perhaps more importantly, the large-scale use of gas involved very complex logistical and management problems. Once released, it posed problems of control because wind and weather conditions could alter the course of the cloud putting one's own soldiers at risk as well as the inhabitants of any nearby towns. The prohibition against biological weapons was included in the treaty at the last moment at the insistence of Poland. The United

States first proposed the treaty in 1922 as part of the Washington Naval Conference negotiations. Even so, the U.S. Senate never ratified the protocol (Holmes 2001, 293).

DOCUMENT: PROTOCOL FOR THE PROHIBITION OF THE USE IN WAR OF ASPHYXIATING GAS AND OF BACTERIOLOGICAL METHODS OF WARFARE

When: June 17, 1925; entry into force February 8, 1928
Where: Geneva, Switzerland
Source: The Avalon Project. Online at http://avalon.law.yale.edu/20th _century/geneva01.asp.
Significance: The use of poison gas in World War I by the Germans surprised and horrified the Allies. Even so, the Allies responded in kind. Keep in mind that in war, your opponent may have the capability of responding in the same way (reciprocity) to a tactic that seemingly offers an advantage.

Protocol for the Prohibition of the Use in War of Asphyxiating, Poisonous or Other Gases, and of Bacteriological Methods of Warfare

Signed at Geneva: 17 June 1925 Entered into force: for each signatory as from the date of

The Undersigned Plenipotentiaries, in the name of their respective Governments: Whereas the use in war of asphyxiating, poisonous or other gases, and of all analogous liquids, materials or devices, has been justly condemned by the general opinion of the civilized world; and

Whereas the prohibition of such use has been declared in Treaties to which the majority of Powers of the world are Parties; and

To the end that this prohibition shall be universally accepted as a part of International Law, binding alike the conscience and the practice of nations;

Declare:

That the High Contracting Parties, so far as they are not already Parties to Treaties prohibiting such use, accept this prohibition, agree to extend this prohibition to the use of bacteriological methods of warfare and agree to be bound as between themselves according to the terms of this declaration.

The High Contracting Parties will exert every effort to induce other States to accede to the present Protocol. Such accession will be notified to the Government of the French Republic, and by the latter to all signatory and acceding Powers, and will take effect on the date of the notification by the Government of the French Republic.

The present Protocol, of which the English and French texts are both authentic, shall be ratified as soon as possible. It shall bear to-day's date.

The ratifications of the present Protocol shall be addressed to the Government of the French Republic, which will at once notify the deposit of such ratification to each of the signatory and acceding Powers.

The instruments of ratification of and accession to the present Protocol will remain deposited in the archives of the Government of the French Republic.

The present Protocol will come into force for each signatory Power as from the date of deposit of its ratification, and, from that moment, each Power will be bound as regards other Powers which have already deposited their ratifications.

In witness whereof the Plenipotentiaries have signed the present Protocol.

PRISONERS OF WAR (POWs)

States had adopted a second Geneva Convention in 1906. The 1907 Hague convention extended its provisions to maritime warfare. Given the significant problems with prisoners of war (POWs) that had arisen during World War I, states felt the 1906 Convention needed further elaboration. The 1929 Geneva Convention gives detailed rules on the following:

- the conditions in which prisoners should be captured and evacuated;
- the organization of camps;
- food and clothing for prisoners;
- hygiene; religious practice;
- mental and physical recreation; discipline inside camps;
- prison labor;
- prisoners' mail, including parcels;
- penal sanctions and legal proceedings concerning prisoners of war; and,
- repatriation at the end of hostilities.

When the Geneva Convention is mentioned in films, books, or other media that focus on events in World War II, the reference is to the 1929 Convention.

DOCUMENT: CONVENTION OF JULY 27, 1929, RELATIVE TO THE TREATMENT OF PRISONERS OF WAR

When:	July 27, 1929
Where:	Geneva, Switzerland
Source:	U.S. Statutes at Large, 47 Stat. 2021. Online at http://avalon.law.yale.edu/20th_century/geneva02.asp.
Significance:	The text of the original document runs to 97 articles plus an annex. The International Committee of the Red Cross reference provides a concise summary of the reasons for the new treaty. The 1929 Convention relative to the Treatment of Prisoners of War was replaced by the third Geneva Convention of August 12, 1949 (Geneva Convention III). It is no longer in operation following the universal acceptance of the Geneva Conventions of 1949.

PART I
General Provisions

Article 1.
The present Convention shall apply without prejudice to the stipulations of Part VII:

(1) To all persons referred to in Articles 1, 2 and 3 of the Regulations annexed to the Hague Convention (IV) of 18 October 1907, concerning the Laws and Customs of War on Land, who are captured by the enemy.

(2) To all persons belonging to the armed forces of belligerents who are captured by the enemy in the course of operations of maritime or aerial war, subject to such exceptions (derogations) as the conditions of such capture render inevitable. Nevertheless these exceptions shall not infringe the fundamental principles of the present Convention; they shall cease from the moment when the captured persons shall have reached a prisoners of war camp.

Article 2.
Prisoners of war are in the power of the hostile Government, but not of the individuals or formation which captured them.

They shall at all times be humanely treated and protected, particularly against acts of violence, from insults and from public curiosity.

Measures of reprisal against them are forbidden [all emphases in document have been added].

Article 3.
Prisoners of war are entitled to respect for their persons and honour. Women shall be treated with all consideration due to their sex.

Prisoners retain their full civil capacity.

Article 4.
The detaining Power is required to provide for the maintenance of prisoners of war in its charge.

Differences of treatment between prisoners are permissible only if such differences are based on the military rank, the state of physical or mental health, the professional abilities, or the sex of those who benefit from them.

PART II
Capture

Article 5.
Every prisoner of war is required to declare, if he is interrogated on the subject, his true names and rank, or his regimental number.

If he infringes this rule, he exposes himself to a restriction of the privileges accorded to prisoners of his category.

No pressure shall be exercised on prisoners to obtain information regarding the situation in their armed forces or their country. Prisoners who refuse to reply may not be threatened, insulted, or exposed to unpleasantness or disadvantages of any kind whatsoever.

If, by reason of his physical or mental condition, a prisoner is incapable of stating his identity, he shall be handed over to the Medical Service.

Article 6.
All personal effects and articles in personal use—except arms, horses, military equipment and military papers—shall remain in the possession of prisoners of war, as well as their metal helmets and gas-masks.

Sums of money carried by prisoners may only be taken from them on the order of an officer and after the amount has been recorded. A receipt shall be given for them. Sums thus impounded shall be placed to the account of each prisoner.

Their identity tokens, badges of rank, decorations and articles of value may not be taken from prisoners.

PART III
Captivity

SECTION I
Evacuation of Prisoners of War

Article 7.
As soon as possible after their capture, prisoners of war shall be evacuated to depots sufficiently removed from the fighting zone for them to be out of danger.

Only prisoners who, by reason of their wounds or maladies, would run greater risks by being evacuated than by remaining may be kept temporarily in a dangerous zone.

Prisoners shall not be unnecessarily exposed to danger while awaiting evacuation from a fighting zone.

The evacuation of prisoners on foot shall in normal circumstances be effected by stages of not more than 20 kilometres per day, unless the necessity for reaching water and food depôts requires longer stages.

Article 8.
Belligerents are bound mutually to notify each other of their capture of prisoners within the shortest period possible, through the intermediary of the information bureaux, such as are organized according to Article 77. They are likewise bound to inform each other of the official addresses to which the correspondence of their families may be sent to prisoners of war.

As soon as possible, every prisoner shall be enabled to correspond personally with his family, in accordance with the conditions prescribed in Article 36 and the following Articles.

As regards prisoners captured at sea, the provisions of the present article shall be observed as soon as possible after arrival in port.

SECTION 2
Prisoners of War Camps

Article 9.
Prisoners of war may be interned in a town, fortress or other place, and may be required not to go beyond certain fixed limits. They may also be interned in fenced camps; they shall not be confined or imprisoned except as a measure indispensable for safety or health, and only so long as circumstances exist which necessitate such a measure.

Prisoners captured in districts which are unhealthy or whose climate is deleterious to persons coming from temperate climates shall be removed as soon as possible to a more favourable climate.

Belligerents shall as far as possible avoid bringing together in the same camp prisoners of different races or nationalities. [emphasis added]

No prisoner may at any time be sent to an area where he would be exposed to the fire of the fighting zone, or be employed to render by his presence certain points or areas immune from bombardment.

[Articles 10 through 97 omitted]

The Convention set some very demanding standards. Many critics felt the Convention mandated treatment for POWs that was totally unrealistic considering the nature of modern warfare. A large number of captives could impose an unwelcome and burdensome responsibility if the captors themselves suffered from serious material resources. The Soviet Union and Japan did not sign the 1929 Convention. In World War II, although Japan stated in 1942 that it would observe the rules, the declaration was little more than propaganda. The Japanese believed that anyone who surrendered instead of fighting to the death had lost their honor. No great effort was expended to house and feed prisoners, nor were POWs provided even minimum medical care. The Japanese became notorious for "death marches" of POWs. For Americans, the Bataan Death March in the Philippines was considered one of the most atrocious war crimes committed by the Japanese during the war.

In the bitter struggle between Germany and the Soviet Union on the Eastern Front, POWS suffered great privation. Of the approximately 5.7 million Red Army POWs taken by the Germans, over 3 million died in captivity from abuse, disease, and starvation. Germans captured by the Red Army fared no better. Approximately 45 percent died. Of the 100,000 POWs taken at Stalingrad by the Soviets, only 5,000 ever returned to Germany (Holmes 2001, 734).

References
Chambers, John Whiteclay, II, ed. 1999. *The Oxford Companion to American Military History.* Oxford: Oxford University Press.

Croddy, Eric. 2001. *Chemical and Biological Warfare: A Comprehensive Survey for the Concerned Citizen.* New York: Copernicus Books.

Holmes, Richard, ed. 2001. *The Oxford Companion to Military History.* Oxford: Oxford University Press.

4

World War II

WHAT CAUSED WORLD WAR II?

The Treaty of Versailles (1919) and others negotiated at the end of World War I left a number of states dissatisfied with the results. Germany saw the treaty as an extreme and unwarranted punishment. The treaty required Germany to reduce its army to 100,000 men, forbade conscription, and the acquisition of tanks, heavy artillery, aircraft, and airships. In addition, the treaty imposed a very large sum (equivalent of $400 billion today) to be paid as reparations. During and after the war, Japan felt that it had not gotten the respect it deserved. Despite criticism, it openly pursued colonial expansion in Korea and China.

The economic impact of the Great Depression (1929) reinforced the reluctance of the victors in World War I to take measures to enforce the terms of the Versailles Treaty. The economic collapse did not just happen in the United States but also impacted almost every country in the Americas and Europe. Putting people back to work in domestic jobs took precedence over concerns about international events. The words of Neville Chamberlain, prime minister of Great Britain, concerning the partition of Czechoslovakia in 1938, expressed the thoughts of many about taking action to resist clear violations of the Treaty of Versailles by Germany. Before flying to Munich to negotiate the partition of Czechoslovakia in 1938 he said: "How horrible, fantastic, incredible it is that we should be digging trenches and trying on gas-masks here because of a quarrel in a far-away country between people of whom we know nothing."

GERMANY

As part of its campaign platform, the Nationalsozialistische Deutsche Arbeiterpartei (NSDAP), or Nazi Party, had promised to rearm and restore Germany to its former status as a great power. Note that during electoral campaigns, Hitler and the Nazi platform attracted popular support for many reasons, the most important of which had nothing to do with the "Jewish problem." It captured and gave coherent direction to the desires of ordinary Germans for national renewal and social reform. They tried to broadcast a broad agenda that had mass appeal. They spoke of programs to put all of the unemployed back to work, strengthening the nation, and ending all threats from groups inside the country. The explicit campaign against Jews began only after Hitler and the party had gained full control of the government in August 1934 when Hitler assumed the position of president in addition to that of chancellor.

Known as the Holocaust, the deliberate slaughter of as many as 6 million Jewish men, women, and children dominates discussions about World War II. To give a number for comparison, 6 million people is equivalent to the combined populations of the U.S. states of Alabama and Georgia in 1945. The *Oxford English Dictionary* gives the modern, secular definition of the term "holocaust" as "destruction or slaughter on a mass scale," with specific reference to "the mass murder of Jews under the German Nazi regime during the period 1941–45." The Germans conquered and occupied thirty-five separate European countries during World War II. In these occupied areas, Nazi forces conducted a systematic slaughter of the Jewish population and other minorities considered inferior.

As shocking as that number may be, the focus on the horrific toll in Jewish lives is only part of the story. The Nazis also deliberately killed another 3 million of other groups also defined as having "alien" blood or otherwise considered unfit or undesirable. R. J. Rummel argues that the Nazis murdered close to 21 million people in all (2009, 111). Among those were Soviet prisoners of war, Gypsies (Roma and Sinti), Negroes (term used in German law), the mentally handicapped, the mentally ill, and the physically disabled. With the outbreak of war in 1939, initial plans lumped Jews and Gypsies together in terms of "cleansing." Some estimates claim that the Holocaust claimed a half million Gypsies as well.

WAR CRIMES

The widespread violations of the laws of war by the Axis Powers and their minor allies in World War II led to demands for immediate postwar punishment of the guilty individuals. The early questions revolved around the appropriate method. Britain at first opposed trials because, as Anthony Eden had observed, the guilt of such individuals is so black that they fall outside and go beyond the scope of any judicial process. U.S. secretary of the treasury Henry Morgenthau Jr. and U.S. secretary of state Cordell Hull supported summary executions. Morgenthau went further by advocating the "pasturalization" of Germany. Germany should be de-industrialized, its people dispersed, and the land plowed under to form a giant pasture. Stalin advocated summary executions. Secretary of War Henry L. Stimson at first embraced executions, then became a strong advocate for trials. Stimson believed that trials were necessary to establish beyond doubt the idea of *organizational responsibility* as well as the guilt of individuals responsible for the worst atrocities. Organizational responsibility meant because of their aims, policies, and orders, the main organizations of the Nazi apparatus, the Gestapo and SS, would be held responsible for the atrocities committed in addition to just the leadership. Eventually Stimson's advocacy for trials would prevail.

NAZI PARTY ORGANIZATIONS

Understanding the role of the Nazi Party requires familiarity with the extensive network of organizations created to carry out their programs. Table 4.1 gives a brief summary of the most important organizations and how they related to each other.

Table 4.1   Nazi Party Organizations

The following were not official agencies of the state. They were answerable to Hitler as head of the Nazi Party and commanded by Nazi Party officials, not by agents of the government. Often they operated as parallel agencies with state counterparts (e.g., the Waffen SS with the Wehrmacht or regular army).

Sturmabteilung (SA)

Known as "Brownshirts" or Storm Troopers (Sturmtruppen), the Sturmabteilung (SA) paramilitary organization played a key role in Adolf Hitler's rise to power before the SS was formed in 1929. The SA protected Party meetings, marched in Nazi rallies, and physically assaulted political opponents. By the time that Hitler came to power in 1933, it had an estimated 400,000 members. On June 30, 1934, the Night of the Long Knives (*die Nacht der langen Messer*), Hitler, using SS forces, carried out a "Blood Purge" of the SA leadership. Dozens of SA leaders were summarily executed. Thereafter the SA, reduced in strength, continued to exist but ceased to play a major political role in Nazi affairs.

Schutzstaffel (SS)

The Schutzstaffel (SS) was established in 1929 as a small paramilitary unit to provide security for Hitler and other party officials. Under Heinrich Himmler, it had expanded to over a million members by 1945. It organized and supervised the activities connected with the "Final Solution." It comprised four sections.

The Security Section

The Geheime Staatspolizei (Gestapo), or Secret Police, were responsible for seeking out and eliminating opposition to the Nazi Party.

Sicherheitsdienst (SD)

The Sicherheitsdienst (SD) was the intelligence agency. In 1938, it became the intelligence organization for the State as well as for the Party. It included the Sicherheitspolizei (Sipo), or security police. The Einsatzgruppen der Sicherheitspolizei und des SD carried out many of the mass executions of Jews during the "Final Solution" in Eastern Europe.

The Military Section: Waffen SS

The Waffen SS had two subgroups: Hitler's personal bodyguards, the Leibstandarte, and the Verfügungstruppen (Troops). Serving as elite combat troops alongside the regular army, the Waffen SS gained a reputation as fanatical fighters.

Concentration Camp Section: Totenkopf verbände

The Death's Head Battalions administered the concentration camps and a vast pool of slave labor drawn from Jews and the populations of the occupied territories. This section was merged into the Waffen SS in 1942.

TRIALS

Two documents developed by the Allied Powers—the United States, United Kingdom (Great Britain), Soviet Union (USSR), and France—provided the authority and guidance for a large number of trials in Europe. In early August 1945, representatives of these four countries met in London to finalize arrangements for trials of the leadership and prominent supporters of the Nazi Party. The Charter of the International Military Tribunal (IMT) that set forth the specific details of structure, jurisdiction, and procedures was contained in an Annex to the Agreement for the Prosecution and Punishment of the Major War Criminals of the European Axis (August 8, 1945). This document will be analyzed in chapter 11, which deals with the IMT trial at Nuremberg.

A second document, Control Council Law No. 10 (CCL No. 10—Punishment of Persons Guilty of War Crimes, Crimes Against Peace and Against Humanity) was signed by the four Allied Powers on December 20, 1945. The Allied Control Council or Allied Control Authority served as the governing body for the Allied Occupation Zones in Germany and Austria. The Preamble of CCL No. 10 states the purpose: "to establish a uniform legal basis in Germany for the prosecution of war criminals and other similar offenders, other than those dealt with by the International Military Tribunal." Using CCL No. 10 as the basis, the United States and Great Britain conducted a second set of twelve trials for those not part of the leadership. These included the Medical Trial (Doctors' Trial) and Einsatzgruppen trials covered later in this book. CCL No. 10 will be discussed in the introduction to the subsequent Nuremberg Trials (chapter 12).

But, post–World War II war crime trials comprised much more than prosecution of the leaders of Germany at Nuremberg and Japan at Tokyo. In fact, the first set of trials occurred before the IMT got underway. The relevant U.S. law identified three types of military tribunals that could be used to prosecute alleged offenders (*Dostler* case, 24): (1) court-martials, (2) Military Commissions, and (3) Provost Courts. A court-martial determines the guilt or innocence of members of the armed forces subject to military law. Court-martials may also be used to try enemy combatants for violations of the law of war prior to their capture. The second type, Military Commissions, may try both enemy combatants and civilians, who do not have protected status (POWs or noncombatants) under the laws of war, for major violations. Provost Courts deal with minor violations. These trials did not rely on either the London Charter or CCL No. 10 for their authority. Instead the authority came from rights under international law to try violations of the law and customs of war. Here the 1907 Hague Regulations as well as the 1929 Geneva Convention provided sufficient authority. Even though the events associated with each of the trials involve horrific details of slaughter and other abuses on a massive scale, the crimes simply involve murder and mistreatment. It is the sheer numbers of victims that overwhelms imagination.

References

Bloxham, Donald. 2009. *The Final Solution: A Genocide*. Oxford: Oxford University Press.

Browning, Christopher R. 2004. *The Origins of the Final Solution: The Evolution of Nazi Jewish Policy, September 1939–March 1942*. Lincoln: University of Nebraska Press.

Dostler Case, Law Reports of Trials of War Criminals. Vol. 1. 1947. London: United Nations War Crimes Commissions. Online at: http://www.loc.gov/rr/frd/Military_Law/pdf/Law-Reports_Vol-1.pdf.

Gellately, Robert. 1990. *The Gestapo and Germany Society: Enforcing Racial Policy 1933–1945.* Oxford: Oxford University Press.

Rummel, R. J. 2009. *Death by Government.* New Brunswick, NJ: Transaction Publishers.

5

Anton Dostler Case

The first individual tried for war crimes in the aftermath of World War II was German general Anton Dostler. The trial was held in Rome, Italy, by a U.S. Military Commission established under the Regulations for the Trial of War Crimes, issued by Headquarters, Mediterranean Theater of Operations on September 23, 1945. As such the regulations established procedures for trials involving Type C war crimes (ordinary war crimes) as defined in the London Charter. The acting supreme allied commander of the Mediterranean Theater, General Joseph T. McNarney, appointed the members of the commission. The commission had nine members. Five senior officers formed the hearing panel. Major-General L. C. Jaynes served as the presiding officer (president). Two officers formed the prosecution team, and two served as defense counsels.

General Dostler was accused of ordering the execution of 15 captured American soldiers without holding a hearing or trial. The strategy of the defense team included three issues that would play a great part in other war crime trials: (1) the Military Commission had no legitimate legal basis; (2) the charges violated the laws and customs of war; and (3) the general carried out a superior order from Berlin based upon a policy (a Führerbefehl) dictated by the führer (supreme leader) Adolf Hitler.

DOCUMENT: THE FÜHRERBEFEHL OF 18 OCTOBER, 1942

When:	October 18, 1942
Where:	Berlin, Germany
Source:	*Law Reports of Trials of War Criminals*, vol. 1 (London: United Nations War Crimes Commissions, 1947), 22–34. Online at http://www.loc.gov/rr/frd/Military_Law/pdf/Law-Reports_Vol-1.pdf.
Significance:	Freely translated a Führerbefehl means a direct order (command) from the *Führer* (supreme leader). The reasoning in the following order justifies the policy by claiming that the enemy is not

observing the laws and customs of war. Therefore, Hitler ordered German military forces to respond in the same way.

1. Recently our adversaries have employed methods of warfare contrary to the provisions of the Geneva Convention. The attitude of the so-called commandos, who are recruited in part among common criminals released from prison, is particularly brutal and underhanded. From captured documents it has been learned that they have orders not only to bind prisoners but to kill them without hesitation should they become an encumbrance or constitute an obstacle to the completion of their mission. Finally, we have captured orders which advocate putting prisoners to death as a matter of principle.

2. For this reason, an addition to the communiqué of the Wehrmacht of 7th October, 1942, is announced; that, in the future, Germany will resort to the same methods in regard to these groups of British saboteurs and their accomplices—that is to say that German troops will exterminate them without mercy wherever they find them.

3. Therefore, I command that: Henceforth all enemy troops encountered by German troops during so-called commando operations, in Europe or in Africa, though they appear to be soldiers in uniform or demolition groups, armed or unarmed, are to be exterminated to the last man, either in combat or in pursuit. It matters not in the least whether they have been landed by ships or planes or dropped by parachute. If such men appear to be about to surrender, no quarter should be given them on general principle. A detailed report on this point is to be addressed in each case to the OKW for inclusion in the Wehrmacht communiqué.

4. If members of such commando units, acting as agents, saboteurs, etc., fall into the hands of the Wehrmacht through different channels (for example, through the police in occupied territories), they are to be handed over to the Sicherheitsdienst without delay. It is formally forbidden to keep them, even temporarily, under military supervision (for example, in POW camps, etc.).

5. These provisions do not apply to enemy soldiers who surrender or are captured in actual combat within the limits of normal combat activities (offensives, large-scale air or seaborne landings). Nor do they apply to enemy troops captured during naval engagements, nor to aviators who, have bailed out to save lives, during aerial combat.

The Führerbefehl raises two important issues. First, can a state (government) abandon accepted rules and customs of war because they believe the enemy has repeatedly violated them? This was an issue evaded by the Courts in the *Dover Castle* and *Llandovery Castle* trials after World War I. Second, what status should the American soldiers have had after their capture? The first issue involves the idea involved in the *tu quoque* defense discussed earlier. In this case, the policy states: "OK, they did it; so in response, we will do it, too." Now as logical as this may sound, the legal situation is somewhat more complicated. The logic that underlies the rules and customs of war relies on the idea that the rules and customs benefit both sides. The answers to this query lie in the legal regulations involving *reprisals*. While generally, reprisals are seen as a method of taking enforcement action against a violation of the laws by an enemy, there is much disagreement over exactly what actions a belligerent may take in reprisal. The later analysis of the case will briefly discuss the law that applies to the use of reprisals in war.

Second, because the capture of these combatants occurred deep in enemy territory, did they still deserve treatment as prisoner of war (POW) status according to the 1929 Geneva Convention; or, did the Germans have the right to treat them as spies and saboteurs? Spies and saboteurs have always been considered as "out in the cold," meaning that they have no official status in or protection if caught. Nonetheless, the corollary question is, even if they were spies and saboteurs, were the Germans within their rights to order summary execution without a hearing?

TRIAL SUMMARY #2: THE *DOSTLER* CASE

An Important Preliminary Consideration: The Legal Basis for the Military Commission (Jurisdiction)

The Defense challenged both the makeup and the jurisdiction of the Military Commission. Thus, the first part of the trial dealt with the legal basis (legitimacy) of the Commission as the appropriate method of trial. The issue involves two different challenges: the first involves the question of *who has the right to establish the tribunal*. The follow-on question then becomes *by what authority* regarded as a source generally accepted as part of the laws and customs of war does this entity have that right to hold a trial? These issues had to be settled before the actual trial on the merits of the case could begin. Please take note because, although such challenges will not be discussed in future cases unless they have some unusual features, they will be part of the defense strategy in most cases covered in this book.

The Defense contended that:

1. Article 63 of the 1929 Geneva Convention meant that, as a prisoner of war, General Dostler should be tried by a court-martial rather than a Military Commission. The rules for court-martials mandate a higher standard for evidence presented and include other safeguards that do not apply to Military Commissions;
2. the American general who had issued the command did not have the authority to do so; and
3. only the President of the United States had the authority to establish a Military Commission, and no such order had been issued.

The Prosecution argued that:

1. With regard to the trial of prisoners of war, the provisions of the 1929 Geneva Convention pertained only to offences committed by a prisoner of war while in captivity. It did not apply to offences committed against the Law of Nations prior to the defendant becoming a prisoner of war.

2. In response to the second set of claims by the Defense, the Prosecution asserted that by long-standing practice, custom, and laws of war the Supreme Commander in the field had the authority to appoint a Military Commission. The belligerent injured by the offense was the United States. The Supreme Commander for all American Forces in that theater was General McNarney, who had appointed the Commission and had referred the case to it. Under the provisions of Rules of Land Warfare, the injured belligerent could bring the captured defendant before a Military Commission.

Military Commission Ruling on Defense Objections to Legality/Jurisdiction

The trial panel accepted the arguments of the Prosecution. Most importantly, they decided that the provisions of Article 63 of the Geneva Convention did not apply to the case. As customary, the Commission did not give any reasons for its decision.

DOCUMENT: THE ANTON DOSTLER CASE

When:	October 8–10, 1945
Where:	Rome, Italy
Court:	United States Military Commission
Defendant:	General Anton Dostler, Commander of the 75th German Army Corps
Source:	*Law Reports of Trials of War Criminals*, vol. 1 (London: United Nations War Crimes Commissions, 1947), 22–34. Online at http://www.loc.gov/rr/frd/Military_Law/pdf/Law-Reports_Vol-1.pdf.
Charge:	Ordering the execution of fifteen American prisoners of war in violation of the Regulations attached to The Hague Convention IV of 1907 and in violation of long-established laws and customs of war
Legal Issue:	Because they were clearly identified as legitimate combatants and engaged on legitimate military missions, did the captured soldiers have the right to be treated as prisoners of war (POWs); that is, was the order for summary execution permissible under the circumstances
Defense:	Defense argued that the defendant, General Dostler, was a "protected person"—a prisoner of war—and thus not subject to prosecution. Defense also contended that the Commission had not been legally established. Later the defendant pled superior orders based upon the Führerbefehl (Fuhrer's orders or commands) of October 18, 1942
Verdict:	Guilty; death by firing squad
Significance:	The issues raised by the defense team in this trial would be raised again and again in subsequent trials.

Facts

On the night of 22nd March, 1944, two officers and 13 men of a special reconnaissance battalion disembarked from some United States Navy boats and landed on the Italian coast about 100 kilometres north of La Spezia. The front at the time was at Cassino with a further front at the Anzio beach head. The place of disembarkation was therefore 250 miles behind the then established front. The 15 members of the United States Army were on a *bona fide* military mission, which was to demolish the railroad tunnel on the mainline between La Spezia and Genoa. On the morning of 24th March, 1944, the entire group was captured by a party consisting of Italian Fascist soldiers and a group of members of the German army. They were brought to La Spezia where they were confined near the headquarters of the 135th Fortress Brigade.

. . .

On the next morning (25th March, 1944) a telegram was received at the headquarters of the 135th Fortress Brigade signed by the accused Dostler, saying in substance "the captured Americans will be shot immediately."

On receiving this cable, the commanding officer of the 135th Fortress Brigade and the Naval Officers interrogating the prisoners got into touch with the 75th Army Corps headquarters in order to bring about a stay of the execution. Late on the afternoon of the 25th March, Colonel Kurt Almers (then commanding the brigade) received another telegram from 75th Army Corps which said in substance that by 7.0 o'clock the next morning (26th March) he would have reported compliance with the order of execution.

Colonel Almers then gave orders for the conduct of the execution, for the digging of a grave, etc. During the night from Saturday 25th to Sunday, 26th March, two attempts were made by officers of the 135th Fortress Brigade and by the Naval Officers to bring about a change in the decision by telephoning to the accused Dostler. All these attempts having been unsuccessful, the 15 Americans were executed on the 26th March, early in the morning.

They were neither tried, nor given any hearing.

Testimony/Evidence

Witnesses for the Prosecution included a Captain in the United States Army who had directed the operation against the tunnel. He stated that the fifteen soldiers had been *bona fide* members of the United States Forces; he also bore witness as to the nature of the mission on which they were sent, and as to the clothing and equipment which they wore. Witnesses for the Prosecution included . . . two German Naval Intelligence Officers who gave further evidence regarding the deceased's clothing. One of the last two identified a document before the Commission as representing in substance the Führerbefehl to which reference was made by the Defence. Three ex-members of the Wehrmacht [German army] gave evidence of attempts made to induce Dostler to change the order regarding the execution, and on the circumstances of the execution. General [Gustav-Adolf von] Zangen [Dostler's immediate superior in the German army chain of command] appeared in the witness box and denied having ordered the execution of the prisoners.

Two depositions and the notes of a preliminary interrogation of General Dostler were also allowed as evidence. The first deposition was made by a German lieutenant in hospital, who bore witness to the contents of the telegram containing Dostler's orders regarding the immediate execution of the prisoners and to the efforts which were made to avert the latter. The second deposition was made by a Captain in the United States Army who had been present at the exhumation of the bodies of the soldiers.

The Defence recalled General Zangen, who bore witness to the accused's merits as a soldier, and called a second Wehrmacht General, von Saenger, who described the oath which officers of the German Army had had to take on the accession of Hitler to power.

...

[T]he decisive facts were not controversial, namely that the victims had been members of the American Forces, carrying out a military mission, that the accused had ordered their shooting without trial, and that they had been so shot.

The Arguments of the Defense and Replies Made by the Prosecution

1. *That the Deceased were not entitled to the Benefits of the Geneva Convention*

   The Defence claimed that for any person to be accorded the rights of a prisoner of war under the Geneva Convention, it was necessary, under Article I thereof, for that person, *inter alia*, "to have a fixed distinctive emblem recognisable at a distance." The submission of the Defence was that the American soldiers had worn no such distinctive emblem, and that their mission had been undertaken for the purpose of sabotage, to be accomplished by stealth and without engaging the enemy. They were not therefore entitled to the privileges of lawful belligerents, though *it was admitted that they were entitled to a lawful trial even if they were treated as spies* [emphasis added].

2. The Plea of Superior Orders

   The accused relied on the defence of superior orders which was based on two alleged facts:

   (a) The Führerbefehl of 18th October, 1942, the text of which is provided in the Appendix [see above]. The Führerbefehl laid down that if members of Allied commando units were encountered by German troops they were to be exterminated either in combat or in pursuit. If they should fall into the hands of the Wehrmacht through different channels they were to be handed over to the Sicherheitsdienst [SS] intelligence and security service) without delay.

...

> (b) Alleged orders received from the Commander of the Army Group, General von Zangen, and from the Commander of the Heeresgruppe [Army Group] South West, Field Marshal Kesselring.

Dostler also claimed that he had revoked his first order to shoot the men and that he had eventually re-issued it on higher order.

The Defence tried to establish the fact that in 1933 all officers of the German Army had to take a special oath of obedience to the Fuhrer, Adolf Hitler. This fact was confirmed both by General von Zangen and Dostler himself in the witness box. The Prosecution put a question to General von Saenger whether he could cite to the Commission, any single case of a general officer in the German Army who was executed for disobedience to an order. Von Saenger replied that he had heard of two cases, one of which he knew; the second was only a rumour. The witness did not know a case in the German Army in which a general officer was executed for disobedience to the Führerbefehl of 18th October, 1942.

General von Saenger admitted that the Fuhrer gave out orders which in their way interfered with International Law. The officers at the front who had to execute these orders were convinced, however, that in those cases Hitler would make a statement or by some other means inform the enemy governments of his decisions, so that the officers were not responsible for crimes committed while carrying out his orders. He also said that during the war officers could not resign from the German Army.

Dostler himself said that under the oath to Hitler he understood that it was mandatory upon him to obey all orders received from the Fuhrer or under his authority.

Issue: Was the Action a Legitimate Act of Reprisal?

Defence Counsel quoted a statement from Oppenheim-Lauterpacht, *International Law*, . . . to the effect that an act otherwise amounting to a war crime might have been executed in obedience to orders conceived as a measure of reprisals, and that a Court was bound to take into consideration such a circumstance.

The Defence invoked the text of the Führerbefehl which in its first sentence itself refers to the Geneva Convention and represents itself as a reprisal order made in view of the alleged illegal methods of warfare employed by the Allies. Counsel claimed that retaliation was recognised by the Geneva Convention as lawful, that the Führerbefehl stated the basis on which it rested and that the accused therefore had a perfect right to believe that the order, as a reprisal order, was legitimate.

The Defence quoted also paragraph 347 of the United States Basic Field Manual F.M.27-10 (*Rules of Land Warfare*), which says that individuals of the armed forces will not be punished for war crimes if they are committed under the orders or sanction of their government or commanders.

In so far as the defence was based on the Führerbefehl, the Prosecution submitted that, apart from an illegal order being no defence, the shooting of the prisoners in the present case had not even been covered by the terms of the Führerbefehl, because the latter ordered that Commandos should be annihilated in combat or in pursuit, but that if they came into the hands of the Wehrmacht, through other channels, they should be handed over without delay to the Sicherheitsdienst [SS/SD]. The prosecuting Counsel pointed out that the deceased had not been killed in combat or in pursuit, and had been executed instead of being given up to the Sicherheitsdienst.

As far as the Defence relied on orders received from Army Group headquarters, and headquarters of the Heeresgruppe [army group] South West, this defence had not been substantiated.

...

With regard to the text of the Führerbefehl of 18th October, 1942, which was used in evidence, the Defence Counsel said: "It is a matter of common knowledge that this Führerbefehl was kept extremely secret. As a matter of fact practically no originals of it have ever been found. This does not purport to be an original we have; it is a copy on which the signature of whoever signed it is illegible. I understand it was secured from the French intelligence and they passed it on, and that one copy is the only one they have been able to find."

During his examination, the accused, on being handed a copy of the text of the Führerbefehl of October, 1942, said that a document which he had received in 1944 through Army Group channels contained substantially everything that was in the 1942 text, but with certain additions. He stated further that "this copy is not the complete Führerbefehl as it was valid in March, 1944. In the order that laid on my desk in March, 1944, it was much more in detail . . . the Führerbefehl which was laying in front of me listed the various categories of operations which may come under the Führerbefehl. In addition there was something said in that Führerbefehl about the interrogation of men belonging to sabotage troops and the shooting of these men after their interrogation. . . . I am not quite clear about the point, whether a new Führerbefehl covering the whole matter came out or whether only a supplement came out and the former Führerbefehl was still in existence."

With regard to the mission of the 15 American soldiers he claimed that, after making consultations with staff officers: "as it appeared without doubt that the operation came under the Führerbefehl an order was given by me and sent out that the men were to be shot."

General von Saenger said that in the Autumn of 1943 he had been acquainted with a Führerbefehl on the same subject which was different in contents from that before the Commission. On the other hand, three witnesses, namely, one of the German Naval Intelligence Officers, an ex-Wehrmacht Adjutant and General von Zangen, could remember no amendments to the Führerbefehl of October, 1942.

THE IMPORTANCE OF THE RULING ON JURISDICTION

Quibbles over procedural matters may not seem as important as the nature of the charges. Yet procedure lies at the heart of the law because the results from trials must be comparable to each other. Think of the rules that apply to evidence and other matters in the same way that you might think of the rules that apply to solving a problem in mathematics. If you apply the rules correctly, you get the "right" result. Consider also that, if the argument of the Defense in the *Dostler* case regarding the interpretation of the 1929 Geneva Convention were found correct, and accepted by the Commission, that decision would have had far-reaching consequences with regard to trials of other war criminals. Regardless of crimes committed, all enemy soldiers would immediately receive immunity from prosecution when they surrendered and became POWs.

The ruling has other implications for jurisdiction as well, but these are not important for this discussion. The other issues involve very technical questions that go beyond the discussion needed to understand the importance of this case.

REPRISALS

While the claim of superior orders forms the central line of defense in the *Dostler* case, *the first issue really turns on the lawfulness of the policy on which the order was based*. To determine if the order General Dostler gave for summary execution was legitimate, the Commission should first have determined the legality of the policy established by the Führerbefehl. That in turn would have involved an examination of the law governing the use of reprisals in warfare. Acts of reprisal are regarded as necessary to enforce the laws and customs of war. A *reprisal is an illegal action* taken by a belligerent to punish a *prior illegal* action by the enemy. Thus, in the very odd universe of international law and warfare, a reprisal (your illegal act) becomes a legitimate (legal) response because of the prior illegal act by your enemy. *Please note this definition because many dictionary definitions equate reprisal with retaliation.* Retaliation is a much broader concept. Reprisal is one type of retaliation. Not all actions in retaliation involve illegal acts.

So, the first issue revolved around the legality (permissibility) of the policy stated in the Führerbefehl—did the provisions of the Führerbefehl violate international law? Referring back to the *Dover Castle* case, the Defense argued that the 1929 Geneva Convention recognized the right of reprisal. Thus, because the Führerbefehl clearly stated the basis for the policy, the accused had a reason to believe the order was legitimate.

In assessing the evidence, the Commission chose not address questions relating to the legality of the directive. Instead, they focused on the situations identified in paragraph 3 of the Führerbefehl as they related to the capture of the Americans. Recall the earlier discussion that emphasized the element of context as a factor in applying law to specific situations. The text of the Führerbefehl states that those "armed or unarmed, are to be exterminated to the last man, *either in combat or in pursuit*." The capture did not involve either of these situations. The panel found that, while the "give no quarter" implications of the policy violated fundamental rules of modern warfare, that issue was not relevant to the case before the Commission. More to the point, the Führerbefehl explicitly said in paragraph 5: "These provisions do not apply to enemy soldiers who surrender or are captured in actual combat within the limits of normal combat activities (offensives, large-scale air or seaborne landings)." The proper actions should have been to hand over the troops to the SS/SD (security police). Dostler should have known that the order did not conform to the established policy stated in the Führerbefehl.

A second important consideration comes from the protected status of POWs. Simply, killing POWs who have surrendered is prohibited. Article 2(3) of the 1929 Geneva Convention also prohibits measures of reprisal against POWs. The notes appended to the case state: "From this it follows that under the law as codified by the 1929 Convention there can be no legitimate reprisals against prisoners of war. No soldier, and still less a Commanding General, can be heard to say that he considered the summary shooting of prisoners of war legitimate even as a reprisal" (32).

In sum, (1) given the situation, the order for summary execution did not reflect the policy as distributed; and (2) summary execution of those who have POW status can never be accepted as a legitimate reprisal.

SUPERIOR ORDERS AS A DEFENSE

Given that the telegram from Berlin sanctioned an illegal action, the specific issue then should have turned on the extent to which a plea of superior orders could mitigate responsibility for the act. The Commission never grappled with potential issues here. Instead they focused on the Führerbefehl. As discussed earlier, and as the Prosecution had pointed out, the 15 American service men had not been killed either in combat or in pursuit. They were dressed as proper combatants. They had been shot 45 hours after capture. This action violated the instructions in the Führerbefehl, which provides in paragraph 4 that if members of such commando units were to fall into the hands of the Wehrmacht through different channels (e.g., through the police in occupied territories) they were to be handed over to the SS/SD without delay. From this it follows that if Dostler had followed the instruction in the Führerbefehl, he should not have ordered execution of the prisoners, but should have handed them over to the SS/SD.

There is one final point of interest raised by this case. Ironically, it should be noted that if Dostler had handed over the Americans to the SS/SD, he still would have committed a war crime. That action would also have violated both the spirit and intent of the 1929 Geneva Convention.

Reference
Lauterpacht, Hersh, ed. 1935. *International Law: A Treatise by L. Oppenheim*. 5th ed. London: Longman.

6

German Concentration and Extermination Camps

The next three trials deal with German concentration and killing camps. After they gained control of the German government in 1933, the Nazis quickly moved to set up concentration camps to imprison those people they saw as opposing their policies. While policies systematically deprived Jews who had German citizenship of their civil rights and property, they were not sent to concentration camps unless they actively opposed the government. In January 1933, Jews comprised less than 1 percent of the country's total population of 67 million (approximately 523,000). Eighty percent had German citizenship. From the time the Nazis gained control of the government in 1934, Jews became subject to harassment in the form of arbitrary arrests, boycotts, localized violence, and police indifference to complaints about grievances. At first, the policy aimed at forcing the Jewish population to emigrate, but then additional regulations over time made emigration more difficult. Gradually, the Nazis sought to exact penalties for the decision to emigrate by depriving Jews of their property, by levying an increasingly heavy emigration tax, and by restricting the amount of money that could be transferred abroad from German banks. The taxes and regulations made emigration almost impossible for any Jew of modest means.

On the other side, other states became increasingly reluctant to accommodate the flood of refugees emanating from Germany. This situation had become worse because of growing anti-Semitism elsewhere. For example, after 1933, about 100,000 Jews annually emigrated from Poland. Massive waves also came from Latvia, Lithuania, Romania, and Hungary (Schleunes 1970, 186). Governments around the world had imposed emigration restrictions because of the economic crisis (the Great Depression). They had little interest in accepting anyone who might become a pubic charge. Extermination replaced emigration only after the invasion of the Soviet Union in 1941.

The invasion of Poland in August 1939 generated a new set of problems—it added large numbers of those considered racially inferior (Slavs and more Jews) to those living under German authority. The conquest of Poland, by adding approximately 2 million Polish Jews, made a tenfold increase in the number of Jews under German control. The total would rise to 3 million by June 1941. Now the Jewish question also became part of the minority question that involved cleaning out the new occupied territories for resettlement by Germans. The problems of cleansing and resettlement would increase with each success of the German army. The cleansing efforts (i.e., the removal of Jews from the territories formally annexed to Germany) moved 250,000 Jews and 600,000 other Poles into the area around Warsaw. This added considerably to the already significant Jewish population of the area. Warsaw alone had 350,000 Jews, about 30 percent of the city's population. With no possibility of deportation to other areas, the Nazis reluctantly embraced the idea of concentrating the Jewish population in ghettos as a temporary solution. Germans did not use the term "ghetto." They called the areas Jewish quarters (*Jüdisches Wohnbezirk*).

The problems revolved around ensuring that maintenance of the ghetto would not be a drain on scarce resources. From an ideological standpoint, many Nazis believed that the arrangement would produce a great windfall because of misperceptions about the accumulated wealth of Jewish communities. Christopher Browning writes that the debate about policy centered on the goal of the temporary arrangement—attrition or production. "Attritionists" saw the ghettos as concentration camps that would extract as much wealth as possible by requiring payment for everything from food to garbage removal while keeping rations at a minimum. "Productionists" argued that until their final dissolution the ghettos ought to be utilized as a source of cheap labor that potentially could make them self-sufficient and perhaps contributors to the German war economy (Browning 2004, 111). The debate really did not matter because many of the ghettos became temporary labor camps.

As the presumed temporary arrangements lingered, the resources of the ghetto populations were exhausted, which then posed a hard choice—taking action to make the ghettos somewhat self-sustaining or to allow starvation and disease to take its inevitable course. In actuality, decisions to evolve self-sustainability did not make a great difference. The conditions created by Nazi policy produced a situation in which:

> Ruthless expropriation and exploitation of labor combined with a totally inadequate food supply, terrible overcrowding in poor housing, and utter inadequate sanitation and medical care turn Polish Jewry into a starving disease-ridden, impoverished community desperately struggling for survival. (Browning 2004, 167)

Even though both types of camps had high death rates, Timothy Snyder (2010, xiii) notes that an important distinction existed between concentration camps and facilities that engaged in wholesale killing as their function. The Nazis had operated concentration camps to intern "political enemies" since the first days of the regime. Dachau had opened almost immediately after Hitler's appointment as chancellor in 1933. Established in the summer of 1936 near Berlin, Sachsenhausen evolved into the administrative center for all the camps.

Beginning with the war, the number of camps rapidly expanded to an estimated 20,000 that served a number of different purposes: forced labor, POW detention, transit, and killing centers. The camps were commanded by the SS Death's Head Units (Totenkopf verbände), so named for their skull and cross bones insignia. During the final solution, the unit would prove the aptness of its name. Auschwitz and its commandant Rudolf Höss (1940–43, 1944–45) endure as two of the most graphic and appalling symbols of the Holocaust.

In the concentration camps, prisoners were required to work. Several of the camps became major sources of slave labor for nearby German industries. I.G. Farben chose a site to construct a plant to manufacture synthetic rubber and oil largely because of its proximity to Auschwitz (established May 1940; overall operation became known as I.G. Auschwitz). The conditions in the camps made it difficult to keep enough prisoners healthy enough to ensure a steady labor supply. As the war had expanded, so had the dilemmas with respect to the impact of removing Jews from productive pursuits. Over time a great tension developed between the policy of extermination and the need for skilled Jewish labor. Wartime had created a labor shortage. The Germans urgently needed to find a way to address the ever-growing shortage of labor because of the manpower needs of the military and paramilitary forces. The commander of the German forces in the General Government in Poland wrote to Heinrich Himmler: "Unless work of military importance is to suffer, Jews cannot be released until replacements have been trained, and then only step by step" (Friedlander 2007, 495). The attempt to satisfy the two incompatible goals produced inconsistent policies until the decision to proceed with total annihilation.

THE "FINAL SOLUTION"

Experiments with gas had begun at Auschwitz in August 1941. On the basis of those experiments, an SS Sonderkommando unit had begun construction of a center at Chelmno from which multiple mobile gassing vans would operate. The SS Sonderkommandos were ad hoc units formed to undertake various special operations. They should not be confused with camp inmates termed *sonderkommandos* who were workers recruited from death camp prisoners (almost all Jewish). These workers were forced to take care of the disposal of gas chamber victims during the Holocaust.

Prior to this, gassing vans had been used to murder asylum inmates. In late autumn 1941, officials began using mobile gassing vans on Russian POWs interned at Sachsenhausen. In mid-October 1941, SS headquarters in Lublin, Poland, received an oral order from Himmler to start immediate construction work on the first killing center at Bełżec in occupied Poland. The order preceded the Wannsee Conference (January 1942) by three months. Browning argues that by the end of October 1941 the outlines for the "final solution" had been decided upon, but the program could not get fully under way until early spring because the necessary administrative and logistical structures had to be set up (2004, 374). The conference at Wannsee (outside Berlin) in January 1942 left no doubt that the plan now included killing every last Jew in Europe.

Table 6.1   Nazi Killing Centers

Auschwitz-Birkenau	1.1 to 1.6 million
Bełżec	601,500
Chelmno	255,000
Majdanek (Lublin)	360,000
Sobibòr	250,000
Treblinka	750,000 to 870,000

Source: Numbers from "The Holocaust Chronicle," http://www.holocaustchronicle.org/holocaustappendices.html.

The plan approved at the Wannsee Conference eventually was given the name Aktion Reinhardt (also Reinhard). Some dispute exists over the origin of the name, but historians generally believe that the name was chosen to honor Reinhard Heydrich, the coordinator of the "Final Solution." In late May 1942, Heydrich was assassinated in Prague by British-trained Czechoslovakian agents. Table 6.1 lists the main extermination camps operated by the Nazis.

Although technically, concentration and POW camps did not serve as killing centers per se, along with the decision to establish killing centers, a decision was made to extend the Aktion T-4 program to rid the camps of "excess prisoners." The program, Special Treatment 14f13 (after its reference number in documents) presumably would proceed on a predetermined hierarchy of victims: dangerous criminals, those medically unworthy of life, and "medicalized" euthanasia of all groups considered by the regime to be undesirable—Jews, homosexuals, Gypsies, Catholic clergy, and others viewed as morally inferior. The use of "special treatment" in the name of the program came from a distinction that made little difference. Supposedly issued to permit discriminating decisions between life and death on the basis of specific criteria set out in the directives from Heydrich, "special handling" became a synonym for the extermination of Jews in the East.

References

Browning, Christopher R. 2004. *The Origins of the Final Solution: The Evolution of Nazi Jewish Policy, September 1939—March 1942*. Lincoln: University of Nebraska Press.

Friedlander, Saul. 2007. *The Years of Extermination: Nazi Germany and the Jews, 1939–1945*. New York: HarperCollins.

Gellately, Robert. 2001. *Backing Hitler: Consent & Coercion in Nazi Germany*. Oxford: Oxford University Press.

Schleunes, Karl A. 1970. *The Twisted Road to Auschwitz: Nazi Policy toward German Jews 1933–1939*. Urbana: University of Illinois Press.

Snyder, Timothy. 2010. *Bloodlands: Europe between Stalin and Hitler*. New York: Basic Books.

Sofsky, Wolfgang. 1997. *The Order of Terror: The Concentration Camp*. Translated by William Templer. Princeton, NJ: Princeton University Press.

7

Zyklon B Trial

This trial raises a number of issues that go far beyond the scope of this book. While these issues will not be discussed in detail, the reader should be familiar with one that considerably impacts our life in contemporary times. In honor of Mary Shelley who wrote the book, it is known as the Frankenstein problem. Obviously, this has little to do with the horror films that emphasize the monster. The original book has a very serious theme. If their creations produce terrible and unanticipated consequences, do scientists bear any responsibility for the results? In the book, when they are stranded together, Dr. Frankenstein is forced to have a very pointed and extended conversation with his creation about the doctor's "responsibility" for creating what others see as a "monster."

The question arose as an issue for the scientists who developed (and continued to develop) chemical warfare agents in World War I and after. It became an issue for those who worked on the Manhattan Project that created the atomic bomb in World War II. On seeing the first test of the atomic bomb, J. Robert Oppenheimer, the director of the project, said that the first thought that entered his mind was from the *Bhagavad Gita*: "I am become Death, the destroyer of worlds."

The question does not have a simple answer. Apart from the direct role of scientists in explicitly working to creating weapons of war, many technologies that now have become regarded as essential to everyday life also have the potential for dual use in the development of more effective and destructive weapons. Without a great deal of elaboration, the same physics that generated the atomic bomb, when controlled, also generates electric power in many areas of the United States and elsewhere. Satellites and computers connect us to the world and each other, but they also enable enhanced capabilities for targeting as well as espionage. Computer chip technology gives us smaller lighter lap tops and "smart" phones, as well as smaller, "smarter" bombs with larger payloads. Cyanide compounds like Zyklon B were first developed as insecticides and pesticides.

FRITZ HABER

Fritz Haber, a German chemist, has been described as the "father of chemical warfare." In World War I, Haber defended gas warfare against accusations that it was inhumane, saying that death is death, by whatever means it occurs. Considering himself a patriotic German, he played a major role in the development of the non-ballistic use of chemical warfare in World War I. Born of Jewish parents, he elected to convert to Christianity (Lutheran) because of the latent prejudice against Jews in Germany. Haber received the Nobel Prize in Chemistry in 1918 for his invention of the Haber–Bosch process, a method used in industry to synthesize ammonia from nitrogen gas and hydrogen gas. This invention permitted the large-scale synthesis of fertilizers and explosives. To emphasize the prior point about dual use, food production for half the current population of the world depends on this method for producing nitrogen fertilizers.

WHAT IS ZYKLON B?

After World War I, Haber continued to be involved in Germany's secret development of chemical weapons. His research led to the founding of Deutsche Gesellschaft für Schädlingsbekämpfung mbH (Degesch), a state-controlled consortium formed to investigate military use of the chemical Hydrogen cyanide (HCN). HCN, also called prussic acid, is a colorless, flammable, and extremely poisonous liquid that becomes a gas at room temperature (75°F). During the early 1920s, scientists working at his institute developed the cyanide gas formulation Zyklon A. It was widely used as an insecticide and as a fumigant pesticide in grain stores. A team of chemists that included Dr. Bruno Tesch developed a method of packaging HCN in sealed canisters. They named the new product Zyklon B to distinguish it from Zyklon A.

In 1924, Tesch and his partner Paul Stabenow formed Tesch & Stabenow (Testa), a pest control company. The company did not manufacture Zyklon B or any other chemicals. It served as a distributor and specialized in the fumigation of commercial properties such as warehouses and ships in the port of Hamburg. Zyklon B was produced by Dessauer Werke and Kaliwerke, a subsidiary of the industrial giant I.G. Farben. In 1925, Testa became the sole distributor of Zyklon B in areas east of the Elbe River. Testa began distributing the gas to the German army at camps located at Auschwitz-Birkenau, Majdanek, Sachsenhausen, Ravensbrück, and Dachau in 1941.

FRITZ HABER AND THE NAZIS

With the rise to power of the Nazis, Haber became increasingly concerned about the possible safety of his friends, associates, and family. In the spring of 1933, all Jewish personnel in the service of the German state (which included university professors and the staff of the Kaiser Wilhelm Institute that Haber directed) were forced to resign. Haber was shocked by these developments, since he had assumed that his conversion to Christianity and his services to the state during World War I should have made him an honored and patriotic German citizen. Ordered to dismiss all Jewish personnel, Haber attempted to delay their departures long enough to find them somewhere to go. Haber left Germany in August 1933. Several members of Haber's extended family, who elected to stay in Germany, died in Nazi concentration camps.

PREPARING FOR THE "FINAL SOLUTION"

One of the earliest laws of the new Nazi government in 1933 related to the "Prevention of Offspring with Hereditary Diseases" (July 1933). Initially, the mentally handicapped, the mentally ill, repeat criminal offenders, the physically disabled along with those who had epilepsy, Huntington's chorea, and various other debilitating physical diseases would be sterilized. An initial list included 410,000. Sterilization policy was justified as "purification of the national body." Hitler had written:

> The *völkisch* state must see to it that only the healthy beget children. . . . Here the state must act as the guardian of a millennial future. . . . It must put the most modern medical means in the service of this knowledge. It must declare unfit for propagation all who are in any way visibly sick or who have inherited a disease and therefore pass it on. (Lifton 1986, 25)

The sterilization regulations would evolve into a more ominous policy based upon the idea that those who have a life not worth living, even if not institutionalized, consume resources that would be better utilized to support and enhance lives worth living. The length of time it took to move from the decision to sterilize (1933) to systematic elimination (1939) indicates a concern for adverse reaction from the German public. As decreed by Nazi law, from 1934 nursing costs for mental patients were reduced. By 1936 the mental homes had become overcrowded, and conditions worsened as a result of the reduced quantity and quality of food supplies. The Hadamar mental hospital building had been designed to accommodate 250 patients, but by 1939 about 600 inmates were crowded into cramped quarters. When the euthanasia program, Aktion T-4, began at Hadamar, it did so with the very young, gradually expanding to include older children before encompassing adults. Yet when Hitler decided that the project should include adults, he did not wish to be publicly identified with it: Hitler and other Nazi leaders were very much aware that they were advocating a policy for which the German public and even the official state bureaucracy were not quite ready.

Beginning in October 1939, the Nazis experimented with new techniques. Before Zyklon B, they had used a variety of lethal injections. When injections proved slow and cumbersome, the handicapped killing centers pioneered the development of gas chambers like those later used at extermination camps. Scientists and doctors developed a mobile killing unit that first used carbon monoxide (CO). The unit had an air-tight chamber on the back of a van. Victims were placed in the chamber and asphyxiated by use of bottled gas. Between October 1939 and May 1940, approximately 10,000 mental patients were killed. The official program lasted through the early summer of 1941. As the public became aware of the program, opposition mounted. The churches had raised strong objections, and widespread public demonstrations had protested the policy.

During late August 1939, following the designation of the facility at Hadamar as a military hospital, patients were distributed to surrounding mental homes. Between November 1940 and January 1941, the Nazis converted the sickrooms into quarters for the medical and administrative personnel. Rooms to receive arriving patients were located on the first floor. A gas chamber disguised as a shower room was installed in the basement of the building, together with a crematorium with two ovens which were attached to a chimney. Gas entered the chamber from an adjacent room through pipes with holes punched in them.

The technology and modes of transportation developed for the euthanasia centers were later utilized in the extermination camps. Many of the physicians who became specialists in the technology of mass murder in the centers became part of the staff of the death camps. Like the handicapped killing centers, the extermination camps installed ovens to dispose of the dead by cremation. Some of the centers had a conveyor belt system to carry the corpses directly from the gas chamber directly to the ovens.

The official conclusion of the T-4 Program in 1941 coincided with the initiation of the "final solution." Unofficially it ran through the end of 1944. Gallagher reports that as the bombing of German cities during the war increased, what Germans referred to as "wild euthanasia" led to widespread, unorganized, and indiscriminate killing of the elderly, orphans, homosexuals, and other considered unfit. The program claimed over 70,000 victims during its two years of open operation, but even more victims between the official conclusion of the program and the fall of the Nazi regime in 1945. The total number killed under the T-4 Program, including the unofficial covert phase, may have reached 275,000.

TRIAL SUMMARY #3: THE ZYKLON B CASE

Jurisdiction

The question of jurisdiction arose because the indictment and prosecution case did not explicitly claim that any of the victims for Allied countries were British nationals. The judge advocate, in his summing up, stated that "among those unfortunate creatures undoubtedly there were." The absence of British nationals did not matter. The British claim to jurisdiction over the case could be based on three valid circumstances:

1. "by the Declaration regarding the defeat of Germany and the assumption of supreme authority with respect to Germany, made in Berlin on the 5th June, 1945, the four Allied Powers occupying Germany assumed supreme authority" over the areas. They became the local sovereign authority in Germany. This included "the right to try German nationals for crimes of any kind wherever committed";
2. by "the general doctrine called Universality of Jurisdiction over War Crimes, under which every independent State has in International Law jurisdiction to punish pirates and war criminals in its custody regardless of the nationality of the victim or the place where the offence was committed"; or
3. by "the doctrine that the United Kingdom has a direct interest in punishing the perpetrators of crimes if the victim was a national of an ally engaged in a common struggle against a common enemy."

DOCUMENT: THE ZYKLON B CASE

When: March 1–8, 1946
Where: Hamburg, Germany
Court: British Military Court
Each of the defendants had a German Counsel who assisted in the defense.
Defendants: Bruno Tesch, Joachim Drosihn, and Karl Weinbacher
Source: *Law Reports of Trials of War Criminals*, vol. 1 (London: United Nations War Crimes Commissions, 1947), 93–103. Online at http://www.loc.gov/rr/frd/Military_Law/pdf/Law-Reports_Vol-1.pdf.
Charge: Defendants knowingly supplied poison gas used for the extermination of Allied nationals interned in concentration camps in violation of Article 46 of the 1907 Hague IV Regulations
Legal Issue: The charges were based upon commercial transactions done by civilians. Do the provisions of the laws and customs of war apply to civilians?
Defense: The defense claimed that the accused did not know how the gas would be used. For Drosihn, the defense argued that the supply of gas was beyond his control.
Verdict: Tesch and Weinbacher were found guilty. Death by hanging. Drosihn was acquitted.
Significance: Article 46 of the Hague Convention of 1907, concerning the Laws and Customs of War on Land, on which the case for the Prosecution was based, provides that "Family honor and rights, individual life and private property, as well as religious convictions and worship must be respected." This article falls under the section heading Military Authority over the Territory of the Hostile State and was intended to refer to acts committed by the occupying authorities in occupied territory. In the trial of Tesch, the acts to which the accused were allegedly accessories before the fact were committed mainly at Auschwitz, in occupied Poland.

FACTS

Dr. Bruno Tesch was by 1942 the sole owner of the firm known as Tesch and Stabenow (Testa), whose activities were divided into three main categories. In the first place, it distributed certain types of gas and gassing equipment for disinfecting various public buildings, including Wehrmacht barracks and S.S. concentration camps. Secondly, it provided, where required, expert technicians to carry out these gassing operations. Lastly, Dr. Tesch and Dr. Drosihn, the firm's senior gassing technician, carried out instruction for the Wehrmacht and the S.S. in the use of the gas which the firm supplied. The predominant importance of these gassing operations in war-time lay in their value in the extermination of lice.

The principal gas supplied was Zyklon B, a highly dangerous poison gas. Tesch and Stabenow did not manufacture the gas. They had the exclusive contract to supply it east of the River Elbe. They acted solely as middlemen. The Zyklon B itself went directly from the manufacturers to the customer. "The contention for the Prosecution was that from 1941 to 1945 Zyklon B was being supplied as a direct result of orders accepted by the accused's firm, Tesch and Stabenow." Vast quantities of Zyklon B were delivered to the largest concentration camps in Germany east of the Elbe. In these camps from 1942 to 1945, the SS Totenkopf verbande systematically killed 4.5 million people by the use of Zyklon B.

Prosecution

Emil Sehm, a former bookkeeper and accountant employed by Tesch and Stabenow, supplied information, regarding the legitimate business activities of the firm and the positions of the three accused therein, which substantially bore out the opening statements of the Prosecutor on these points. He went on to state that in the Autumn of 1942 he saw in the files of the firm's registry one of the reports, dictated by Tesch, which gave accounts of his business journeys. In this travel report, Tesch recorded an interview with leading members of the Wehrmacht, during which he was told that the burial, after shooting, of Jews in increasing numbers was proving more and more unhygienic, and that it was proposed to kill them with prussic acid. Dr. Tesch, when asked for his views, had proposed to use the same method, involving the release of prussic acid gas in an enclosed space, as was used in the extermination of vermin. He undertook to train the S.S. men in this new method of killing human beings.

Sehm had written down a note of these facts and taken it away with him, but had burnt it the next day on the advice of an old friend, named Wilhelm Pook, to whom he had related what he had seen.

Dr. Marx, a German Barrister practising since 1934, who was called upon to define the status of a Procurist in German law, said:

> The procurist had the right to act in the name and on behalf of the firm. He is a man who, out of all the others mentioned in the law who have also the right to act on behalf of the firm, has most of these rights. He has the right to act on behalf of the firm and to conclude any transactions or any sort of act on behalf of the firm, and to conclude any transactions or any sort of legal proceedings in which the firm might find itself involved. One can say that anybody who has any sort of transactions with a man who holds the "Procura" and who is called the Procurist is in exactly the same position as if he had had that transaction with the head of the firm.

Erna Biagini, a former stenographer of the firm, who was also in charge of the registry, claimed to have read, in "approximately 1942," a travel report of Dr. Tesch which stated that Zyklon B could be used for killing human beings as well as vermin.

Anna Uenzelmann, a former stenographer of the firm, said that in about June 1942 Tesch, after he had dictated a travel report on returning from Berlin, had told her that Zyklon B was being used for gassing human beings, and had appeared to be as terrified and shocked about the matter as she was.

Karl Ruehmling, who had been a bookkeeper and assistant gassing master with the firm, said that Zyklon B was sent by the concern to the concentration camps at Auschwitz, Sachsenhausen and Neuengamme, but Auschwitz was sent the largest consignments.

Alfred Zaun, who was in charge of the firm's bookkeeping, said that, in his opinion; Auschwitz of all the concentration camps had received the most Zyklon B during the war.

...

Perry Broad, who had been a Rottenführer [squad leader in the SS/SD] in the Kommandatur [commandant's headquarter] of the Auschwitz camp from June 1942 until early 1945, described how persons were gassed there with Zyklon B. The people being gassed, to his knowledge, at Auschwitz and Birkenau were German deportees, Jews from Belgium, Holland, France, North Italy, Czechoslovakia and Poland, and Gypsies.

Dr. Bendel, who had been a prisoner at Auschwitz and had acted as a doctor to the inmates, said that from February 1944 to January 1945 a million people had been killed there by Zyklon B.

...

The Prosecution, acting in accordance with Regulation 8(i)(a) of the Royal Warrant, submitted to the Court a sworn affidavit in which Dr. Diels, a former high-ranking German government official, stated that it was common knowledge in 1943 in Germany that gas was being used for killing people.

SETTING THE STAGE FOR THE DEFENSE

The English translation of the statement given by the Defense Counsel for Dr. Tesch summarizes the issues: "I have two duties to perform. The first would be to try to prove that Tesch supplied this gas not knowing for what purposes it might be used. My second duty is that, even if he knew something about it, still the laws of this procedure would not suffice to find him guilty."

The Defense

All three accused gave evidence on oath. Dr. Tesch stated that he had heard nothing and had known nothing about human beings being killed in concentration camps with prussic acid. He denied ever having attended any conference, or having been approached by any official or military authority on the subject, or having written in any document that human beings should be killed by prussic acid. He specifically denied that he had made the remarks referred to by Anna Uenzelmann. He had never been to Auschwitz himself and had had no reason to believe that the camps were incorrectly run.

He did not think that deliveries to Auschwitz were very high because it was a large camp and, further, it "administered more camps in the General Government of Poland." He [Dr. Tesch] could not remember Dr. Drosihn ever having instructed S.S. men. Although the witness had paid subscriptions to both the S.S. and the Nazi Party, he had never been an active member of either. He thought that the passage in the travel report which Erna Biagini had read might have been a record of an answer put to him by pupil.

Drosihn, stated Tesch, was a technical expert and was not concerned with the administration of the firm or the office. Weinbacher, however, had complete control when Tesch was away from the office.

[Karl Weinbacher,] giving evidence on oath, said that his work was, briefly, to look after the current business affairs in the absence of Dr. Tesch, seeing to the incoming and the outgoing mail, answering any queries, and confirming any orders received. He read some of Dr. Tesch's travel reports but not all, because there were too many; in particular, he had not read any dealing with the possibility of destroying Jews with Zyklon B. Dr. Tesch had not mentioned any such possibility to him, nor had the witness heard during the war that Jews were being gassed. He had never been inside a concentration camp, nor had he received unfavourable reports during the war about such camps. He, too, stated that Drosihn had nothing to do with the business management. He could not agree that the S.S. would necessarily come to Dr. Tesch for advice on the extermination of human beings with Zyklon B, since, although Dr. Tesch was an expert on the use of the gas, there were plenty of books available on prussic acid.

Drosihn claimed that his part in the activities of the firm consisted in collaborating on scientific issues, being in charge of the gassing, for instance, of ships in Hamburg docks, and examining delousing chambers to see whether they were working correctly. He spent about 150 to 200 days a year in travelling on business. He had been to check the working of the delousing chambers in Sachsenhausen and Ravensbruck and had been to Neuengamme; but had neither been to Auschwitz, nor given instructions to the S.S. in any place. He knew nothing of the size of consignments of gas to Auschwitz. Contrary to Tesch's evidence, the witness claimed to have reported to him once that he had seen happening in the camps things that were contrary to human dignity.

The Remaining Defense Witnesses
Nine other witnesses called by the Defence did not add substantially to the evidence before the Court. . . .

SOME ADDITIONAL NOTES FOR FUTURE REFERENCE
Auschwitz-Birkenau

Located in southern Poland, Auschwitz actually consisted of a network of Nazi concentration camps and extermination camps built and operated in Polish areas annexed by Nazi Germany during World War II. It consisted of Auschwitz I, Auschwitz II–Birkenau, Auschwitz III–Monowitz, and forty-five satellite camps. The complex had three different types of camps: a prison camp, an extermination camp, and a slave-labor camp. Buna-Monowitz (Auschwitz III) served as a slave-labor camp supplying workers for the nearby chemical and synthetic-rubber works of I.G. Farben. The forty-five smaller subcamps mostly housed slave laborers. Camp guards were members of the Nazi paramilitary SS Totenkopf verbände (Death's Head Unit).

During most of the period from 1940 to 1945 Captain (SS Hauptsturmführer) Rudolf Franz Höss (Hoess) served as commandant. Höss testified to his activities before the International Military Tribunal in Nuremberg. In one of the more chilling statements in his testimony he boasted of the efficiency of his killing operation in comparison with others: "Another improvement we made over Treblinka was that we built our gas chambers to accommodate 2,000 people at one time, whereas at Treblinka their 10 gas chambers only accommodated 200 people each." In his own trial (Case No. 38), held before a Polish Special Criminal Court in Krakow (March 11–29, 1947), Höss was convicted and sentenced to death. He was executed on April 16, 1947.

As the most lethal of the Nazi extermination camps, after the war, Auschwitz rapidly became a virtual synonym for the Holocaust. From 1941 until the liberation of the camp in 1945, between 1.1 and 1.5 million people died at Auschwitz. Ninety percent of those killed were Jews. Totals also included 19,000 Gypsies (Roma), who were held at the camp as slave laborers until the Nazis gassed them in July 1944. The Poles constituted the second largest victim group at Auschwitz—83,000 were killed or died. Between 1941 and the liberation of the camp in 1945, an estimated 1.1 million of those interned there were killed.

In addition to the function of the camp as an extermination center, it became infamous for the "medical" experiments carried out on prisoners. The research of Dr. Josef Mengele and his physician colleagues added to the horrors of the camp. Hundreds of prisoners suffered and died, or were executed in brutally cruel, painful experiments conducted in attempts to validate Nazi beliefs about the superiority of the Aryan race. After the war, Mengele managed to escape to South America where he lived until his death in 1979.

The Nazis were not the only ones to use extermination camps. From 1941 until the end of the war, the Ustaše (Croatian military) operated one of the largest concentration-elimination camps in Europe at Jasenovac in Slavonia. Croatian authorities murdered between 320,000 and 340,000 ethnic Serb residents of Croatia and Bosnia during the period.

I.G. Farben

I.G. Farben was a German chemical and pharmaceutical industry conglomerate. Formed in 1925 from the merger of a number of major chemical companies that had been working together closely since World War I, it was both the largest company in Europe, and the largest chemical and pharmaceutical company in the world. Auschwitz began to grow with an initiative by the company to build its third large plant for synthetic rubber and liquid fuels. The new plant would be located in Silesia, beyond the range of Allied bombers at the time. The final location was chosen for its access to railroad lines, water supply (the Vistula), the availability of nearby raw materials, and the access to prisoners from the nearby Auschwitz concentration camp, who would provide low-cost labor.

The company bought the land from the Treasury for a pittance after German occupation forces had taken it without compensation to its Polish owners. The German authorities also systematically expelled Jews from the villages and towns, confiscated their homes, and sold them to the company as housing for company employees brought in from Germany. I.G. Farben officials reached an agreement with the concentration camp commandant to hire prisoners at 3 to 4 marks per day for the labor of auxiliary and skilled construction workers. In a letter to his colleagues about the negotiations, I.G. Farben director Otto Ambros wrote that "our new friendship with the SS is very fruitful" (Memorial Museum, n.d.). The I.G. Farben Trial (*The United States of America v. Carl Krauch, et al.*), was the sixth subsequent Nuremberg proceeding, under CCL No. 10.

References

Hayes, Peter. 2004. *From Cooperation to Complicity: Degussa in the Third Reich*. Cambridge: Cambridge University Press.

Holocaust Education & Archive Research Team. n.d. "Hadamar Euthanasia Center." http://www.holocaustresearchproject.org/euthan/hadamar.html.

Lifton, Robert J. 1986. *The Nazi Doctors: Medical Killing and the Psychology of Genocide*. New York: Basic Books.

Longerich, Peter. 2010. *Holocaust: The Nazi Persecution and Murder of the Jews*. New York: Oxford University Press.

Memorial Museum, Auschwitz-Birkenau. n.d. "I G Farben." http://auschwitz.org/en/history/auschwitz-iii/ig-farben.

Modern History Sourcebook: Rudolf Hoess, Commandant of Auschwitz: Testimony at Nuremburg, 1946, http://sourcebooks.fordham.edu/halsall/mod/1946Hoess.html.

Rees, Lawrence. 2005. *Auschwitz: A New History*. New York: MJF.

8

Belsen Trial

In part, the Zyklon B trial addressed activities at Auschwitz. However, even though Auschwitz became the ultimate symbol of the Holocaust, none of the Allied Powers held a trial that dealt only with Auschwitz. This happened because the Red Army (Soviet Union) liberated the camp, and it remained within the Soviet sphere of control after the war. Because of their own anti-Semitic sentiments, the Soviets had little incentive to undertake prosecutions for the crimes committed in the camp. This did not mean that those responsible went unpunished. The commandant of Auschwitz emphasized the central role the camp played in "The Final Solution." Testifying for the defense at the IMT trial at Nuremberg, the commandant of Auschwitz, Rudolf Höss, testified:

> I estimate that at least 2,500,000 victims were executed and exterminated there by gassing and burning, and at least another half million succumbed to starvation and disease, making a total dead of about 3,000,000. This figure represents about 70% or 80% of all persons sent to Auschwitz as prisoners, the remainder having been selected and used for slave labor in the concentration camp industries.

Many of the camp commandants, senior supervisors, and guards had been moved back into camps in Germany as Allied forces advanced. When the western Allied Forces liberated camps, they arrested and tried a large number of those who actively operated the camps. The Bergen-Belsen trials, the first trial by a military tribunal in Germany, specifically addressed the Auschwitz crimes in its indictments, as did the Dachau trial (November 1945).

Bergen-Belsen, more familiarly Belsen, was a Nazi concentration camp in northern Germany. Located southwest of the town of Bergen in the province of Lower Saxony, the Nazis established the camp in 1940 as a prisoner of war (POW) camp for French and Belgian prisoners. In 1941, it housed about 20,000 Russian POWs. In 1943, sections were converted into a concentration camp. In theory, Jews with foreign passports were kept there to be exchanged for German nationals imprisoned abroad. Not surprisingly very few exchanges ever happened. The camp was later expanded to accommodate Jews from other concentration camps. The camp was not a killing center and thus, had no ovens.

By reports, initially the conditions in the camp were good by comparison with those in other concentration camps. Most prisoners did not have to endure forced labor. However, beginning in the spring of 1944 the situation rapidly changed for the worse. In March, the Nazis redesignated Belsen as a "Recovery Camp." In theory this meant that prisoners in other camps who were too sick to work would be sent to Belsen, even though no records indicate that any prisoner ever received treatment. Yet, as with several other camps, Nazi doctors carried out so-called medical experiments on prisoners.

As the German Army began to retreat on both the Eastern and Western Fronts, late in 1944 the Germans began to evacuate concentration camps in the areas they abandoned. Trapped in the middle between the Soviet Army in the East and the Allied Army in the West, the SS decided to abandon the concentration and extermination camps in Poland and moved or destroyed evidence of the atrocities they had committed there. They killed thousands of prisoners before the forced transfers of the survivors to other camps began.

The transfers became known as "death marches." Most of the surviving prisoners were very weak or ill after enduring the routine violence, overwork, and starvation of concentration camp life. The transfers involved long marches, often through snow, to railway stations. They then had to endure a journey of days without food, water, or shelter in freight carriages originally designed for cattle. On arrival at their destination, the survivors again had to march to their new camps. The guards killed prisoners who could not keep up due to fatigue or illness.

The facilities at Belsen could not accommodate the sudden influx of thousands of prisoners. Basic infrastructure and services, such as food supply, water, and sanitation, collapsed. The deterioration of living conditions caused an outbreak of disease. Along with other prisoners, in March 1945, Anne Frank and her sister Margot died in a typhus epidemic.

Bergen-Belsen contained no gas chambers, but an estimated 50,000 prisoners died of starvation, overwork, disease, brutality, and sadistic medical experiments. By April 1945, more than 60,000 prisoners were imprisoned in two camps. Camp No. 2 opened only a few weeks before the liberation. Timothy Snyder observes:

> In the last few months of war, from January to May 1945, the inmates of the German concentration camps died in very large numbers. Perhaps *three hundred thousand* people died in this period, from hunger and neglect. The American and British soldiers who liberated the dying inmates from camps in Germany believed that they had discovered the horrors of Nazism. The images their photographers and cameramen capture of the corpses and the living skeletons at Bergen-Belsen and Buchenwald seemed to convey the worst crimes of Hitler. As the Jews and Poles of Warsaw knew ... and the Red Army soldiers knew, this was far from the truth. (2010, 311–312)

Lieutenant-Colonel J. Douglas Paybody, one of the first British soldiers in the camp, wrote of his experience:

> What we saw was a nightmare which beggars description. . . . It's often assumed that liberation means people celebrating and coming to hug you, but they were too far gone. They would just sit and rock back and forth. As you watched, you saw one die in front of you. (Quoted in Celinscak 2015, 44)

CHARGES

The British Army liberated the camp in April 1945. It was the only camp in the area that came directly under the control of the British Army. All the defendants at the Belsen Trial were provided with defense counsel. Eleven of the defense attorneys were British and one was Polish. The charges here require some explanation. Because Josef Kramer and several of the guards and supervisors had worked at Auschwitz-Birkenau before coming to Belsen, the charges against the forty-five defendants consisted of two separate categories—crimes committed at Belsen and crimes committed at Auschwitz-Birkenau. Kramer was a camp leader (*Lagerführer*) at Birkenau prior to being transferred to Bergen-Belsen. He, along with eleven others who had worked with him there, was charged under both categories.

After Kramer, the most high-profile defendants were Dr. Fritz Klein, camp doctor, Franz Hössler (Hoessler), deputy camp commandant, Irma Grese, and Elisabeth Volkenrath. Peter Weingartner had also been a guard and a supervisor of a women's work detail (*Arbeitskommando Weber*) at Auschwitz before coming to Belsen in February 1945.

In his very brief tenure as commandant, Josef Kramer, became known as the Beast of Belsen. Prior to assignment to Bergen-Belsen in December 1944, he served as *Lagerführer* in charge of the gassing operations at Auschwitz II-Birkenau, the main killing center within the Auschwitz concentration camp complex.

The two women also had a reputation for extreme cruelty. The inmates had nicknamed Grese the "hyena of Buchenwald." At age 19, she had become a supervisor at Ravensbrück used as a training camp for many female SS guards. She came to Bergen-Belsen in March 1945. She had been promoted to the rank of Senior Supervisor (*Oberaufseherin*) in the autumn of 1943. She had charge of around 30,000 women prisoners, mainly Polish and Hungarian Jews. In her testimony, Grese admitted that she regarded the inmates of the concentration camps as subhuman rubbish; and said that, as someone might kill an insect without feeling guilty about it, she saw nothing inherently wrong in what she was doing. She denied selecting prisoners for the gas chambers but admitted she knew of their existence. She also admitted to whipping prisoners and beating them with a walking stick, despite knowing that both practices were contrary to the camp rules. At age 22, she was the youngest woman executed by British authorities during the twentieth century.

Elisabeth Volkenrath had also begun her SS career at Ravensbrück. In March 1942, she went to Auschwitz-Birkenau where she participated in the selection of prisoners for the gas chambers. In November 1944, she was promoted to *Oberaufseherin* for all camp sections for female prisoners at Auschwitz. She came to Bergen in February 1945, where she served as the most senior supervisor for the women's camps. In that short time, she became known as the most hated woman in the Bergen-Belsen camp.

Dr. Fritz Klein had actively participated in the "selection" process that determined which prisoners would go to the gas chamber at both Auschwitz-Birkenau and at Belsen after his arrival in January 1945. He is remembered for an exchange he had at Auschwitz with another doctor. When asked how he could reconcile the

Hippocratic Oath that doctors work to save lives with his role in sending large numbers of individuals to their death, he answered: "Of course I am a doctor and I want to preserve life. And out of respect for human life, I would remove a gangrenous appendix from a diseased body. The Jew is the gangrenous appendix in the body of mankind" (quoted in Lifton, 1986, 16).

TRIAL SUMMARY #4: BELSEN TRIAL

The condition of the prisoners found in Belsen and in Auschwitz was brought about by criminal neglect and by deliberate starvation and ill-treatment that clearly would cause death or lasting physical injury. Each of those charged with crimes at Auschwitz had directly participated in the deliberate killing of thousands of people. The persons who suffered these wrongs came from ten different nationalities. The principal causes of death in Belsen were lack of food and lack of washing and sanitary facilities which in its turn led to lice and the spread of typhus and other diseases. A very large store of medical supplies was found at Belsen, but very little was used for the prisoners. In addition, guards and other officers of the camp had deliberately killed a large number of prisoners, particularly in the days before liberation of the camp.

DOCUMENT: BELSEN TRIAL: JOSEF KRAMER AND 44 OTHERS

When:	September 17–November 13, 1945
Where:	Lüneburg, Germany (Lower Saxony)
Court:	British Military Court
Defendant:	Josef Kramer, et al.
Source:	*Law-Reports of Trials of War Criminals, The United Nations War Crimes Commission*, Vol. 2 (London, HMSO, 1947). Transcript of the Official Shorthand Notes of "The Trial of Josef Kramer and Forty-Four Others." Online at http://www.bergenbelsen.co.uk/pages/TrialTranscript/Trial_Contents.html.
Charges:	The basic charge was that all were "members of the staff of one or other of two concentration camps, Bergen-Belsen or Auschwitz-Birkenau, and as such, responsible for the well-being of the prisoners interned there, in violation of the law and usages of war they were together concerned as parties to the ill-treatment of certain of the persons interned in the camp; and by that ill-treatment, they caused the death of some and they caused physical suffering to others." The indictment separated liability on the basis of where individuals had served. The first involved the twelve individuals (including Kramer) who worked at Auschwitz prior to coming to Belsen and included their activities at Belsen. The second involved all of those who were at Belsen until the liberation of the camp.
Legal Issues:	The defense did raise the issue of jurisdiction but did not pursue it. They petitioned for separate trials for each of the two counts

of the indictment. The Court, while thanking the lead defense counsel for his "very clear and cogent argument" denied the petition. Otherwise, the questions all revolved around proving the charges.

Defense: Superior orders and lack of knowledge

National Socialism demanded two things: implicit obedience and trust on the part of the person carrying out the order. Josef Kramer took an oath on the day Hitler first became Chancellor and President of the Reich: "I swear to you, Adolf Hitler, as Führer and Chancellor of the Reich, faith and steadfastness. I pledge to you and to those to whom you entrust your orders unwavering obedience unto death. So help me God."

As members of the National Socialist Party, members of the SS, and a part of the armed forces of Germany, all were bound by the so-called Führer principle, which was that the person at the top gave the orders and that the person at the bottom obeyed these orders, not because they were orders but because they came from the top.

Verdicts: Thirty of the forty-four defendants were found guilty. Ten of the twelve defendants who were charged under both counts were found guilty. Two, George Kraft and Ilse Lothe, were acquitted on all charges. Thirty-two of the forty-four defendants were charged only for crimes committed at Bergen-Belsen. Out of this group of thirty-two, twelve were acquitted. Of the six found guilty on both Counts 1 and 2, five received a death sentence and were hanged: Josef Kramer, Dr. Fritz Klein, Peter Weingartner, Elisabeth Volkenrath, and Irma Grese.

Testimony

Brigadier Glyn Hughes said that, shortly before the 15th April, 1945, certain German officers came to the headquarters of 8th Corps and asked for a truce in respect of Belsen camp. In pursuance of the arrangement arrived at, he went on the same day to Belsen camp, after it had been captured. There were piles of corpses lying all over the camp. Even within the huts there were numbers of bodies, some even in the same bunks as the living. Most of the internees were suffering from some form of gastro-enteritis and were too weak to leave the huts. The lavatories in the huts had long been out of use. Those who were strong enough could get into the appropriate compounds but others performed their natural actions from where they were. The compounds were one mass of human excreta. Some of the huts had bunks, but not many, and they were filled absolutely to overflowing with prisoners in every state of emaciation and disease. There was not room for them to lie down at full length in the huts. In the most crowded there were anything from 600 to 1,000 people in accommodation which should only have taken 100. There were large medical supplies in the stores at Belsen, but issues for the use of the prisoners were inadequate. The witness had made a tour of the camp accompanied by

Kramer, the Kommandant of Belsen; the latter seemed to be quite callous and indifferent to what they saw.

Mr. Harold O. Le Druillenec . . ., a British subject from Jersey, stated that he had been arrested by the Germans in June, 1944, and was sent to Belsen on about April 5th, 1945. He was put into Block 13 with five or six hundred others, and there were more on the following night. The floor was wet and foul through having been used as a latrine. The internees were so crowded that they could not lie down. Sleep was impossible, and the atmosphere was vile. Seven or eight died in the first night.

. . .

On his fifth day at the camp and during about four days following, he and others had to drag corpses and put them in large burial pits. This went on from sunrise to dusk and many died in the process. He thought that the operation was intended to clear up the camp before the British arrived. Anybody who faltered was struck. He had altogether a pint of soup during his first four days at the camp. During the last five days before the liberation, which were spent in burying the dead, he had neither food nor water. Nearly every minute of the day, shots were going off about the camp; guards would shoot internees usually for no reason at all.

Dr. Ada Bimko, . . . a Jewess from Poland, stated that she was arrested and sent to Auschwitz on 4th August, 1943. She was transferred to Belsen on 23rd November, 1944. In both camps she worked in a hospital. At a point later than her own arrival Kramer became Kommandant of Birkenau which was that part of Auschwitz which contained the camp's five crematoria. She testified that records which had been secretly compiled by internees working in the sonderkommando (Special Fatigue Party) at the Auschwitz crematoria showed, according to a member of the sonderkommando to whom she had spoken, that about four million people had been destroyed in the crematoria. Experiments had been carried out in Block 10 in Auschwitz; one woman had told her that an experiment in artificial insemination had been carried out on her. Prisoners selected for the gas chamber were sent first to Block 25, where they often waited days without food and drink, before the lorries arrived for them.

Kramer, Klein and Hoessler, the witness said, took an active part in selections made at Auschwitz, a process whereby numbers of prisoners were chosen from the rest and sent to the gas chambers. She had seen Kramer at Belsen kicking four Russians who were too weak to work. Kramer arrived at Belsen early in December, 1944, and on his arrival roll-calls and beatings commenced.

. . .

Sophia Litwinska, . . . a Jewess from Poland, said that she was sent to Auschwitz as a prisoner at the beginning of the Autumn of 1941, and was transferred to Belsen about three months before its liberation. Litwinska said that on the 24th December, 1941, at a selection at Auschwitz there was a parade of 3,000 Jewesses at which Hoessler was present. The women were naked, and those selected were taken to the gas chamber, a room equipped to look like a bath-house.

...

Gertrude Diament, a Jewess from Czechoslovakia, stated that during 1942 she had seen Volkenrath make selections; she would give orders that prisoners be loaded on to lorries and transported to the gas chamber. Grese was also responsible for selecting victims for the gas chambers at Auschwitz. Grese, at both Auschwitz and Belsen, when in charge of working parties, beat women with sticks and when they fell to the ground she kicked them as hard as she could with her heavy boots. She frequently caused blood to flow and in the deponent's opinion many of the people she injured were likely to die from such injuries, but she had no direct evidence of such deaths.

...

Klara Lobowitz, a Czech, said that Grese was in charge of roll-calls and that she made internees go on their knees for hours and hold stones above their heads, and that she kicked people on the ground. . . . The deponent had often seen the accused with Dr. Mengele selecting people for the gas chamber and for forced labour in Germany.

Excerpt from Statement of Josef Kramer
AUSCHWITZ: 10 to 15 May 1944 till 29 November 1944

Auschwitz was an enormous camp to which many smaller camps in the vicinity belonged. As the responsibility for the whole camp could not be taken by one man it was split and I was put in charge of one part of the camp. I was camp commander of that part but as I came under the supreme commander of the whole camp who was my superior officer, my duties were those of a Lagerführer (camp leader), though my appointment was called Camp Kommandant. I had under me in my part of the camp the hospital and the agricultural camp which was an enormous camp and contained many thousand acres. The number of prisoners under my immediate control varied between 15000 and 16000, and 35000 and 40000, comprising male and female.

There were between 350 and 500 deaths a week. The death rate was higher among the men, the reason being that the influx from the working camp consisted mainly of sick people. When I speak of the death rate in Auschwitz, I mean that all these people died of natural causes, that is to say either from illness or old age. The death rate was slightly above normal due to the fact that I had a camp with sick people who came from other parts of the camp. The only reason I can see for the higher death rate, not only at Auschwitz but at all concentration camps in comparison with civil prisons, was that prisoners had to work whereas in civil prisons they had not to work.

In Auschwitz the prisoners went out to work at 5 a.m. in the summer and returned at 8 p.m., sometimes even later. They worked seven days a week, but on Sundays they returned at 1, 2 or 3 o'clock in the afternoon. The work was of an agricultural nature and all the work there was done by prisoners. . . . There were men, women and children in the camp. The majority of prisoners under my immediate control were Easterners, i.e. Poles and Russians. I have no reason to believe that there were any prisoners of war among them although there might have been without my knowing it.

...

All prisoners who died were cremated. There was no sort of service held when they died. They were just burnt. The cremations were carried out by prisoners. All I had to do when a prisoner died was to inform Obersturmbannführer Hoess and he would deal with it. I had no administration in Auschwitz. All the prisoners were known by numbers only. I had nothing to do with meting out punishment in Auschwitz; that was all done through Hoess. When I came to Auschwitz there was no corporal punishment for women, but I have heard it mentioned, and it was talked about in the camp that there had been corporal punishment for women before and that it had been abolished. The only way in which I was informed corporal punishment for women was not allowed was that conversation in the camp to which I have referred. . . . Even if corporal punishment for women would have been allowed I would never have put it into practice as such a thing is inconceivable to me. The punishment administered to women, if they had committed any of the crimes for which men were beaten, was that they were transferred to another working party where they had a dirtier type of work or longer hours.

...

I have heard of the allegations of former prisoners in Auschwitz referring to a gas chamber there, the mass executions and whippings, the cruelty of the guards employed, and that all this took place either in my presence or with my knowledge. All I can say to all this is that it is untrue from beginning to end.

BELSEN - 1 December 1944 till 15 April 1945

I do not know of what nationality the prisoners were when I arrived, because there were no files or papers of any kind in the camp. It was impossible for me to know what kind of prisoners there were as they had been sent to Belsen because they were ill, from all concentration camps over the country. Many of them had lost their identification marks, and as there were no records it was absolutely impossible to tell who was who. I started to keep my own records of the prisoners, but these records were all destroyed on orders which I received from Berlin about the end of March. I do not remember who signed these orders.

...

I do not know the number of deaths which occurred in this period at all, but the conditions in Belsen got worse from the middle of February till the middle of April, 1945, when the Allies came. I inspected the camp daily during this period and was fully aware of the conditions and the great number of people who were dying. The death rate during the months of February, March and April gradually mounted until it reached 400 or 500 a day. This figure was due to the fact that if people were healthy I had to send them out on working parties and only retain the sick and dying.

. . .

There was a crematorium in the camp and as long as coke was available all dead bodies were cremated. When there was no more coke available they were buried in mass graves.

. . .

When Belsen Camp was eventually taken over by the Allies I was quite satisfied that I had done all I possibly could under the circumstances to remedy the conditions in the camp.

Excerpt from Statement of Irma Gese

I know from the prisoners that there were gas chambers at Auschwitz and that prisoners were gassed there. Dr. Mengele came in the camp at Birkenau and sorted out the people unfit for work for these transports. I knew what was happening and have hidden mothers and children away in order that they should not be chosen. I was once denounced by the Jews for having done this and was put under arrest for two days in my room. Jews were used as spies in this camp and had certain privileges. I never took part in choosing people and was only on parade for roll call and seeing that no one escaped.

I have never beaten or kicked any prisoners.

SOME OBSERVATIONS ABOUT THE TESTIMONY

In examining Kramer's testimony and that of the other defendants who received the death penalty, two important points stand out. First, none of the senior officers of the camp relied upon superior orders as a defense. Instead they simply denied that the incidents described by witnesses happened as related, had no knowledge, or conveniently could not remember. The following exchange between Peter Weingartner and the Prosecutor illustrates this:

> **Major Winwood**: Were not the people who were selected for the gas chamber taken down the road right along the side of the women's camp where you were working, to get to the crematoria?
>
> **Weingartner**: Yes, I have seen people there, but whether they went to the bathhouse or the crematorium I cannot say.

Many of those accused only of crimes at Bergen-Belsen were of lower rank and did rely on superior orders. As noted earlier, superior orders could not excuse a defendant's actions, but in certain circumstances could be used as a factor in moderating the sentence given.

A NOTE ON CAMP ORGANIZATION

Among those prosecuted in the trial were several prisoners who had been heads or overseers (*Kapos*). The Kapo system recruited prisoners as staff who then became the active agents of control for the SS—the enforcers of rules in return for privileges. Among the first prisoners to arrive at Auschwitz in June 1940 were a number of German criminals transferred from Sachsenhausen. The SS immediately recruited them as Kapos. Lawrence Rees notes that "murderous behavior by the Kapos had been a feature of Auschwitz from the very beginning" (2005, 98) Nonetheless, the Kapos themselves had to continue to please their SS bosses. They also were at risk. Heinrich Himmler summarized their position:

> His [the Kapo's] job is to see that the work gets done . . . thus he has to push his men. As soon as we are no longer satisfied with him, he is no longer a Kapo and returns to the other inmates. He knows that they will beat him to death his first night back. (Quoted in Rees 2005, 7)

Very few Kapos were prosecuted after the war, due to the difficulty in determining which Kapo atrocities had been performed under SS orders and which had been individual actions.

References

Celinscak, Mark. 2015. *Distance from the Belsen Heap: Allied Forces and the Liberation of a Concentration Camp.* Toronto: University of Toronto Press.

"Death Marches." n.d. *Holocaust Encyclopedia* (United States Memorial Holocaust Museum, Washington, DC). https://www.ushmm.org/wlc/en/article.php?ModuleId=10005162.

Lengyel, Olga. 1995. *Five Chimneys: A Woman Survivor's True Story of Auschwitz.* 2nd ed. Chicago: Chicago Review Press.

Lifton, Robert Jay. 1986. *The Nazi Doctors: Medical Killing and the Psychology of Genocide.* New York: Basic Books.

Rees, Lawrence. 2005. *Auschwitz: A New History.* New York: MJF Books.

Snyder, Timothy. 2010. *Bloodlands: Europe between Hitler and Stalin.* New York: Basic Books.

Steinbacher, Sybille. 2005. *Auschwitz: A History.* New York: Harper-Collins.

9

Buchenwald Trial

The Buchenwald Trial was one of a large number of trials for various German civilians, concentration camp personnel, medical personnel, and members of SS units held at the site of the former Dachau concentration camp between November 1945 and December 1947. The Dachau series of 465 trials included civilian and military personnel from the main camps of Dachau, Buchenwald, Flossenbürg, Mauthausen, Nordhausen, and Mühldorf, as well as the sprawling network of subsidiary camps attached to each. Dachau was chosen as the site because many of the accused were associated with the camp and because its facilities were adequate to accommodate the trial participants. But perhaps just as important at the time, Dachau had become the place that Americans most associated with the worst German atrocities in World War II.

Dachau and Buchenwald were the first two concentration camps established after the Nazis gained control of the government. By the end of World War II in 1945, the Nazis ran a system of 20,000 concentration camps in Germany and German-Occupied Europe. A point made earlier in the introduction to the three cases that involve concentration or extermination camps needs to be emphasized again. Discussions often use "concentration camp" as a general term for all German camps. This misses some important distinctions. Historians make a clear distinction between death camps and concentration camps. Although large numbers of people died in each type of facility, as noted in the general introduction to these trials, concentration camps differed from extermination camps in purpose. Concentration camps held large groups of prisoners without trial or judicial process. In the period before Germany invaded Poland to start World War II (1934–1939), most prisoners consisted of member of opposition political parties—German Communists, Socialists, and Social Democrats, and marginal groups such as the Gypsies (Roma), Jehovah's Witnesses, homosexuals, and persons accused of asocial or socially "deviant" behavior by the Nazis. They served a number of war-related purposes, including prison facilities, labor camps, prisoner of war camps, and transit camps among others. Deaths in these camps came from systemic brutality, starvation, forced labor, murder, and illness due to the harsh conditions in the camp. As discussed in the Zyklon B case, the principal purpose of extermination camps was to kill prisoners on a massive scale through the use of poison gas and other means.

Buchenwald was constructed in 1937, about five miles northwest of Weimar in east-central Germany. It eventually comprised 88 camps. For the first six years or so of its existence, it housed males only. During World War II, the Buchenwald camp system became an important source of forced labor. Females arrived sometime in late 1943. Most of the early inmates at Buchenwald were political prisoners. This changed in 1938. In the aftermath of Kristallnacht, the camp received almost 10,000 Jews. Camp authorities subjected them to extraordinarily cruel treatment: "Periodically, the SS staff conducted selections throughout the Buchenwald camp system and dispatched those too weak or disabled to work to so-called euthanasia facilities" (Buchenwald, n.d.). Beginning in 1941, a number of physicians and scientists carried out a varied program of medical experimentation on prisoners at Buchenwald in special barracks. Presumably the medical experiments tested the efficacy of vaccines and treatments against contagious diseases such as typhus, typhoid, cholera, and diphtheria. They resulted in hundreds of deaths (Buchenwald, n.d.).

As Allied forces advanced, the Germans destroyed a large number of records in an attempt to hide the evidence of war crimes and crimes against humanity. Between April 1938 and April 1945, the Nazis had imprisoned a total of 238,000 people of various nationalities including some Western Allied prisoners of war in Buchenwald. Similar to Belsen-Bergen, Buchenwald had received large numbers of prisoners from other camps located in areas from which the German forces had to retreat. Historians estimate that 56,000 died at Buchenwald.

Elie Wiesel, a Nobel Peace Prize honoree, and the recipient of the Presidential Medal of Freedom, survived both internment at Auschwitz and a transfer to Buchenwald as Soviet forces advanced in Poland. Almost immediately upon the family's arrival at Auschwitz, his mother and sister were murdered. He and his father escaped because they were able-bodied and able to work. They both survived the trip to Buchenwald but just before liberation forces reached Buchenwald, Wiesel's father died.

DEFENDANTS

Buchenwald often surfaces in narratives about the camps because of the stories of excessive cruelty associated with its first commandant, Karl-Otto Koch and his wife Ilse (1937–1941). When Koch became commandant, Ilse Koch also received an appointment as an *Oberaufseherin*. She played an active role in the atrocities committed there, becoming infamous as the "Witch of Buchenwald" (*Die Hexe von Buchenwald*). Under Koch's command, living conditions had deteriorated to a state considered deplorable even by Nazi standards, as had the mistreatment of prisoners.

Koch and his wife were arrested by the Gestapo at the request of SS judge Josias Prince zu Waldeck-Pyrmont. Koch was charged with the unauthorized murder of three prisoners and Ilse with embezzling more than 700,000

Reichsmarks and illegally appropriating other property. Although Ilse was acquitted of these charges by the German court, it convicted her husband. A firing squad at Buchenwald executed Koch just a week before the Allies liberated the camp. In a bit of irony, his body was cremated in the crematorium there.

Ilse Koch would again stand trial in 1947 before an American Military Court after the war for "wrongfully" participating in a "common plan" to commit war crimes by beatings, killings, torture, and other abuses of prisoners. Along with Koch, Prince Josias, Hermann Pister (defendant #21) the commandant who succeeded Koch and ran the camp from 1942 to 1945, and twenty-eight other defendants were charged. In the testimony, Ilse Koch is defendant #15.

TRIAL SUMMARY #5: BUCHENWALD TRIAL

The transcript contains thirteen pages that systematically detail abuses at the camps, which included beatings, executions, and general mistreatment. Among the most gruesome practiced were the collection of human skins for their colorful tattoos and other bizarre medical experiments.

DOCUMENT: BUCHENWALD TRIAL (*UNITED STATES OF AMERICA V. JOSIAS PRINCE ZU WALDECK ET AL.*)

When:	April 11–August 14, 1947
Where:	Dachau Concentration Camp
Court:	General Military Government Court
Defendants:	Josias Prince zu Waldeck, Ilse Koch, Hermann Pister, and 28 others
Source:	Archive, International Criminal Court. Online at https://www.legal-tools.org/en/browse/record/8ff3d8/.
Jurisdiction:	CCL No. 10; Office of Military Government for Germany, "Legal and Penal Administration of Military Government Regulations," Title 5, §300.3 (March 21, 1947): "Military Government Courts have jurisdiction over all offenses committed in the U.S. Zone against the regulations enacted by Military Government, the existing German law, and the laws and usages of war . . ."
Charges:	Violation of the Laws and Usages of War The accused "in pursuance of a common design . . . did wrongfully and unlawfully, encourage, aid, abet, and participate in the operation of Concentration Camp Buchenwald and its subcamps. . . ." Prisoners were subjected to "killings, beatings, tortures, starvation, abuses and indignities, the exact names and numbers of such persons being unknown but aggregating many thousands."
Defense:	The defense claimed that after Pister assumed command of the camp, conditions materially improved. SS men and capos (kapos) were punished for any mistreatment. In addition to "superior orders," defense claimed that an "informal camp administration"

	run by inmate gangs was primarily responsible for most of the violence against prisoners.
Verdicts:	Waldeck and Koch received life sentences; 22 others, including Pister, received the death penalty. Of these, 12 were eventually executed. Waldeck's sentence was commuted to 20 years; he served 3.

Selected Testimony and Evidence

Prosecution

Medical Experiments and Treatment (pp. 8–9)

It was a matter of general knowledge among the inmates of the camp that the camp physician frequently called healthy inmates to the camp hospital and performed surgical operations on them. The inmates were usually killed by injections shortly thereafter. . . . If an inmate patient did not have cigarettes, food or other gifts for the chief doctor (accused #13) . . . he would not treat him. When asked by inmates why he refused to treat them, he answered, "You are here in a concentration camp and not in a sanatorium. You are just like your comrades here to die like a dog and not to be cured."

. . .

On one occasion, an escaped Polish inmate when recaptured, was executed and decapitated. His head was shrunken and later displayed. . . .

Human Skins (pp. 9–10)

In the pathological department, camp personnel worked on tattooed human skins. By December 1943 they had a large collection of these skins. This work continued until April 1945. Tattooed skins of human being were taken from the dissecting room to this collection. The skins were cleaned, dried and stretched on frames in the pathological department. Many habitual criminal inmates at Buchenwald had obscene pictures tattooed on their skins. This type of tattoo seemed to arouse the most interest among the personnel who worked with the skin collection.

. . .

Inmates in charge of the dissecting room determined whether the tattooed skin was sufficiently colorful or interesting, when the bodies were brought to the pathological department. One week after a certain healthy inmate arrived, his tattooed skin was in the pathological department. This inmate was called to the hospital from the bath by Dr. Mueller. . . . A short time thereafter, the same witness saw the inmate's tattooed skin in the pathological department. Still later he saw a lamp shade made from the tattooed skin from his arm.

There were two lamp shades in the lounge of the home of Camp Commander Koch which were said to have been made out of human skin. There was a human skull between two lamps. The son of the camp commander played with this skull. A witness testified that accused No. 15, wife of the camp commander, had a photo album, a brief case, and a pair of gloves made from tattooed human skin. The same witness testified that in the summer of 1940 a French or Belgian inmate, who was known throughout camp for his tattoos . . . including a colored cobra winging all the way up his left arm and an exceptionally cleanly tattooed sail boat with four masts on this chest. Accused No. 15 saw him and took down his number. . . . He was not seen again, but about six months later a skin with the same sail boat was seen in the pathological department.

Extermination (pp. 12–13)

Purported executions were carried out by shooting at the rifle range in the German Armament Works . . . by shooting by detail 99 at the horse stables, and by hanging at the crematory.

All executions, except those in the horse stables, were said to be exclusively in charge of the adjutant and the acting first sergeant. The executions in the horse stables were in charge of the prison compound leader. . . . No trials preceded the executions pursuant to orders from Berlin. Accused Nos. 1 and 21 knew that inmates were being executed without trial. There was a "court commissioner" in the Reichs Security Head Office who summarily imposed penalties upon without color of judicial proceedings.

. . .

In September 1941, and on several other occasions at other times, inmates wearing foreign military uniforms were seen going into the German Armament Works. . . . After a few minutes shots were heard and shortly thereafter dead bodies were seen being carried into the crematory. One witness counted about 180 Russian and Polish inmates who were apparently killed in this manner. . . . The extermination of Russian prisoners of war in the horse stables by detail 99 began in 1942 and continued until the fall of 1944. . . .

Testimony for the Defense

The following summarizes testimony in support of the defense.

Medical Experiments (pp. 19–20)

The experimental station at Buchenwald was directly under the command of the Reichs Physician of the SS I Berlin. The camp commander at Buchenwald had no control over it. Most of the experiments in block 46 were for the purpose of finding a protective vaccination for typhus. Only German habitual criminal inmates were used for the typhus experiments. Non-Germans were not used. In this connection it could be assumed that eastern nationals had experienced typhus in their youth and were immune and, in any event, it was impossible to get a proper case history on them. Many other non-Germans were very sick from typhus upon arrival . . .

Killing and Mistreatment (pp. 20–21)

The camp commander issued orders in the spring of 1942 directing that mistreatment of inmates cease immediately. Thereafter, he punished SS men and capos when he saw them mistreating inmates. . . . Each member of the guard had to sign a regulation which recited that it was an offense to talk with, beat, or mistreat an inmate.

. . .

Inmates were beaten by camp personnel for infractions of the camp rules and regulations. This was a favor to the inmates because, if the infraction had been reported, the punishment report would have remained in the inmates' personnel files causing their release to be delayed. . . .

Executions (pp. 21–22)

Eastern nationals were executed at Buchenwald under a law of the German Reich in the form of a decree issued about the middle of 1942 entitled "Decree about the punishment of Poles and Jews." Under that decree the cases were investigated by the police and witnesses were heard both for and against the accused. [decision/review process described] . . . In the opinion of a defense witness, who was a doctor of law and formerly a judge in a Germany state court, a written execution order based on this decree concerning Poles and Jews was legal under German law.

. . .

Russian political organizers and commissars were executed by detail 99 in the horse stables. They were not inmates of Buchenwald. Accused no. 21 asserted that they came to Buchenwald through policy channels from prisoner of war camps, but were not prisoners of war, inasmuch as they had no prisoner of war tag number and only a number from the prison camp from which they came. . . . As the victims had never been admitted as inmates to Buchenwald, no death certificates were executed. The bodies were cremated. These victims . . . were executed by detail 99 as reprisal for crimes committed against the German Wehrmacht by the Russians. The execution orders entitled "special treatment" always came from the Reichs Security Head Office.

SOME ADDITIONAL FINDINGS OF THE COURT

The Court found that "It is the ruling of this Tribunal, that neither the Charter of the International Military Tribunal nor Control Counsel [*sic*] Law No. 10 has defined *conspiracy to commit a war crime or crime against humanity* as a separate substantive crime; therefore this Tribunal has no jurisdiction to try any defendant upon a charge of conspiracy considered as a separate substantive offense." The fact that the Court rejected in whole one part of the indictment did not place any great burden on the prosecution because both international law and CCL No. 10 provided sufficient authority. The conspiracy charge added very little of substance to the indictment.

The defense claim that conditions at the end of the war had deteriorated because Allied operations had caused a shortage of food and other essential supplies was acknowledged by the Court. However, the Court concluded that Allied operations were only a minor contributing factor to the conditions found at liberation. Testimony of inmates clearly indicated long-standing and ongoing patterns of abuse and neglect.

Superior Orders and Executions

The defense claimed that executions involved prisoners duly sentenced by German civilian courts who were sent to Buchenwald to have the sentence carried out or for inmate violations of German law. The alleged executions of Russian POWs presumably were carried out by a special Gestapo unit, not personnel assigned to the camp. Alternatively, the defense claimed that these executions were carried out in compliance with orders from Head Office of the Gestapo. As in the Belsen Trial, witnesses could not remember many alleged incidents or denied knowledge of them.

The Court found that: "The law of war is addressed not only to combatants and public authorities of a state but to anybody regardless of status or nationality who assists or participates in violation thereof . . . (p. 31). That German law may have sanctioned the executions is irrelevant." Citing the Charter for the IMT, the Court stated further that: "the very essence of the Charter is that individuals have international duties that transcend the national obligations imposed by the individual state. He who violates the laws of war cannot obtain immunity while acting in pursuance of the authority of the state if the state in authorizing action moves outside its competence in international law" (p. 32).

Ilse Koch

Despite her reputation for cruelty, the panel reviewing the trial did not find that the evidence supported many of the accusations against Ilse Koch. Moreover, despite her isolation, she now was seven months pregnant. In an action that caused considerable outrage at the time, on the basis of the case review, General Lucius Clay reduced her original sentence of life imprisonment to four years. Even so she would be again tried by a German court in 1950 on charges of incitement to murder, incitement to attempted murder and incitement to the crime of committing grievous bodily harm, against German and Austrian citizens. In 1951, she again received a life sentence. She committed suicide in prison in 1967.

References

"Buchenwald." n.d. *Holocaust Encyclopedia* (United States Holocaust Museum) https://www.ushmm.org/wlc/en/article.php?ModuleId=10005198.

"Nazi War Crimes Trials: The Dachau Trials (1945–1948)." n.d. *Jewish Virtual Library.* http://www.jewishvirtuallibrary.org/the-dachau-trials.

10

The Malmedy Massacre Trial

The incident known as the Malmedy Massacre occurred in Belgium during the Battle of the Bulge (Ardennes campaign, December 1944), the largest land battle on the Western Front during World War II. The war had reached a critical point. The German Eastern Front (Soviet Union/Russia) was largely deadlocked, but the Allies were gaining ground in the west. German leader Adolf Hitler ordered a massive counteroffensive into this lightly defended area in Belgium in order to drive a wedge between British and American forces and retake the port of Antwerp. By this move, Hitler hoped to stall the Allied advance in the West and thereby gain three or four additional months to deal with the advancing Soviets. Preparations for the German offensive began in September 1944 with strict security and no radio communication. As a result, the attack achieved total surprise. The German forces created a "bulge" in the Allied lines of advance some 50 miles wide and 70 miles deep. Several fragments of U.S. forces were surrounded and destroyed. American forces in the town of Bastogne were completely encircled by German Troops for several days, until General George Patton arrived with the American 3rd Army to break the standoff. During the struggle for Bastogne, General Anthony McAuliffe became an instant American hero for his one-word response to a demand from the Germans that American troops surrender. General McAuliffe said, "Nuts."

MALMEDY

The Malmedy incidents involve war crimes committed during active field operations around the town by a German Waffen SS Panzer (mechanized) brigade, Kampfgruppe (Combat Group) Peiper, commanded by SS Obersturmbannführer (Lt. Colonel) Joachim Peiper. The unit consisted of 140 tanks supported by a battalion (800 men) of motorized infantry. During the service of the unit on the Eastern Front (against Soviet troops), it had earned the nickname of "the blowtorch battalion." Presumably the nickname stemmed from an action where the unit had burned two Russian villages (Mitcham 2006, 33).

The first event occurred on December 17, 1944. German soldiers surprised and captured an American motor convoy belonging to Battery B of the 285th Field Artillery Observation Battalion at a road intersection south of the Belgian town of Malmedy. The exact number of soldiers who surrendered to the Germans is unknown; but, according to various accounts, it was somewhere between 85 and 125. Eighty-four American prisoners of war (POWs) were killed by their German captors. As the unit advanced, reports of further incidents of killing POWs were reported on December 18, 19, and 20. Other killings of POWs were reported on December 31, and again between January 10 and 13, 1944, in the area south of Malmedy. Allegedly, many of these were ordered personally by Peiper.

TRIAL SUMMARY #6: MALMEDY MASSACRE

All the accused were members of the *Waffen* SS. Although presumably under the tactical control of the regular army (*Wehrmacht*), matters of philosophy and personnel still rested with the head office of the SS. Testimony indicated that at least one tactical order came directly from Heinrich Himmler during the campaign.

A Note on Prosecution Strategy

The Prosecution went to great lengths to show that officers of the Waffen SS had been taught that instilling terror and panic in the enemy population through ruthless tactics was the primary goal of an attack. Inhabitants and enemy soldiers should come to feel that resistance was futile. Prosecutors quoted extensively from the findings of the International Military Tribunal (IMT) concerning the German vision of total war. The IMT had concluded: "Everything is made subordinate to the overmastering dictates of war. Rules, regulations, assurances, and treaties all alike are of no moment; and so, freed from the restraining influence of international law, the aggressive war is conducted by the Nazi leaders in the most barbaric way." In discussing the treatment of Soviet POWs, the IMT panel had determined that the deaths of so many men resulted from "systematic plans to murder." Further it stated, "There is evidence that the shooting of unarmed prisoners of war was the general practice in some Waffen SS divisions" (pp. 7–8).

The Prosecution listed thirteen specific episodes with testimony from witnesses to support the charges. In reviewing the testimony, the reader should note that the evidence is linked to the specific places around Malmedy: Honsfeld, Bullingen, The Crossroads (4 km southeast of Malmedy), Ligneuville, Ligeneuville-Stavelot Road, Stavelot, Cheneux, La Gleize, Stoumont, Wanne, Lutrebois, Trois Ponts, and Petit Thier.

DOCUMENT: MALMEDY MASSACRE (*UNITED STATES V. VALENTIN BERSIN, ET AL.*)

When: May 16–July 16, 1946
Where: Dachau Concentration Camp

Court:	General Military Government Court
Defendants:	Joachim Peiper and 72 others
Source:	*United States v. Valentin Bersin, et al.* Review and Recommendations of the Deputy Judge Advocate for War Crimes Jewish Virtual Library. Online at http://www.jewishvirtuallibrary.org/jsource/Holocaust/dachautrial/fs11.pdf.
Jurisdiction:	CCL No. 10; Office of Military Government for Germany, "Legal and Penal Administration of Military Government Regulations," Title 5, §300.3 (March 21, 1947): "Military Government Courts have jurisdiction over all offenses committed in the U.S. Zone against the regulations enacted by Military Government, the existing German law, and the laws and usages of war . . ."
Charges:	Violation of the Laws and Usages of War "The accused were involved in the execution of a common plan, which contemplated the application of terroristic methods in combat curing the Ardennes counteroffensive" (pp. 4–5). The Prosecution listed thirteen alleged episodes of execution of POWs (p. 13).
Defense:	Challenge to the Jurisdiction of the Court on basis that the accused were POWs, so thus should be tried by a General Court Martial (denied—see Buchenwald case) Defense raised a number of procedural issues regarding the validity of some forms of evidence permitted (these motions denied) Denied that any orders verbal or written had been issued that mandated the deliberate killing of POWs. Troops were instructed to observe the Geneva Convention (1929). Superior orders
Verdicts:	Forty-three sentenced to death by hanging, including Peiper; twenty-two sentenced to life imprisonment; two sentenced to twenty years' imprisonment; one sentenced to fifteen years; five sentenced to ten years

Testimony

Private First Class Willie Braun (Machine Gunner)

The accused . . . related that on the morning of 19 December 1944 in the vicinity of Stoumont seven American prisoners of war were turned over to Sergeant Schumacher, commander of the troop carrier of which he was a crew member. Schumacher ordered the entire crew to dismount with hand weapons and kill the prisoners. In conformity with this order the crew dismounted and, including the accused who was using a fast firing rife, shot the prisoners. This is corroborated by the . . . statement of Friedrichs. (p. 54)

[Author comment: Verdict: guilty, life imprisonment reduced to fifteen years on review.]

Sergeant Valentin Bursin (Tank Commander)

The accused stated in his . . . sworn statement that on either 19 or 20 December 1944 when the tank commanded by himself was in Wanne, Belgium, he received an order from Second Lieutenant Heubeck, his commanding officer, to take two men from each of the crews of two tanks and round up all male civilians over sixteen years of age who were able to bear arms and have them shot. The accused stated that he remonstrated against this order; but when Heubeck insisted upon it, he passed the order on to two members of his own crew and to Sergeant Pflueger who assigned two men from his crew to help carry out the mission. Although the accused was not present at the execution of the order, he later heard from some soldiers that two Belgian male civilians had been shot. On the evening of the same day he reported to Heubeck: "Orders executed, Belgian civilians have been shot." This statement is corroborated by the extrajudicial sworn statements of Kotzur, Trettin, Clotten, Brecht; and by the testimony of Schneider, Hemroulle, Milburs, and Englebert. Kotzur stated that the two civilians were shot almost in the immediate vicinity of the accused (pp. 50–51).

[**Author comment:** *Verdict: guilty, death penalty, upheld on review.*]

First Lieutenant Friedrich Christ (commander 2nd Panzer company)

Instructions to Subordinates: The accused in his . . . sworn statement stated that on 15 December 1944 he reported the talk of Poetschke to his company to the effect that the impending offensive was a decisive one; that the troops were to behave toward the enemy so that panic and terror would precede them and discourage the enemy from resisting.; and that no prisoners were to be taken. The fact that this talk was given by the accused to his company . . . is corroborated by the . . . statements of Wikolischer, Ritzer, Szyperski, and Werner.

The Crossroads: Rumpf . . . stated that he arrived at the Crossroads about noon 17 December 1944 and that about five minutes after his arrival the accused requested a few men for a detail which apparently was for the purpose of shooting prisoners of war. Rehagel stated . . . that at the Crossroads the accused gave an order to shoot surrendered and unarmed American prisoners of war.

La Gleize: One witness testified that at La Gleize the accused ordered the shooting of about 30 American prisoners of war. This incident is corroborated by the . . . statement of Ritzer who stated that at La Gleize he recognized the accused's voice giving an order to take 20 to 30 surrendered and unarmed American prisoners of war into a pasture and to "bump them off." Ritzer also stated . . . that he did not see the accused at this time, nor did he see the prisoners shot, but he knew that the guards marched off with the prisoners. Later he talked with a messenger who showed him an American watch which the messenger said had been taken from an American prisoner who was shot by the accused.

Stoumont: Wikolischer stated . . . that many shootings of prisoners of war took place at Stoumont on 19 December 1944 upon orders of a platoon leader who had received an order from the accused over the radio to shoot prisoners of war. This is corroborated by the . . . statement of Werner. A witness testified that 12 to 18 unarmed and surrendered prisoners of war standing before a grocery store in

Stoumont were fired upon from the turret machine gun of the accused's tank. (pp. 58–59)

[Author comment: Sufficiency of Evidence: In this case, the court made a statement that applied across the board to the defense case except for those like Willi Braun who freely admitted participation.]

Apparently the theory of the defense as to the accused is that he did not participate, but if he did, it was pursuant to superior orders. There is no element of superior orders present, except for the campaign plans and orders of the various levels of command for the application of terrorism, which the accused as an officer in an essential Nazi organization actively supported. There is nothing in mitigation. (p. 62)

[Author comment: Verdict: guilty, death penalty, upheld.]

General Josef Dietrich (Commander, 6th SS Panzer Army)

Instructions to Subordinates: The accused stated in his . . . sworn statement that preceding the Ardennes Offensive, he issued an Army Order of the Day directing that the troops were to be preceded by a wave or terror and fright, that no human inhibitions were to be shown, and that every resistance was to be broken by terror but did not order that prisoners of war should be shot. Peiper stated in his . . . sworn statement that he was nearly certain that the Army Order of the Day contained express directions that prisoners of war were to be shot when local conditions of combat required it. Gruhle state in his . . . sworn statement that the Army Order of the Day directed that the fight was to be conducted stubbornly with no regard for Allied prisoners of war, who were to be shot if necessary in very compelling situations. (pp. 69–70)

[Author comment: Verdict: guilty, life imprisonment, upheld.]

Lieutenant Colonel Joachim Peiper (Commander, Combat Group Peiper, 1st Panzer Division)

Instructions to Subordinates: The accused stated in one of his . . . sworn statements that the Army Order of the Day provided that a wave of terror and fright was to precede the attacking troops; that the German soldier was to recall the victims of the bombing terror; and that the enemy resistance was to be broken by terror. The accused also stated that he was nearly certain that the Army Order of the Day expressly provided that prisoners of war were to be shot where the local conditions of combat required it. A regimental order was drawn by Gruhle, his adjutant, based on information received from the division commander and from the Army Order of the Day. The regimental order included substantially the same wording concerning prisoners of war as existed in the Army Order of the Day. The regimental order was transmitted to the battalion commanders. . . . [Corroborated by the statements of seven other officers.]

Honsfeld: Elements of Combat Group Peiper entered Honsfeld in the early morning of 17 December 1944. Two enlisted men, Technician Fifth Grad Morris and Private White, of the 612th Tank Destroyer Battalion, U.S. Army, stated in their . . .

statements that they were in Honsfeld on the morning of 17 December 1944. Just as it was getting daylight a German tank started firing at a house. Later a group of American soldiers came [out] of the house and approached the tank unarmed and with their hands raised in surrender. As the group approached the tank the crew opened fire upon them and they all fell to the ground. After the first burst of fire the German tank commander motioned to and ordered those still alive to surrender. Those who were not hit by the first burst again attempted to surrender and were shot down as they approached.

Another American enlisted man, Sergeant Wilson, stated . . . that he was with a group of Americans in a house in Honsfeld about 0800 hours 17 December 1944 when a German tank started firing at the house. The lieutenant in charge of the American surrendered and the group was ordered out of the house and lined up in a row facing the house. A German corporal started shooting the Americans and after two had fallen to the ground Sergeant Wilson escaped by running across country.

[Testimony on Chenoux omitted]

La Gleize: The accused stated . . . that while in La Gleize he had a conversation with Poetachke, Diffenthal, and Von Westerhagen concerning what was to be done with American prisoners of war if aid was not received and they had to fight to the finish. It was determined that prisoners would be shot. . . . The accused ordered the formation of a detail for shooting prisoners of war at La Gleize, according to the . . . sworn statements of Rumpf, Hennecke, and Reiser.

Stoumont: The accused stated in his . . . statement that at Stoumont on 19 December 1944 he gave Hillig an order to shoot an American prisoner of war. This is corroborated by the . . . sworn statement of Hillig, who carried out the order and killed the prisoner; and by the . . . sworn statement of Gruhle, who stated that he saw the body and heard from the accused himself that the prisoner was shot on the accused's order. It is also corroborated by the testimony of Landfried and Ebeling. . . .

[Testimony on Chenoux omitted]

[**Author comment:** *Verdict: guilty, death penalty, upheld.*]

THE REST OF THE STORY

None of the convicted SS soldiers received the death penalty were ever executed. By 1956, all of them had been released from prison. The Malmedy Massacre trial at Dachau intended to show the world that the Waffen SS soldiers were heartless killers. Instead, it turned into a controversial case that dragged on for over ten years and generated criticism of the American occupation, the war crimes military tribunals, the Jewish prosecutors at Dachau, and the entire American system of justice.

Most of the scrutiny stemmed from the efforts of the defense attorney, Lt. Col. Willis M. Everett who felt strongly that the proceeding had been "mock trials"—no more than a hollow "victor's justice." In addition to the inadequacy of the prior investigation and alleged defects in trial procedures, Everett also claimed that the German defendants had been subjected to brutal treatment and torture in order to gain confessions. Everett's efforts prompted a third in-house review by a judge employed by the American Occupation Army. Taking Everett's contentions seriously, the judge recommended commutation of the death sentences and a reduction in the others. General Lucius Clay, Commander of the American Zone of Occupation accepted the recommendations. Nonetheless, the commotion around the case resulted in an investigation by a subcommittee of the Armed Services Committee of the U.S. Senate. In its report, the subcommittee made a number of recommendations for the future, but said:

> The subcommittee is impressed by the thoroughness of General Clay's final review. . . . It is the considered opinion of the subcommittee that the Army in reaching its final conclusion in these cases ruled out any evidence secured by improper procedures during the pretrial interrogation, or as a result of procedural errors by the court. (p. 31)

References

Malmedy Massacre Investigation. Hearings before a Subcommittee of the Committee on Armed Services, United States Senate, 81st Congress, 1st sess. (1949). [Investigation of Action of Army with Respect to Trial of Persons Responsible for the Massacre of American Soldiers, Battle of the Bulge, Near Malmedy, Belgium, December 1944]. https://www.loc.gov/rr/frd/Military_Law/pdf/Malmedy_report.pdf.

"Massacre at Malmedy: War Crimes Trial." n.d. Jewish Virtual Library. Online at http://www.jewishvirtuallibrary.org/background-and-overview-of-massacre-at-malm-eacute-dy-2.

Mitcham, Samuel W. 2006. *Panzers in Winter: Hitler's Army and the Battle of the Bulge.* Westport, CT: Praeger.

Remy, Steven P. 2017. *The Malmedy Massacre: The War Crimes Trial Controversy.* Cambridge, MA: Harvard University Press.

Weingartner, James J. 2000. *A Peculiar Crusade: Willis M. Everett and the Malmedy Massacre.* New York: New York University Press.

11

The Nuremberg Trial

Historians generally regard the trial of the "Major War Criminals of the European Axis" before the International Military Tribunal (IMT) as the most important of the trials held after World War II. After the Allied Powers decided on trials as the method of proceeding, they met in London in August 1945 to draw up a blueprint for the trials. This conference resulted in the agreement generally referred to as the London Charter (sometimes called the Nuremberg Charter).

DOCUMENT: INTERNATIONAL CONFERENCE ON MILITARY TRIALS (LONDON CHARTER)

When:	August 8, 1945
Where:	London, England
Source:	Report of Robert H. Jackson, U.S. Representative to the International Conference on Military Trials, London, 1945 (Washington, DC: Government Printing Office, 1949). Online at http://avalon.law.yale.edu/imt/jack60.asp.
Significance:	The Annex to this agreement, The Charter of the International Military Tribunal (sometimes referred to as the London Charter or Nuremberg Charter) established the composition of the court, its procedures, its specific jurisdiction, and its authority to undertake certain activities in order to facilitate the trials. This Charter represented a ground-breaking document in the development of international criminal law. The following excerpt forms the heart of the document.

AGREEMENT by the Government of the UNITED STATES OF AMERICA, the Provisional Government of the FRENCH REPUBLIC, the Government of the UNITED KINGDOM OF GREAT BRITAIN AND NORTHERN IRELAND and the Government of the UNI0N Of SOVIET SOCIALIST REPUPLICS for the Prosecution and Punishment of the MAJOR WAR CRIMINALS of the EUROPEAN Axis....

[Part I omitted]

II. JURISDICTION AND GENERAL PRINCIPLES

Article 6. The Tribunal established by the Agreement referred to in Article I hereof for the trial and punishment of the major war criminals of the European Axis countries shall have the power to try and punish persons who, acting in the interests of the European Axis countries, whether as individuals or as members of organizations, committed any of the following crimes.

The following acts, or any of them, are crimes coming within the jurisdiction of the Tribunal for which, there shall be individual responsibility:

(a) *Crimes against peace*: namely, planning, preparation, initiation or waging of a war of aggression, or a war in violation of international treaties, agreements or assurances, or participation in a common plan or conspiracy for the accomplishment of any of the foregoing;

(b) *War crimes*: namely, violations of the laws or customs of war. Such violations shall include, but not be limited to, murder, ill-treatment or deportation to slave labor or for any other purpose of civilian population of or in occupied territory, murder or ill-treatment of prisoners of war or persons on the seas, killing of hostages, plunder of public or private property, wanton destruction of cities, towns or villages, or devastation not justified by military necessity;

(c) *Crimes against humanity*: namely, murder, extermination, enslavement, deportation, and other inhumane acts committed against any civilian population, before or during the war; or persecutions on political, racial or religious grounds in execution of or in connection with any crime within the jurisdiction of the Tribunal, whether or not in violation of the domestic law of the country where perpetrated.
Leaders, organizers, instigators and accomplices participating in the formulation or execution of a common plan or conspiracy to commit any of the foregoing crimes are responsible for all acts performed by any persons in execution of such plan.

Article 7. The official position of defendants, whether as Heads of State or responsible officials in Government Departments, shall not be considered as freeing them from responsibility or mitigating punishment.

Article 8. The fact that the Defendant acted pursuant to order of his Government or of a superior shall not free him from responsibility, but may be considered in mitigation of punishment if the Tribunal determines that justice so requires.

Article 9. At the trial of any individual member of any group or organization the Tribunal may declare (in connection with any act of which the individual may be convicted) that the group or organization of which the individual was a member was a criminal organization.

After receipt of the Indictment the Tribunal shall give such notice as it thinks fit that the prosecution intends to ask the Tribunal to make such declaration and any member of the organization will be entitled to apply to the Tribunal for leave to be heard by the Tribunal upon the question of the criminal character of the organization. The Tribunal shall have power to allow or reject the application. If the application is allowed, the Tribunal may direct in what manner the applicants shall be represented and heard.

Article 10. In cases where a group or organization is declared criminal by the Tribunal, the competent national authority of any Signatory shall have the right to bring individuals to trial for membership therein before national, military or occupation courts. In any such case the criminal nature of the group or organization is considered proved and shall not be questioned.

Article 11. Any person convicted by the Tribunal may be charged before a national, military or occupation court, referred to in Article 10 of this Charter, with a crime other than of membership in a criminal group or organization and such court may, after convicting him, impose upon him punishment independent of and additional to the punishment imposed by the Tribunal for participation in the criminal activities of such group or organization.

A NOTE ON THE TOKYO TRIALS

The focus on Nuremberg often overshadows the other set of trials held in Tokyo and other venues across the Pacific. The International Military Tribunal for the Far East (IMTFE) mirrored the Nuremberg trial (IMT) in that it focused on those who planned, initiated, and directed Japan's war effort. Although it was not the product of an international agreement, the Charter for the IMTFE took much of its language from the London Charter.

At the Moscow Conference, held in December 1945, the Soviet Union, the United Kingdom, and the United States (with concurrence from China) agreed to a basic structure for the occupation of Japan. The agreement gave General Douglas MacArthur, as supreme commander of the Allied Powers, the authority to "issue all orders for the implementation of the Terms of Surrender, the occupation and control of Japan, and all directives supplementary thereto."

In January 1946, acting on this grant of authority, General MacArthur issued a special proclamation that established the IMTFE. The Charter for the IMTFE was added as an annex to the special proclamation. Like the Nuremberg Charter, it laid out the composition, jurisdiction, and functions of the tribunal. The trials began in May 1946 and lasted until November 1948. These trials will be analyzed in the section following the discussion of CCL No. 10.

NUREMBERG: JURISDICTION AND PROCEDURE

The London Charter stipulated that crimes of the European Axis Powers could be tried. It limited the temporal scope (time frame) of crimes that could be prosecuted to those committed between September 1, 1939 (the invasion of Poland) and the end of the war. The paragraphs in Article 6 defined three categories of crimes: crimes against peace, war crimes, and crimes against humanity. Because of how they are labelled, other discussions and descriptions of trials will refer to these categories as class A, class B, and class C war crimes. Crimes against peace, crimes against humanity, and the idea that certain organizations were criminal enterprises represented innovations in terms of charges because of questions about the validity of their legal origins.

The Charter stated that holding an official position did not give immunity for war crimes. Obedience to *superior orders* could only be considered in mitigation of punishment if the Tribunal determined that justice so required. The procedures used by the Tribunal drew more on the *civil law* (European continental courts) model than on *common law* (United States and the United Kingdom) practices. This meant that the trials would be held before a panel of judges rather than a jury. The decision also meant that the prosecution had a very wide allowance for types of evidence permitted. Unlike common law proceedings, hearsay evidence would be permitted.

Each of the four Allied nations—the United States, Great Britain, the Soviet Union, and France—appointed a judge, an alternate judge, and a prosecution team. Lord Justice Geoffrey Lawrence of Great Britain served as the court's presiding judge. Each prosecution team had a Chief Prosecutor. President Harry Truman appointed Supreme Court justice Robert H. Jackson. Colonel Telford Taylor served as one of Jackson's assistant prosecutors. Taylor would gain a promotion to brigadier general and oversee the twelve subsequent trials held at Nuremberg for the trials held under CCL No. 10. The British prosecutor, Sir Hartley Shawcross, would play an important role in the cross-examination of Hermann Göring.

NUREMBERG

For both political and practical reasons, the Allies chose the Palace of Justice at Nuremberg, Germany, for the trial site. The proclamation of the Third Reich's racial laws against the Jews had been made at Nuremberg. Just as important, the Palace of Justice there had received only minimal damage during the war. The large stone structure had 80 courtrooms and over 500 offices, which provided sufficient space for a major international legal proceeding. An undestroyed prison was part of the justice building complex, so all prospective defendants could be housed on site. U.S. Army personnel prepared the Palace of Justice for the trial, repairing damage and laying thousands of feet of electrical wire. The Trial of the Major War Criminals (IMT) began on November 14, 1945 and ended on October 1, 1946.

The prosecution presented indictments against twenty-four major criminals and six organizations. The indicted organizations were the Nazi Party (NSDAP), the Schutzstaffel (SS), the SD, the Gestapo, the General Staff, and Hitler's cabinet. The defendants were entitled to a legal counsel of their choosing. One defendant, Robert Ley, head of the German Labor Front, committed suicide on the eve of the trial. Adolf Hitler, Heinrich Himmler, and Joseph Goebbels never stood trial because they had committed suicide before the end of the war. The IMT decided not to try the three posthumously because they did not wish to give an impression that they might still be alive.

The trial itself lasted 218 days with 360 witnesses giving either written or verbal testimony. A new simultaneous translation system allowed the trial to proceed

Table 11.1   Nuremberg Defendants

- Martin Bormann, deputy führer after 1941 (tried in absentia)
- Karl Dönitz, admiral and commander of the Navy from 1943 to 1945
- Hans Frank, governor-general of Poland
- Wilhelm Frick, minister for internal affairs
- Hans Fritzsche, head of the Radio Division of the Ministry of Propaganda
- Walther Funk, minister of economic affairs
- Hermann Göring, Reich marshal and commander of the Luftwaffe
- Rudolf Hess, deputy führer until May 1941
- Alfred Jodl, army general, Oberkommando der Wehrmacht (OKW)
- Ernst Kaltenbrunner, head of SD, Security Service
- Wilhelm Keitel, field marshal—Army chief of staff
- Gustav Krupp von Bohlen und Halbach, head of Krupp armaments
- Robert Ley, head of the Labor Front (committed suicide on October 16, 1945)
- Konstantin Neurath, protector of Bohemia and Moravia from 1939 to 1943
- Franz von Papen, former vice chancellor and ambassador to Turkey
- Erich Raeder, grand admiral and commander of the Navy until 1943
- Joachim von Ribbentrop, foreign minister
- Alfred Rosenberg, minister for the Occupied Territories in the East until 1941
- Fritz Saukel, plenipotentiary for the mobilization of labor
- Hjalmar Schacht, president of the Reichsbank from 1933 to 1939 and minister of economics from 1934 to 1937
- Arthur Seyss-Inquart, commissioner for the Netherlands from 1940 to 1945
- Baldur von Shirach, leader of the Hitler Youth and *Gauleiter* (area commander) of Vienna
- Albert Speer, minister of armaments from 1942 to 1945
- Julius Streicher, publisher of the newspaper *Der Sturmer*

The indicted organizations were the Nazi Party (NSDAP), the Schutzstaffel (SS), the SD, the Gestapo, the General Staff, and Hitler's cabinet.

---

efficiently and swiftly in four languages. Although the defense had the right to call its own witnesses, it could not introduce any evidence against the Allies. This prevented the defense from using what is known as the *tu quoque* defense. *Tu quoque* means "you did it too." This form of defense does not try to refute the truth of the accusations but asserts that those conducting the trial are guilty of hypocrisy because they also engaged in the same type of behavior. The individuals and organizations charged are listed in Table 11.1.

HERMANN GÖRING

Hermann Göring (Goering) was the highest-ranking member of the NSDAP to face trial at Nuremberg. At the close of World War II, Göring's official titles included Reich marshal, commander-in-chief of the Luftwaffe, Reichstag president, minister president of Prussia, and second in command in the leadership of the NSDAP. He had a distinguished war record in World War I (1914–1918). At the beginning, he was an infantry lieutenant but soon transferred to the air corps. During the war, he scored twenty-two aerial kills, earning one of Germany's highest military decorations, the Blue Max (*Pour le Mérite*). When Manfred von

Richthofen (the Red Baron), commander of the fighter squadron nicknamed the "Flying Circus," died in action in 1918, Göring assumed command of the unit.

Göring joined the Nazi Party in 1921 and soon became one of Hitler's most trusted advisers and leader of the SA (Stormtroopers or "Brownshirts"), the NSDAP's private army. When the Nazi Party gained control of the government in 1933, Hitler appointed Göring commissioner for aviation. In 1935, he became commander in chief of the newly established German Air Force (the Luftwaffe). By the opening days of World War II, the Luftwaffe had become the largest air force in the world. Along with Heinrich Himmler, Göring was primarily responsible for developing the legislation that led to the systematic elimination of the Jewish population in Germany and other occupied areas.

RUDOLF HÖSS (HOESS)

Although not a defendant, the most graphic testimony given during the trial came from Rudolf Höss, the commandant (*Obersturmbannführer*) of the Auschwitz concentration camp during much of World War II (May 1940–November 1943). As a witness called by the defense, Höss readily admitted his part in testing and putting into practice various methods to accelerate the effort to exterminate the Jewish population of Nazi-occupied Europe (see the *Zyklon B* case). He was responsible for introducing Zyklon B into the killing process and developing the equivalent of an assembly line for mass murder. Höss wrote his autobiography while he awaited execution after his own trial before a British military court (1947). In describing his role in the process, he said:

> During Eichmann's next visit I told him about this use of Cyclon B [Zyklon B] and we decided to employ it for the mass extermination operation. The killing by Cyclon B gas of the Russian prisoners of war transported to Auschwitz was continued, but no longer in block II, since after the gassing the whole building had to be ventilated for at least two days. The mortuary of the crematorium next to the hospital block was therefore used as a gassing room, after the door had been made gasproof and some holes had been pierced in the ceiling through which the gas could be discharged. I can however only recall one transport consisting of nine hundred Russian prisoners being gassed there and I remember that it took several days to cremate their corpses. (p. 185–186)

TRIAL SUMMARY #7: TRIAL OF THE MAJOR WAR CRIMINALS

DOCUMENT: TRIAL OF MAJOR WAR CRIMINALS

When: November 14, 1945–October 1, 1946
Where: Nuremberg, Germany
Court: International Military Tribunal
Defendants: 24 leaders of Nazi Germany and 6 Nazi organizations
Source: Rudolf Franz Ferdinand Hoess, "Affidavit, 5 April 1946," in Trial of the Major War Criminals before the International Tribunal, Nuremberg, 14 November 1945–1 October 1946 (Nuremberg:

	Secretariat of the International Military Tribunal, 1949), Doc. 3868PS, vol. 33, 27579. Online at https://www.loc.gov/rr/frd/Military_Law/NT_major-war-criminals.html.
Jurisdiction:	London Charter (International Agreement) Note the limited temporal jurisdiction—no crime committed before September 1, 1945.
Charges:	Crimes against peace Violation of the laws and usages of war Crimes against humanity Conspiracy to commit crimes against peace, war crimes, and crimes against humanity
Defense:	Rejection of jurisdiction Rejection of idea that crimes against humanity and crimes against peace have a basis in international law (acts of state) *Führer* principle (superior orders)—sometimes referred to as "the Nuremberg Defense" in discussions of other war crime trials
Verdicts:	Three were acquitted (Fritzsche, Papen, and Schacht); twelve received the death penalty; Göring committed suicide the night before his scheduled execution; three were sentenced to life imprisonment and four to prison terms ranging from ten to twenty years. Gustav Krupp considered not competent to stand trial. Later evidence confirmed that Martin Bormann had died in an air raid on Berlin in the last days of the war. The International Military Tribunal declared three of the indicted organizations criminal enterprises: the Leadership Corps of the Nazi Party, the Gestapo/ *Sicherheitsdienst* (SD), and the SS. They acquitted the Reich cabinet because it consisted of a small group of senior personnel who could be prosecuted individually. The IMT determined that the General Staff/High Command was an instrumentality of the state rather than a membership organization or institutional entity. The IMT acquitted the SA (Stormtroopers) because its criminal actions fell outside the tribunal's temporal (specified time frame) jurisdiction.

Testimony

I, Rudolf Franz Ferdinand Hoess, being first duly sworn, depose and say as follows:

1. I am forty-six years old, and have been a member of the NSDAP since 1922; a member of the SS since 1934; a member of the Waffen-SS since 1939. I was a member from 1 December 1934 of the SS Guard Unit, the so-called Deathshead Formation (*Totenkopf Verband*).

2. I have been constantly associated with the administration of concentration camps since 1934, serving at Dachau until 1938; then as Adjutant in Sachsenhausen from 1938 to 1 May, 1940, when I was appointed

Commandant of Auschwitz. I commanded Auschwitz until 1 December, 1943, and estimate that at least 2,500,000 victims were executed and exterminated there by gassing and burning, and at least another half million succumbed to starvation and disease, making a total dead of about 3,000,000. This figure represents about 70% or 80% of all persons sent to Auschwitz as prisoners, the remainder having been selected and used for slave labor in the concentration camp industries. Included among the executed and burnt were approximately 20,000 Russian prisoners of war (previously screened out of Prisoner of War cages by the Gestapo) who were delivered at Auschwitz in Wehrmacht transports operated by regular Wehrmacht officers and men. The remainder of the total number of victims included about 100,000 German Jews, and great numbers of citizens (mostly Jewish) from Holland, France, Belgium, Poland, Hungary, Czechoslovakia, Greece, or other countries. We executed about 400,000 Hungarian Jews alone at Auschwitz in the summer of 1944.

[Paragraph 3 omitted]

4. Mass executions by gassing commenced during the summer 1941 and continued until fall 1944. I personally supervised executions at Auschwitz until the first of December 1943 and know by reason of my continued duties in the Inspectorate of Concentration Camps WVHA that these mass executions continued as stated above. All mass executions by gassing took place under the direct order, supervision and responsibility of RSHA. I received all orders for carrying out these mass executions directly from RSHA.

[Paragraph 5 omitted]

6. The "final solution" of the Jewish question meant the complete extermination of all Jews in Europe. I was ordered to establish extermination facilities at Auschwitz in June 1941. At that time there were already in the general government three other extermination camps; BELZEK, TREBLINKA and WOLZEK. These camps were under the *Einsatzkommando* of the Security Police and SD. I visited Treblinka to find out how they carried out their exterminations. The Camp Commandant at Treblinka told me that he had liquidated 80,000 in the course of one-half year. He was principally concerned with liquidating all the Jews from the Warsaw Ghetto. He used monoxide gas and I did not think that his methods were very efficient. So when I set up the extermination building at Auschwitz, I used Cyclon B, which was a crystallized Prussic Acid which we dropped into the death chamber from a small opening. It took from 3 to 15 minutes to kill the people in the death chamber depending upon climatic conditions. We knew when the people were dead because their screaming stopped. We usually waited about one-half hour before we opened the doors and removed the bodies. After the bodies were removed our special commandos took off the rings and extracted the gold from the teeth of the corpses.

7. Another improvement we made over Treblinka was that we built our gas chambers to accommodate 2,000 people at one time, whereas at Treblinka their 10 gas chambers only accommodated 200 people each. The way we selected our victims was as follows: we had two SS doctors on duty at Auschwitz to examine the incoming transports of prisoners. The prisoners would be marched by one of the doctors who would make spot decisions as they walked by. Those who were fit for work were sent into the Camp. Others were sent immediately to the extermination plants. Children of tender years were invariably exterminated since by reason of their youth they were unable to work. Still another improvement we made over Treblinka was that at Treblinka the victims almost always knew that they were to be exterminated and at Auschwitz we endeavored to fool the victims into thinking that they were to go through a delousing process. Of course, frequently they realized our true intentions and we sometimes had riots and difficulties due to that fact. Very frequently women would hide their children under the clothes but of course when we found them we would send the children in to be exterminated. We were required to carry out these exterminations in secrecy but of course the foul and nauseating stench from the continuous burning of bodies permeated the entire area and all of the people living in the surrounding communities knew that exterminations were going on at Auschwitz.

8. We received from time to time special prisoners from the local Gestapo office. The SS doctors killed such prisoners by injections of benzine. Doctors had orders to write ordinary death certificates and could put down any reason at all for the cause of death.

9. From time to time we conducted medical experiments on women inmates, including sterilization and experiments relating to cancer. Most of the people who died under these experiments had been already condemned to death by the Gestapo.

10. Rudolf Mildner was the chief of the Gestapo at Kattowicz and as such was head of the political department at Auschwitz which conducted third degree methods of interrogation from approximately March 1941 until September 1943. As such, he frequently sent prisoners to Auschwitz for incarceration or execution. He visited Auschwitz on several occasions. The Gestapo Court, the SS Standgericht, which tried persons accused of various crimes, such as escaping Prisoners of War, etc., frequently met within Auschwitz, and Mildner often attended the trial of such persons, who usually were executed in Auschwitz following their sentence. I showed Mildner throughout the extermination plant at Auschwitz and he was directly interested in it since he had to send the Jews from his territory for execution at Auschwitz.

I understand English as it is written above. The above statements are true; this declaration is made by me voluntarily and without compulsion;

after reading over the statement, I have signed and executed the same at Nuremberg, Germany on the fifth day of April 1946.

WAS THE NUREMBERG TRIAL AN EXERCISE IN VICTOR'S JUSTICE?

This trial was a first. History had not seen such a tribunal before. As the trial proceeded, it came under very heavy criticism from lawyers, judges, and others. The chief justice of the Supreme Court of the United States, Harlan Fiske Stone, described the proceedings as a fraud.

> Jackson [Associate Justice Robert Jackson, chief U.S. prosecutor] is away conducting his high-grade lynching party in Nuremberg. . . . I don't mind what he does to the Nazis, but I hate to see the pretense that he is running a court and proceeding according to common law. This is a little too sanctimonious a fraud to meet my old-fashioned ideas. (Mason 1956, 716)

In an oblique criticism of what he saw as a purely political exercise, Hermann Göring wrote, "The victor will always be the judge and the vanquished the accused" (Bass 2003, 8), implying that after a war, might and victory substitute for "right" and justice.

Space does not permit a thorough discussion of these issues here. For the most part, the criticisms came from those who thought the hybrid procedures violated basic principles of "fairness." A very real question arose with respect to the validity of the charges of "crimes against humanity" and "crimes against peace" ("waging aggressive war"). The question was: Had international law and practice actually developed a clear and firm rationale between 1914 and the onset of World War II in 1939 that would permit prosecution for offenses involving either category? This question reflects a very fundamental principle of law because a basic principle of modern law is *nullum crimen sine lege*, or no crime without a law (sometimes *nullum poenae sine lege*, or no penalty without law). The principle means that individuals should face criminal punishment only for an act that was criminalized by law before they performed the act. In the Constitution of the United States, the prohibition against *ex post facto laws* (after the fact) embodies that principle (Article I.10). The London Charter itself, as a hybrid of procedures from Allied countries, also violated other fundamental common law principles. For example, Article 19 of the London Charter states: "The Tribunal shall not be bound by technical rules of evidence." This permitted hearsay evidence to be introduced without any confirmation of its validity from other sources.

Criticism also stemmed from what many perceived as a double standard. The Allies were prosecuting Germans for offenses that they themselves had committed. The charge of crimes against humanity included the indiscriminate bombing of civilian populations. Yet, Americans dropped the atomic bomb on Hiroshima and Nagasaki, bombed cities in Japan, and participated with the British in systematically destroying the industrial cities of Germany. The indictment charged German defendants with conspiracy to commit aggression against Poland in 1939 but ignored the role of the Soviet Union as a participant in the same conspiracy (see previous discussion of *tu quoque* arguments).

Despite the criticisms, the record clearly indicates that this trial and others were not political purges of those seen as enemies. Even with the flawed process, the issue centered on the question of the appropriate punishment for "guilt so black" that it falls outside the scope of the judicial process. Consider the scope of the crimes that Rudolf Höss openly and publicly acknowledged. Additionally, a clear dividing line exists between political "show" trials and those that adhere to a principled approach. At Nuremberg and in other trials, some defendants were acquitted. Finally, even under very close retrospective examination, the trials did not produce outcomes that were manifestly "unjust." The Court did not find any defendant guilty solely on charges that had questionable origins.

SIGNIFICANCE

The desire of the Allies to punish Germany for its criminal behavior in starting the war and the tactics they used, furnished the principal justification for the trials. Many have later seen the Nuremberg trials as resulting from the Allied reaction to the Holocaust; however, the events associated with the decimation of European Jewry had very little part in the determination to hold Germany responsible for the devastation caused by Nazi aggression. For the Americans and the British, the fundamental purpose of the trials was to punish Nazi leaders for waging "aggressive war." In contrast, the Soviet Union saw the trials as exercises in propaganda (Bass 2003, 202).

The charges in the London Charter, sections II.6(a) and II.6(c), "crimes again peace" and "crimes against humanity," represented two entirely new areas of war crimes aimed at holding the leaders and planners accountable. In the past, war crime trials had focused primarily on the *ius in bello*, conduct in field during active hostilities, not on the *ius ad bellum*, the planning and initiation of interstate conflict. This had meant that although the soldiers in the field were individually responsible for any breach of law, the leaders and planners who planned, initiated, and directed the conflict had no individual liability for their actions. International Law considered the initiation of war an *act of state* that might engage *collective responsibility* (i.e., Germany as a state might have liability, just as a corporation might have liability in domestic law) but individual officials would have no personal liability. True, the efforts to try Kaiser Wilhelm of Germany after World War I had relied upon a charge of "waging aggressive war," but no trial occurred. At that time, that charge itself drew upon very questionable precedents in international law. In fact, the United States had strenuously objected to a trial, arguing that the trial would have had no justifiable basis in existing international law.

In spite of the questions, the Nuremberg and Tokyo trials gave a jump start to an entirely new area of international law—international criminal law (ICL). Traditional international law rests upon the idea of collective responsibility, that is, that the "state" as a whole is responsible for any breach of law, not the individuals who actually performed the actions. This meant that until World War II, the individuals who planned and started a war bore no direct individual responsibility for what they did.

In contrast, crimes under ICL involve individual criminal liability for planning and initiating an international conflict. It holds leaders directly responsible, and potentially punishable, for any violations. Most important here, the term "genocide," coined during World War II by a Polish international lawyer, Raphael Lemkin, had not yet entered into general usage. Along with Lemkin's pioneering work, the definition of "crimes against humanity" in the London Charter formed the basis for the development of the post–World War II Genocide Convention (1948).

References

Bass, Gary. 2003. *Stay the Hand of Vengeance: The Politics of War Crimes Tribunals*. Princeton, NJ: Princeton University Press.

Goldensohn, Leon. 2004. *The Nuremberg Interviews: An American Psychiatrist's Conversations with the Defendants and Witnesses*, edited by Robert Gellately. New York: Vintage.

Hoess, Rudolf. 1959/2000. *Commandant of Auschwitz. London*: Weidenfeld & Nicolson.

Mason, Alpheus Thomas. 1956. *Harlan Fiske Stone: Pillar of the Law*. New York: Viking Press

"The Nuremberg Trials: An International Responsibility to Uphold Justice." n.d. http://nuremberg-trials.org/.

Taulbee, James Larry. 2017. "Nazi Germany: The Holocaust." In *Genocide, Mass Atrocity, and War Crimes in Modern History*, vol. 1, pp. 141–173. Santa Barbara, CA: Praeger.

Taylor, Telford. 1992. *The Anatomy of the Nuremberg Trials: A Personal Memoir*. Boston: Little, Brown.

12

Allied Control Council Law No. 10

Initially, Allied plans included more than just one international trial at the IMT. However, the growing friction between the victorious Allied Powers made this impossible. The Soviet Union (USSR) had become increasingly uncooperative with respect to establishing uniform policies for the four occupation zones (British, French, U.S., and USSR). Frustrated by the situation, in December 1945, the three Western allies, Britain, France, and the United States, pushed for the adoption of Allied Control Council Law No. 10 (CCL 10), which authorized every occupying power to use its own legal system to try war criminals in their respective zones of occupation in Germany independently of the IMT. The stated purpose was to establish a "uniform legal basis in Germany for the prosecution of war criminals and other similar offenders other than those dealt with by the International Military Tribunal." Based on this law, after the IMT ended, U.S. authorities held another twelve trials in Nuremberg. The IMT had already established the criminality of war crimes, aggressive war, and crimes against humanity. These trials focused on determining the guilt of second-tier Nazis accused of those crimes. These trials differed from the IMT in that they involved U.S. military tribunals rather than the international tribunal that decided the fate of the major Nazi leaders. In total, the United States indicted 183 defendants in 12 subsequent trials. The judges and prosecutors in all of these trials were American. Brigadier General Telford Taylor, who had served as a deputy prosecutor at the IMT, served as chief of counsel for the prosecution.

Similar trials took place in the other occupation zones. U.S. military tribunal trials at Dachau tried 1,941 defendants with 1,517 found guilty. Of these, 324 were sentenced to death; 278 of these sentences were actually carried out. In the British Occupation Zone, in Lüneburg, Hamburg, and Wuppertal, 1,085 defendants were tried before British military tribunals yielding 240 death sentences. In the French Zone, 2,107 defendants were tried; 104 sentenced to death. The total number of Nazi criminals convicted in the three Western occupation zones between 1945 and 1949 was 5,025, of whom 806 were sentenced to death. Four hundred eighty-six death sentences were carried out; the remaining sentences were commuted to prison terms of varying lengths. No comparable figures (official or unofficial) are available for the trials of Nazis in the Soviet Occupation Zone. It is assumed, however, that tens of thousands of Germans were tried there and that most of them were convicted and either executed or transported to Soviet territories to serve their sentences (Jewish Virtual Library, n.d.). In addition to the efforts by the Allies in Germany, many countries initiated proceedings against those who had committed war crimes within their sovereign jurisdiction.

Before the trials concluded, the political climate changed. The Cold War had begun and for many Americans the Korean War quickly relegated concern with the Nazi period to the past. John J. McCloy, a former assistant secretary of war who became U.S. high commissioner for Germany in 1949, promulgated the Clemency Act in January 1951, commuting many of the sentences of those convicted. By 1958, nearly all prisoners had been freed.

DOCUMENT: ALLIED CONTROL COUNCIL LAW NO. 10 (CCL NO. 10)—
PUNISHMENT OF PERSONS GUILTY OF WAR CRIMES, CRIMES AGAINST
PEACE AND AGAINST HUMANITY

When: December 20, 1945
Where: Berlin, Germany
Source: Telford Taylor, *Final Report to the Secretary of the Army on the Nurenberg War Crimes Trials under Control Council Law No. 10* (Washington, DC: Government Printing Office, 1949). Online at http://avalon.law.yale.edu/imt/imt10.asp.
Significance: This order formed the basis for trials of individuals other than those brought before the IMT at Nuremberg.

Article II

1. Each of the following acts is recognized as a crime:

    (a) Crimes against Peace. Initiation of invasions of other countries and wars of aggression in violation of international laws and treaties, including but not limited to planning, preparation, initiation or waging a war of aggression, or a war of violation of international treaties, agreements or assurances, or participation in a common plan or conspiracy for the accomplishment of any of the foregoing.

    (b) War Crimes. Atrocities or offenses against persons or property constituting violations of the laws or customs of war, including but not limited to, murder, ill treatment or deportation to slave labour or for any other purpose, of civilian population from occupied territory, murder or ill treatment of prisoners of war or persons on the seas, killing of hostages, plunder of public or private property, wanton destruction of cities, towns or villages, or devastation not justified by military necessity.

    (c) Crimes against Humanity. Atrocities and offenses, including but not limited to murder, extermination, enslavement, deportation, imprisonment, torture, rape, or other inhumane acts committed against any civilian population, or persecutions on political, racial or religious grounds whether or not in violation of the domestic laws of the country where perpetrated.

    (d) Membership in categories of a criminal group or organization declared criminal by the International Military Tribunal.

2. Any person without regard to nationality or the capacity in which he acted, is deemed to have committed a crime as defined in paragraph 1 of this Article, if he was (a) a principal or (b) was an accessory to the commission of any such crime or ordered or abetted the same or (c) took a consenting part therein or (d) was connected with plans or enterprises involving its commission or (e) was a member of any organization or group connected with the commission of any such crime or (f) with reference to paragraph 1(a) if he held a high political, civil or military (including General Staff) position in Germany or in one of its Allies, co-belligerents or satellites or held high position in the financial, industrial or economic life of any such country.

...

4. (a) The official position of any person, whether as Head of State or as a responsible official in a Government Department, does not free him from responsibility for a crime or entitle him to mitigation of punishment.

    (b) The fact that any person acted pursuant to the order of his Government or of a superior does not free him from responsibility for a crime, but may be considered in mitigation.

5. In any trial or prosecution for a crime herein referred to, the accused shall not be entitled to the benefits of any statute of limitation in respect to the period from 30 January 1933 to 1 July 1945, nor shall any immunity, pardon or amnesty granted under the Nazi regime be admitted as a bar to trial or punishment.

Article III

1. Each occupying authority, within its Zone of Occupation,

    (a) shall have the right to cause persons within such Zone suspected of having committed a crime, including those charged with crime by one of the United Nations, to be arrested and shall take under control the property, real and personal, owned or controlled by the said persons, pending decisions as to its eventual disposition.

    (b) shall report to the Legal Directorate the name of all suspected criminals, the reasons for and the places of their detention, if they are detained, and the names and location of witnesses.

(c) shall take appropriate measures to see that witnesses and evidence will be available when required.

(d) shall have the right to cause all persons so arrested and charged, and not delivered to another authority as herein provided, or released, to be brought to trial before an appropriate tribunal. Such tribunal may, in the case of crimes committed by persons of German citizenship or nationality against other persons of German citizenship or nationality, or stateless persons, be a German Court, if authorized by the occupying authorities.

2. The tribunal by which persons charged with offenses hereunder shall be tried and the rules and procedure thereof shall be determined or designated by each Zone Commander for his respective Zone. Nothing herein is intended to, or shall impair or limit the Jurisdiction or power of any court or tribunal now or hereafter established in any Zone by the Commander thereof, or of the International Military Tribunal established by the London Agreement of 8 August 1945.

Table 12.1 summarizes the trials at Nuremberg under CCL No. 10.

Table 12.1 Trials of War Criminals before the Nuremberg Military Tribunals

#	Designations	Dates	Defendants
1	Doctors' trial	December 9, 1946–August 20, 1947	23 Nazi physicians Action T4 Program
2	Milch trial	January 2, 1947–April 14, 1947	Luftwaffe Field Marshal Erhard Milch
3	Judges' trial	March 5, 1947–December 4, 1947	16 Nazi German jurists
4	Pohl trial	April 8, 1947–November 3, 1947	Oswald Pohl and 17 SS officers
5	Flick trial	April 19, 1947–December 22, 1947	Friedrich Flick and 5 directors of his companies
6	I.G. Farben trial	August 27, 1947–July 30, 1948	Directors of I.G. Farben, maker of Zyklon B
7	Hostages trial	July 8, 1947–February 19, 1948	12 German generals—Balkan Campaign
8	RuSHA trial	October 20, 1947–March 10, 1948	14 racial cleansing and resettlement officials
9	Einsatzgruppen trial	September 29, 1947–April 10, 1948	24 officers of *Einsatzgruppen*
10	Krupp trial	December 8, 1947–July 31, 1948	12 directors of the Krupp Group
11	Ministries trial	January 6, 1948–April 13, 1949	21 officials of Reich ministries
12	High Command trial	December 30, 1947–October 28, 1948	14 High Command (OKW) generals

References

Heller, Kevin John. 2011. *The Nuremberg Military Tribunals and the Origins of International Criminal Law.* Oxford: Oxford University Press.

"Nazi War Crimes: War Crimes Trials." n.d. Jewish Virtual Library. https://www.jewishvirtuallibrary.org/war-crimes-trials.

Priemel, Kim C., and Alexa Stiller, eds. 2012. *Reassessing the Nuremberg Military Tribunals: Transitional Justice, Trial Narratives, and Historiography.* New York and Oxford: Berghahn Books.

13

The Medical Case (Doctors' Trial): *United States v. Karl Brandt, et al.*

This case, the first of twelve that dealt with the second tier of the Nazi elite, tried twenty leading German physicians and three medical administrators for their willing participation in war crimes and crimes against humanity. The trial developed from evidence originally gathered to prosecute Hermann Göring at the International Military Tribunal. That evidence included a large amount of material implicating the Luftwaffe's physicians in tortuous and fatal experiments, and routine abuse of concentration camp inmates in similar experiments by other branches of the military.

The lead defendant, Dr. Karl Brandt had served as Hitler's personal physician and advisor. German physicians planned and enacted an involuntary Euthanasia Program (Aktion T-4) that systematically killed those they deemed "unworthy of life." The victims included people with severe psychiatric, neurological, or physical disabilities. During World War II, German physicians also conducted pseudo-scientific medical experiments utilizing thousands of concentration camp prisoners without their consent. Most died and a great many were permanently injured as a result. Most of the victims were Jews, Poles, Russians, and Roma (Gypsies). Technology developed under Aktion T-4, particularly the use of lethal gas to commit mass murder, was the basis for the methods later used in the extermination camps.

Robert J. Lifton states that Hitler had an "intense interest in direct medical killing" (1986, 50). In his testimony at Nuremberg, Karl Brandt stated that Hitler thought the demands of war would overcome religious and moral opposition to the euthanasia program. The program began sometime in 1939, first targeting children. Hitler formally extended the program to include adults in a Führer Decree (October 1939). This permitted physicians to grant patients, who were considered "incurable according to the best available human judgment," a "mercy death." Lifton writes that "the T-4 program . . . involved virtually the entire German psychiatric community and related portions of the general medical community"

(1986, 65). In one sense, it is a relatively small step from justifying the deliberate killing of the weak and infirm to justification of a broader rationale for killing the unwanted.

The prosecution had access to an enormous number of original documents. Allied troops had seized thousands of photostats, microfilms, and other archival material. The Germans had kept meticulous records. In his opening statement, the chief prosecutor, General Telford Taylor, listed a number of "experiments" that involved extreme risk or death, noting that those selected had not given their consent. On the face of it, many of these would seemingly have addressed important topics of interest to the military. Experiments on the effects of high altitude and cold, the potability of processed sea water, the effects of mustard gas and phosphorous, and the healing value of sulfanilamide for wounds can all be related to potential medical problems in military operation. In addition, malaria, epidemic jaundice, and typhus were among the principal diseases that afflicted the German Armed Forces and German authorities in occupied territories.

No one disputed that the subject matter and stated goals of the experiments seemed legitimate. Taylor stressed that the methods and practices associated with the experiments raised very troubling questions. He asserted that the prosecution would clearly establish that "in some instances the true object of these experiments was not how to rescue or to cure, but how to destroy and kill" (p. 37).

> Mankind has not heretofore felt the need of a word to denominate the science of how to kill prisoners most rapidly and subjugated people in large numbers. This case and these defendants have created this gruesome question for the lexicographer. For the moment we will christen this macabre science "thanatology," the science of producing death. The thanatological [from the Greek God of death, Thanatos] knowledge, derived in part from these experiments, supplied the techniques for genocide, a policy of the Third Reich, exemplified in the "euthanasia" program and in the widespread slaughter of Jews, gypsies, Poles, and Russians. This policy of mass extermination could not have been so effectively carried out without the active participation of German medical scientists. (p. 38)

In addition, Taylor asserted that the charges with respect to "euthanasia" and the deliberate slaughter of tubercular Poles obviously had no relation to research or experimentation. In summing up their case, the prosecution asserted that:

> These experiments revealed nothing which civilized medicine can use. It was, indeed, ascertained that phenol or gasoline injected intravenously will kill a man inexpensively and within 60 seconds. This and a few other "advances" are all in the field of thanatology. There is no doubt that a number of these new methods may be useful to criminals everywhere and there is no doubt that they may be useful to a criminal state. (p. 73)

The American prosecution team preparing for the Medical Trial asked the secretary of war, Robert P. Patterson, for a medical expert. That request in turn triggered contact with the American Medical Association (AMA). After some deliberation, the AMA appointed Dr. Andrew C. Ivy, a well-known medical researcher, as the AMA's official consultant to the Nuremberg prosecutors. In a lengthy memo, Ivy laid out what he termed "the rules" of human experimentation. He stated without equivocation that these standards had been "well established by custom, social usage and the ethics of medical conduct." In their verdict, the judges accepted Ivy's standards almost in their entirety. Significantly, the judges also reiterated Ivy's assertion that these rules were already widely understood and followed by ethical medical researchers. Ivy's standards for human experimentation served as more than the primary textual foundation for the Nuremberg Code. His set of rules also formed the basis for the AMA's first formal statement on human experimentation.

Some notorious figures did not face prosecution. These included Leonardo Conti (suicide), Sigmund Rascher (executed on Himmler's orders), and Josef Mengele (escaped to South America).

TRIAL SUMMARY #8: THE MEDICAL CASE

The defendants fell into three main groups. Eight of them were members of the medical service of the German Air Force. Seven were members of the medical service of the SS. The remaining eight included the defendants Karl Brandt and Siegfried Handloser, who occupied top positions in the medical hierarchy; it also included the three defendants who were not doctors: Paul Rostock, who was an immediate subordinate of Karl Brandt; Kurt Blome, a medical official of the Nazi Party; and Adolf Pokorny, who was simply grouped under SS authority.

When General Taylor was asked about the selection of defendants, he made a statement that applies to all of the World War II crimes:

> The choice of defendants and choices of subjects in the Nuremberg Trials were largely determined by factors not altogether under the control of the people who were organizing the trials. To put it bluntly, a great deal depended upon who was available to be tried. A great many people who might have been tried had either been killed or died in the war. Right at the end there had been quite a number of suicides of people who would have been very much in demand at Nuremberg. Other people were hiding and could not be found. (Quoted in Freyhofer 2004, 49)

DOCUMENT: *UNITED STATES V. KARL BRANDT, ET AL.*

When:	December 9, 1946–August 20, 1947
Where:	Nuremberg, Germany
Court:	U.S. Military Court
Defendants:	Dr. Karl Brandt and 22 others
Source:	*Trials of War Criminals before the Nuremberg Military Tribunals under Control Council Law No. 10.* Vol. 1 (Washington, DC: Government Printing Office, 1949, 61–62, 64. Online at https://www.loc.gov/rr/frd/Military_Law/NT_major-war-criminals.html and http://nuremberg.law.harvard.edu/transcripts/1-transcript-for-nmt-1-medical-case?seq=5094.
Charges:	Murders, brutalities, cruelties, tortures, atrocities, and other inhumane acts as part of a common design to commit war crimes and crimes against humanity War crimes Crimes against humanity

	Membership in a criminal organization
Defense:	Superior Order, Defense of the State

Defendants who were in high positions in the German medical service refused to take any responsibility for the alleged criminal conduct of their subordinates

Necessity of war

Tu quoque

Verdicts: Sixteen were guilty, seven were acquitted. Of the guilty, seven (including K. Brandt) received the death penalty; seven were sentenced to life imprisonment, one was sentenced to fifteen years, and one to ten years' imprisonment. All of those who received the death penalty were hanged.

Evidence and Testimony

Prosecutor: I call the Tribunal's special attention to the German word "*Sonderbehandlung.*" In the next document, as will be shown, it occurs frequently in Nazi correspondence and was used by them to mean extermination. In May 1942, Greiser [A German Governor in Occupied Poland] wrote to Himmler as follows:

> The special treatment [*Sonderbehandlung*] of about 100,000 Jews in the territory of my district approved by you in agreement with the Chief of the Reich Security Main Office, SS Obergruppenfuehrer Heydrich, can be completed within the next 2 to 3 months. I ask you for permission to rescue the district immediately after the measures are taken against the Jews, from a menace, which is increasing week by week, and to use the existing and efficient special commandos for that purpose.
>
> There are about 230,000 people of Polish nationality in my district who were diagnosed to suffer from tuberculosis. The number of persons infected with open tuberculosis is estimated at about 35,000. This fact has led in an increasing frightening measure to the infection of Germans, who came to the Warthegau perfectly healthy. In particular, reports are received with ever-increasing effect of German children in danger of infection. . . . The ever-increasing risks were also recognized and appreciated by the deputy of the Reich Leader for Public Health (Reichsgesundheitsfuehrer) Comrade Professor Dr. Blome. . . .
>
> Considering the urgency of this project I ask for your approval in principle as soon as possible. This would enable us to make the preparations with all necessary precautions now to get the action against the Poles suffering from open tuberculosis under way, while the action against the Jews is in its closing stages.

. . .

Late in June, Himmler sent a "favorable" reply to Greiser cautioning him, however, that the exterminations should be carried out inconspicuously.

Euthanasia Program

Prosecution: On . . . the day of the German attack on Poland, and after a great deal of discussion between Dr. Karl Brandt, Dr. Leonardo Conti, Philipp Bouhler, the Chief of the Chancellery of the Fuehrer, and others, Hitler issued the following authority to the defendant Karl Brandt:

Reichsleiter Bouhler and Dr. Brandt, M. D., are charged with the responsibility of enlarging the authority of certain physicians to be designated by name in such a manner that persons who, according to human judgment, are incurable can, upon a most careful diagnosis of their condition of sickness, be accorded a mercy death.
  [Signed] ADOLF HITLER

After the receipt of this order, an organization was set up to execute this program, Karl Brandt headed the medical section and Philipp Bouhler, the administrative section. The defendant Hoven, as chief surgeon of the Buchenwald concentration camp, took part in the program and personally ordered the transfer of at least 300 to 400 Jewish inmates of different nationalities, mostly non-German, to their death in the euthanasia station at Bernburg. The defendants Brack and Blome participated in their capacities as assistants to Bouhler and Conti.

[Author comment: Superior Orders. The defense of superior orders formed a common thread in all of the twelve subsequent trials. The following exchange characterizes the testimony of every defendant in this case. The question concerns the experimentation with deadly viruses at Buchenwald. The defendant is Joachim Mrugowsky, oberführer (Senior Colonel) in the Waffen SS and chief hygienist of the Reich Physician SS and Police.]

Q: In your opinion did the State have the right to dispose of the health and lives of the inmates by placing them at the disposal of medical experiments, as a result of which permanent disturbances of their health or even death could occur?
A: In normal times the State certainly does not have that right. But the experiments here . . . were carried on during the war.

Q: When making these presumptions [necessities associated with war] do you think that a physician is entitled to carry out experiments on human being using drugs or new vaccine even if he knows that the life of the experimental subject is being endangered by that procedure?
A: I don't think that a physician is justified to do that . . . [on] his own initiative. I think, however, that *he is obliged to obey the order given by his State when the highest responsible member of the state is ordering such experiments* [emphasis added] for any specific purpose and defines explicitly the circle of persons to be used.

WHY?

Despite the strong statements of General Taylor concerning the worth of the experiments—that bad ethics result in bad science, the testimony in the trial raised many ethical issues that go beyond the scope of this discussion. The issues proved not as simple as Taylor had characterized them even though his perspective still provided the critical underpinning for the verdicts. Again, the tribunal consistently refused to permit any testimony that would have allowed a *tu quoque* defense, but under cross-examination Dr. Ivy admitted that the United States had also engaged in some experiments similar to those detailed in the indictment against the defendants.

After the horrors of the Holocaust became widely known, the question quickly became: How could ordinary people commit such extraordinary crimes? A great many felt that the only explanation of the colossal extent of the brutality and policy of deliberate extermination had to rely on a great number of insanely evil individuals who coerced others into following orders. How else could they have engaged in these horrendous practices? To this explanation, Horst Freyhofer made a rather chilling point that applied to many professions other than doctors and individuals as well. He asserted that many of those on trial had lived personal lives of exemplary civility and service. He answered the question with a disturbing observation about human behavior that he argued generally has held true for other eras in history: We should not underestimate the ability of human beings to relegate those regarded as "not us" to the status of experimental mice without damage to their own humanity (2004, 164).

Ever though the prosecution clearly tried to convict all of the defendants, the acquittals testify to the fairness of the trial. In summary, all of the Nuremberg trials were held to "teach a lesson" by showing step by step how a supposedly civilized and informed society can be politically hijacked by totalitarian-minded individuals and groups. General Taylor argued that: "It is our deep obligation to all peoples of the world to show how and why these things happened. It is incumbent upon us to set forth with conspicuous clarity the ideas and motives which moved these defendants to treat their fellow men as less than beasts" (p. 28).

References

"The American Expert, the American Medical Association, and the Nuremburg Medical Trial." n.d. Advisory Committee on Human Radiation Experiments, The Law, Science & Public Health Law Site, Louisiana State University, http://biotech.law.lsu.edu/research/reports/ACHRE/chap2_2.html.

Freyhofer, Horst. 2004. *The Nuremberg Medical Trial: The Holocaust and the Origin of the Nuremberg Medical Code.* New York: Peter Lang.

Lifton, Robert J. 1986. *The Nazi Doctors: Medical Killing and the Psychology of Genocide.* New York: Basic Books.

14

Einsatzgruppen Case: *United States of America v. Otto Ohlendorf, et al.*

The Einsatzgruppen were special extermination squads under the command of the German Security Police (Sicherheitspolizei; Sipo) and Security Service (Sicherheitsdienst; SD), which followed the advance of the German Army into areas to be occupied. These units followed the German advance into Poland in September 1939 and followed in the wake of the invasion of the Soviet Union in June 1941. The squads were composed primarily of German SS and police personnel.

In Poland, between 1939 and 1941, the squads rounded up Jews, communists, and Polish dissidents, and placed them into ghettos (segregated areas) or concentration camps. However, after the German invasion of the Soviet Union on June 22, 1941, the Einsatzgruppen's activities increased dramatically. Their primary mission changed to one of extermination of those perceived to be racial or political enemies found behind German combat lines. In addition to targeting the Jewish population of occupied areas, the victims included Roma (Gypsies), officials of the Soviet state and the Communist party, and thousands of residents of institutions for the mentally and physically disabled. Although many think of the Holocaust only in terms of the systematized extermination of Jews and others at Nazi death camps, the fact is that many were killed in or near their home towns or villages by the Einsatzgruppen. It is estimated that mobile killing squads murdered as many as 1.3 million people between 1939 and 1945.

The killing squads followed close on the heels of advancing German Army troops, moving into towns and villages rapidly to take the civilian population by surprise. Often with the help of local informants and interpreters, Jews in a given locality were identified and taken to collection points. Thereafter they were marched or transported by truck to the execution site, where trenches had been prepared. In some cases the captive victims had to dig their own graves. After the victims had handed over their valuables and undressed, all were shot, either standing before the open trench, or lying face down in the prepared pit. Many of the victims included women and children. In places like Ukraine, Lithuania, and Latvia, the killing squads were aided by non-Jews and others not targeted by the

Nazis. Perhaps the worst single atrocity occurred at Babi Yar (Ukraine) during September 29–30, 1941, when some 34,000 Jews were shot to death.

The Einsatzgruppen used shooting as the most common form of killing. In the late summer of 1941, Heinrich Himmler (Reichsführer of the Schutzstaffel), noting the psychological burden that mass shootings had inflicted on these men, requested that a more convenient and efficient method of killing be found. The mobile killing methods, particularly shooting, had proved psychologically burdensome to the killers. Alcoholism, desertion, and suicide were common problems. This order resulted in the development of a mobile gas van—a gas chamber surmounted on the chassis of a cargo truck—which first employed carbon monoxide from the truck's exhaust to kill its victims. Gas vans made their first appearance on the Eastern Front in late fall 1941 and were eventually utilized, along with shooting, to murder Jews and other victims in most areas where the Einsatzgruppen operated. By the spring of 1943, the Einsatzgruppen and Order Police battalions (reserve units) had killed over a million Soviet Jews and tens of thousands of Soviet political commissars, partisans, Roma, and institutionalized disabled persons.

OTTO OHLENDORF

Otto Ohlendorf had joined the Schutzstaffel (SS) in 1926. In June 1941, upon the German invasion of the Soviet Union, Ohlendorf was assigned to command Einsatzgruppen D, a mobile killing squad unit assigned to the Crimea and southern Ukraine. Among other tasks, Ohlendorf's men were responsible for the mass killing of Jews in Kherson, Nikolaiev, and Podilia. At Simferopol, on December 13, 1941, the unit massacred some 14,300 civilians, mainly Jews. Ohlendorf testified he had ordered numerous men to fire on victims simultaneously, so that it would be impossible to establish personal responsibility for any single killing.

In June 1942, Ohlendorf left the war front and returned to his work for the SS in Germany. According to written records of the unit, during his one-year tenure as commander, the squad killed roughly 90,000 civilians. At the end of the war in 1945, Allied authorities took Ohlendorf and placed him on trial for war crimes. At the Nuremberg Trial of several Einsatzgruppen officials, Ohlendorf was the lead defendant. He testified calmly and accurately at the proceedings. At one point he asserted that his unit had committed crimes no less odious than the "push-button" killers who had unleashed the atomic bombs over Japan in 1945. He never indicated any regret or remorse for his actions.

TRIAL SUMMARY #9: EINSATZGRUPPEN CASE

Prosecution Case

The prosecution's case concentrated on four main areas:

1. *The task of the Einsatzgruppen.* The prosecution alleged the primary task of the Einsatzgruppen was to carry out Hitler's order calling for the extermination of Jews, Communists, Gypsies, and other racial or national groups considered by the Nazis as "racially inferior" or "politically undesirable."

2. *The magnitude of the enterprise.* Of the contemporaneous documents on this point one reports the killing of more than 220,000 people, another of more than 130,000, still others more than 91,000 persons, 80,000 persons, and 60,000 persons, respectively.
3. *Methods of execution.* It was alleged by the prosecution that mass exterminations of Jews and other undesirables were carried out mainly by shooting and that gas vans were also used for this purpose.
4. *Membership in criminal organizations.* Charged with membership in organizations declared to be criminal by the International Military Tribunal (the SS, the SD, and the Gestapo).

DOCUMENT: *UNITED STATES V. OTTO OHLENDORF, ET AL.*

When:	September 29, 1947–April 10, 1948
Where:	Nuremberg, Germany
Court:	U.S. Military Court
Defendants:	Otto Ohlendorf and 23 others
Source:	Library of Congress, Trials of War Criminals before the Nuernberg Military Tribunals under Control Council Law No. 10, https://www.loc.gov/rr/frd/Military_Law/pdf/NT_war-criminals_Vol-IV.pdf.
Charges:	Crimes against humanity and war crimes, as defined in Control Council Law No. 10. These crimes included the murder of more than one million persons, tortures, atrocities, and other inhumane acts, as set forth in counts one and two of this indictment. Membership in criminal organizations, as set forth in count three of this indictment.
Defense:	The *Führerbefehl*. All defendants argued that they acted under superior orders and had no means of opposing or refusing to execute them. Self-defense. Several defendants declared that they considered the order itself justified. *Tu quoque* argument: Justification because Allied air raids killed noncombatants. Justified action against partisans and as measures of reprisal.
Verdict:	Twenty-two were guilty on all charges; two (Ruhl and Graf) guilty only on membership in a criminal organization; fourteen received the death penalty (only four, including Ohlendorf were executed; sentences of other defendants were commuted). By 1958, all defendants had been released from prison.

Testimony of Otto Ohlendorf

Q: When was the area of operation made public?
A: It was made known shortly before the units left for Russia, about three days before.

Q: When was the order given for the liquidation of certain elements of the population in the U.S.S.R. and by whom was it handed over?
A: As far as I recollect, this order was given at the same time when the area of operations was made known. In Pretzsch, the chiefs of offices I and IV, the then Lieutenant Colonels [Obersturmbannfuehrers] Streckenbach and Mueller gave the order which had been issued by Himmler and Heydrich.

Q: What was the wording of this order?
A: This special order, for such it is, read as follows: That in addition to our general task the Security Police and SD, the Einsatzgruppen and the Einsatzkommandos had the mission to protect the rear of the troops by killing the Jews, gypsies, Communist functionaries, active Communists, and all persons who would endanger the security.

Q: What were your thoughts when you received this order of killings?
A: The immediate feeling with me and with the other men was one of general protest. Lieutenant Colonel Streckenbach listened to this protest, and, even gave us a few different points which we could not know, but at the same time he told us that even he himself had protested most strenuously against a similar order in the Polish campaign, but that *Himmler had rebuked him just as severely by stating that this was a Fuehrer order, which must be carried out* [emphasis added], in order to achieve the war aim of destroying communism for all times, therefore, this order was to be accepted without hesitation.

Q: Did you consider this order as justified?
A: No; I did not. I did not consider it justified because quite independently from the necessity of taking such measures, these measures would have moral and ethical consequences which would deteriorate the mind.

. . .

Q: Did you give any thought to the legality of such a Fuehrer order?
A: Of course I did. I knew the history of communism. From the theory of Lenin and Stalin and from the strategy and tactics of the Bolshevist world revolution, I knew that bolshevism was to let no rules prevail other than those which would further and promote its aim. The practice of bolshevism in the Russian Civil War, in the war with Finland, in the war with Poland, in the occupation of the Baltic countries and Bessarabia, gave us the assurance and certainty that this was not only theory, but that this was carried out in practice, and in the same manner it therefore was to be expected that in this war no other laws would have any validity. This was true for the international conventions which Russia officially denounced to the German Government, as well as the international customs and usages of war, and it was true because according to this same communist ideology the customs and usages could only develop between partners who were on the same ideological basis.

. . .

Q: Is, in your opinion, the man who receives these orders obliged to examine them when they are given to him?
A: This is not possible, legally or actually. According to the general legal interpretation in Germany, not even a judge had the possibility of examining the legality of a law or an order, as little as an administrative official could examine the administrative edict of a supreme authority. But even actually it would have been presumptuous because in the position in which every one of the defendants found themselves, we did not have the possibility of actually judging the situation. It also corresponds to the moral concept which I have learned as a European tradition, that no subordinate can take it upon himself to examine the authority of the supreme commander and chief of state. He only faces his God and history.

Q: Didn't Article 47 of the Military Penal Code give you an occasion to interpret this execution order differently?
A: It is impossible for me to imagine that an article which was created to prevent excesses by individual officers or men leaves open the possibility to consider the supreme order of the supreme commander a crime. Apart from this, again according to continental concept, the chief of state cannot commit a crime.

Q: What is your conviction about the actual background of the Fuehrer order which was given to you?
A: I have had no cause, and I still have no cause today to think that any other goal was aimed at than the goal of any war, namely, an immediate and permanent security of our own realm against that realm with which the belligerent conflict is taking place.

. . .

Every time I found the same facts which I considered with great respect, that the Jews who were executed went to their death singing the "International" and hailing Stalin. That the Communist functionaries and the active leaders of the Communists in the occupied area of Russia posed an actual continuous danger for the German occupation the documents of the prosecution have shown. It was absolutely certain that by these persons the call of Stalin for ruthless partisan warfare would be followed without any reservation.

Q: What orders did you give to the Einsatzgruppen and Einsatzkommandos for the security of the rear area concerning the killing certain elements of the civilian population?
A: Before I testify to the various facts, I would like to say the following: The men of my group who are under indictment here were under my military command. If they had not executed the orders which they were given, they would have been ordered by me to execute them. If they had refused to execute the orders they would have had to be called to account for it by me. There could be no doubt about it. Whoever refused anything in the front lines would have met immediate death. If the refusal would have come about in any other way, a court martial of the Higher SS and Police Leader would have brought about the same consequences.

DISCUSSION

Although the word had not yet entered the general vocabulary, this trial was the first that dealt with *genocide*. The Court expressed its horror at the testimony:

> [I]t was left to the twentieth century to produce so extraordinary a killing that even a new word had to be created to define it.
>
> One of counsel has characterized this trial as the biggest murder trial in history. Certainly never before have twenty-three men been brought into court to answer to the charge of destroying over one million of their fellow human beings. There have been other trials imputing to administrators and officials responsibility for mass murder, but in this case the defendants are not simply accused of planning or directing wholesale killings through channels. They are not charged with sitting in an office hundreds and thousands of miles away from the slaughter. It is asserted with particularity that these men were in the field actively superintending, controlling, directing, and taking an active part in the bloody harvest.
>
> If what the prosecution maintains is true, we have here participation in a crime of such unprecedented brutality and of such inconceivable savagery that the mind rebels against its own thought image and the imagination staggers in the contemplation of a human degradation beyond the power of language to adequately portray. The crime did not exclude the immolation of women and children, heretofore regarded the special object of solicitude even on the part of an implacable and primitive foe. (p. 412)

Many of the defendants readily admitted their participation in the mass killings. Their testimony paralleled Ohlendorf's in relying primarily on the "Führer (Nuremberg) defense." Defendants relied upon the Führerbefehl (Hitler Order) to justify their actions—one cannot question orders that come from the highest authority. Moreover, no matter how strange it may sound, they did regard every member of the targeted groups as potential subversives who, if not presently part of a resistance effort, could be in the future. In this sense, the defendants considered their actions as an exercise in *anticipatory* (preventive) *self-defense*. Take care of these individuals now so they cannot cause a problem in the future.

The other striking evidence comes from Ohlendorf's statement about deterioration of the mind. As mentioned above, the day after day slaughter took a terrible mental toll on the members of the killing units. Recall, that Himmler had sought an alternative because he recognized the debilitating impact on those soldiers ordered to kill in large numbers again and again.

A CURIOUS DEFENSE

The defense team called an expert witness who gave a very lengthy analysis of the German law on self-defense; yet, curiously, the defense then claimed that Soviet law justified their actions. The Court said: "One cannot avoid noting the paradox of the defendant's invoking the law of a country whose jurisprudence, ideologies, government and social system were all declared antagonistic to Germany, and which very laws, ideologies, government, and social system the defendants, with the rest of the German Armed Forces, had set out to destroy" (p. 462).

The defense also claimed: "Acts of necessity are unrestrictedly admissible if they are necessary for the protection of higher interests insofar as the danger could not be averted by any other means." The Court rejected this line of reasoning because: "Under this theory of law any belligerent who is hard-pressed would be allowed unilaterally to abrogate the laws and customs of war. And it takes no great amount of foresight to see that with such facile disregarding of restrictions, the rules of war would quickly disappear. Every belligerent could find a reason to assume that it had higher interests to protect" (p. 463).

Given the provisions of the London Charter as well as CCL No. 10, the Court could only consider the superior order defense in terms of mitigation of punishment. It had to reject the *tu quoque* plea altogether. The Court noted:

> The subject of superior orders is not so confusing and complicated as it had been made by some legal commentators. In considering the law in this matter, we must keep in mind that fundamentally there are some legal principles that stand out like oak trees . . .
>
> 1. Every man is presumed to intend the consequences of his act.
> 2. Every man is responsible for those acts unless it be shown that he did not act of his own free will.
> 3. Deciding the question of free will, all the circumstances of the case must be considered because it is impossible to read what is in a man's heart. (p. 488)

As a final note here, the defense of superior orders from a supreme leader played a prominent part in the trials of Japanese war criminals as well. In the case of Japan, the justification relied on the argument that any order issued in the Emperor's name had to be obeyed without question.

References

Browning, Christopher. 1993. *Ordinary Men: Reserve Battalion 101 and the Final Solution in Poland.* New York: Harper Perennial.

Mendelsohn, John, ed. 1982. *The Einsatzgruppen or Murder Commandos.* New York: Garland Publishing.

Rhodes, Richard. 2002. *Masters of Death: The SS-Einsatzgruppen and the Invention of the Holocaust.* New York: Knopf.

15

Tokyo War Crimes Trial

INTERNATIONAL MILITARY TRIBUNAL FOR THE FAR EAST

Less well known than the International Military Tribunal at Nuremberg, the International Military Tribunal for the Far East (IMTFE) tried 28 Japanese military and political leaders charged with crimes against peace, crimes against humanity, and responsibility for conventional war crimes. The Potsdam Declaration (July 26, 1945) signed by the United States, China, and Great Britain had called for "unconditional surrender" and the elimination for "all time [of] the authority and influence of those who have deceived and misled the Japanese people." Point 10 of that declaration stated: "We do not intend that the Japanese shall be enslaved as a race or destroyed as a nation, but stern justice shall be meted out to all war criminals."

At the subsequent Moscow Conference in December 1945, the Soviet Union, the United Kingdom, and the United States (with the concurrence of China) agreed to a basic structure for the occupation of Japan. General Douglas MacArthur, Supreme Commander of the Allied Powers in the East, was granted authority to "issue all orders for the implementation of the Terms of Surrender, the occupation and control of Japan, and all directives supplementary thereto." On this authority, General MacArthur issued a special proclamation that established the IMTFE in January 1946. The Charter for the IMTFE was attached as an annex to the proclamation. The jurisdiction, powers, and procedures of the Tokyo Tribunal were essentially the same as those of the Nuremberg Tribunal. Article 5 of the IMTFE Charter (reproduced below), which specifies "Jurisdiction and Offenses," is identical to Article 6 of the Nuremberg Charter.

DOCUMENT: CHARTER OF THE INTERNATIONAL MILITARY TRIBUNAL FOR THE FAR EAST

When: January 19, 1946
Where: Tokyo, Japan
Source: Online at https://www.macalester.edu/~tam/HIST194%20War%20Crimes/documents/Nuremberg/Charter%20of%20the%20International%20Military%20Tribunal%20Far%20East.htm

Significance: The IMTFE was the Eastern counterpart to the IMT at Nuremberg. Like its European counterpart in Germany, the court tried those considered the architects of the Japanese war effort.

CONSTITUTION OF THE TRIBUNAL

[Part I, Articles 1–5 defined the structure and composition of the court]

II

JURISDICTION AND GENERAL PROVISIONS

Article 5. Jurisdiction over Persons and Offenses. The Tribunal shall have the power to try and punish Far Eastern war criminals who as individuals or as members of organizations are charged with offenses which include Crimes against Peace.

The following acts, or any of them, are crimes coming within the jurisdiction of the Tribunal for which there shall be individual responsibility:

(a) *Crimes against Peace*: Namely, the planning, preparation, initiation or waging of a declared or undeclared war of aggression, or a war in violation of international law, treaties, agreements or assurances, or participation in a common plan or conspiracy for the accomplishment of any of the foregoing;

(b) *Conventional War Crimes*: Namely, violations of the laws or customs of war;

(c) *Crimes against Humanity*: Namely, murder, extermination, enslavement, deportation, and other inhumane acts committed against any civilian population, before or during the war, or persecutions on political or racial grounds in execution of or in connection with any crime within the jurisdiction of the Tribunal, whether or not in violation of the domestic law of the country where perpetrated. Leaders, organizers, instigators and accomplices participating in the formulation or execution of a common plan or conspiracy to commit any of the foregoing crimes are responsible for all acts performed by any person in execution of such plan.

Article 6. Responsibility of Accused. Neither the official position, at any time, of an accused, nor the fact that an accused acted pursuant to order of his government or of a superior shall, of itself, be sufficient to free such accused from responsibility for any crime with which he is charged, but such circumstances may be considered in mitigation of punishment if the Tribunal determines that justice so requires.

ALLIANCE WITH GERMANY

Japan's ties with Germany predated the Meiji restoration (1868), generally understood to be the event that propelled Japan toward industrialization and "modernization" of its political and military institutions. Because the Japanese saw parallels with their own history, German industrialization provided an attractive model for the Japanese. The German connection soured when Japan allied with Britain and France in World War I. Relations warmed again after Hitler came to power. In late November 1936, Germany and Japan signed the Anti-Comintern Pact, a treaty that opposed the spread of communism by the Soviet Union. Relations somewhat soured again when Hitler signed the Treaty of Non-aggression between Germany and the Union of Soviet Socialist Republics (Molotov-Ribbentrop Pact) in August 1939. Still, in September 1940, Germany, Italy, and Japan signed the Tripartite Pact that created the Axis alliance. Interestingly, Japan did not declare war on the Soviet Union when Hitler invaded it in June 1941. The Soviet Union did not declare war on Japan until August 8, 1945, shortly before it surrendered on August 15, 1945.

THE WAR IN THE PACIFIC

Characterized by President Franklin Roosevelt as "a day which will live in infamy," the surprise Japanese attack on Pearl Harbor on December 7, 1941, shocked the United States. The attack sank or disabled 19 ships (including 8 battleships), killing 2,335 military and civilian personnel, and wounding another 1,178. Because the attack happened without a declaration of war and without explicit warning, the Tokyo Tribunal found the attack to be a war crime.

The war in the Pacific was fought with great brutality. Over time, the concepts of loyalty and duty embodied in the Japanese code of *bushido* had become defined as blind obedience to orders and dying for the Emperor. In the period between the Russo-Japanese War (1904–1905) and World War I, the Japanese military drastically changed its existing military training and strategic concepts to mirror French and German ideas. The most prominent changes resulted in instilling the importance of "fighting spirit" and the will to achieve victory at any cost at every level of the military services. The Japanese Field Service Code now required soldiers to commit suicide rather than surrender. Historians have attributed the change in interpretation to a *generational* change in the senior ranks that occurred because of retirements. The retirement of those who had long served in senior leadership positions resulted in a top echelon leadership that had very different class origins and education from those who had guided policy over the previous fifty years. The traditional version emphasized the values of benevolence and right conduct with the heaviest burdens falling on leadership. The new breed had learned the words of the code but had not been schooled to understand the true meaning of the concepts.

William Manchester, who fought in the Pacific as a sergeant in the Marine Corps, reports that General Alexander Vandergrift wrote his superior: "General, I have never heard or read of this kind of fighting. These people refuse to surrender." Manchester observed:

> Having been introduced to the enemy's code of total resistance, defiance to the last man, the Marines had no choice; they had to adopt themselves. From then on until

the end of the war, neither side took prisoners except under freakish circumstances. It was war without quarter: none was asked, none was given. (220)

Propaganda told the Japanese recruit that he had joined a family where the company formed a household headed by a "father" company commander and a "mother" senior NCO. The Emperor, now considered a living god, sat atop the hierarchy. Recruits had gained a new status by becoming soldiers in the Emperor's personal army. All equipment and orders were issued in the name of the Emperor. Dying in service to the Emperor became a soldier's most honorable duty. The Japanese had signed the 1929 Geneva Convention but had never ratified it. Imbued with the new ideological commitment to self-sacrifice for the Emperor, the Japanese military opposed ratification because they expected Japanese soldiers to fight to the death; and, if placed in untenable situations, they should commit suicide rather than surrender.

The idea that surrender was shameful carried over to their attitude toward prisoners of war (POWs) in World War II. The contempt Japanese soldiers felt for those who had surrendered was reflected in their treatment of POWs. Anyone who had surrendered had forfeited their honor. For the Japanese, POWs had shamed themselves and their families because they had given up rather than electing to fight to their death. Prisoners, even those used as forced labor, received little food and virtually no medical attention. At best, Japanese forces treated POWs as military supplies to be used up or discarded as necessary. The impact of the harsh training and indoctrination in the emperor cult became apparent from the very first land engagements. At Guadalcanal (1942–1943), the first battle for territory initially occupied by the Japanese, all but 128 of the original 917 members of the Ichiki Regiment's First Element died fighting.

In the month after the surrender agreement was signed, Japanese political and military officials engaged in mass suicides. The reasons varied—guilt for their collective crimes, shame for their defeat by the Allies, loyalty to their conquered leaders, or simply because they wanted to avoid being held accountable by the Allies. Other Japanese either faked or, in the case of General Tōjō, failed in their attempts to commit suicide. In total, over 1,000 high-ranking Japanese officials committed suicide. Table 15.1 lists those officials chosen for trial before the IMTFE.

EMPEROR HIROHITO

Even before the beginning of the trials, controversy erupted over MacArthur's decision to exempt the Japanese emperor Hirohito and members of the imperial family from indictment and trial. General MacArthur argued that preserving the institution of emperor would help establish the legitimacy of the reconstruction effort with respect to Japanese public opinion. The problem in exempting the Emperor stemmed from his active participation in operational planning during the war. Herbert Bix writes, "Although Hirohito never visited the war theaters as did other commanders in chief, he exercised a decisive and controlling influence on theater operations, both in planning and execution, whenever he chose to do so" (2000, 441). Although the emperor had actively engaged in strategic planning and

Table 15.1 Tokyo Defendants

Military

- General Hideki Tōjō, prime minister (1941–1944)
- General Seishirō Itagaki, war minister (1938–1939)
- General Sadao Araki, war minister (1931–1934)
- Field Marshal Shunroku Hata, war minister (1939–1940)
- Admiral Shigetarō Shimada, Navy minister (1941–1944), chief of the Imperial Japanese Navy General Staff (1944)
- Lieutenant General Kenryō Satō, chief of the Military Affairs Bureau
- General Kuniaki Koiso, prime minister (1944–1945), governor-general of Korea (1942–1944)
- Vice Admiral Takazumi Oka, chief of the Bureau of Naval Affairs
- Lieutenant General Hiroshi Ōshima, ambassador to Germany
- Fleet Admiral Osami Nagano, Navy minister (1936–1937), chief of the Imperial Japanese Navy General Staff (1941–1944)
- General Jirō Minami, governor-general of Korea (1936–1942)
- General Kenji Doihara, chief of the intelligence service in Manchukuo
- General Heitarō Kimura, commander of the Burma Area Army
- General Iwane Matsui, commander of the Shanghai Expeditionary Force and Central China Area Army
- Lieutenant General Akira Mutō, chief of staff of the 14th Area Army
- Lieutenant Colonel Kingorō Hashimoto, founder of Sakurakai
- General Yoshijirō Umezu, commander of the Kwantung Army, chief of the Imperial Japanese Army General Staff Office (1944–1945)
- Lieutenant General Teiichi Suzuki, chief of the Cabinet Planning Board

Civilian

- Kōki Hirota, prime minister (1936–1937), foreign minister (1933–1936, 1937–1938)
- Kiichirō Hiranuma, prime minister (1939), president of the privy council
- Naoki Hoshino, chief cabinet secretary
- Kōichi Kido, lord keeper of the Privy Seal
- Toshio Shiratori, ambassador to Italy
- Shigenori Tōgō, foreign minister (1941–1942, 1945)
- Mamoru Shigemitsu, foreign minister (1943–1945)
- Okinori Kaya, finance minister (1941–1944)
- Yōsuke Matsuoka, foreign minister (1940–1941)

decisions before and during the war, in the aftermath of the surrender, he also continually avoided acknowledging any moral or political responsibility for the war. At the time of his death in 1989, Hirohito had the longest reign of any Japanese emperor (1926–1989). According to Japanese custom, after his death the era of his rule was assigned the name *Shōwa* ("radiant/glorious" Japan).

Other political decisions also limited the scope of jurisdiction. Unlike the IMT at Nuremberg, the IMTFE had a temporal jurisdiction (January 1, 1928, to September 2, 1945) that began before the beginning of the war with the United States; prosecutors ignored a host of crimes committed again Koreans; and, Allied authorities also had not indicted many prominent Japanese business leaders who had been deeply involved in the war effort.

GENERAL HIDEKI TŌJŌ

General Hideki Tōjō served as prime minister of Japan during most of the war (1941–1944). An ardent militarist and supporter of imperial expansion, he was dedicated to advancing Japanese power by force of arms. Tōjō was a zealous supporter of the invasion of Korea and subsequent expansion of the war into China. During the last cabinet meetings of the government headed by Prince Fumimaro Konoe, Tōjō had emerged as a hawkish voice who advocated resisting all American demands. He portrayed Americans as arrogant bullies, racists, and hypocrites. He became prime minister in mid-October 1941, when Konoe resigned after admitting failure to resolve the diplomatic deadlock with the United States over Japan's occupation of China. The Tōjō government ordered the attack on Pearl Harbor six weeks later (December 7). He was removed as prime minister in mid-July 1944 after a series of Japanese reverses. Tōjō spent the remainder of the war in the military reserve, far from the center of power. General Kuniaki Koiso served as prime minister until the end of the war.

COMPOSITION OF THE COURT

General MacArthur appointed eleven judges to the IMTFE—one nominated by each of the nine members states who had signed the Instrument of Surrender (Australia, Canada, China, France, the Netherlands, New Zealand, the Soviet Union, the United Kingdom, and the United States), plus one judge each from India and the Philippine Commonwealth. MacArthur also designated the Australian judge, Sir William Webb, as president of the Court. Each of the nine signatories also appointed a prosecutor. Joseph Keenan, a former assistant attorney general of the United States and a highly respected trial lawyer, served as the lead prosecutor.

TRIAL SUMMARY #10: TRIAL OF MAJOR JAPANESE WAR CRIMINALS

To emphasize an important feature of the trials, all the testimony by those accused maintained that they truly believed that an order given in the name of the emperor could not be disobeyed. This contention mirrored similar claims by defendants in the Nuremberg trials that an order from the Führer (Hitler) had to be obeyed without question. For the most part, the defense arguments played a minor role in this trial.

Document: Trial of Major Japanese War Criminals

When: April 29, 1946, to November 12, 1948
Where: Tokyo, Japan
Court: International Military Tribunal, Far East (IMTFE)
Jurisdiction: Cairo Declaration (1943), the Declaration of Potsdam (1945), the Instrument of Surrender (September 1945), the Moscow Conference (December 1945), and the Charter of the Tribunal
Defendants: Hideki Tōjō and 27 other high-ranking military and civilians
Source: Final Judgement of November 12, 1948. From John Pritchard and Sonia M. Zaide, *The Tokyo War Crimes Trial*, Vol. 22 (New York: Garland, 1981). Online at http://werle.rewi.hu-berlin.de/tokio.pdf. Dissentient Judgement of R. B. Pal available online at https://www.cwporter.com/pal2.htm.
Charges: Crimes against humanity
Crimes against peace
War crimes
Under these three headings prosecutors elaborated 54 subcounts
Defense: No basis for jurisdiction
No relevant law—actions were acts of state
Rejected ideas of conspiracy and "command responsibility" as defined in indictment
Tu quoque
Preemptive Self defense
Superior orders ("Emperor principle")
Verdicts: No acquittals; seven defendants received the death penalty; sixteen received life imprisonment, and one received twenty years' imprisonment, one received seven years' imprisonment. Two (Yōsuke Matsuoka and Osami Nagano) died of natural causes during the trial. One (Shumei Okawa) had a mental breakdown on the first day of trial, was sent to a psychiatric ward, and was released in 1948 a free man.

Testimony

Overview

The final judgment of the majority begins:

After carefully examining and considering all the evidence we find that it is not practicable in a judgment such as this to state fully the mass of oral and documentary evidence presented; for a complete statement of the scale and character of the atrocities reference must be had to the record of the trial. The evidence relating to atrocities and other Conventional War Crimes presented before the Tribunal establishes that from the opening of the war in China until the surrender of Japan in August 1945 torture, murder, rape and other cruelties of the most inhumane and barbarous character were freely practiced by the Japanese Army and Navy. During a period of several months the Tribunal heard evidence, orally or by affidavit, from witnesses who testified in detail to atrocities committed in all theaters of war on a scale so vast, yet following so common a pattern in all theaters, that only one conclusion is possible—the atrocities were either secretly ordered or wilfully permitted by the Japanese Government or individual members thereof and by the leaders of the armed forces.

. . .

Prisoners of War

At the beginning of the Pacific War in December 1941 the Japanese Government did institute a system and an organization for dealing with prisoners of war and civilian internees. Superficially, the system would appear to have been appropriate; however, from beginning to end the customary and conventional rules of war designed to prevent inhumanity were flagrantly disregarded. Ruthless killing of prisoners by shooting, decapitation, drowning, and other methods; death marches in which prisoners including the sick were forced to march long distances under conditions which not even well-conditioned troops could stand, many of those dropping out being shot or bayonetted by the guards; forced labor in tropical heat without protection from the sun; complete lack of housing and medical supplies in many cases resulting in thousands of deaths from disease; beatings and torture of all kinds to extract information or confessions or for minor offences; killing without trial of recaptured prisoners after escape or for attempt to escape; killing without trial of captured aviators; and even cannibalism. These are some of the atrocities of which proof was made before the Tribunal.

The extent of the atrocities and the result of the lack of food and medical supplies is exemplified by a comparison of the number of deaths of prisoners of war in the European Theater with the number of deaths in the Pacific Theater. Of United States and United Kingdom forces 235,473 were taken prisoners by the German and Italian Armies; of these 9,348 or 4 per cent died in captivity. In the Pacific Theater 132,134 prisoners were taken by the Japanese from the United States and United Kingdom forces alone of whom 35,756 or 27 per cent died in captivity.

. . .

The Japanese Government signed and ratified the Fourth Hague Convention of 1907 Respecting the Laws and Customs of War on Land, which provided for humane treatment of prisoners of war and condemned treacherous and inhumane conduct of war. The reason for the failure of the Japanese Government to ratify and enforce the Geneva Prisoner of War Convention which it signed at Geneva in 1929 is to be found in the fundamental training of the Japanese Soldier. Long before the beginning of the period covered by the Indictment, the young men of Japan had been taught that "The greatest honor is to die for the Emperor," a precept which we find ARAKI repeating in his speeches and propaganda motion pictures. An additional precept was taught that it is an ignominy to surrender to the enemy. The combined effect of these two precepts was to inculcate in the Japanese soldier a spirit of contempt for Allied soldiers who surrendered, which, in defiance of the rules of war was demonstrated in their ill-treatment of prisoners. In this spirit they made no distinction between the soldier who fought honorably and courageously up to an inevitable surrender and the soldier who surrendered without a fight. All enemy soldiers who surrendered under any circumstance were to be regarded as being disgraced and entitled to live only by the tolerance of their captors.

China

Captives Taken in The China War Were Treated as Bandits: The Japanese delegate at Geneva in accepting the resolution of the League of Nations of 10 December 1931... stated that his acceptance was based on the understanding that the resolution would not preclude the Japanese Army from taking action against "bandits" in Manchuria. It was under this exception to the resolution that the Japanese military continued hostilities against the Chinese troops in Manchuria. They maintained that no state of war existed between Japan and China; that the conflict was a mere "incident" to which the laws of war did not apply; and that those Chinese troops who resisted the Japanese Army were not lawful combatants but were merely "bandits." A ruthless campaign for the extermination of these "bandits" in Manchuria was inaugurated.

...

On 16 September 1932 the Japanese forces in pursuit of defeated Chinese volunteer units arrived at the towns of Pingtingshan, Chienchinpao and Litsekou in the vicinity of Fushun. The inhabitants of these towns were accused of harboring the volunteers or "bandits" as they were called by the Japanese. In each town the Japanese troops assembled people along ditches and forced them to kneel; they then killed these civilians, men, women and children; with machine guns; those who survived the machine-gunning being promptly bayoneted to death, Over 2,700 civilians perished in this massacre, which the Japanese Kwantung Army claimed to be justified under its program of exterminating "bandits." Shortly thereafter, KOISO sent to the Vice Minister of War an "Outline for Guiding Manchukuo" in which he said:

> Racial struggle between Japanese and Chinese is to be expected. Therefore, we must never hesitate to wield military power in case of necessity.

In this spirit the practice of massacring, or "punishing" as the Japanese termed it, the inhabitants of cities and towns in retaliation for actual or supposed aid rendered to Chinese troops was applied. This Practice continued throughout the China War—the worst example being the massacre of the inhabitants of Nanking in December 1937.

[Author comment: *One of the most interesting aspects of the trial resulted from the dissenting opinion of the judge from India, Radhabinod Pal. His dissent comprised 1,235 pages. He found all of the defendants not guilty. Pal objected to what he saw as dangerous innovations in the law but also stands as a forerunner to those who later argued for a distinctive "Third World" perspective on international law.]*

Concerns of the Accused

[After dismissing concerns about racial bias and other emotions as factors, Justice Pal turned to the essence of his objections. The emphasis is in the original.]

The defense also took several other objections to the trial; of these the substantial ones may be subdivided under two heads:

1. Those relating strictly to the jurisdiction of the Tribunal.
2. Those which, while assuming the jurisdiction of the Tribunal, call on the Tribunal to discharge the accused of the charges contained in several counts on the ground that they do not disclose any offence at all . . .

The first substantial objection relating to the jurisdiction of the Tribunal is that the CRIMES TRIABLE BY THIS TRIBUNAL MUST BE LIMITED TO THOSE COMMITTED IN OR IN CONNECTION WITH THE WAR WHICH ENDED IN THE SURRENDER on 2 September, 1945. In my judgment this objection must be sustained. It is preposterous to think that defeat in a war should subject the defeated nation and its nationals to trial for all the delinquencies of their entire existence. There is nothing in the Potsdam Declaration and in the Instrument of Surrender which would entitle the Supreme Commander or the Allied Powers to proceed against the persons who might have committed crimes in or in connection with ANY OTHER WAR.

. . .

We have been set up as an International Military Tribunal. The clear intention is that we are to be "a judicial tribunal" and not "a manifestation of power." The intention is that we are to act as a court of law and act under international law. We are to find out, by the application of the appropriate rules of international law, whether the acts constitute any crime under the already existing law, dehors the Declaration, the Agreement or, the Charter. Even if the Charter, the Agreement or the Declaration schedules them as crimes, it would only be the decision of the relevant authorities that they are crimes under the already existing law. But the Tribunal must come to its own decision. It was never intended to bind the Tribunal by the decision of these bodies, for otherwise the Tribunal will not be a "judicial tribunal" but a mere tool for the manifestation of power.

The so-called trial held according to the definition of crime now given by the victors obliterates the centuries of civilization which stretch between us and the summary slaying of the defeated in a war. A trial with law thus prescribed will only be a sham employment of legal process for the satisfaction of a thirst for revenge. It does not correspond to any idea of justice. Such a trial may justly create the feeling that the setting up of a tribunal like the present is much more a political than a legal affair, an essentially political objective having thus been cloaked by a juridical appearance. Formalized vengeance can bring only an ephemeral satisfaction, with every probability of ultimate regret; but vindication of law through genuine legal process alone may contribute substantially to the re-establishment of order and decency in international relations.

. . .

[Quoting Professor Hans Kelsen]: "I. That general international law does not establish individual, but collective responsibility for the acts concerned, and 2. That the acts for which the guilty persons shall be punished are acts of state—that is, according to general international law, acts of the government or performed at the government's command or with its authorization."

. . .

I cannot accept the view that by such a treaty ex post facto law can always be created and applied to the case of such persons. It is, however, not necessary for me to quarrel with this proposition in the present connection. HERE THERE is NO SUCH TREATY; and the terms of authority of the Supreme Commander make it expressly clear that any power conferred on him is not in any way derived from the vanquished through any contractual relationship.

[Author comment: As an ironic note, Hans Kelsen supported both the Nuremberg and Tokyo trials.]

THE TOKYO TRIALS AND VICTOR'S JUSTICE

By the time the Tokyo trials began, the Nuremberg Charter and Indictment had already been critically analyzed by jurists and others who had raised significant issues. The Allied Powers knew that "crimes against peace" and "crimes again humanity" had broken new ground. The United States and Britain particularly focused on "crimes against peace" and hoped that the Tokyo Judgement would confirm Nuremberg's condemnation of aggressive war. As a consequence, every possible measure was taken to ensure that the Tokyo trial backed Nuremberg on this charge.

As with Nuremberg, the trial generated a great deal of criticism. Consider that the Court had to deal with a complex case that had colossal dimensions. The transcript of the trial contains over 45,000 pages. Unlike Nuremberg, five judges wrote separate opinions. Justice Pal wrote the only opinion that totally rejected the verdict. Two justices differed from the majority only on relatively minor points or on reasoning. Another Justice questioned the absence of Hirohito among the accused and had some problems with what he saw as procedural deficiencies. Justice Bert Röling (Netherlands) had more serious reservations. Agreeing with Judge Pal, he rejected the validity of "crimes against peace" on the basis that the charge was not established in international law.

As previously discussed, Pal's dissent addressed two of the more questionable charges. First, supporting Justice Röling, he rejected the claim that clear rules of international law relating to "crimes against peace" had evolved since the beginning of World War I. The Kellogg-Briand Pact did prohibit the waging of aggressive war, but no provision of that treaty held individuals criminally responsible for violations. He noted that the presumed legal basis for crimes against humanity had an even murkier origin. Interestingly "crimes against humanity" did not play a major role in the prosecution. The indictment has only one mention, and the majority Judgement addresses it only in passing. Still, though resting on shaky grounds, the IMT and the IMTFE still helped establish these two charges as the foundation of a future international criminal law. Along these same lines, the allegations of a broadly drawn conspiracy that underpinned much of the prosecution had no basis in international law other than its use at the Nuremberg (IMT) trial.

As with Nuremberg, many critics saw the Tokyo trials as simply "show" trials. In this respect, however, consider the comment of Herbert Bix that if the Tokyo trial was a political "show" trial, it was a joint American-Japanese effort. Bix observes:

> [T]he Tokyo trial was never a straightforward adversarial proceeding, pitting victors against vanquished. The charge of "victors' justice" leveled most vehemently by Pal, was and remains extremely simplistic. . . . During its preparatory stage Hirohito and those closest to him participated behind the scenes helping to select and influence the persons charged with war crimes. (2000, 613)

The Nuremberg trial (IMT) will have always a simple legacy. Despite the criticisms, it detailed the evils of Nazis aggression and brought attention to the horrors of the Holocaust. In contrast, while the IMTFE did document Japanese war crimes in great detail, the Tokyo trials left a more complex and ambiguous message. Part of this stems from the dissent of Justice Pal. While, aggression and war crimes are wrong, Pal went beyond this to say that so is colonialism and the use of the atomic bomb. His dissent highlighted what he considered to be the "war crimes" of the Allies that could not be acknowledged as a defense because of the prohibition on *tu quoque* arguments. Pal's dissent thus served to focus attention on the idea of "victor's justice" in that the Japanese were punished, while Americans who committed similar crimes were not.

References

Bix, Herbert. 2000. *Hirohito and the Making of Modern Japan*. New York: Harper.
Boister, Neil, and Robert Cryer. 2008. *The Tokyo International Military Tribunal: A Reappraisal*. Oxford: Oxford University Press.
Manchester, William. 1981. *Goodbye, Darkness: A Memoir of the Pacific War*. London: Penguin.
Porter, C. W. n.d. *Dissentient Judgement of Justice R. B. Pal*. Tokyo Tribunal. http://www.cwporter.com/pal1.htm.
Totani, Yuki. 2009. *The Tokyo War Crimes Trial: The Pursuit of Justice in the Wake of World War II*. Cambridge, MA: Harvard University Press.

16

General Tomoyuki Yamashita

THE *YAMASHITA* CASE: COMMAND RESPONSIBILITY

The *Yamashita* case stands out as the most controversial trials among a host of controversial trials. General Tomoyuki Yamashita and General Masaharu Homma were both charged with failure to exert effective control over their troops. General Homma commanded the Japanese force that had forced U.S. general Douglas MacArthur from the Philippines in 1942. General Yamashita held command of the troops that captured Malaya and Singapore. The quick victory of Japanese forces earned him the nickname of "The Tiger of Malaya." Later in the war, he had the task of commanding the Japanese troops defending the Philippines from advancing U.S. forces. While Yamashita did not stop the U.S. advance at the end of the war, he did hold on to part of Luzon until the formal Japanese surrender in August 1945. The two cases raise the same issue of *command responsibility*. Command responsibility is the opposite of superior orders. Superior orders raise the question of: to what extent can *subordinates* be held responsible for carrying out the *unlawful orders of their superiors*. Command responsibility raises the question: to what extent can *commanders* be held responsible for the *unlawful actions of their subordinates*?

Because of the extensive controversy associated with the final Supreme Court review of the Yamashita case, the analysis will focus on it alone. After his surrender on September 3, 1945, Yamashita was charged with unlawfully disregarding his duty as commander to control the operations of the members of his command, permitting them to commit brutal atrocities and other high crimes that constituted violations of the laws of war.

No one denied the scope and nature of the atrocities that had occurred. Japanese troops had committed rape, torture, and murder on a massive scale against both civilians and POWs. Some evidence suggested that many of the atrocities had been carried out on an organized and systematic basis on orders of Japanese commissioned officers. The questions revolved around the extent to which Yamashita could be held accountable for not stopping the criminal behavior, or afterward, for not punishing those soldiers who had committed the crimes. To assess this, the trial panel had to determine *what did General Yamashita know, and what could he have done, if he had known*? General Yamashita contended that he had no knowledge of what had happened. Most of the atrocities were committed by units or commanders distant from his headquarters, both geographically and in the chain of command. The prosecution argued that the crimes were so widespread and egregious that Yamashita had to have known.

The trial commission consisted of six army officers, five of them generals. George Guy, a member of the defense team, noted: "The Military Commission which tried General Yamashita had no judge learned in the law sitting with it. True, one of the officers was designated as a 'law member' but he is not a lawyer . . . and not a member of the legal profession" (pp. 161–162). The defense team (six army officers) had approximately three weeks to locate witnesses, conduct research on the 123 charges, and prepare for trial.

TRIAL SUMMARY #11: TRIAL OF GENERAL TOMOYUKI YAMASHITA

Because of the standard used to determine the extent of "command responsibility"—that is the liability/accountability that a superior officer may bear for the actions of his subordinates, this trial ranks among the most controversial held after World War II. In a book assessing the relevance of the World War II war crime trials for Vietnam, Telford Taylor, the chief prosecutor for trials held under the authority of Allied Control Council Order No. 10, argued that if the standard used in the Yamashita case were applied to any number of incidents in Vietnam, U.S. officers at the highest level of command should have been subject to court-martial proceedings.

DOCUMENT: *IN RE YAMASHITA* 327 U.S. 1 (1946)

When:	October 8, 1945–December 7, 1945
Where:	Manila, Philippines
Court:	United States Military Commission; U.S. Supreme Court
Defendant:	General Tomoyuki Yamashita, Commanding General of the 14th Army Group of the Imperial Japanese Army
Source:	*Law Reports of Trials of War Criminals*, Vol. 4 (London: Published for the United Nations War Crimes Commission by His Majesty's Stationery Office, 1948). Online at https://www.loc.gov/rr/frd/Military_Law/pdf/Law-Reports_Vol-4.pdf.
Charges:	He "unlawfully disregarded and failed to discharge his duty as commander to control the operations of the members of his command, permitting them to commit brutal atrocities and other high crimes." This charge was later supplemented with 123 specifications, all of which alleged specific war crimes committed by members of Yamashita's command. Combined, they alleged the murder and mistreatment of over 36,500 Filipino civilians and captured Americans, hundreds of rapes, and the arbitrary destruction of private property.

Defense: See introductory discussion

Verdict: In its judgement, the Commission accepted certain of the geographical and communications difficulties alleged by Yamashita but concluded that these problems were not quite as insurmountable as he contended. The commission found Yamashita guilty on all charges (December 7, 1945). It sentenced him to death.

Defense Arguments

1. Argument that Yamashita did not commit a war crime

It is an incontrovertible fact that the branding of military personnel as war criminals did not rest upon the mere fact of the command of troops, but rather upon the improper exercise of that command. This point was recognised officially by the U.S. War Department in its publication, Rules of Land Warfare (FM 27-10, Section 345, 1), which provided as follows: "Liability of Offending Individuals. Individuals and organisations who violate the accepted laws and customs of war may be punished therefor. However, the fact that the acts complained of were done pursuant to order of a superior or government sanction may be taken into consideration in determining culpability, either by way of defence or in mitigation of punishment. The person giving such orders may also be punished."

There was nothing said in that provision concerning the Commanding General of a force being responsible, under the Laws of War, for any offences committed by members of his command without his sanction. Liability for war crimes was imposed on the persons who committed the crimes and on the officers who ordered the commission thereof. The war crime of a subordinate, committed without the order, authority or knowledge of his superior, was not a war crime on the part of the superior. The pleadings now before the Commission did not allege that the accused ordered, authorised or had knowledge of the commission of any of the alleged atrocities or war crimes. Without such an allegation, it was submitted, the cause must be dismissed as not stating an offence under the Laws of War. The Defence claimed that if a violation of the Laws of War was not alleged, the Military Commission had no jurisdiction to hear the case" (12–13).

. . .

2. Argument that the commission lacked jurisdiction

Counsel said there existed neither martial law nor military government in the Philippines, and hostilities had ceased on or about 2nd September, 1945. There was no justification in law for the exercise by the Commander-in-Chief of the Army Forces, Pacific, of the extraordinary power by virtue of which the Commission was set up. The fundamental principle involved was apparently within the contemplation of the Commander-in-Chief, Army Forces, Pacific, when he issued the letter of 24th September, 1945, upon which the Commission based its authority, because paragraph 3 of his letter read as follows: "The Military Commissions established hereunder shall have jurisdiction over all Japan and all other areas occupied by the armed forces commanded by the Commander-in-Chief, Army Forces, Pacific." The Philippine Islands, Counsel pointed out, were not areas occupied by the armed forces. The above-mentioned letter, consequently, did not grant authority to set up military commissions in the Philippine Islands; and Special Orders No. 112, Headquarters, United States Army Forces, Western Pacific, dated 1st October, 1945, was therefore without authority" (13–14).

The United States was not and never had been a hostile army with respect to the Philippine Islands. The re-entry into the Philippine Islands in 1944 and 1945 had constituted a recovery of territory, not an occupation. From the date of re-entry on Philippine soil, General MacArthur had consistently affirmed and recognised the full governmental responsibility of the Philippine Commonwealth. This was evidenced by publications in the Official Gazette, April 1945, page 86; May 1945, pages 145 to 148; and September 1945, page 494. On 22nd August, 1945, General MacArthur issued the following proclamation: "Effective on 1st September, 1945, United States Army Forces in the Pacific shall cease from further participation in the self-administration of the Philippines, as such is no longer necessary."

3. *Defense Case*
The Defense did not deny that troops under the command of the accused had committed these various atrocities. Defence will show that the accused never ordered the commission of any crime or atrocity; that the accused never gave permission to anyone to commit any crimes or atrocities; that the accused had no knowledge of the commission of the alleged crimes or atrocities; that the accused had no actual control of the perpetrators of the atrocities at any time that they occurred, and that the accused did not then and does not now condone, excuse or justify any atrocities or violation of the laws of war. On the matter of control we shall elaborate upon a number of facts that have already been suggested to the Commission in our cross examination of the Prosecution's witnesses:

1. That widespread, devastating guerilla activities created an atmosphere in which control of troops by high ranking officers became difficult or impossible.
2. That guerilla activities and American air and combat activities disrupted communications and in many areas destroyed them altogether, making control by the accused a meaningless concept. And
3. That in many of the atrocities alleged in the Bill of Particulars there was not even paper control; the chain did not channel through the accused at all.

. . .

Prosecution Case

1. *Prosecution goals*
We will show also that he had overall command of the prisoner-of-war camps and civilian internment camps, labour camps, and other installations containing prisoners of war and other internees in all the Philippine Islands. . . . We will show that his area or territory of command included all of the Philippine Islands, the

entire area so known. We will show that at times he also commanded Navy forces and air forces, particularly when engaged as ground troops. . . . We will then show that various elements, individuals, units, organisations, officers, being a part of those forces under the command of the accused, did commit a wide pattern of widespread, notorious, repeated, constant atrocities of the most violent character; that those atrocities were spread from the northern portion of the Philippine Islands to the southern portion; that they continued, as I say, repeatedly throughout the period of Yamashita's command; that they were so notorious and so flagrant and so enormous, both as to the scope of their operation and as to the inhumanity, the bestiality involved, that they must have been known to the accused if he were making any effort whatever to meet the responsibilities of his command or his position; and that if he did not know of those acts, notorious, widespread, repeated, constant as they were, it was simply because he took affirmative action not to know. That is our case.

2. *Witnesses for the Prosecution*
Narciso Lapus stated that he had been private secretary to the Philippine General Artemio Ricarte, who had supported and worked for the Japanese during their occupation of the Philippine Islands. During the period from October 1944 and 31st December, 1944, Ricarte maintained contact with Yamashita as Commander-in-Chief of the Japanese forces in the Philippines. Ricarte told the witness that Yamashita, as the highest commander of the Japanese forces in the Philippines, had control over the army the navy and the air force. Four or five days after Yamashita arrived in the Philippines, Ricarte had a conversation with him, and on returning to his house, the latter told Lapus that Yamashita had issued a general order to all the commanders of the military posts in the Philippine Islands "to wipe out the whole Philippines, if possible," and to destroy Manila, since everyone in the Islands were either guerrillas or active supporters of the guerrillas; wherever the population gave signs of favouring the Americans the whole population of that area should be exterminated. Yamashita subsequently rejected Ricarte's plea that he should withdraw these orders.

Joaquin Galang, who claimed to have been a friend of Ricarte, stated that in December 1944, Yamashita visited Ricarte, and the former rejected Ricarte's request that the order to kill all Philippine inhabitants and destroy Manila be revoked; speaking through Ricarte's grandson as interpreter, Yamashita said: "An order is an order, it is my order, and because of that it should not be broken or disobeyed."

THE REST OF THE STORY

After the guilty verdict, Yamashita's defense team filed an immediate appeal to the Philippine Supreme Court, which rejected it on the basis that the court had no jurisdiction over the U.S. Army. The defense then sent a wire to the U.S. Supreme Court requesting a stay of execution, pending the submission of a writ of habeas corpus. The four issues raised by the defense had already been argued unsuccessfully in almost every case before a military commission. The Court had systematically refused to take up any of the previous applications for reviews of the European war crime trials; but, surprisingly, in this case the Court granted the stay and issued a *writ of certiorari*. Oral arguments in the case occurred on January 9, 1946.

Before the Supreme Court, the defense argued four issues:

(1) the creation of the military commission was unlawful because hostilities had ceased;
(2) the charges did not contain a violation of the law of war;
(3) the commission lacked authority and jurisdiction because the rules of evidence used (permitting hearsay and other "opinion" evidence) violated both U.S. military law (due process) and the Geneva Convention; and,
(4) the commission lacked authority and jurisdiction because of the failure to give advance notice of Yamashita's trial to the neutral power presenting the interests of Japan as required by Article 60 of the Geneva Convention.

Chief Justice Harlan Fiske Stone delivered the majority opinion (6–2), upholding the legality of the commission, the verdict, and the sentence. Associate Justices William Francis (Frank) Murphy and Wiley Rutledge delivered strong dissenting opinions.

The majority opinion ruled that the order convening the Commission which tried Yamashita was a lawful order under both United States and International Law, that the Commission was lawfully constituted, that the offence of which Yamashita was charged constituted a violation of the laws of war, and that the procedural safeguards of the United States Articles of War and of the provisions of the Geneva Prisoners of War Convention relating to Judicial Proceedings had no application to war crime trials.

In his dissent Justice Frank Murphy said: "The Fifth Amendment guarantee of due process of law applies to any person who is accused of a crime by the Federal Government or any of its agencies. No exception is made as to those who are accused of war crimes or as those who possess the status of an enemy belligerent" (p. 26). He thought that Yamashita had been denied the right to prepare an adequate defense and had not received the benefit of the most elementary rules of evidence. "No military necessity or other emergency demanded the suspension of the safeguards of due process" (pp. 27–28). The more important argument was his view that "had there been some element or *knowledge or direct connection* with the atrocities, the problems would be different" (p. 30). This last statement captures the subsequent evolution of command responsibility.

In 1948, two subsequent cases tried before the Nuremberg Military Tribunals adopted more limited liability standards for commanders. In the *Hostage* case (*United States v. Wilhelm List*), the standard became "must have known" to a more lenient "*should have* known." This meant that a commander's knowledge of widespread atrocities was presumed but could be offset by testimony citing mitigating factors, rather than presumed as an irrefutable fact. In the *High Command* case (*The United States of America v. Wilhelm von Leeb, et al.*), another Nuremberg Tribunal espoused a standard apparently giving commanders the benefit of the doubt on the knowledge issue. That panel stated, "Noting that modern warfare is highly decentralized, this court held that a commander *cannot know* everything that happens within the command, so the prosecution must prove knowledge" (Landrum 1995, 298). This court emphasized that in order to hold commanders criminally responsible for the actions of subordinates, the prosecution must prove criminal neglect in their supervision. A 1995 commentary noted:

> Even in United States courts, Yamashita has lost favor. If it ever stood for a strict liability standard, that strict standard never has been enforced again. The Protocol I standard [1977] is probably the best indication of what the international community would find acceptable, and that standard rejects any strict liability. Comparing the Protocol I standard with that established by the United Nations Security Council in creating the International Criminal Tribunal for the Former Yugoslavia, the two appear to be quite similar. (Landrum 1995, 297)

The provisions of Additional Protocol I (1977) to the 1949 Geneva Conventions will be discussed later in conjunction with cases before the International Criminal Court for the Former Yugoslavia (ICTY).

References

Lael, Richard L. 1982. *The Yamashita Precedent: War Crimes and Command Responsibility.* Wilmington, DE: Scholarly Resources.

Landrum, Major Bruce D. 1995. "The Yamashita War Crimes Trial: Command Responsibility Then and Now." *Military Law Review* 149: 293–301.

Reel, A. Frank. 1949. *The Case of General Yamashita.* Chicago: University of Chicago Press.

Taylor, Telford. 1971. *Nuremberg and Vietnam: An American Tragedy.* New York: Bantam.

17

Khabarovsk War Crime Trial

In addition to the IMTFE, separate trials convened by Australia, China, France, the Netherlands, the Philippines, the United Kingdom and the United States tried more than 5,700 lower-ranking personnel for conventional war crimes committed in the Asian theater during World War II. Due to factors such as distance and language, these trials did not generate the same level of interest as the European trials. The drama surrounding this trial reflects the interplay of competing and conflicting goals at the end of the war. Although U.S. forces had arrested the founder of the Japanese biological warfare program, General Shirō Ishii (also Ishii Shirō), he never stood trial. Actually, the United States never held a trial for many of the captured participants in the Japanese biological warfare program in their custody. Instead, General Douglas MacArthur and others petitioned for immunity for these individuals because the U.S. military wished to tap the data and expertise developed by the Japanese researchers to assist in the development of the U.S. biological warfare program. When the Soviet Union decided to hold a trial (1949) that focused on the Japanese program, the United States denounced it as a "show trial" and "communist propaganda." Given the destruction of records at the end of the war, the lack of survivors, and the extreme secrecy associated with the program, the extent of Japanese activities in developing biological weapons become known in the West only when participants began to talk fifty years later.

JAPANESE BACTERIOLOGICAL WEAPONS PROGRAM

Until the late nineteenth century, disease often claimed more victims in war than wounds in combat. During the Russo-Japanese War (1904–1905), Western observers took note of Japanese medical practices because of the low incidence of disease among their troops. The early concerns of Japan centered on prevention of outbreaks of typhus and dysentery by concentrating on the purity of the water supply to troops. An American doctor wrote that "Japan put into use the most elaborate and effective system of sanitation ever used in war" (Gold 1996, 19). With respect to wartime medicine and hygiene, Japan led the world. Soon after the end of the Russo-Japanese War, the Japanese established a Department of Field Disease Prevention.

It was a short step from a focus on prevention and cure to begin thinking about the impact disease might have on an enemy. Japan signed the 1925 Geneva Protocol (Chemical and Bacteriological Weapons, CBW) but did not ratify it.

SHIRŌ ISHII AND UNIT 731

Shirō Ishii became interested in bacteriology during his medical studies at Kyoto University. After his graduation in 1920, he enlisted in the army. Impressed with his dedication, the army sent him back to Kyoto where Shirō earned a Ph.D. in microbiology. An article on the 1925 Geneva Protocol aroused his interest in the possibilities of using disease as a weapon. Over the next few years, he searched for information on the use of CBW weapons and became a strong and persistent advocate for their development and introduction into the Japanese arsenal. His persistence paid off. In 1932, the army set up an Epidemic Prevention Research Laboratory within an army hospital in Tokyo under Shirō's direction.

The Japanese seizure of Manchuria in 1931 provided an opportunity to conduct experiments that would not have been possible in Tokyo. In late 1932, the Japanese General Staff and Ministry for War set up a bacteriological research laboratory in Pingfang District (Harbin) under command of the Kwantung Army. Ostensibly, it focused on protection and prevention, but the primary purpose was investigating and developing the possible uses of infectious diseases as a weapon. Today the building is a museum honoring the victims. Known informally as Unit 731 (Epidemic Prevention and Water Supply Unit 731), the laboratory used civilians of various ethnicities, mainly Chinese, as live subjects. Unit 731 did not comprise the entire Japanese biological warfare program. Other units existed, but Unit 731 is the unit within the Japanese biological warfare program that historians know the most about. Shirō Ishii, now promoted to general, served as director and one of the chief researchers. The exact number of subordinate units that operated under Shirō or made up Japan's biological warfare program still remains an open question at present.

During World War II, researchers also utilized prisoners of war (POWs) as human subjects. From 1942 to 1945, this involved more than 1,000 Allied soldiers. Consistent with the emperor cult discussed in the chapter on the Tokyo trials (IMTFE), Ishii saw POWs as cowards lacking honor and the Chinese as subhuman and expendable. Japan had refused to ratify the 1929 Geneva Convention because of the belief that Japanese soldiers would choose death before the dishonor of capture. The Japanese viewed captured enemy soldiers as having lost their honor by acting in a cowardly fashion. Accordingly, prisoners did not deserve humane treatment. In addition to using Chinese as human subjects for experiments, the Japanese Army had regularly used live Chinese for instructing troops in the use of the bayonet and as live targets for weapons training.

The detachments of Unit 731 and their branches carried on systematic bacteriological research with the object of determining which types of germs would be most effective to use as bacteriological weapons. The units also worked to devise methods for breeding the cultures on a massive scale as well as developing the necessary methods for employing them to kill people in large numbers and to inflict economic damage by infecting cattle and crops.

The biological experiments included live dissection without anesthesia to assess the progress of various communicable diseases deliberately injected into subjects. The doctors did not wait for death because they felt the results would not be as conclusive after the blood stopped flowing. Scientists experimented with cholera, anthrax, bubonic plague, smallpox, typhoid fever, tularemia (rabbit fever), as well various venereal diseases. Live subjects were also used to assess the effects of frostbite and to test the effectiveness and effects of grenades and flamethrowers. The full extent of the programs will never be known because the Japanese made sure there were no survivors. Unlike Nazi Germany, the surviving records did not surface until late in the 1990s. Sheldon Harris estimates the experiments involved 10,000–12,000 individuals. As a comparison, these figures mean that the Japanese program was 10–12 times larger than that of the Nazis.

The Japanese actively employed biological weapons against Chinese troops and cities. In 1939–1940, an estimated 1,000 Manchurian water wells were infected with typhoid bacteria. Casualties ranged from single deaths to outbreaks of typhoid that devastated entire villages. One 1942 campaign that used strains of cholera, dysentery, typhoid, plague, and anthrax caused "inestimable" losses among the Chinese. Because the Chinese were starving, they used food to distribute the deadly toxins as a very effective and low-cost method of delivery. Ishii would personally pass chocolates filled with anthrax bacilli to the local children (Harris 1994, 77). As Japan faced defeat at the end of the war, the Japanese initiated a wholesale dumping of the toxins into reservoirs, rivers, and wells. This tainted the water supply and caused the deaths of Chinese for many years after the war ended. They also released a horde of plague-infested rats on Manchurian communities. These rats caused outbreaks of the plague that killed at least 30,000 people in Harbin from 1946 to 1948.

GENERAL OTOZŌ YAMADA

General Yamada became the commanding officer of the Kwantung Army in July 1944. In this role, he was a strong advocate of the work done by Unit 731. He felt that because Japan lacked resources to build large amounts of conventional armament, it must develop inexpensive unconventional alternatives such as chemical and biological weapons. General Yamada raised a large conscript army in the final days of the war in an attempt to buy his regular troops time to prepare defenses against the Soviet advance; but, the untrained conscript force was defeated within days. When Yamada realized that Japan would have to surrender, he ordered Unit 731 personnel to destroy equipment and records that could be used as evidence of Japanese experiments. Soviet agents convinced Yamada to surrender on August 19, 1945.

TRIAL SUMMARY #12: GENERAL OTOZŌ YAMADA AND ELEVEN OTHERS

As did the United States, the Soviet Union (U.S.S.R.) had a great interest in acquiring the data and information on methodology for its own biological weapons program. By the time the trial began, the split between the U.S.S.R. and the United States and its Western European allies had evolved into the Cold War. Consequently, the arms competition, including the development of chemical and biological weapons (CBW) of mass destruction, became perceived as necessary. The reasoning behind the development forms the reverse of a *tu quoque* defense: "They are doing it, so we *must* do it also in order to defend ourselves."

DOCUMENT: GENERAL OTOZŌ YAMADA AND ELEVEN OTHERS

When: December 25–31, 1949
Where: Khabarovsk, Union of Soviet Socialist Republics (U.S.S.R., Russia)
Court: Military Tribunal of the Primorye Military Area
Defendants: General Otozō Yamada and 11 others
Source: *Materials on the Trial of Former Servicemen of the Japanese Army Charged with Manufacturing and Employing Bacteriological Weapons* (Moscow: Foreign Languages Publishing House, 1950). Online at https://books.google.com/books?id=ARojAAAAMAAJ.
Charges: Accomplices to the Nazi plan of aggression
Gross violations of the laws and customs of war
Participating in human experiments involving bacteriological agents and weapons for the "mass extermination of troops and the civilian population"
Development, production, and use of bacteriological weapons
Murder of subjects of human experiments
Defense: Culture of obedience and hatred of other peoples
Superior orders
Verdict: All found guilty; none received the death penalty. Kawashima Kiyoshi received a 25-year sentence for his role as Chief of Production and an additional 25 years for the activities associated with the development and production of the weapons. General Otozō and two others received 25-year sentences. Other sentences ranged from 3 years to 18 years.

TESTIMONY

In an interview in 2007, a member of Unit 731 who had escaped prosecution said unapologetically: "We removed some of the organs and amputated legs and arms. Two of the victims were young women, 18 or 19 years old. I hesitate to say it but we opened up their wombs to show the younger soldiers. They knew little about women—it was sex education" (Felton 2012, Introduction). The testimony from the trial is equally graphic.

State Prosecutor: Accused Nishi, what positions did you hold in Detachment 731, and at what times?

Accused Nishi [Medical Service lieutenant colonel Nishi Toshihide, formerly chief of a division of Detachment 731]: From January 1943 to July 1944, I was Chief of Detachment 731's branch in the town of Sunyu. From July 1944 to July 1945, I was Chief of the Training Division of Detachment 731.

Q: What did Detachment 731 do? What were its functions?
A: Most of the work of Detachment 731 was concerned with preparation for waging bacteriological warfare.

Q: Which of Detachment 731's divisions were engaged in preparations for waging bacteriological warfare?
A: The 1st, 2nd and 4th divisions conducted preparations for waging bacteriological warfare.

Q: What bacteriological means did Detachment 731 employ?
A: Its accepted weapons were the germs of plague, anthrax and gas gangrene.

Q: Which of these disease carriers were considered the most effective?
A: Plague bacteria.

Q: What methods of employing these bacteriological means were adopted by the detachment?
A: First, spraying bacteria from aircraft, second, dropping of porcelain bacteria bombs.

Q: Were plague fleas employed to infect human beings?
A: Yes, they were employed in China.

. . .

Q: What instructions regarding the development of bacteriological means of warfare did General Ishii bring with him when he came to the detachment as its Chief?
A: After he assumed his duties, Lieutenant General Ishii used to tell us almost daily that the work on plague must be activized.

Q: On plague?
A: On plague and the breeding of fleas. After Ishii's arrival, and in connection with the instructions received by the detachment to expand the mass production of fleas, special courses of training on the mass breeding of these parasites were instituted.

. . .

Accused **Nishi Toshihide** . . . testified:

"In January 1945, in my presence, Lieutenant Colonel **Ikari**, Chief of the 2nd Division of Detachment 731, and **Futaki**, a research official of this division, performed an experiment at the detachment's proving ground near Anta Station in infecting ten Chinese war prisoners with gas gangrene. The ten Chinese prisoners were tied to stakes from 10 to 20 metres apart, and a bomb was then exploded by electricity. All ten were injured by shrapnel contaminated with gas gangrene germs, and within a week they all died in severe torment." . . .

The corpses of the victims were burned in a special incinerator which Detachment 731 had built in close proximity to the prison.

. . .

Witness **Furuichi** testified that experiments had been performed in infecting human beings with typhoid. He said:

". . . It was about the beginning of 1943 that, on the orders of **Tabei**, Chief of the 1st Division, I first took part in typhoid-infection experiments on people confined in the prison of Detachment 731. I prepared one litre of sweetened water, which I infected with typhoid germs. This litre I then mixed with more water, and this was administered to about 50 imprisoned Chinese, war prisoners, if I remember rightly, only some of whom had been inoculated against typhoid."

. . .

Questioned as to the activities of the 1st Division of Detachment 731, accused **Kawashima Kiyoshi** said:

"Detachment 731 experimented widely in the action of all lethal bacteria on human beings. For these purposes we used imprisoned Chinese patriots and Russians whom the Japanese counterespionage service had condemned to extinction. . . ."

" . . . Detachment 731 had a special prison, where the persons designated for experimentation were kept under a strict regime and in close isolation; for purposes of secrecy, the detachment personnel usually referred to them as 'logs.'"

. . .

Accused **Karasawa** testified:

". . . I personally was present on two occasions at the Anta proving ground when the action of bacteria was tested on human beings under field conditions. The first time I was there towards the end of 1943. Some ten persons were brought to the proving ground, were tied to stakes which had been previously driven into the ground five metres apart, and a fragmentation bomb was exploded by electric current about 50 metres away from them. A number of the experimentees were injured by bomb splinters and simultaneously, as I afterwards learned, infected with anthrax, since the bomb was charged with these bacteria. . . ."

"The second time I visited the proving ground was in the spring of 1944; about ten people were brought there, and, as on the first occasion, tied to stakes. A cylinder filled with plague germs was then exploded at a distance of roughly ten metres from the experimentees."

WAR CRIMES AND THE POLITICS OF SELF-INTEREST

Although the trial provides us with an example of a Soviet "show" trial, it still serves to document the activities associated with the Japanese research program. As part of the script for the "show," each of the accused made an explicit confession of his crimes and gave an apology before sentencing. The following excerpt is a plea to the court made by one of the Soviet defense attorneys on behalf of his "client." Look carefully at the language the attorney used to request a light sentence.

> Kikuchi Norimitsu is a Japanese subject. Under the law of compulsory military service he was drafted into the ranks of the Japanese Army. I must say that service in the Japanese Army did not depend upon Kikuchi's wishes, he was obliged to serve, but he, of course, should not have carried out the obviously criminal orders of his superiors to perfect the methods of breeding lethal bacteria. In this case he was an accomplice of his superiors.
>
> Thus, the defence, and Kikuchi Norimitsu himself, admit guilt and regard the definition of the crime according to Art. 1 of the Decree of the Presidium of the Supreme Soviet of the U.S.S.R. of April 19, 1943, as correct.
>
> As regards the penalty, I ask the Military Tribunal, when discussing this question, to take into consideration that Kikuchi was born and brought up in capitalist society. He lived according to the jungle laws of capitalist society. This ideology was fostered in his mind by the Command of the Kwantung Army.
>
> I ask that you also take into consideration the minor degree of his guilt compared with that of the generals sitting at Kikuchi's side (incidentally, this is the first time in his life that he has had the opportunity of sitting next to top-rank generals).

The United States did denounce the trial but it did raise questions about U.S. actions in not prosecuting those Japanese in American custody who had been employed by the program. Many of these went on to have successful high-profile careers in Japan after the war. These included two university presidents (one of a medical university) and a number who became professors of medicine (Gold 1996, 142–143).

References

Felton, Mark. 2012. *The Devil's Doctors: Japanese Human Experiments on Allied Prisoners of War.* Barnsley, UK: Pen & Sword Books.

Gold, Hal. 1996. *Unit 731 Testimony: Japan's Wartime Human Experimentation Program.* Boston: Charles Tuttle.

Harris, Sheldon H. 1994. *Factories of Death: Japanese Biological Warfare 1932–1945 and the American Cover Up.* New York: Routledge.

Williams, Peter, and David Wallace. 1989. *Unit 731: Japan's Secret Biological Warfare in World War II.* New York: Free Press.

18

The Eichmann Trial

The pursuit of Nazi war criminals did not end with the prosecutions immediately after World War II. The Israeli government and others undertook the mission to seek out and bring to trial those associated with any aspect of the Holocaust. As late as January 2016, Germany still had four trials scheduled. These trials have become somewhat problematic because of the age of the defendants and the ages (and numbers) of witnesses. Many of those sought, if not dead, may now be mentally unfit to stand trial. Memories of aged witnesses about events of 70 years ago may still be vivid but lacking essential details.

In the United States, the most prominent case involved John Demjanjuk. In 1986, after a number of Holocaust survivors identified him as a guard at the Treblinka death camp nicknamed "Ivan the Terrible," the United States deported him to Israel to stand trial. Upon his conviction in 1988, the United States revoked his naturalized citizenship. On appeal, the Israeli Supreme Court reversed the trial verdict on the basis of new evidence that cast reasonable doubt on the validity of the original charge. The United States restored his citizenship and he returned to his home in Cleveland, Ohio.

Demjanjuk's return did not end the story. In 2001, new evidence surfaced. Demjanjuk was charged again, on evidence that he had worked at the Sobibor and Majdanek camps under the name Ivan Demjanjuk. After lengthy legal maneuvering, he again lost his naturalized U.S. citizenship and in 2009, he was deported to Germany to stand trial. German prosecutors charged him with being an *accessory* to approximately 28,000 murders while employed as a guard at Sobibor (1943). The German trial court found him guilty. Before the Appellate Court could confirm the verdict of the trial court, Demjanjuk died in a German nursing home in 2012. Under German law, because the case had not been completed, Demjanjuk thus technically remained not guilty. This case still stood as a landmark because the prosecution did not claim that Demjanjuk had committed any specific act such as a beating or a murder. He was convicted for being an accessory—that is, of acts that aided others in the commission of crimes.

THE EICHMANN SAGA

The RuSHA trial, one of the subsequent Nuremberg proceedings, had indicted and tried officials of Gestapo Section IV B4, the Race and Resettlement Section (*Rasse und Siedlungshauptamt*, RuSHA) of the Reich Main Security Office (RSHA). Adolf Eichmann, the head of the section, had been detained in a U.S. internment camp, but managed to escape and hide. In 1950, with the help of the SS underground, he fled to Argentina and adopted the name Ricardo Klement. Ten years later, Eichmann's current location came to the attention of the Israeli government. Mossad (National Intelligence Agency of Israel) agents kidnapped him on May 11, 1960. Heavily sedated, he was taken aboard an airliner to Israel disguised as a sick passenger. His trial began in April 1961 and lasted 56 days. In December 1961, after lengthy deliberation, the three judges announced a verdict of guilty on all charges.

Career

Karl Adolf Eichmann was born in Austria. His biographers note that he grew up in a political and social environment that routinely disparaged Jews. Anti-Semitism had long been an acceptable prejudice in both German and Austrian society, though seldom overtly stated in public. Propaganda after World War I played to the prejudice. Many Austrians and Germans firmly believed that a Jewish conspiracy had been the root cause of their defeat in World War I.

Eichmann did not join the Nazi Party until the spring of 1932, after it became respectable through its electoral success. After losing his job in early 1933, perhaps because of an Austrian government effort to suppress the Nazi Party, he immigrated to Germany where he volunteered for the Schutzstaffel (SS). In early 1934, Eichmann applied to the Sicherheitdienst (SD) and was accepted. While working for the SD, he met individuals who were deeply anti-Semitic, but who also encouraged him to learn more about Judaism. He learned Hebrew and did extensive research on Jewish culture and the Zionist movement. Although they would be among the principal players in the "Final Solution," the most important personages in the SD, Heinrich Himmler and Reinhard Heydrich, did not play an influential role in the early formulation and development of Nazi anti-Jewish policy. In one of the ironic twists produced by the conflicted politics at the end of World War II, Hans Globke, one of the principal architects of the early Nazi anti-Semitic policies, avoided prosecution. He was serving as chief of staff for Chancellor Konrad Adenauer when Eichmann went on trial.

Impressed with Eichmann's presence and work, Leopold (Edler) von Mildenstein invited him to work in the newly formed SS Jewish Affairs Office. Von Mildenstein vigorously advocated the "Zionist" solution, which encouraged Jewish emigration to Israel. Eichmann continued to champion emigration until circumstances made the policy unworkable. Eventually, anti-Semitic attitudes along with economic hard times diminished the willingness of other countries to admit emigrants under any circumstances. As late as July 1940, Eichmann still favored deportation or forced emigration. He proposed the Madagascar Plan to settle European Jews on the island off the east coast of Africa. The plan was considered, but never implemented. After the German invasion of the Soviet Union (Russia), another plan would advocate moving them into Siberia after the German Army prevailed. When the Soviet Army stopped the German advance, this eliminated that possible option.

Eichmann's work in the SD attracted the attention of both Heinrich Himmler and Reinhard Heydrich. Himmler appointed him to head the newly created SD Scientific Museum of Jewish Affairs. From this point on, Eichmann became the SD authority on Jewish affairs. After the German annexation of Austria (Anschluss) in March 1938, Eichmann, now head of the SS Office for Jewish Emigration, was sent to Vienna to promote Jewish emigration from Austria. In 1939, Hitler appointed him to the directorship of Section IV B4, the Reich Central Office for Jewish Affairs and Evacuation (RuSHA). Eichmann now had responsibility for implementing the Nazi policy toward Jews in Germany and all of its occupied territories (eventually comprising sixteen countries). He became chiefly responsible for the mass deportation of Jews and other undesirables (Gypsies) from Germany as well as other parts of Europe to labor and extermination camps. David Cesarani attributes his rapid rise to his having "the right objective, problem-solving and managerial outlook in combination with a fierce German nationalism grounded in racial pride" (2004, 47).

Moving toward the "Final Solution" (Endlösung der Judenfrage)

"What to do with the Jews" had become a major problem for the Nazis. When the war started, the initial success of German armies in taking and occupying new territory had markedly increased the number of "inferior" and "undesirable" people under German rule. The larger numbers placed even more serious constraints on efforts to carry out deportation and resettlement programs. The cleansing efforts in the annexed territories had displaced 250,000 Jews in addition to the 350,000 Jews in Warsaw. With no possibility of deportation or emigration to other areas, the Nazis reluctantly embraced the idea of concentrating the Jewish population in ghettos as a temporary solution. Eichmann had stated that the number of Jews who had to be removed from the "living space of the German people" had risen from 5.8 million in mid-1940 to 11 million in the summer of 1941. Moving large numbers to other places no longer formed a viable option.

The problems centered on ensuring that maintenance of the ghettoes would not be a drain on resources. From an ideological standpoint, many Nazis had believed that the arrangement would produce a great windfall because of their misperceptions about the accumulated assets of the Jewish communities. An ensuing debate about policy focused on the main goal of the temporary arrangement. Some advocated a policy of letting those in the ghettos starve to death after the Reich had collected everything of value. Others had argued that, given the shortage of labor cause by the number of individuals called to military and government duties, the ghettos should be utilized as a source of cheap labor that potentially could make them self-sufficient and positive contributors to the German war economy. The "final solution" would occur only when the state no longer needed them. As the presumed temporary arrangements lingered on, the resources of the ghetto populations were exhausted. This situation then did reduce to the choice between taking action to make the ghettos somewhat self-sustaining or allowing starvation and disease to take its inevitable course. In actuality, no choice existed. Doing nothing had already produced a starving, impoverished community desperately struggling for survival.

THE WANNSEE CONFERENCE

As noted in the discussion of previous trials, by December 1941, the precedent for systematic mass killing had taken root. From the middle of 1941 until the beginning of Aktion Reinhard (the operational name for the "Final Solution") in July 1942, the killing fields were mainly in Nazi-occupied Soviet territory. The euthanasia campaign and the mass butchery in Eastern Europe had set the stage. Two problems had arisen in the course of the operations in Eastern Europe. First, given the large numbers of Jews alone, continuing executions by using only firing squads presented what seemed to be an insurmountable logistical problem. Second, participation in the bloodbaths of mass slaughter on a routine basis had exacted a huge psychological toll on the men who were directly engaged (see Einsatzgruppen Trial). Frustration combined with racial hatred provided the final impetus.

In late July 1941, Reichsführer Hermann Göring instructed Heydrich to draw up a plan for a "total solution of the Jewish question" in territories under German control. Heydrich was also to arrange and ensure the necessary participation of all government agencies necessary to accomplish the goals of the plan. The plan, named Generalplan Ost (General Plan for the East), called for collection at central points and deportation (originally to Siberia for slave labor) but left the question of extermination open. Heydrich organized the Wannsee Conference to present the plan. Initially scheduled for early December, several important events forced postponement. Soviet resistance to the German invasion in June had eliminated the possibility of using Siberia as an outlet. Japan had bombed Pearl Harbor, and America had declared war on the Axis Powers. Finally, at some point before the rescheduled meeting in Wannsee, Hitler had decided on extermination as the solution to the problem. That decision was not discussed at the conference.

The central part of the plan remained intact. Jews would be rounded up and herded to collection points, and then transported to "housing" centers located in occupied Poland. The scale of the "Final Solution" would not have been possible without mass transport. The success of the extermination effort depended on the railway system as much as on the efficiency of the killing centers. Rail shipments allowed the Nazis to build and operate bigger and more efficient death camps. German authorities used rail systems across the continent to transport Jews from their homes to the camps. Once the systematic slaughter had begun, Jews were moved to these facilities primarily by train but also by truck or on foot if the distances were short or trains not available. Given transport conditions, many deaths occurred during the "evacuation" process.

IMPLEMENTING THE "FINAL SOLUTION"

To carry out the task, the Nazis had established camps close by the ghettos. Three had begun operations by late mid-March 1942. The camps did not substitute for the other ongoing methods of massacre but added another dimension and capability far beyond what the mobile death squads could accomplish. The seven weeks from late July to mid-September stand out as the most murderous in the period of active extermination during the Holocaust as the Nazis sent those in the ghettos in Poland to the killing centers. By September, 310,000 of the 380,000 Jews in the Warsaw ghetto had perished. During their operational period, approximately 1.7 million Jewish residents went to the gas chambers at the Aktion Reinhard camps. Add to this total the thousands shot by units still operating under SS instructions and orders.

Historians still quibble over the depth of Eichmann's ideological commitment to the "Final Solution." In terms of his subsequent actions, whether he "truly believed" or "was just following orders" produced the same result. Every day, Eichmann personally oversaw the massive logistical operation of rounding up, transporting, murdering, and disposing of millions of Jews. He was a very efficient bureaucrat who often complained about delays caused by the lack of zeal in some of the occupied zones. The Germans have a word, s*chreibtischtäter* ("desk criminal"), that describes a person who authorizes or organizes the commission of a crime, but who does not directly participate in any action directly connected to the crime. Eichmann's behavior presents a good example to illustrate the term.

TRIAL SUMMARY #13: KARL ADOLF EICHMANN

Eichmann, who testified from a bulletproof glass booth, used the defense that he was just obeying orders. Over one hundred witnesses, however, testified to Eichmann's willing participation in the Final Solution. On December 2, 1961, the Court sentenced Eichmann to death for crimes against the Jewish people and crimes against humanity. On June 1, 1962, Eichmann was executed by hanging. His body was cremated and the ashes were spread at sea, beyond Israel's territorial waters. The execution of Adolf Eichmann remains the only time that Israel has overtly enacted a death sentence.

DOCUMENT: *THE ATTORNEY GENERAL V. ADOLF EICHMANN*

When:	April 11, 1961–December 11, 1961
Where:	Jerusalem, Israel
Court:	District Court of Jerusalem
Defendants:	Karl Adolf Eichmann
Source:	The Nizkor Project: The Trial of Adolf Eichmann http://www.nizkor.org/hweb/people/e/eichmann-adolf/transcripts/.
Charges:	A 15 count indictment alleged crimes against the Jewish People, crimes against humanity, and war crimes. "The period of the crimes ascribed to him, and their historical background, is that of the Hitler regime in Germany and in Europe, and the counts of

	the indictment encompass the catastrophe which befell the Jewish People during that period."
Defense:	Superior Orders
Verdict:	Guilty; death penalty
Significance:	The Eichmann trial reinforced the horrors of the Holocaust. Occurring as it did, some years after the end of World War II, it encouraged a greater openness among Israelis in discussing the Holocaust and what it meant for Jews and humanity as a whole. Indeed, many Holocaust survivors were more willing to open up about their experiences.

TESTIMONY

Before examining the testimony, the statement of the District Court bears repeating, not only as a perspective on the Eichmann trial but also on the historical value of war crime trials in general. The Court noted:

> How could this happen in the light of day, and why was it just the German people from which this great evil sprang? Could the Nazis have carried out their evil designs without the help given them by other peoples in whose midst the Jews dwelt? Would it have been possible to avert the Holocaust, at least in part, if the Allies had displayed a greater will to assist the persecuted Jews? Did the Jewish People in the lands of freedom do all in its power to rally to the rescue of its brethren and to sound the alarm for help? What are the psychological and social causes of the group-hatred which is known as anti-Semitism? Can this ancient disease be cured, and by what means? What is the lesson which the Jews and other nations must draw from all this, as well as every person in his relationship to others? There are many other questions of various kinds which cannot even all be listed.

The following is an excerpt of Eichmann's cross-examination by the attorney general of Israel. In his testimony, Eichmann consistently denied having any direct responsibility for other than being a middleman responsible for arranging transportation.

Attorney General: When you returned from this trip, during which you saw the Operations Units in action, you said to Mueller that this was not the right way, that "our people would become sadists," another method for executions had to be found. Is that correct?

Accused: I am not familiar with the last phrase, "another method for executions had to be found"—this is the first time I have heard this.

Q. Very well: "the first time." During your examination in Bureau 06 you were shown T/47, the article in Life, for your perusal, and in T/48 you indicated your reaction. On page 31 of the manuscript you were shown, with no comments on the comments sheet, practically without your taking exception to this matter, the following is recorded as your words on page 31 of the typed copy:

> Gruppenfuehrer, the solution should have been a political one; but since the Fuehrer has now issued orders for a physical solution, clearly it will have to be a physical one. But we cannot continue carrying out the executions as at Minsk and, I believe,

elsewhere. That would train our people to become sadists. We cannot solve the Jewish Question by putting a bullet through the head of a defenceless woman holding her child up to us.

So you were saying that if the extermination had to be physical, then let it be physical, but not by means of shooting, and not with a woman throwing her baby at your leather coat, as in Minsk, is that true?

A. No, that is a completely wrong interpretation of what I said. This meaning can, in literal terms, be deduced from this statement by me, but that is not how I made it, because the meaning was that there could be no question here of killing people. I made the point without beating about the bush; in principle it makes no difference whether this was by means of gas or with a bullet. I was against that.

Q. But it is more elegant with gas—that was the opinion of the gentlemen from the Ministry for the Eastern Occupied Territories. It is more elegant with gas, is that not true?

A. Yes, but that was definitely not my opinion. This is also quite obvious from the phrases I have just heard. Who added this business of physical extermination here, I do not know, I do not know. But the point I was trying to make . . . I should be believed that I really did express it as I felt it inside me.

Q. You say, "but since the Fuehrer has now issued orders for a physical solution, it will have to be a physical one," a physical solution?

A. Did I sign it? I do not believe I did.

Q. You made no comment on this; only on the word "offensichtlich" (obviously) did you make a comment by underlining it. That is all. There is no comment here on these words. You may look at it.

A. [Accused] Here in Israel?

Q. [Attorney General] Yes, here in Israel.

A. [Accused] Then I definitely failed to notice this matter. That is also in the nature of things, because otherwise I would definitely have corrected this, if I had noticed it.

Q. You spoke with the people from Rosenberg's Ministry about gas matters, didn't you?

A. No, I really do not believe that I spoke to anybody about gas matters. That is what was strange to me when I was shown this matter here.

Q. So how do you know, and why do you imagine, that these people saw this as a more elegant solution, if you did not talk to them at all?

A. Because at that time there was a great deal of talk about such things in the Head Office for Reich Security.

Q. Between whom?

A. Between whom? There were . . . at meetings between Section Heads and so on, there was talk of this, of this matter.

Q. About gas?

A. About everything, about the entire question in the East. . . .

Q. I am asking you about exterminating Jews by means of gas.

A. That was also under discussion at the time. Someone must have spoken one way or the other about it, because otherwise I would not have known about it.

. . .

Q. Do you agree that what you have told me fits what Wetzel described in his letter? The people who shoot Jews are being morally poisoned; another solution must be found—the solution is found by extermination through gassing. You are asked about this. You give your authorization, and thus this all fits perfectly.

A. No, I had nothing at all to do with these matters; I did not deal at all with this.

Q. But Wetzel does refer to you, does he not?

[Exchange with Judge omitted]

Accused: That was known not only to Wetzel. All sorts of central authorities knew about this which were dealing with these waves of deportations to Riga and Minsk, and in fact there was a whole list of central authorities which were dealing with this directly.

Q. True, but only Wetzel knew that you had given your consent on behalf of the Head Office for Reich Security to extermination by gassing.

A. I did not give my consent, because I could not give any such consent—I had nothing to do with the killing. I have said as much here time and again, I cannot say anything further on this. This is also correct.

Q. In your Section, you had a typist called Werlmann? And also a man who worked in Registry, called Martin?

A. Yes.

Q. I am going to read out a passage to you. Will you please tell me whether this is correct or not?

> I was given orders to produce a letter for Globocnik. A letter I would have to hand over in person, I constantly kept an eye on. I dictated the letter to Mrs. Werlmann, after which this letter was received by Unterscharfuehrer Martin as Head of Registry, who gave this communication its number as Secret State Business and entered it in the Registry. No copy was made, there was only the original, and then I took this letter with me and either handed it to Heydrich in person or gave it to Mueller, who in turn handed it to Heydrich, and then I received this letter back through official channels.

Is what you said here correct?

A. Not verbatim, but the meaning is correct. Things were as follows: As I explained, I received orders to draft a letter of this kind which either Mueller or Heydrich—I believe Heydrich—signed, and I had to deliver that to Globocnik.

Q. So here Sassen did not falsify your words?

A. The words are not verbatim, but the meaning is quite clear. What is not in here is that . . . *if one reads this, the impression might be that I drafted such a letter on my own initiative*, and then, ex post facto. . . .

Judge Halevi: No, no, it does say "im Auftrage" (per pro) after all? It does say im Auftrage, [*by proxy*] does it not?

Accused: It does say im Auftrage.

Attorney General: It does indeed say im Auftrage.

Accused: I should also like to say that I have already long since referred to this matter here in my Statement.

Q. This letter—that was an order to execute a quarter of a million Jews?

A. No, they were already dead. Globocnik wanted to have some form of cover from Heydrich after the event, and that is how this came about; I was ordered to produce this communication, and Heydrich, or Mueller . . . I do not think . . . signed it, and then I had to take it to the Generalgouvernement.

Q. And you wrote such letters two or three times?

A. In my Statement I also said here . . . I do not know . . . twice . . . I think . . . I do not think it was three times . . . I believe I remember it was twice . . . but I do not know if it was 250,000 or 150,000 . . . that I never knew.

Q. In your memoirs which you have written, T/44, pages 116 and 117, you mention that Globocnik wanted further instructions to kill Jews—that is, he was given the assignment to kill such and such a number of Jews, and he also wanted a retroactive confirmation for the Jews he had already killed. Is that correct?

A. No, of that I am not aware. But Globocnik did want a confirmation for the Jews he had killed, as a cover. That I do remember.

[*exchanges with Judge omitted*]

Attorney General: Did you ever bring Globocnik an order to kill Jews—not a post factum order, but an order to kill Jews?

Accused: No, I did not do that. If I had done so, when I wrote these memoirs, I . . . if I had not felt like writing down everything I knew, I would have written that down as well.

Q. It will do, if you say no. Which concentration camps did you visit?

A. After this station, which was being built, I received orders to go to Kulm, to Kulmhof. After that I was sent to Minsk, and now I know that with time . . . no, at that time I travelled via Lemberg.

Q. Did you go to Majdanek?

A. Yes, but that was later.

Q. All right; in general terms I should like to know which concentration camps you went to. Did you go to Majdanek?

A. Majdanek, . . .

Q. Did you go to Treblinka?

A. No, that I do not know. . . .

Q. Sobibor?

A. I went to Auschwitz. . . .

Q. You wrote somewhere that you went repeatedly to Auschwitz, didn't you?

A. Yes, and I have also admitted that; I went there some five or six times, I am not sure of the exact number.

Q. And Hoess showed you the entire extermination process from A to Z, did he not?

A. No, that is just not true.

Q. No? That is what Hoess writes about it, you know that.

A. That is possible, but it is not true. Hoess was wrong by an entire year, and I have proved that, by going through all the literature about it, because it struck me as odd, and I also managed to prove this by means of facts.

Q. Very well. Let us therefore assume that Hoess got the date wrong. But was he also wrong about the fact that he showed you the extermination plant? He writes that he showed you the entire process. Did he ever show it to you? Ever?

A. "Show" is not the right word; he told me about it, and I saw part of it, that is, how the bodies were burned. That I did see.

Q. Did you have any authority for the extermination camps?

A. No, no authority whatsoever.

SOME QUESTIONS WITHOUT GOOD ANSWERS

The Israeli Court asked the essential question: "How could this happen in the light of day . . .?" The answers offer little comfort. The simplest explanation springs to mind is that those involved were criminal psychopaths who forced others to do their bidding. How otherwise could anyone have condoned deliberate slaughter on such a massive scale? The difficulty with this explanation comes from the large number of people involved.

In his essay on Eichmann, Thomas Merton made an observation that raised a great deal of controversy. Merton noted that one of the most disturbing aspects of the trial was that a psychiatrist had examined Eichmann and found him *"perfectly sane."* He characterized Eichmann as a "calm . . . unperturbed official conscientiously going about his desk work, his administrative work which happened to be the supervision of mass murder" (1966, 45). Hannah Arendt, a prominent Jewish academician, who observed the trial, received a great deal of very hostile criticism from the worldwide Jewish community for her description of Eichmann's activity as the "banality of evil," a phrase that emphasized the ordinary nature of what Eichmann did. To use Merton's words again: "He [Eichmann] was thoughtful, orderly, unimaginative. He had a profound respect for system, for law and order. He was obedient, loyal, a faithful officer of a great state. He served his government very well." But, Merton's next words highlight the most troublesome part of Eichmann's testimony: *"He was not bothered much by guilt"* [emphasis added] (1966, 45). How could any sane person be so deeply involved in such a horrific enterprise without expressing any remorse even in a situation where some expression of regret might have saved his life?

This last question does not have a simple answer. How typical was Eichmann of those who orchestrated the slaughter, operated the camps, or served in the Einsatzgruppen? As chilling as Eichmann's testimony was, those who helped to plan and implement the genocide were not simple, uneducated ideologues and thugs. They came from the educated middle class. Among the men in the leadership corps of the SS, two-thirds held the equivalent of a college B.A., nearly one-third had a Ph.D. They created the Holocaust and gave it that strange combination of personalized brutality and efficient character. Education may widen one's horizons, but it can also provide the tools to construct more sophisticated justifications to validate one's beliefs. Certainly this was the case with Eichmann with respect to the studies and research that led to his becoming the "Jewish expert" in the SS.

Still, sorting out motives is difficult. Racism and hatred do not necessarily translate directly into toleration, support for, or participation in, mass killing even if individuals do share the animosity toward a specific group in whole or in part. The real questions involve those individuals who were not members of the SS who willingly aided, abetted, and benefited. The issues concern how anyone can participate in actions that contribute to a policy that violates a fundamental moral conviction. The answers to this question are not comforting. These issues will arise again in the later discussion of Rwanda and Bosnia.

Cesarani argues that even though Eichmann probably shared the negative attitudes of the Nazi Party toward Jews, that attitude did not play a decisive role in his initial decision to become a member. Nothing at that moment suggested that the party offered a path to advancement and influence. A combination of chance and choice over time opened up unexpected paths for advancement. Cesarani sees Eichmann's experience in Vienna as the critical point where: "As a good National Socialist and SD man, he was able to divorce what would normally be regarded as the moral and human consequences of his actions from his purely formal and 'legal' remit" (2004, 363). Anyone who has worked in a rigid bureaucratic environment for any length of time will understand this dynamic. The process, the routine, the rules become the focus, not the ultimate goal(s) of the organization. Within the RUSHA, promotion and recognition were tied to performance.

In Eichmann's case, his own words undermined his claim of just being a small cog in the larger complex of machinery. Whatever his deepest motivation, in his own words, his task became one of not just obtaining freight cars and constructing timetables, but of ensuring "that the freight cars should be used to their maximum capacity" (Lipstadt 2011, 143). While couched in the language of a bureaucrat, this admission goes beyond simple arranging to actively "facilitating." Nonetheless, in his final statement, Eichmann still portrayed himself as a victim and placed all blame on the political leaders.

References

Arendt, Hannah. 2006. *Adolf Eichmann in Jerusalem: A Report on the Banality of Evil.* Rev. ed. New York: Penguin.

Cesarani, David. 2004. *Becoming Eichmann.* Cambridge, MA: Da Capo Books.

Gouri, Haim. 2004. *Facing the Glass Booth: The Jerusalem Trial of Adolf Eichmann.* Detroit: Wayne State University Press.

Lipstadt, Deborah E. 2011. *The Eichmann Trial.* New York: Schocken Books.

Merton, Thomas. 1966. "A Devout Meditation in Memory of Adolf Eichmann." In *Raids on the Unspeakable*, 45–49. New York: New Directions.

19

My Lai Massacre: Vietnam War

The trial of Second Lieutenant William Laws Calley Jr. for the My Lai Massacre raises the same central issue as the Leipzig Trials discussed earlier: *superior orders*. In this case, the relevant body of law is the Uniform Code of Military Justice (UCMJ). Article 1(8) of the U.S. Constitution gives Congress the power "To make Rules for the Government and Regulation of the land and naval Forces." As passed by the Congress, the UCMJ (64 Stat. 109, 10 U.S.C. §§ 801–946) applies to all men and women in any branch of the U.S. military services. It defines procedures in the military justice system and lists and defines criminal offenses under military law. The UCMJ includes the international law of armed conflict (laws and customs of war) as adopted by the United States through ratification of treaties and conventions and recognition of customary practices through decisions in court cases.

The military court system, created under Article I of the U.S. Constitution, stands totally apart from the Federal Court system created under Article III. It includes military court-martials, a Criminal Court of Appeals for each branch of the armed services, and the U.S. Court of Appeals for the Armed Forces (CAAF). The CAAF has a *discretionary* appellate jurisdiction over military cases from each branch. Discretionary means the Court does not have to review a case unless it chooses to do so. With the exception of a potential final review by the U.S. Supreme Court, military courts handle all appeals of trial decisions in military cases. The Supreme Court will normally not consider a military case unless the CAAF has heard the appeal.

CONSCRIPTION (THE DRAFT)

From 1940 until 1973, the United States "drafted" men to fill manpower needs of the U.S. Armed Forces not otherwise satisfied through voluntary enlistment. At the end of World War II, the Congress did suspend conscription for a short time but had to reinstate it because the U.S. Army needed soldiers to serve in the U.S. areas of occupation in Germany and Japan. The onset of the Cold War (1948) with the USSR and the Korean War (1949–1953) underlined the necessity of having a strong military to stop the expansion of Communism.

Protests against the draft began as U.S. troop strength in South Vietnam increased. Many saw the war as an unnecessary war to protect a corrupt government and sought means of avoiding the draft by filing for "conscientious objector" status or leaving the United States to live in other countries. The Congress enacted legislation that ended conscription. With the official end of the Vietnam War in January 1973, the Congress enacted legislation that ended conscription and made service in the armed forces voluntary. The end of conscription did not end the eligibility for compulsory military service in the event of a national emergency. Every male citizen of the United States still has a requirement to register with the Selective Service System on or shortly after his 18th birthday.

THE DEFENDANT

William Laws ("Rusty") Calley Jr. was drafted in 1966. After basic training he served as a clerk-typist at Fort Lewis, Washington. Private First Class Calley attracted the attention of his superiors who, on the basis of his Armed Forces Qualification tests, encouraged him to apply for Officer Candidate School (OCS) at Fort Benning, Georgia. Calley was graduated and commissioned a Second Lieutenant in September 1967. In Vietnam, he commanded a platoon (25–30 soldiers) in Company C ("Charlie Company) of the 1st Battalion, 20th Infantry, 23rd Infantry (Americal) Division.

Commanded by Captain Ernest Medina, Charlie Company came to Vietnam in December 1967 as one of three companies in Task Force Barker. Named for its overall commander, Lieutenant Colonel (LTC) Frank Barker, the Task Force was assigned to Quang Ngai Province. The United States had targeted the province as a stronghold of the Viet Cong (South Vietnamese Communist army). Task Force Barker had the specific mission to deal with resistance in an area around Son My village. Son My had been nicknamed "Pinkville" because of the concentration of Communist sympathizers and the extent of Viet Cong (VC) activity in the area.

ARMY OPERATIONS IN VIETNAM

Distinguishing noncombatants from enemy fighters formed an everyday problem for American soldiers because the Viet Cong often wore the same clothing as villagers. As a solution to the problem, the U.S. military had designated areas seen as enemy "strongholds" as "free fire zones." A "free fire zone" was an area where all friendly forces had supposedly been evacuated. Any remaining people were then presumed hostile. Within the borders of a free fire zone, military action could be used for complete destruction of objectives on the initiative of local commanders. The evacuation of "friendly" villagers necessary for establishing a free fire zone generated resentment in the local population, as did the destruction afterwards from frequent bombing missions and artillery attacks. "Pinkville" was in a free fire zone.

THE MY LAI OPERATION

The My Lai Massacre stands out as the most notorious U.S. military incident of the Vietnam War. Still, any discussion of the violations of the law of war in general, and at My Lai in particular, must be viewed against the background of the enemy's activities. As emphasized in previous cases, while the actions of an enemy *may explain a reaction, they do not justify it*. The My Lai operation was designed as a classic search-and-destroy sweep intended to trap some of the estimated 250 Viet Cong operating in the area. Prior to this operation, such sweeps had not generated sustained direct contact with the VC, but Charlie Company still had suffered a significant number of losses to snipers, mines, and booby-trap incidents.

My Lai 4 comprised a cluster of hamlets (small groups of houses) that formed part of the larger Son My village complex. The Americans believed that My Lai housed the headquarters of the Viet Cong local-force 48th Battalion, which had inflicted heavy losses on Charlie Company during the previous weeks. The U.S. plan called for an airmobile assault (delivery of troops by helicopter) into My Lai 4 to arrive shortly after the local women had departed for market.

Instead when Calley's platoon entered the hamlet, they found the village occupied by noncombatants, mainly the elderly, children, and women still cooking breakfast. The U.S. soldiers began indiscriminately shooting people as they ran from their huts. Survivors were systematically rounded up, led to a nearby ditch, and executed. As the unit continued its sweep of the hamlet, more villagers were killed and huts and bunkers destroyed by fire and explosives. The killing stopped only when Warrant Officer Hugh Thompson, an aero-scout pilot supporting the operation, landed his helicopter between the Americans and some fleeing Vietnamese and confronted the soldiers. By this time, Lt. Calley and the platoon had killed an estimated 350–500 Vietnamese civilians. One American soldier in Charlie Company had been wounded by friendly fire.

THE INVESTIGATION

Due to a massive cover-up by the brigade and division staffs, details of the massacre only came to light a year later, thanks to the efforts of a former soldier, Ronald Ridenhour. Ridenhour, a veteran of the 11th Infantry Brigade in Vietnam, had learned of the events by talking to members of Charlie Company, who had participated in it. His letters to various officials generated a number of news stories. The publicity finally prompted the Secretary of the Army to open an investigation under the direction of Lieutenant General Williams Peers.

By the time the investigation had ended, several officers and men who had been involved had been killed in action. This included LTC Barker. Others had already received honorable discharges. The Peers Inquiry identified thirty persons who were aware of the atrocities. Decisions were made to prosecute a total of twenty-five officers and enlisted men, including Major General Samuel Koster, Colonel Oran Henderson, and Captain Ernest Medina; however, only fourteen were charged with crimes. All but Lt. Calley, the most junior officer, either had the charges dropped or were acquitted by a court-martial.

THE UNIFORM CODE OF MILITARY JUSTICE

Calley was tried at a general court-martial as prescribed in the UCMJ. The UCMJ defines the military justice system and lists criminal offenses under military law. A general court-martial is reserved for the most serious offenses, such as murder, rape, or robbery. A general court-martial includes a military judge, the accused, prosecuting and defense attorneys, and a panel of at least five members. A general court-martial may impose any sentence authorized by the *Manual for Courts-Martial* if the defendant is found guilty of the offenses charged.

DOCUMENT: THE UNIFORM CODE OF MILITARY JUSTICE

What:	The Congressional Code of Military Criminal Law applicable to all military members worldwide.
Where:	Washington, D.C.
Source:	*Manual for Courts-Martial, United States* (2012 ed.). Online at http://www.au.af.mil/au/awc/awcgate/law/mcm.pdf.
Significance:	The UCMJ includes the relevant law from international treaties the United States has ratified as well as laws, regulations, and procedures duly enacted by the Congress. Procedures in a court-martial reflect those of civilian trials. Accused are presumed innocent until proven guilty, have a right of representation, the right to know the evidence against them, the right to call witnesses on their behalf, and to give testimony of their own. The following excerpt deals with the trial record and sentencing.

SUBCHAPTER VIII
SENTENCES

854. Art. 54. Record of Trial

(a) Each general court-martial shall deep a separate record of the proceedings in each case brought before it, and the record shall be authenticated by the signature of the military judge. If the record cannot be authenticated by the military judge by reason of his death, disability, or absence, it shall be authenticated by the signature of the trial counsel or by that of a member if the trial counsel is unable to authenticate it by reason of his death, disability, or absence. In a court-martial consisting of only a military judge the record shall be authenticated by the court reporter under the same conditions which would impose such a duty on a member under the subsection.

(b) Each special and summary court-martial shall keep a separate record of the proceedings in each case, and the record shall be authenticated in the manner required by such regulations as the President may prescribe.

(c) (1) A complete record of the proceedings and testimony shall be prepared—

(A) in each general court-martial case in which the sentence adjudged includes death, a dismissal, a discharge, or (if the sentence adjudged does not include a discharge) or any other punishment which exceeds that which may otherwise be adjudged by a special court-martial; and

(B) in each special court-martial case in which the sentence includes a bad-conduct discharge.

(2) In all other court-martial cases, the record shall contain such matters as may be prescribed by regulations of the President.

(d) A copy of the record of the proceedings of each general and special court-martial shall be given to the accused as soon as it is authenticated.

SUBCHAPTER VIII
SENTENCES

855. Art. 55. Cruel and Unusual Punishments Prohibited.

Punishment by flogging, or by branding, marking, or tattooing on the body, or any other cruel or unusual punishment, may not be adjudged by a court-martial or inflicted upon any person subject to this chapter. The use of irons, single or double, except for the purpose of safe custody, is prohibited.

856. Art. 56. Maximum Limits

The punishment which a court-martial may direct for an offense may not exceed such limits as the President may prescribe for that offense.

857. Art. 57. Effective Date of Sentences

(a) No forfeiture may extend to any pay or allowances accrued before the date on which the sentence is approved by the person acting under section 860(c) of this title (article 60(c)).

(b) Any period of confinement included in a sentence of a court-martial begins to run from the date the sentence is adjudged by the court-martial, but periods during which the sentence to confinement is suspended or deferred shall be excluded in computing the service of the term of confinement.

(c) All other sentences of courts-martial are effective on the date ordered executed.

(d) On application by an accused who is under sentence to confinement that has not been ordered executed, the convening authority, or, if the accused is no longer under his jurisdiction, the officer exercising general court-martial jurisdiction over the command to which the accused is currently assigned, may in his sole discretion defer service of the sentence to confinement. The deferment shall terminate when the sentence is ordered executed. The deferment may be rescinded at any time by the officer who granted it or, if the accused is no longer under his jurisdiction, by the officer exercising general court-martial jurisdiction over the command to which the accused is currently assigned.

858. Art. 58. Execution of Confinement

(a) Under such instructions as the Secretary concerned may prescribe, a sentence of confinement adjudged by a court-martial or other military tribunal, whether or not the sentence includes discharge or dismissal, and whether or not the discharge or dismissal has been executed, may be carried into execution by confinement in any place of confinement under the control of any of the armed forces or in any penal or correctional institution under the control of the United States, or which the United States may be allowed to use. Persons so confined in a penal or correctional institution not under the control of one of the armed forces are subject to the same discipline and treatment as persons confined or committed by the courts of the United States or of the State, Territory, District of Columbia, or place in which the institution is situated.

(b) The omission of the words "hard labor" from any sentence of a court-martial adjudging confinement does not deprive the authority executing that sentence of the power to require hard labor as a part of the punishment.

TRIAL SUMMARY #14: *UNITED STATES V. CALLEY*

As the full extent of My Lai unfolded, the senior military commanders in Vietnam had to think about the verdict and reasoning in the trial of General Tomoyuki Yamashita. Calley's defense turned on superior orders, but the validity of superior orders depends on the principle of *command responsibility*. The U.S. Tribunal had convicted Yamashita of war crimes for the mass murders, rapes, and other atrocities committed by Japanese troops in Manila. The court found Yamashita guilty for not exercising command responsibility even though testimony showed that he did not personally give orders and that the actions of enemy forces had hindered his ability to communicate with the units involved. In upholding the *Yamashita* decision, the U.S. Supreme Court had adopted the very strict standard that General Yamashita "should have known." From a practical standpoint, the decision in the *Yamashita* case set a very bad precedent because it assigned ultimate command responsibility to the most senior commanders who may not have issued any orders or had any constructive information about the incident. This may explain why none of the trials associated with the My Lai incident raised the issue of command responsibility.

DOCUMENT: *UNITED STATES V. WILLIAM LAWS CALLEY JR.*

When:	December 21, 1970–March 29, 1971
Where:	Ft. Benning, Georgia
Court:	U.S. Military Court Martial
Defendant:	Lt. William L. Calley
Source:	*United States v. Calley*, 48 C.M.R. 19 (C.M.A. 1973), United States National Archives. Online at http://www.famous-trials.com/mylaicourts/1608-myl-calt.
Charge:	Four specifications alleging premeditated murder in violation of Article 118 of Uniform Code of Military Justice:
Defense:	Superior orders
Verdict:	Guilty in twenty-two cases; life imprisonment; reduced to twenty years on appeal.

Significance: Of fourteen originally charged, Lt. Calley, the most junior officer, was the only one convicted.

Facts: Colonel Oran K. Henderson visited the Task Force Barker command post prior to the attack. In a briefing with the senior officers, he stressed the importance of locating and eliminating the 48th LF Battalion. After his remarks, Lt. Colonel (LTC) Barker and his staff gave an intelligence briefing and issued an operations order. The intelligence briefing identified most of the population of Son My as "VC or VC sympathizers." It assumed that most of the civilian inhabitants would be away from Son My and on their way to market by 7:00 a.m. The operation would begin at 7:25 a.m. At some undetermined point either during, or shortly after, the briefing, LTC Barker ordered the company commanders to burn the houses, kill the livestock, destroy foodstuffs, and perhaps to close the wells. No instructions were given concerning the treatment of noncombatants found there. The subsequent briefing by Captain Medina to his men emphasized that only the enemy would be present in My Lai and that the enemy was to be destroyed.

Testimony

Paul Meadlo, Witness for the Prosecution

Q: Where did you get these people?
A: Some of them was in hooches and some was in rice paddies when we gathered them up.
Q: Why did you gather them up?
A: We suspected them of being Viet Cong. And as far as I'm concerned, they're still Viet Cong. . . .
Q: What did you do when you got there?
A: Just guarded them.
Q: Did you see Lieutenant Calley?
A: Yes.
Q: What did he do?
A: He came up to me and he said, "You know what to do with them, Meadlo," and I assumed he wanted me to guard them. That's what I did.
Q: What were the people doing?
A: They were just standing there. . . .
A: [Calley] said, "How come they're not dead?" I said, I didn't know we were supposed to kill them." He said, "I want them dead." He backed off twenty or thirty feet and started shooting into the people—the Viet Cong—shooting automatic. He was beside me. He burned four or five magazines. I burned off a few, about there. I helped shoot 'em.
Q: What were the people doing after you shot them?
A: They were lying down.

Q: Why were they lying down?
A: They was mortally wounded.
Q: How were you feeling at that time?
A: I was mortally upset, scared, because of the briefing we had the day before.
Q: Were you crying?
A: I imagine I was . . .
Q: Were there any Vietnamese there?
A: Yes, there was Viet Cong there. About seventy-five to a hundred, standing outside the ravine. . . .
A: Then Lieutenant Calley said to me, "We've got another job to do, Meadlo."
Q: What happened then?
A: He started shoving them off and shooting them in the ravine.
Q: How many times did he shoot?
A: I can't remember.
Q: Did you shoot?
A: Yes. I shot the Viet Cong. He ordered me to help kill people. I started shoving them off and shooting.
Q: How long did you fire?
A: I don't know.
Q: Did you change magazines?
A: Yes.
Q: Did Lieutenant Calley change magazines?
A: Yes.
Q: How many times did he change magazines?
A: Ten to fifteen times.
Q: How many bullets in a magazine?
A: Twenty, normally.
Q: How was Lieutenant Calley armed?
A: He had a M-16.

Lt. William Calley questioned by his defense attorney [emphasis added]

Q: Now, I will ask you if during these periods of instruction and training, you were instructed by anybody in connection with the Geneva Conference [*sic*]?
A: Yes, sir, I was.
Q: And what was it—do you have a recollection, what was the extent and nature of that tutoring?
A: I know there were classes. I can't remember any of the classes. Nothing stands out in my mind what was covered in the classes, sir.
Q: Did you learn anything in those classes of what actually the Geneva Convention covered as far as rules and regulations of warfare are concerned?
A: No, sir. Laws and rules of warfare, sir.
Q: Did you receive any training in any of those places which had to do with obedience to orders?
A: Yes, sir.

Q: What were the nature of the—what were you informed was the principles involved in that field?
A: That all orders were to be assumed legal, that the soldier's job was to carry out any order given him to the best of his ability.
Q: Did you tell your doctor or inform him anything about what might occur if you disobeyed an order by a senior officer?
A: You could be court-martialed for refusing an order and refusing an order in the face of the enemy, you could be sent to death, sir.
Q: Well, let me ask you this: what I am talking and asking is whether or not you were given any instructions on the necessity for— or whether you were required in any way, shape or form to make a determination of the legality or illegality of an order?
A: No, sir. I was never told that I had the choice, sir.
Q: If you had a doubt about the order, what were you supposed to do?
A: If I had—questioned an order, I was supposed to carry the order out and then come back and make my complaint later.
Q: Now, during the course of your movement through the village, had you seen any Vietnamese dead, or dead bodies?
A: Yes, sir.
Q: And how would you classify it as to whether it was a few, many, how would you—what descriptive phrase would you use for your own impression?
A: Many.
Q: Now, did you see some live Vietnamese while you were going through the village?
A: I saw two, sir.
Q: All right. Now, tell us, was there an incident concerning those two?
A: Yes, sir. I shot and killed both of them.
Q: Under what circumstances?
A: There was a large concrete house and I kind of stepped up on the porch and looked in the window. There was about six to eight individuals laying on the floor, apparently dead. And one man was going for the window. I shot him. There was another man standing in a fireplace. He looked like he had just come out of the fireplace, or out of the chimney. And I shot him, sir. He was in a bright green uniform. . . .
Q: All right. Now that you gave that incident, did you see any other live individuals who were in the village itself as you made through the sweep?
A: Well, when I got to the eastern edge of the village, I saw a group of Vietnamese just standing right outside the eastern edge of the village, sir, the southeastern edge.
Q: All right. Was there anybody there with that group of individuals that you saw at that time?
A: I recollect that there were GI's there with them. . . .
A: I heard a considerable volume of firing to my north, and I moved along the edge of the ditch and around a hootch and I broke into the clearing, and my men had a number of Vietnamese in the ditch and were firing upon them.
Q: When you say your men, can you identify any of the men?
A: I spoke to Dursi and I spoke to Meadlo, sir.

Q: Was there anybody else there that you can identify by name?
A: No, sir. There was a few other troops, but it was insignificant to me at the time and I didn't—
Q: What was your best impression of how many were there at the ditch?
A: Four to five, sir.
Q: Two of whom you can specifically identify, Meadlo and Dursi?
A: Yes, sir. I spoke to those two.
Q: What did you do after you saw them shooting in the ditch?
A: Well, I fired into the ditch also sir . . .
Q: Now, did you have a chance to look and observe what was in the ditch?
A: Yes, sir.
Q: And what did you see?
A: Dead people, sir.
Q: Let me ask you, at any time that you were alone and near the ditch, did you push or help push people into the ditch?
A: Yes and no, sir.
Q: Give us the yes part first.
A: Well, when I came out of this hedgerow, I came right up—came right up about the last man to go into the ditch. I didn't physically touch him, but if he would have stopped, I guess I would have.
Q: Well, did he—was somebody there with him to order him in or push him in?
A: They had been ordered in—to go to the ditch, sir.
Q: Do you know who gave them that information?
A: Well, indirectly, I did, sir.
Q: And indirectly, what do you mean by that, was it through somebody?
A: I had told Meadlo to get them on the other side of the ditch, sir. . . .
Q: All right. Then what did you do?
A: I butt-stroked him in the mouth, sir.
Q: With what effect?
A: It knocked him down.
Q: Did you shoot him?
A: No, sir, I did not. . . .
Q: Let me ask you another—your impressions of another incident. There has been some testimony in the record to the effect that there was a child running from the ditch, that you threw him back into the ditch and you shot him. Did you participate in any such event?
A: No, sir, I did not.
Q: Did you see a boy or a child running from the ditch?
A: Wait, let me backtrack. Now this child that I supposedly said I shot, now, was running away from the ditch, but it is not in the same location. It is east of the ditch, but he was running away from the ditch. Now, I don't—
Q: To the extent that you shot and it turned out ultimately to be a child, is that the only impression you have of any incident which involved a child?
A: Yes, sir, I do.
Q: There has been some information disclosed that you heard before the court that you stood there at the ditch for a considerable period of time; that you waited and had your troops organized, groups of Vietnamese thrown in the

ditch and knocked them down in the ditch or pushed them in the ditch and that you fired there for approximately and hour and a half as those groups were marched up. Did you participate in any such shooting or any such event?
A: No, sir, I did not.
Q: Did you at any time direct anybody to push people in the ditch?
A: Like I said, I gave the order to take those people through the ditch and had also told Meadlo if he couldn't move them, to waste them, and I directly— other than that, there was only that one incident. I never stood up there for any period of time. The main mission was to get my men on the other side of the ditch and get in that defensive position, and that is what I did, sir.
Q: Now, why did you give Meadlo a message or the order that if he couldn't get rid of them to waste them?
A: Because that was my order, sir. That as the order of the day, sir.
Q: Who gave you that order?
A: My commanding officer, sir.
Q: He was?
A: Captain Medina, sir.
Q: And stated in that posture, in substantially those words, how many times did you receive such an order from Captain Medina?
A: The night before in the company briefing, platoon leaders' briefing, the following morning before we lifted off and twice there in the village.

AFTERMATH

Despite direct testimony and the findings of the Peers Report, the convictions in the My Lai case went no further up the chain of command than to Lt. Calley. As the only conviction resulting from the investigation and indictments, the military system of justice essentially declared that Calley bore full responsibility for the events at My Lai. The Army dropped all charges against General Koster because the investigation determined that his actions "did not show any intentional abrogation of responsibilities." Koster, who served as the Superintendent of the U.S. Military Academy at West Point at the time, was slated for promotion to the rank of lieutenant general. Because of his involvement in the My Lai cover-up he did not receive the promotion. Instead, further inquiries led to his censure and demotion one rank (to Brigadier General) for failing to conduct an adequate investigation. Court-martials found Colonel Henderson and Captain Medina not guilty on all charges. In Medina's case, the *New York Times* (September 23, 1971) reported that the jury of five combat officers deliberated only 60 minutes before reaching a verdict of not guilty.

Calley was found guilty of murdering twenty-two civilians and sentenced to life imprisonment. Public opinion saw Calley as the scapegoat because his superior officers had escaped punishment. After he had served only three months in the stockade, President Richard Nixon ordered him confined to quarters pending review of the case. The Court of Military Appeals reduced his sentence to twenty years. The Secretary of the Army further reduced the sentence to ten years. In

November 1974, a Federal District Court judge in Georgia, citing "prejudicial publicity," ruled that Calley was convicted unjustly and granted bail (*Calley v. Callaway*, 382 F. Supp. 650 (M.D. Ga. 1974)). The army vigorously disputed the intervention of the civilian court, arguing lack of jurisdiction. When the Fifth Circuit Court of Appeals reinstated the conviction in 1975 (496 F.2d 701 (5th Cir. 1974)), the Secretary of the Army brought closure to the case by granting Calley a parole for "good behavior." Calley actually served a total of only three and a half years, with most of that time under house arrest in his quarters at Fort Benning, Georgia.

The intervention of the Federal District Court prior to the hearing by the CAAF in this case was highly unusual. Normally, only military verdicts that impose the death penalty or raise serious constitutional issues are subject to review; and, in those cases, the Supreme Court has exclusive jurisdiction (see *Yamashita* case). Otherwise, as discussed earlier, the two systems of justice run parallel on totally separate tracks.

The prosecution did find a Supreme Court decision dealing with Korean War POWs limited its ability to indict some of those accused. Once individuals have been discharged from military service, they are no longer subject to the UCMJ unless they maintain some essential connection such as reserve status. While former service personnel may be subpoenaed as witnesses, they cannot be charged for offenses committed while in uniform (*United States ex rel. Toth v. Quarles*, 350 U.S. 11 (1955)). Because of the limited territorial and subject matter jurisdiction of U.S. civilian courts with respect to alleged offenses committed outside the United States, former service members are literally "home free" when discharged.

CHANGES

Answers to the obvious question of "why did My Lai happen" fall outside the rather narrow scope of this discussion; however, the shocks to the Army caused by the war in Vietnam in general, and My Lai in particular, led to major changes. To its credit, the Army immediately began to initiate upgrades in training for both officers and enlisted personnel aimed at building a more professional army. In particular, everyone now received extensive instruction and training in appropriate battlefield conduct which included: "the reporting of war crimes; the proper treatment of civilians, non-combatants, and prisoners of war; the protection of property; the adherence to the rules of engagement; and the enforcement of the Hague and Geneva Conventions as integral parts of the law of war" (Jones 2017, 346). A career soldier recently stated that sometimes he felt that he needed his own personal lawyer to accompany him on a combat mission.

In the first chapter of this book, the objections to the idea that conduct in war can be governed by rules were examined. The emphasis on ethical conduct on the battlefield has been tested again and again by contemporary conflicts that have graphically raised the question: "Why should we conduct ourselves according to the rules when the other side does not?" The enemies may have changed, but the answers have not.

References

Belknap, Michael R. 2002. *The Vietnam War on Trial: The My Lai Massacre and the Court-Martial of Lieutenant Calley.* Lawrence: University Press of Kansas.

Jones, Howard. 2017. *My Lai: Vietnam 1968, and the Descent into Darkness.* New York: Oxford University Press.

Linder, Douglas O. n.d. "Famous Trials: The My Lai Massacre and Courts-Martial: An Account." http://famous-trials.com/mylaicourts/1656-myl-intro.

Olson, James S., and Randy Roberts. 1998. *My Lai: A Brief History with Documents.* New York: Bedford/St. Martin's.

Report of the Department of the Army Review of the Preliminary Investigations into the My Lai Incident (Peers Report). https://www.loc.gov/rr/frd/Military_Law/Peers_inquiry.html.

Uniform Code of Military Justice, 64 Stat.109, 10 U.S.C. §§ 801–946. http://www.ucmj.us/.

20

Updating the Rules of War after World War II

WHAT CHANGED?

World War I changed attitudes about the utility of war as a useful tool of foreign policy. Advances in technology made World War II even more devastating. The destruction of Dresden in Europe and the use of the atomic bomb on Hiroshima and Nagasaki outlined a very grim future for the world if the resort to force was not controlled.

THE UNITED NATIONS CHARTER

The Covenant of the League of Nations did not outlaw the resort to force. Much debate has occurred over the impact and relevance of the Kellogg-Briand Pact. Many saw this instrument as providing the legal basis for prosecuting Nazi and Japanese Leaders for "crimes against peace." Others have steadfastly insisted that because it did not have enforcement measures, the treaty had little legal significance beyond being a statement of vague aspirations. In contrast, the Charter of the United Nations set up a system of collective security that clearly meant to restrict the unilateral use of force by states to only *self-defense*. The model draws upon the basic premise of domestic systems of law and order where the lawful use of armed force against criminal violators rests with the community in the form of a police function. Within specified limits, individual members of the community do have a right to act to protect themselves in emergency situations until the police arrive.

Similarly, under the UN Charter if an armed conflict occurs, states have the right to use self-defense until the central organization takes appropriate action to help subdue the aggressor. Within the United Nations, the 15-member Security Council has the special duty to assess situations that may threaten "peace and security" and recommend appropriate action. If the Security Council determines that a threat exists and passes a resolution that lays out a course of action, all 193 member states have a positive duty to assist in the action.

Document: The Charter of the United Nations

When:	August 12, 1945
Where:	San Francisco, October 24, 1945
Source:	Charter of the United Nations. Signed June 26, 1945; Came into force October 24, 1945. Online at http://www.un.org/en/charter-united-nations/.
Status:	193 members. The extent of acceptance means that the provisions of the Charter may also be considered as customary law, thus binding those states and other entities that have not signed and ratified.
Significance:	The first truly comprehensive attempt to outlaw the unilateral use of force by states in pursuit of conquest or other aggressive policy goals. As do the Geneva Conventions discussed later in this chapter, the Charter avoids use of the word "war," speaking instead of armed conflict or armed attack.

CHAPTER II

MEMBERSHIP

Article 2.3

All Members shall settle their international disputes by peaceful means in such a manner that international peace and security, and justice, are not endangered.

Article 2.4

All Members shall refrain in their international relations from the *threat or use of force* [emphasis added] against the territorial integrity or political independence of any state, or in any other manner inconsistent with the Purposes of the United Nations.

CHAPTER VII

ACTION WITH RESPECT TO THREATS TO THE PEACE, BREACHES OF THE PEACE, AND ACTS OF AGGRESSION

Article 39

The Security Council shall determine the existence of any threat to the peace, breach of the peace, or act of aggression and shall make recommendations, or decide what measures shall be taken in accordance with Articles 41 and 42, to maintain or restore international peace and security.

Article 40

In order to prevent an aggravation of the situation, the Security Council may, before making the recommendations or deciding upon the measures provided for in Article 39, call upon the parties concerned to comply with such provisional measures as it deems necessary or desirable. Such provisional measures shall be without prejudice to the rights, claims, or position of the parties concerned. The Security Council shall duly take account of failure to comply with such provisional measures.

Article 41

The Security Council may decide what measures not involving the use of armed force are to be employed to give effect to its decisions, and it may call upon the Members of the United Nations to apply such measures. These may include complete or partial interruption of economic relations and of rail, sea, air, postal, telegraphic, radio, and other means of communication, and the severance of diplomatic relations.

. . .

Article 48.1

The action required to carry out the decisions of the Security Council for the maintenance of international peace and security shall be taken by all the Members of the United Nations or by some of them, as the Security Council may determine.

Article 48. 2

Such decisions shall be carried out by the Members of the United Nations directly and through their action in the appropriate international agencies of which they are members.

Article 49

The Members of the United Nations shall join in affording mutual assistance in carrying out the measures decided upon by the Security Council.

. . .

Article 51

Nothing in the present Charter shall impair the inherent right of *individual or collective self-defense if an armed attack occurs* [emphasis added] against a Member of the United Nations, until the Security Council has taken the measures necessary to maintain international peace and security. Measures taken by Members in the exercise of this right of self-defense shall be immediately reported to the Security Council and shall not in any way affect the authority and responsibility of the Security Council under the present Charter to take at any time such action as it deems necessary in order to maintain or restore international peace and security.

CHAPTER VIII
REGIONAL ARRANGEMENTS
Article 52.1
Nothing in the present Charter precludes the existence of regional arrangements or agencies for dealing with such matters relating to the maintenance of international peace and security as are appropriate for regional action, provided that such arrangements or agencies and their activities are consistent with the Purposes and Principles of the United Nations.

Article 52.2
The Members of the United Nations entering into such arrangements or constituting such agencies shall make every effort to achieve pacific settlement of local disputes through such regional arrangements or by such regional agencies before referring them to the Security Council.

. . .

Article 53.1
The Security Council shall, where appropriate, utilize such regional arrangements or agencies for enforcement action under its authority. But no enforcement action shall be taken under regional arrangements or by regional agencies without the authorization of the Security Council.

THE GENEVA CONVENTIONS

While the word "war" continues to be used to describe situations of extreme conflict, the term now has little juridical content. In the post–World War II world, because the UN Charter limits the use of force to self-defense, states have attempted to delete the term "war" from their diplomatic vocabulary when justifying the resort to force. To use the United States as an example, history texts may refer to the Korean War, but officially, even though ostensibly authorized by the UN, President Truman and the U.S. Senate chose to label it a "police action." The U.S. Congress never officially enacted a formal declaration of war for Korea nor has it done so for any of the major conflicts after. The international conventions that form the basis of contemporary law use *armed conflict* in place of war to avoid extended debates about whether a situation meets the formal criteria for war. The International Committee of the Red Cross (ICRC) maintains that the application of international humanitarian law (IHL) does not depend on the existence of a formal state of war.

Once again, calls to strengthen and extend the law of armed conflict followed World War II. The effort produced a fourth Geneva Convention in 1949, and three additional Protocols or amendments (two in 1977, one in 2005) that establish the standards of international law for humanitarian treatment in armed conflicts (IHL). These conventions do not deal with weapons or potential weapons. They focus on providing protection for individuals in an armed conflict who should be considered noncombatants or for those who can no longer take part because of capture (POWs), wounds, incapacitating illness, or shipwreck.

DOCUMENT: THE 1949 GENEVA CONVENTIONS

When:	August 12, 1949
Where:	Geneva, Switzerland
Source:	International Committee of the Red Cross. Online at https://www.icrc.org/eng/assets/files/publications/icrc-002-0173.pdf.
Status:	196 ratifications. The extent of acceptance means that the provisions of the Convention may also be considered as customary law, thus binding those states that have not signed and ratified.
Significance:	The convention updates, expands, and incorporates three prior treaties and adds a fourth to provide explicit protections for civilians/noncombatants, an area not directly addressed in prior treaties. The four Conventions were designed to govern conduct during all armed conflicts. The overall treaty constitutes an innovation in that the Geneva Diplomatic Conference sought to group together and amplify the common provisions. Now all four have certain basic provisions that apply to everyone. For example, no individual can lose or give up the rights granted to them by the Conventions. All states parties to the Convention must observe its provisions even if they are involved in a conflict with another party who has not formally accepted the Conventions. The Conventions also contain procedures for their application and for the settlement of disputes.

GENEVA CONVENTION FOR THE AMELIORATION OF THE CONDITIONS OF THE WOUNDED AND SICK IN ARMED FORCES IN THE FIELD OF AUGUST 12, 1949 (GENEVA I)

This Convention aims to ensure the protection of and respect for the rights of the wounded and sick during times of war, including making all possible effort to find the sick and wounded; keeping records of sick, wounded, and dead; identifying the dead; and providing humane burials. It also covers civilians who are sick and wounded in the field. Article 14 states: "The wounded and sick of a belligerent who fall into enemy hands shall be prisoners of war, and the provisions of international law concerning prisoners of war shall apply to them." The Convention outlines acts that may not be carried out against the people covered by the Convention, including murder, torture, hostage-taking, and humiliating treatment. The Convention also establishes the rights and obligations of medical units and medical establishments, designates who constitutes medical personnel, delineates what buildings and materials are covered, and demands respect for medical transports.

CHAPTER II
WOUNDED AND SICK
Article 12

Members of the armed forces and other persons mentioned in the following Article, who are wounded or sick, shall be respected and protected in all circumstances. They shall be treated humanely and cared for by the Party to the conflict in whose power they may be, without any adverse distinction founded on sex, race, nationality, religion, political opinions, or any other similar criteria. Any attempts upon their lives, or violence to their persons, shall be strictly prohibited; in particular, they shall not be murdered or exterminated, subjected to torture or to biological experiments; they shall not willfully be left without medical assistance and care, nor shall conditions exposing them to contagion or infection be created. Only urgent medical reasons will authorize priority in the order of treatment to be administered. Women shall be treated with all consideration due to their sex. The Party to the conflict which is compelled to abandon wounded or sick to the enemy shall, as far as military considerations permit, leave with them a part of its medical personnel and material to assist in their care.

...

Article 14

Subject to the provisions of Article 12, the wounded and sick of a belligerent who fall into enemy hands shall be prisoners of war, and the provisions of international law concerning prisoners of war shall apply to them.

Article 15

At all times, and particularly after an engagement, Parties to the conflict shall, without delay, take all possible measures to search for and collect the wounded and sick, to protect them against pillage and ill-treatment, to ensure their adequate care, and to search for the dead and prevent their being despoiled. Whenever circumstances permit, an armistice or a suspension of fire shall be arranged, or local arrangements made, to permit the removal, exchange and transport of the wounded left on the battlefield. Likewise, local arrangements may be concluded between Parties to the conflict for the removal or exchange of wounded and sick from a besieged or encircled area, and for the passage of medical and religious personnel and equipment on their way to that area.

GENEVA CONVENTION FOR THE AMELIORATION OF THE CONDITIONS OF WOUNDED, SICK, AND SHIPWRECKED MEMBERS OF ARMED FORCES AT SEA OF AUGUST 12, 1949 (GENEVA II)

This is a revision of the 10th Hague Convention of October 18, 1907 and an adaptation of the Maritime Warfare of the Principles of the Geneva Convention of

1906. It applies to all forces on board ship and outlines the rights of a belligerent to demand the surrender of the sick, wounded, and shipwrecked. The Convention also establishes rules governing the disposition of prisoners of war; seeking out the wounded; recording and burying the dead (including burial on land if dead people were landed); protection of hospital ships, including the rights of a belligerent to search a ship and remove the sick and wounded if there is an appropriate place to put them and the current vessel is needed. In addition, it delineates what medical personnel are covered and specifies the rights of medical transports.

WOUNDED, SICK AND SHIPWRECKED
Article 12

Members of the armed forces and other persons mentioned in the following Article, who are at sea and who are wounded, sick or shipwrecked, shall be respected and protected in all circumstances, it being understood that the term "shipwreck" means shipwreck from any cause and includes forced landings at sea by or from aircraft . . . (See Convention I, Article 12)

HOSPITAL SHIPS
Article 22

Military hospital ships, that is to say, ships built or equipped by the Powers specially and solely with a view to assisting the wounded, sick and shipwrecked, to treating them and to transporting them, may in no circumstances be attacked or captured, but shall at all times be respected and protected, on condition that their names and descriptions have been notified to the Parties to the conflict ten days before those ships are employed.

The characteristics which must appear in the notification shall include registered gross tonnage, the length from stem to stern and the number of masts and funnels.

GENEVA CONVENTION RELATIVE TO THE TREATMENT OF PRISONERS OF WAR OF AUGUST 12, 1949 (GENEVA III)

This Convention includes a description of who constitutes a prisoner of war, what acts may not be carried out against a prisoner of war, under what conditions the Convention applies to prisoners of war, and the requirement for humane treatment. Article 14 states: "Women shall be treated with all the regard due to their sex and shall in all cases benefit by treatment as favorable as that granted to men." The Convention requires that medical treatment be available if necessary and protects the personal effects of prisoners of war. It also sets out the living conditions under which prisoners of war may be held, relating to shelter, hygiene, water provision, food, clothing, etc. It addresses the status of medical and religious personnel, and questions of rank. The Convention permits appropriate types of paid labor and establishes procedures for securing the financial resources of prisoners of war and keeping accounts. It outlines what relations a prisoner of war may have with the exterior, including mail, censorship, and packages. It provides rights for prisoners to complain about the conditions of their captivity and establishes what disciplinary sanctions may be taken against prisoners of war. The Convention specifies that seriously wounded or sick prisoners should be repatriated, that death certificates must be completed for any prisoners of war who die in captivity, and that suspicious deaths must be subjected to inquiry. The Convention requires all parties to a conflict to establish an information agency for prisoners of war and states that all prisoners must be released and repatriated at the end of hostilities.

Article 4

A. Prisoners of war, in the sense of the present Convention, are persons belonging to one of the following categories, who have fallen into the power of the enemy:

1) Members of the armed forces of a Party to the conflict as well as members of militias or volunteer corps forming part of such armed forces.

2) Members of other militias and members of other volunteer corps, including those of organized resistance movements, belonging to a Party to the conflict and operating in or outside their own territory, even if this territory is occupied, provided that such militias or volunteer corps, including such organized resistance movements, fulfil the following conditions:

    a) that of being commanded by a person responsible for his subordinates;
    b) that of having a fixed distinctive sign recognizable at a distance;
    c) that of carrying arms openly;
    d) that of conducting their operations in accordance with the laws and customs of war.

3) Members of regular armed forces who profess allegiance to a government or an authority not recognized by the Detaining Power.

4) Persons who accompany the armed forces without actually being members thereof, such as civilian members of military aircraft crews, war correspondents, supply contractors, members of labour units or of services responsible for the welfare of the armed forces, provided that they have received authorization from the armed forces which they accompany, who shall provide them for that purpose with an identity card similar to the annexed model.

5) Members of crews, including masters, pilots and apprentices of the merchant marine and the crews of civil aircraft of the Parties to the conflict, who do not benefit by more favourable treatment under any other provisions of international law.

6) Inhabitants of a non-occupied territory who, on the approach of the enemy, spontaneously take up arms to resist the invading forces, without having had time to form themselves into regular armed units, provided they carry arms openly and respect the laws and customs of war.

B. The following shall likewise be treated as prisoners of war under the present Convention:

1) Persons belonging, or having belonged, to the armed forces of the occupied country, if the occupying Power considers it necessary by reason of such allegiance to intern them, even though it has originally liberated them while hostilities were going on outside the territory it occupies, in particular where such persons have made an unsuccessful attempt to rejoin the armed forces to which they belong and which are engaged in combat, or where they fail to comply with a summons made to them with a view to internment.

2) The persons belonging to one of the categories enumerated in the present Article, who have been received by neutral or non-belligerent Powers on their territory and whom these Powers are required to intern under international law . . . [text omitted]

GENEVA CONVENTION FOR THE PROTECTION OF CIVILIAN PERSONS IN TIME OF WAR OF AUGUST 12, 1949 (GENEVA IV)

This is the first convention that explicitly addresses the idea that civilians should enjoy immunity from deliberate attack. It was a response to tactics and strategies in World War II, which made large numbers of civilian subject to indiscriminate attack, mass extermination, deportation, and hostage-taking. This Convention does not protect anyone who benefits from the provisions of any of the other three Conventions, or who is suspected of carrying out activities hostile to the party in whose territory they are situated. It is directed at protecting populations of countries that are party to a conflict, including those in occupied areas. Provisions entail the right to protect safe zones for the wounded and sick, children, the elderly, mothers of young children, or pregnant women. The Convention denotes that civilian hospitals must not be attacked and that medical personnel and other related personnel must be protected even if they are resident in an occupied area. Article 27 states, "Women shall be especially protected against any attack on their honor, in particular against rape, enforced prostitution, or any form of indecent assault."

The Convention outlines the rights of people living in occupied territories, specifying that the occupying power cannot put protected civilians at risk and noting the obligation to facilitate the education of children and medical care for all protected people. It establishes grounds for internment, provides regulations for how internees must be treated, and guarantees the personal property of internees. The Convention governs relations with the exterior. It includes procedures for informing interned people of their status and what their rights are under the Convention.

Article 4

Persons protected by the Convention are those who at a given moment and in any manner whatsoever, find themselves, in case of a conflict or occupation, in the hands of persons a Party to the conflict or Occupying Power of which they are not nationals. Nationals of a State which is not bound by the Convention are not protected by it. Nationals of a neutral State who find themselves in the territory of a belligerent State, and nationals of a co-belligerent State, shall not be regarded as protected persons while the State of which they are nationals has normal diplomatic representation in the State in whose hands they are. The provisions of Part II are, however, wider in application, as defined in Article 13. Persons protected by the Geneva Convention for the Amelioration of the Condition of the Wounded and Sick in Armed Forces in the Field of August 12, 1949, or by the Geneva Convention for the Amelioration of the Condition of Wounded, Sick and Shipwrecked Members of Armed Forces at Sea of August 12, 1949, or by the Geneva Convention relative to the Treatment of Prisoners of War of August 12, 1949, shall not be considered as protected persons within the meaning of the present Convention.

THE COMMON ARTICLES

All four of the 1949 Geneva Convention treaties contain the following two articles. The ICRC maintains that the provisions apply to both sides in a conflict regardless of how the war started; that is, it does not matter if one side started the conflict through the resort to an illegal use of force. Common Article 2 of the 1949 Geneva Conventions states:

Article 2

In addition to the provisions which shall be implemented in peacetime, the present Convention shall apply to all cases of declared war or of any other armed conflict which may arise between two or more of the High Contracting Parties, even if the state of war is not recognized by one of them. The Convention shall also apply to all cases of partial or total occupation of the territory of a High Contracting Party, even if the said occupation meets with no armed resistance. Although one of the Powers in conflict may not be a party to the present Convention, the Powers who are parties thereto shall remain bound by it in their mutual relations. They shall furthermore be bound by the Convention in relation to the said Power, if the latter accepts and applies the provisions thereof.

Common Article 3 extends the scope of the Conventions to "armed conflict not of an international character." *It is the only article in the four Geneva Convention treaties that specifically references non-international conflicts.* Some have described the article as a mini-convention within itself because it contains the essential rules of the Geneva Conventions in a condensed format and makes them applicable to conflicts *not of an international character* (i.e., civil wars). In another weird twist of international law, when Common Article 3 applies, it totally governs—no other parts of the Geneva Convention apply.

Article 3

In the case of armed conflict not of an international character occurring in the territory of one of the High Contracting Parties, each Party to the conflict shall be bound to apply, as a minimum, the following provisions:

1) Persons taking no active part in the hostilities, including members of armed forces who have laid down their arms and those placed hors de combat by sickness, wounds, detention, or any other cause, shall in all circumstances be treated humanely, without any adverse distinction founded on race, colour, religion or faith, sex, birth or wealth, or any other similar criteria. To this end, the following acts are and shall remain prohibited at any time and in any place whatsoever with respect to the above-mentioned persons:

   a) violence to life and person, in particular murder of all kinds, mutilation, cruel treatment and torture;
   b) taking of hostages;
   c) outrages upon personal dignity, in particular humiliating and degrading treatment;
   d) the passing of sentences and the carrying out of executions without previous judgment pronounced by a regularly constituted court, affording all the judicial guarantees which are recognized as indispensable by civilized peoples.

2) The wounded and sick shall be collected and cared for. An impartial humanitarian body, such as the International Committee of the Red Cross, may offer its services to the Parties to the conflict. The Parties to the conflict should further endeavour to bring into force, by means of special agreements, all or part of the other provisions of the present Convention. The application of the preceding provisions shall not affect the legal status of the Parties to the conflict.

THE ADDITIONAL PROTOCOLS

Post–World War II, non-international conflicts have been far more prevalent than traditional state versus state clashes. A study conducted by the Department of Peace and Conflict Research at Uppsala University categorized and analyzed all armed conflicts that had occurred following World War II. Of the 225 armed conflicts that had taken place between 1946 and 2001, 163 were internal armed conflicts. Only forty-two qualified as inter-state or international armed conflicts. The remaining conflicts were categorized as "extra-state," defined as a conflict involving a state and a non-state group. Often the non-state group was acting from the territory of a third state. In most of these conflicts, civilian/noncombatant casualties have far outnumbered the military losses. At present, dealing with non-state armed groups such as ISIS forms a prime dilemma for contemporary law-makers and policy-makers.

Prior to the Geneva conference that met in 1974, no systematic effort to update the laws and customs of war had occurred since the Hague Conventions of 1899 and 1907. The reaffirmation and enhancement were important because of the age of the Hague Conventions and the fact that the anticolonial movement had more than doubled the number of states. Former colonies had now become independent and demanded the right to participate in the revision of rules in which they originally had no input in making. These states felt that the 1949 Geneva Convention did not sufficiently address many of their concerns. Another diplomatic conference in Geneva (1974–1977) produced two additional treaties regarded as amendments to the original 1949 Conventions:

- Protocol Additional to the Geneva Conventions of 12 August 1949, and relating to the Protection of Victims of International Armed Conflicts (Protocol Additional I), 8 June 1977, and
- Protocol Additional to the Geneva Conventions of 12 August 1949, and relating to the Protection of Victims of Non-International Armed Conflicts (Protocol Additional II), 8 June 1977.

DOCUMENT: GENEVA PROTOCOL ADDITIONAL I

When; June 8, 1977
Where: Geneva, Switzerland
Source: International Committee of the Red Cross. Online at https://ihl-databases.icrc.org/ihl/INTRO/470.
Status: 174 States Parties; the United States has ratified.
Significance: Primarily sponsored by the states that had become newly independent during the "anticolonial" revolution beginning in the mid-1950s, Protocol Additional I extends the definition of *international armed conflicts* by adding those "in which peoples are fighting against colonial domination, alien occupation or racist regimes."

Article 1

General principles and scope of application

1. The High Contracting Parties undertake to respect and to ensure respect for this Protocol in all circumstances.

2. In cases not covered by this Protocol or by other international agreements, civilians and combatants remain under the protection and authority of the principles of international law derived from established custom, from the principles of humanity and from the dictates of public conscience.

3. This Protocol, which supplements the Geneva Conventions of 12 August 1949 for the protection of war victims, shall apply in the situations referred to in Article 2 common to those Conventions.

4. The situations referred to in the preceding paragraph include armed conflicts in which peoples are fighting against *colonial domination and alien occupation and against racist régimes in the exercise of their right of self-determination, as enshrined in the Charter of the United Nations and the Declaration on Principles of International Law concerning Friendly Relations and Co-operation among States in accordance with the Charter of the United Nations* [emphasis added].

[Articles 5–34 omitted]

Article 35

Basic Rules

1. In any armed conflict, the right of the Parties to the conflict to choose methods or means of warfare is not unlimited.

2. It is prohibited to employ weapons, projectiles and material and methods of warfare of a nature to cause superfluous injury or unnecessary suffering.

3. It is prohibited to employ methods or means of warfare which are intended, or may be expected, to cause widespread, long-term and severe damage to the natural environment.

[Articles 36–42 omitted]

Article 43

Armed Forces

1. The armed forces of a Party to a conflict consist of all organized armed forces, groups and units which are under a command responsible to that Party for the conduct of its subordinates, even if that Party is represented by a government or an authority not recognized by an adverse Party. Such armed forces shall be subject to an internal disciplinary system which, "inter alia," shall enforce compliance with the rules of international law applicable in armed conflict.

2. Members of the armed forces of a Party to a conflict (other than medical personnel and chaplains covered by Article 33 of the Third Convention) are combatants, that is to say, they have the right to participate directly in hostilities.

3. Whenever a Party to a conflict incorporates a paramilitary or armed law enforcement agency into its armed forces it shall so notify the other Parties to the conflict.

[Articles 44–46 omitted]

Article 47

Mercenaries

1. *A mercenary shall not have the right to be a combatant or a prisoner of war* [emphasis added].

2. A mercenary is any person who:
   (a) is specially recruited locally or abroad in order to fight in an armed conflict;
   (b) does, in fact, take a direct part in the hostilities;
   (c) is motivated to take part in the hostilities essentially by the desire for private gain and, in fact, is promised, by or on behalf of a Party to the conflict, material compensation substantially in excess of that promised or paid to combatants of similar ranks and functions in the armed forces of that Party;
   (d) is neither a national of a Party to the conflict nor a resident of territory controlled by a Party to the conflict;
   (e) is not a member of the armed forces of a Party to the conflict; and
   (f) has not been sent by a State which is not a Party to the conflict on official duty as a member of its armed forces.

[Articles 48–51 omitted]

Article 52

General Protection of Civilian Objects

1. Civilian objects shall not be the object of attack or of reprisals. Civilian objects are all objects which are not military objectives as defined in paragraph 2.

2. Attacks shall be limited strictly to military objectives. In so far as objects are concerned, military objectives are limited to those objects which by their nature, location, purpose or use make an effective contribution to military action and whose total or partial destruction, capture or neutralization, in the circumstances ruling at the time, offers a definite military advantage.

3. In case of doubt whether an object which is normally dedicated to civilian purposes, such as a place of worship, a house or other dwelling or a school, is being used to make an effective contribution to military action, it shall be presumed not to be so used.

Article 1.4 embodies the concerns of the new states by adding struggles against "colonial domination, alien occupation or racist regimes" to the legitimate uses of armed force. Articles 8–34 extend the rules of the First and the Second Geneva Conventions (1949) on wounded, sick, and shipwrecked to civilian medical transport, personnel, equipment, and supplies. Articles 25–60 update rules on the conduct of hostilities. In particular, Article 43 gives a new definition of armed forces and combatants. It defines "the armed forces of a Party to a conflict" and provides that the members of such armed forces are combatants, subject to some exceptions.

Article 47 outlawing mercenaries came from concerns generated by the extensive use of mercenary forces in the Congolese and Nigerian civil wars that ensued after they became independent states. Even today, mercenaries have found their way into conflicts in many countries in Africa and elsewhere. Article 47 led to the creation of a separate treaty that sought to ban the recruitment, use, financing, and training of mercenaries. Unfortunately, the Convention simply incorporated the definition of mercenary contained in Article 47.2 (https://treaties.un.org/pages/

ViewDetails.aspx?src=TREATY&mtdsg_no=XVIII-6&chapter=18&clang=_en). Most legal commentaries view the definition as deeply flawed because of potential loopholes and issues in application. The treaty opened for signature and ratification in 1989 but did not enter into force until October 2001. The Convention currently has 35 States Parties. No major military power has ratified the treaty.

Among the most important provisions are Articles 48–60, which deal with the protection of the civilian population from the effects of hostilities. They contain a precise definition of military objectives (Article 52) and strengthen the prohibition against attacks on civilian persons and objects. Articles 61–79 deal with the protection of civil defense organizations, relief actions, and the treatment of persons in the power of a party to a conflict.

DOCUMENT: GENEVA PROTOCOL ADDITIONAL II

When:	June 8, 1977
Where:	Geneva, Switzerland
Source:	International Committee of the Red Cross. Online at https://ihl-databases.icrc.org/ihl/INTRO/475.
Status:	168 Parties. The United States has not ratified this treaty.
Significance:	Protocol Additional II attempts to provide better protection for victims of internal armed conflicts—those that take place within the borders of a single country. The scope of Protocol Additional II is much more limited than the provisions in the rest of the Geneva Conventions because of limitations imposed by respect for the sovereign rights and duties of national governments. The treaty refines and extends the obligations in Common Article 3 of the 1949 Conventions. Nonetheless, since end of World War II in 1945, non-international armed conflict has been responsible for 80 percent of the victims of armed conflict.

Article 1

Material Field of Application

1. This Protocol, which develops and supplements Article 3 common to the Geneva Conventions of 12 August 1949 without modifying its existing conditions of applications, shall apply to all armed conflicts which are not covered by Article 1 of the Protocol Additional to the Geneva Conventions of 12 August 1949, and relating to the Protection of Victims of International Armed Conflicts (Protocol I) and which take place in the territory of a High Contracting Party between its armed forces and dissident armed forces or other organized armed groups which, under responsible command, exercise such control over a part of its territory as to enable them to carry out sustained and concerted military operations and to implement this Protocol.

2. This Protocol shall not apply to situations of internal disturbances and tensions, such as riots, isolated and sporadic acts of violence and other acts of a similar nature, as not being armed conflicts.

[Article 2 omitted]

Article 3

Non-intervention

1. Nothing in this Protocol shall be invoked for the purpose of affecting the sovereignty of a State or the responsibility of the government, by all legitimate means, to maintain or re-establish law and order in the State or to defend the national unity and territorial integrity of the State.

2. Nothing in this Protocol shall be invoked as a justification for intervening, directly or indirectly, for any reason whatever, in the armed conflict or in the internal or external affairs of the High Contracting Party in the territory of which that conflict occurs.

Article 4

Fundamental Guarantees

1. All persons who do not take a direct part or who have ceased to take part in hostilities, whether or not their liberty has been restricted, are entitled to respect for their person, honour and convictions and religious practices. They shall in all circumstances be treated humanely, without any adverse distinction. It is prohibited to order that there shall be no survivors.

2. Without prejudice to the generality of the foregoing, the following acts against the persons referred to in paragraph 1 are and shall remain prohibited at any time and in any place whatsoever:

    a) violence to the life, health and physical or mental well-being of persons, in particular murder as well as cruel treatment such as torture, mutilation or any form of corporal punishment;
    b) collective punishments;
    c) taking of hostages,
    d) acts of terrorism;
    e) outrages upon personal dignity, in particular humiliating and degrading treatment, rape, enforced prostitution and any form of indecent assault;
    f) slavery and the slave trade in all their forms;
    g) pillage;
    h) threats to commit any of the foregoing acts.

3. Children shall be provided with the care and aid they require, and in particular:

    a) they shall receive an education, including religious and moral education, in keeping with the wishes of their parents, or in the absence of parents of those responsible for their care;
    b) all appropriate steps shall be taken to facilitate the reunion of families temporarily separated;
    c) children who have not attained the age of fifteen years shall neither be recruited in the armed forces or groups nor allowed to take part in hostilities;
    d) the special protection provided by this Article to children who have not attained the age of fifteen years shall remain applicable to them if they

take a direct part in hostilities despite the provisions of sub-paragraph c) and are captured;

e) measures shall be taken, if necessary, and whenever possible with the consent of their parents or persons who by law or custom are primarily responsible for their care, to remove children temporarily from the area in which hostilities are taking place to a safer area within the country and ensure that they are accompanied by persons responsible for their safety and well-being.

[Article 5 omitted]

Article 6

Penal Prosecutions

1. This Article applies to the prosecution and punishment of criminal offences related to the armed conflict.

2. No sentence shall be passed and no penalty shall be executed on a person found guilty of an offence except pursuant to a conviction pronounced by a court offering the essential guarantees of independence and impartiality. In particular:

   a) the procedure shall provide for an accused to be informed without delay of the particulars of the offence alleged against him and shall afford the accused before and during his trial all necessary rights and means of defence;
   b) no one shall be convicted of an offence except on the basis of individual penal responsibility;
   c) no one shall be held guilty of any criminal offence on account of any act or omission which did not constitute a criminal offence, under the law, at the time when it was committed; nor shall a heavier penalty be imposed than that which was applicable at the time when the criminal offence was committed; if, after the commission of the offence, provision is made by law for the imposition of a lighter penalty, the offender shall benefit thereby;
   d) anyone charged with an offence is presumed innocent until proved guilty according to law;
   e) anyone charged with an offence shall have the right to be tried in his presence;
   f) no one shall be compelled to testify against himself or to confess guilt.

3. A convicted person shall be advised on conviction of his judicial and other remedies and of the time-limits within which they may be exercised.

4. The death penalty shall not be pronounced on persons who were under the age of eighteen years at the time of the offence and shall not be carried out on pregnant women or mothers of young children.

5. At the end of hostilities, the authorities in power shall endeavour to grant the broadest possible amnesty to persons who have participated in the armed conflict, or those deprived of their liberty for reasons related to the armed conflict, whether they are interned or detained.

[Articles 7–12 omitted]

PROTECTION OF CIVILIAN POPULATION

Article 13

Protection of the Civilian Population

1. The civilian population and individual civilians shall enjoy general protection against the dangers arising from military operations. To give effect to this protection, the following rules shall be observed in all circumstances.

2. The civilian population as such, as well as individual civilians, shall not be the object of attack. Acts or threats of violence the primary purpose of which is to spread terror among the civilian population are prohibited.

3. Civilians shall enjoy the protection afforded by this Part, unless and for such time as they take a direct part in hostilities.

Article 14

Protection of Objects Indispensable to the Survival of the Civilian Population

Starvation of civilians as a method of combat is prohibited. It is therefore prohibited to attack, destroy, remove or render useless, for that purpose, objects indispensable to the survival of the civilian population, such as foodstuffs, agricultural areas for the production of foodstuffs, crops, livestock, drinking water installations and supplies and irrigation works.

[Articles 15–16 omitted]

Article 17

Prohibition of Forced Movement of Civilians

1. The displacement of the civilian population shall not be ordered for reasons related to the conflict unless the security of the civilians involved or imperative military reasons so demand. Should such displacements have to be carried out, all possible measures shall be taken in order that the civilian population may be received under satisfactory conditions of shelter, hygiene, health, safety and nutrition.

2. Civilians shall not be compelled to leave their own territory for reasons connected with the conflict.

Article 18

Relief Societies and Relief Actions

1. Relief societies located in the territory of the High Contracting Party, such as Red Cross (Red Crescent, Red Lion and Sun) organizations, may offer their services for the performance of their traditional functions in relation to the victims of the armed conflict. The civilian population may, even on its own initiative, offer to collect and care for the wounded, sick and shipwrecked.

2. If the civilian population is suffering undue hardship owing to a lack of the supplies essential for its survival, such as foodstuffs and medical supplies, relief actions for the civilian population which are of an exclusively humanitarian and impartial nature and which are conducted without any adverse distinction shall be undertaken subject to the consent of the High Contracting Party concerned.

Article 3.1 illustrates the inherent tension between sovereign rights and the interests of the greater international community in trying to design rules that regulate major internal disturbances. States are particularly sensitive to any new initiative that might diminish prerogatives that they perceive as an absolute right. The sections on the protection of civilian population also point up a significant problem. Combatants in civil wars often intentionally intermingle with the civilian population or use ostensibly civilian facilities for parts of their campaigns. Terroristic actions against civilians is a common tactic, not only by rebels, but sometimes by governments against people seen as shielding or aiding those involved in a conflict. Actions in internal wars tend to be more brutal than in inter-state wars.

DOCUMENT: PROTOCOL ADDITIONAL III (2005)

When: December 8, 2005
Where: Geneva, Switzerland
Source: International Committee of the Red Cross. Online at https://ihl-databases.icrc.org/ihl/INTRO/615.
Significance: Set rules for the adoption of a distinctive protective symbol to designate medical personnel and facilities as well as other qualified persons and places.

The egoism of twentieth-century international politics produced a controversy over the distinctive protective symbol used to designate medical and other personnel. The First Geneva Convention recognized the Red Cross on a white background as the single distinctive emblem. Since the emblem needed to reflect the neutrality of the medical services of all countries and the protection conferred on them, the new emblem reversed the colors of the Swiss flag. During the war between Russia and Turkey, the Ottoman Empire declared that it would use the Red Crescent on a white background in place of the Red Cross. While respecting the Red Cross symbol, the Ottoman authorities believed that the Red Cross was, by its very nature, offensive to Muslim soldiers. The Red Crescent was temporarily accepted for the duration of this conflict.

After the World War I, a 1929 Diplomatic Conference was called to revise the Geneva Conventions. The Turkish, Persian, and Egyptian delegations requested that the Red Crescent and the Red Lion and Sun be recognized. After lengthy discussions, the Conference agreed to recognize them as distinctive emblems in addition to the Red Cross; but, to avoid any proliferation of emblems, it limited the authorization to the three countries that already used them.

At the 1949 Geneva Conference, Israel proposed to add the red Shield of David. Arab States resisted on the basis that the six-point star was a religious symbol. Other emerging states proposed their own new protective emblems: Afghanistan proposed a red archway, India a red wheel, Lebanon a red cypress tree, Sudan a red rhinoceros, Zaire a red lamb, and Sri Lanka a red swastika. A December 2005 conference in Geneva produced Protocol Additional III (PA-III) to the 1949 Geneva Conventions that added the *red crystal*. A state that opts to use the red crystal may add its own smaller emblem inside the open diamond. The convention entered into force in January 2007. At this writing the Convention has 70 State Parties.

Article 2

Distinctive Emblems

1. This Protocol recognizes an additional distinctive emblem in addition to, and for the same purposes as, the distinctive emblems of the Geneva Conventions. The distinctive emblems shall enjoy equal status.

2. This additional distinctive emblem, composed of a red frame in the shape of a square on edge on a white ground, shall conform to the illustration in the Annex to this Protocol. This distinctive emblem is referred to in this Protocol as the "third Protocol emblem"

3. The conditions for use of and respect for the third Protocol emblem are identical to those for the distinctive emblems established by the Geneva Conventions and, where applicable, the 1977 Additional Protocols.

4. The medical services and religious personnel of armed forces of High Contracting Parties may, without prejudice to their current emblems, make temporary use of any distinctive emblem referred to in paragraph 1 of this Article where this may enhance protection.

Article 3

Indicative Use of the Third Protocol Emblem

1. National Societies of those High Contracting Parties which decide to use the third Protocol emblem may, in using the emblem in conformity with relevant national legislation, choose to incorporate within it, for indicative purposes:

   a) a distinctive emblem recognized by the Geneva Conventions or a combination of these emblems; or
   b) another emblem which has been in effective use by a High Contracting Party and was the subject of a communication to the other High Contracting Parties and the International Committee of the Red Cross through the depositary prior to the adoption of this Protocol.

   Incorporation shall conform to the illustration in the Annex to this Protocol.

GRAVE BREACHES AND WAR CRIMES

The Conventions distinguish between minor violations and serious crimes. The most serious crimes are termed grave breaches and provide a legal definition of a war crime. For example, grave breaches identified in all four treaties of the 1949 Convention include the following acts if committed against a person protected by the convention:

- willful killing;
- torture or inhuman treatment;
- biological experiments;
- willfully causing great suffering;
- causing serious injury to body or health;

States Parties to these treaties must enact and enforce legislation penalizing these crimes. Nations are obligated to search for and bring to trial persons alleged to have committed these crimes and persons who ordered them to be committed. This obligation authorizes states to exercise jurisdiction regardless of the nationality of the accused or the specific place where the alleged crimes took place.

MOVING FROM THE LAW ON THE BOOKS TO MAKING THE LAW WORK IN ACTION

Four important observations apply here. First, for IHL to apply, someone in authority must make a determination that an armed conflict exists. Do hostilities between states require a certain level of intensity and protracted time frame before IHL applies, or does it apply to any resort to force between states? Opinion remains divided on this issue. No clear guidelines defining specific threshold conditions for international armed conflict have emerged from the practice of the ad hoc tribunals. Prosecutors have treated this issue as an *evidentiary* one to be determined with respect to the specific circumstances of each individual case.

Second, to what extent do the rules applicable to international armed conflicts apply to internal armed conflicts? Here we see an interesting evolution. While Geneva PA-II significantly extended the regulations applicable to internal armed conflict, many still questioned whether the law of war crimes applied. The early 1990s witnessed an upsurge in internal conflicts that often had severe consequences for surrounding states. In drafting the Statute for the International Criminal Tribunal for Rwanda (ICTR), the Security Council had to deal expressly with the question of war crimes and internal armed conflict. It did so by directly incorporating common Article 3 of the Geneva conventions and most of the provisions of PA-II into the Statute. Shortly after, the ICTY Appeals Chamber in the *Tadić* case took the issue head on suggesting that a number of rules and principles (including common Article 3) applied to internal conflicts. The Rome Statute of the International Criminal Court explicitly identified and incorporated some core rules, indicating some convergence between the two regimes.

Third, the question of distinguishing an internal conflict where the rules would apply from a riot or other relatively minor disorders remains an open question. Authorities agree that, time (conflict is of a protracted nature), intensity, and level of organization are the essential criteria. Many other technical questions not germane to this discussion remain open.

Fourth, *not all crimes committed during an armed conflict are war crimes.* The criminal conduct must be not only within the context of the conflict but also associated with the conflict. Ordinary crimes remain ordinary crimes to be prosecuted by local authorities if they do not meet the twin test. A rape or murder committed by a civilian against another civilian within the geographic and temporal area of a conflict does not necessarily constitute a war crime. To assess the nature of the crime, one must take into account the status of the perpetrator, the status of the victim, and the intent of the act.

References

Corn, Geoffrey S., Victor Hansen, Richard Jackson, and M. Christopher Jenks. 2012. *The Law of Armed Conflict: An Operational Approach.* New York: Wolters Kluwer.

Sandoz, Yves. 2014. "Land Warfare." In *The Oxford Handbook of International Law in Armed Conflict*, edited by Andrew Clapham and Paolo Gaeta, 81–117. Oxford: Oxford University Press.

Solis, Gary D. 2009. *The Law of Armed Conflict: International Humanitarian Law in War.* Cambridge: Cambridge University Press.

Taulbee, James Larry. 2017. "The Contemporary Law Relating to Armed Conflict: What Is a War Crime?" In *Genocide, Mass Atrocity, and War Crimes in Modern History*, vol. 2, *War Crimes*, 71–104. Santa Barbara, CA: Praeger.

21

The Genocide Convention

THE GENOCIDE CONVENTION: THE POLITICS OF DEFINITION

Prior to World War II, no single term encompassed all aspects of the Holocaust. Raphael Lemkin coined the term *genocide* by combining the Greek word *genos* (race, tribe) and the Latin *cide* (killing). Lemkin's own brief definition was simple: "the destruction of a nation or of an ethnic group." Individuals become victims solely because of their identity as members of the national or ethnic group. Although the Genocide Convention was crafted and adopted immediately after World War II, the first indictment, trial, and conviction for genocide by an international court did not occur until fifty years later when the International Criminal Tribunal for Rwanda (ICTR) found Jean-Paul Akayesu guilty for his actions during the 1994 Rwandan conflict.

After World War II, the move to create an international agreement to deal with the new crime of genocide rapidly gained ground among the members of the newly formed United Nations. In one of its first acts, in 1946 the UN General Assembly (UNGA) approved Resolution 95(1) entitled "Affirmation of the Principles of International Law Recognized by the Nuremberg Charter." This Resolution did not attempt to formulate the Nuremberg principles in detail. The General Assembly adopted Resolution 96(1) "The Crime of Genocide" on the same day. The first paragraph of the resolution defined genocide as: "the denial of the right of existence of entire human groups, as homicide is the denial of the right to live of individual human beings." The resolution also noted that "Many instances of such crimes of genocide have occurred when racial, religious, political, and other groups have been destroyed entirely, or in part."

The important point here is that the UN General Assembly does not have any authority to legislate in the sense of making new rules of binding law for member states of the UN. Even so, Resolution 96(1) stands as an important symbol in terms of the actual drafting of the convention. Because it passed unanimously and without debate, Resolution 96(1) had enormous value in that it provided a strong expression of sentiment concerning the issue, as does the relatively quick adoption of the Genocide Convention. Despite its revolutionary subject matter, the treaty entered into force within three years after it opened for signature.

First, the treaty separated genocide from the broader "crimes against humanity" and eliminated the inadvertent, but unfortunate, Nuremberg connection with the precondition of international armed conflict. *Genocide may occur in a time of peace as well as a strategy during war.* Second, it clearly stated that genocide constituted a crime for which both private individuals and public officials could be prosecuted. Official position could not be used as a defense to avoid liability. Third, it established the principle that individuals could be punished under international law even if no breach of domestic law had occurred.

But, the fifty-year gap where states ignored many massacres such as those in Uganda and Cambodia underlines the fact that a considerable gap existed between rhetorical support and effective action. We can see this in that, almost immediately, divisions appeared over what groups and what actions should be included in the proposed convention. These divisions had much to do with the evolving post–World War II political climate. The increasing split between the USSR and the Western powers that became the Cold War, the issues of Palestine, India/Pakistan/Kashmir, and the rising anticolonial movement all played a part. Consider also that between 1960 and 1980, the number of independent states almost doubled. In 1958, the United Nations had 82 members; at the end of 1980, it had 154 members.

Document: Convention on the Prevention and Punishment of the Crime of Genocide

When: Approved December 9, 1948, entered into force January 12, 1951
Where: New York City, New York
Source: A/RES/260 (III). 9 December 1948. United Nations. Online at http://www.ohchr.org/EN/ProfessionalInterest/Pages/CrimeOfGenocide.aspx
Significance: Defines the crime of genocide for the international community

The Contracting Parties,

Having considered the declaration made by the General Assembly of the United Nations in its resolution 96 (I) dated 11 December 1946 that genocide is a crime under international law, contrary to the spirit and aims of the United Nations and condemned by the civilized world,

Recognizing that at all periods of history genocide has inflicted great losses on humanity, and

Being convinced that, in order to liberate mankind from such an odious scourge, international co-operation is required,

Hereby agree as hereinafter provided:

Article I
The Contracting Parties confirm that genocide, whether committed in time of peace or in time of war, is a crime under international law which they undertake to prevent and to punish.

Article II
In the present Convention, genocide means any of the following acts committed with intent to destroy, in whole or in part, a national, ethnical, racial or religious group, as such:

(a) Killing members of the group;
(b) Causing serious bodily or mental harm to members of the group;
(c) Deliberately inflicting on the group conditions of life calculated to bring about its physical destruction in whole or in part;
(d) Imposing measures intended to prevent births within the group;
(e) Forcibly transferring children of the group to another group.

Article III
The following acts shall be punishable:

(a) Genocide;
(b) Conspiracy to commit genocide;
(c) Direct and public incitement to commit genocide;
(d) Attempt to commit genocide;
(e) Complicity in genocide.

Article IV
Persons committing genocide or any of the other acts enumerated in article III shall be punished, whether they are constitutionally responsible rulers, public officials or private individuals.

Article V
The Contracting Parties undertake to enact, in accordance with their respective Constitutions, the necessary legislation to give effect to the provisions of the present Convention, and, in particular, to provide effective penalties for persons guilty of genocide or any of the other acts enumerated in article III.

Article VI
Persons charged with genocide or any of the other acts enumerated in article III shall be tried by a competent tribunal of the State in the territory of which the act was committed, or by such international penal tribunal as may have jurisdiction with respect to those Contracting Parties which shall have accepted its jurisdiction.

Article VII
Genocide and the other acts enumerated in article III shall not be considered as political crimes for the purpose of extradition.

The Contracting Parties pledge themselves in such cases to grant extradition in accordance with their laws and treaties in force.

Article VIII
Any Contracting Party may call upon the competent organs of the United Nations to take such action under the Charter of the United Nations as they consider

appropriate for the prevention and suppression of acts of genocide or any of the other acts enumerated in article III.

Article IX
Disputes between the Contracting Parties relating to the interpretation, application or fulfilment of the present Convention, including those relating to the responsibility of a State for genocide or for any of the other acts enumerated in article III, shall be submitted to the International Court of Justice at the request of any of the parties to the dispute.

Article X
The present Convention, of which the Chinese, English, French, Russian and Spanish texts are equally authentic, shall bear the date of 9 December 1948.

Article XI
The present Convention shall be open until 31 December 1949 for signature on behalf of any Member of the United Nations and of any non-member State to which an invitation to sign has been addressed by the General Assembly.

The present Convention shall be ratified, and the instruments of ratification shall be deposited with the Secretary-General of the United Nations.

After 1 January 1950, the present Convention may be acceded to on behalf of any Member of the United Nations and of any non-member State which has received an invitation as aforesaid.

Instruments of accession shall be deposited with the Secretary-General of the United Nations.

Article XII
Any Contracting Party may at any time, by notification addressed to the Secretary-General of the United Nations, extend the application of the present Convention to all or any of the territories for the conduct of whose foreign relations that Contracting Party is responsible.

Article XIII
On the day when the first twenty instruments of ratification or accession have been deposited, the Secretary-General shall draw up a procès-verbal and transmit a copy thereof to each Member of the United Nations and to each of the non-member States contemplated in article XI.

The present Convention shall come into force on the ninetieth day following the date of deposit of the twentieth instrument of ratification or accession.

Any ratification or accession effected subsequent to the latter date shall become effective on the ninetieth day following the deposit of the instrument of ratification or accession.

Article XIV

The present Convention shall remain in effect for a period of ten years as from the date of its coming into force.

It shall thereafter remain in force for successive periods of five years for such Contracting Parties as have not denounced it at least six months before the expiration of the current period.

Denunciation shall be effected by a written notification addressed to the Secretary-General of the United Nations.

Article XV

If, as a result of denunciations, the number of Parties to the present Convention should become less than sixteen, the Convention shall cease to be in force as from the date on which the last of these denunciations shall become effective.

Article XVI

A request for the revision of the present Convention may be made at any time by any Contracting Party by means of a notification in writing addressed to the Secretary-General.

The General Assembly shall decide upon the steps, if any, to be taken in respect of such request.

[Articles XVII–XIX on "housekeeping arrangements" omitted]

INNOVATIONS AND PROBLEMS

Lemkin's 1944 book had a major impact, even though the term *genocide* had not yet entered into general usage at the time the Allies prepared the Charter for the Nuremberg trial of Nazi leaders. The definition adopted in Article II of the Convention on the Prevention and Punishment of the Crime of Genocide drew primarily on Lemkin's original formulation. Not unexpectedly, the definition received much criticism for being a political compromise, and hence, much too narrow. Compare the difference between the inclusive thrust of the definition in Resolution 96(1), "entire human groups," and the strict specification of groups protected by Article II of the convention. The Convention does not include cultural genocide (ethnocide) or actions taken against political groups. It does not specify criteria that give substance to many of the operative terms. For example, does genocide entail a certain number or a certain percentage of a certain number of a targeted group? It does not spell out who has the right to assess a violation, then apprehend, try, and punish the alleged crime. The Convention defines a crime but has no provisions for punishment. The original proposals did envisage an international court that would have jurisdiction to try offenses under the proposed Code of Crimes against the Peace and Security of Mankind that would presumably include genocide. After a rocky start, the effort to develop the code and the court lay in abeyance until resurrected in the late 1980s. Spurred by the end of the Cold War and events in Yugoslavia and Rwanda, a renewed effort in the 1990s would result in the establishment of the International Criminal Court (ICC).

References

LeBlanc, Lawrence J. 1991. *The United States and the Genocide Convention.* Durham, NC: Duke University Press.

Lemkin, Raphael. 1944. *Axis Rule in Occupied Europe: Laws of Occupation, Analysis of Government, Proposals for Redress.* Washington, DC: Carnegie Endowment for International Peace.

Taulbee, James Larry. 2017. *Genocide, Mass Atrocity and War Crimes in Modern History: Blood and Conscience.* Vol. 1: *Genocide and Mass Atrocity.* Santa Barbara, CA: Praeger.

22

The International Criminal Tribunal for the Former Yugoslavia

Between the end of the trials conducted at Nuremberg and the genocidal wars in the former Yugoslavia and Rwanda in the early 1990s, war crimes prosecution remained within the domain of the state. No international court existed that had the jurisdiction and mandate to try offenses for charges under the newly emergent "international criminal law" (ICL), which had gained acceptance from the prosecutions at Nuremberg and Tokyo, and from other trials in the wake of World War II. Beginning in the mid-1950s, the anticolonial movement produced many new states as former colonies gained their independence. After independence these new states jealously guarded their sovereignty. Their sensitivity to any hint of intervention in their domestic affairs by those who had been their former imperial masters combined with the politics of the Cold War produced a climate that precluded any overt intervention in the affairs of other states that enforcement would have required. The international community paid little attention to situations where massive violations of human rights had occurred until Yugoslavia began to disintegrate in 1991. The situation produced two great ironies. First, the promise of "never again" became "again and again" as Idi Amin (Uganda), Pol Pot (Cambodia), and Jean-Bédel Bokassa (Central African Republic), among many others carried out their murderous schemes with impunity (for a summary, see Genocide Watch 2008)).

The second irony stems from the fact that these killings occurred during the same period that witnessed major achievements in the development of international human rights—at least on paper. The landmark treaties generally considered as the "International Bill of Human Rights" were all developed, signed, and ratified in this period.

YUGOSLAVIA

The end of the Cold War (1989–1990) saw the development of several conflicts caused by the breakup of Yugoslavia. From its creation after World War I until the country finally broke apart in the early 1990s, Yugoslavia was an unstable state composed of many ethnic (cultural) and religious groups. The Kingdom of Serbs, Croats, and Slovenes was officially established immediately after the end of World War I (December 1918) under the leadership of Serbian king Peter Karađorđević (Karageorgevich). Although a unified Slavic state was never the goal of these Balkan ethnic groups, most political leaders realized that unification was their best option, at the moment. These hopes proved overly optimistic, however. Over the protests of both Croats and Slovenes, a constitution adopted in 1921 created a centralized government predominantly under Serbian control. Over the next several years, non-Serbian groups grew increasingly bitter and disenchanted with the kingdom's government. They opposed the dominant influence of the Serbs in the central government and wanted more authority to make decisions about their own affairs.

Yugoslavia came close to total disintegration during World War II when ethnic tensions resulted in mutual slaughter by Serbs and Croats in a bloody civil war. Marshal Tito (Josip Broz), a communist leader who had led a partisan Serbian faction that successfully fought against the Axis during World War II, became prime minister in the immediate postwar government. He became president in 1953 and president for life in 1960. His political skills and personality kept the country relatively peaceful until his death in 1980. Tito dealt with national aspirations by creating a federation of six nominally equal republics: Croatia, Montenegro, Serbia, Slovenia, Bosnia and Herzegovina, and Macedonia. In Serbia the two provinces of Kosovo and Vojvodina were given autonomous status. The increased autonomy given to Kosovo by changes in the Yugoslav Constitution would eventually be one of the issues that led to the unraveling of the federation. Communist rule restored stability and good relations with the West and ensured a steady stream of loans and aid.

After Tito's death, his successors, in attempts to increase their own personal influence, adopted policies that divided rather than united. Reacting to what they perceived as a Serbian ambition to dominate the federation, in 1991 first Slovenia, then Croatia declared independence. Slobodan Milošević, president of Serbia, sought to ensure Serbian dominance in areas in Bosnia and Croatia inhabited by large Serb populations. With their campaign of ethnic cleansing, the Serbs succeeded in killing or forcing out much of the Muslim Bosniak and Croatian populations from large parts of Bosnia. The drive by Serbia to resist secession and maintain its authority over these areas and produced a number of ugly incidents that included the shelling of Dubrovnik and Sarajevo, the devastation of Vukovar, and the massacre at Srebrenica.

The international community was extremely slow in reacting to the conflicts. In October 1992, the UN Security Council voted to establish a five-member commission of experts to investigate war crimes in the former Yugoslavia. Even though the Security Council provided almost no funding and did little to assist the investigators, the commission raised 3 million dollars from private sources. It submitted the longest report in Security Council history: 3,500 written pages and 300 hours of videotaped interviews and other evidence. Other UN agencies had joined in the investigation as well. The UN Commission on Human Rights (UNCHR) convened a first ever special session and appointed a special rapporteur. The Commission broke new ground in its statements on the conflict by referring to concern about the possibility of genocide in Bosnia and Herzegovina.

This contrasted with the reluctance of the Security Council to use the word *genocide*. None of the permanent members of the Security Council seemed to have any interest in bringing the issue to discussion until media reports detailing the carnage began to appear and influence public opinion. Even then, many questions remained. Diplomats working to resolve the crisis were dead set against trials. They believed the threat of prosecution would deal a severe blow to efforts to negotiate a settlement *because many of those who might be accused of committing or condoning serious crimes were seen as necessary players in resolving the conflict*. The friction between those involved in the diplomatic process of resolving a situation and those who desire to bring individuals seen as criminals to justice has been a major problem in a number of high-profile cases.

Given the ambiguities of its jurisdiction to deal with internal conflicts, the Security Council faced other questions related to its authority to establish a court of any type. This is a different issue from that in the Tadić trial (discussed in the next chapter), where the question became the applicability of certain parts of international humanitarian law to internal conflicts. This issue raised the question, did the conflict affect international peace and security to the extent that Article 2(7) (domestic jurisdiction clause in the UN Charter) did not rule out action by the Security Council.

The question whether the Security Council had the power to create an ad hoc court did not have a simple answer. Article 29 of the UN Charter would seem to grant broad powers to the Security Council: "The Security Council may establish such subsidiary organs as it deems necessary for the performance of its functions." Article 41 provides that:

> The Security Council may decide what measures *not involving* the use of armed force are to be employed to give effect to its decisions, and it may call upon the Members of the United Nations to apply such measures. These may include complete or partial interruption of economic relations and of rail, sea, air, postal, telegraphic, radio, and other means of communication, and the severance of diplomatic relations. (emphasis added)

Reading Article 41 as a list of examples, not as one exhausting all possibilities, would clearly establish authority to establish any entities deemed necessary to the work of the Security Council. Additionally a 1954 Advisory Opinion from the International Court of Justice had upheld the right of the Security Council to establish subsidiary bodies, including tribunals. The technical problem lay in the fact the court would not wholly be a Security Council operation. The General Assembly would elect the judges and the secretary general would nominate the prosecutor. Extended negotiations finally made the arrangements palatable.

Only in February 1993, by Resolution 827, did the Security Council establish the International Tribunal for the Prosecution of Persons Responsible for Serious Violations of International Humanitarian Law Committed in the Territory of the Former Yugoslavia since 1991 (ICTY). It took an additional year for the Court to get up and running. Judges had to be elected, a site selected, facilities acquired, and rules and procedures developed and written. A prosecutor was not named until November. Even then, the establishment of the court seemed a token gesture. While prosecutions began with the Tadić trial, the political climate did not really support the tribunal until 1998. It took a courageous and principled political decision by the U.K.'s prime minister, Tony Blair, to jump start an active pursuit of those indicted.

MANDATE

The ICTY had authority to prosecute four clusters of offences committed on the territory of the former Yugoslavia since 1991:

- grave breaches of the 1949 Geneva Conventions
- violations of the laws or customs of war
- genocide
- crimes against humanity

Unlike Nuremberg, the court had jurisdiction only over natural persons. It could not prosecute organizations, political parties, administrative entities, corporations, or other entities that might have legal status. The ICTY and national courts had concurrent jurisdiction over serious violations of international humanitarian law committed in the former Yugoslavia, but the ICTY could claim primacy over national courts and take over national investigations and proceedings at any stage if it believed that doing so would prove to be "in the interest of international justice." The Court could also refer cases back to national courts, having done so with eight cases (involving thirteen individuals).

DOCUMENT: THE STATUTE OF THE INTERNATIONAL TRIBUNAL FOR THE PROSECUTION OF THE PERSONS RESPONSIBLE FOR SERIOUS VIOLATIONS OF INTERNATIONAL HUMANITARIAN LAW COMMITTED IN THE TERRITORY OF THE FORMER YUGOSLAVIA SINCE 1991

When: Adopted May 25, 1993, by Security Council Resolution 827
Where: New York City, New York
Source: http://www.icty.org/x/file/Legal%20Library/Statute/statute_sept09_en.pdf.
Jurisdiction: The International Tribunal shall have the power to prosecute persons responsible for serious violations of international humanitarian law committed in the territory of the former Yugoslavia since 1991 in accordance with the provisions of the present Statute. (Article 1)

The International Tribunal shall have jurisdiction over naturl persons pursuant to the provisions of the present Statute. (Article 6)

The *territorial jurisdiction* of the International Tribunal shall extend to the territory of the former Socialist Federal Republic of Yugoslavia, including its land surface, airspace and territorial waters. The *temporal jurisdiction* of the International Tribunal shall extend to a period beginning on 1 January 1991. (Article 8) (emphasis added)

Significance: The ICTY was the first UN-created war crimes court and the first international war crimes tribunal since the Tribunals of Nuremberg and Tokyo, following World War II. The Statute establishes the jurisdiction, organization, and procedures for the International Tribunal for the Former Yugoslavia (ICTY).

Article 1
Competence of the International Tribunal

The International Tribunal shall have the power to prosecute persons responsible for serious violations of international humanitarian law committed in the territory of the former Yugoslavia since 1991 in accordance with the provisions of the present Statute.

Article 2
Grave Breaches of the Geneva Conventions of 1949

The International Tribunal shall have the power to prosecute persons committing or ordering to be committed grave breaches of the Geneva Conventions of 12 August 1949, namely the following acts against persons or property protected under the provisions of the relevant Geneva Convention:

(a) willful killing;
(b) torture or inhuman treatment, including biological experiments;
(c) willfully causing great suffering or serious injury to body or health;
(d) extensive destruction and appropriation of property, not justified by military necessity and carried out unlawfully and wantonly;
(e) compelling a prisoner of war or a civilian to serve in the forces of a hostile power;
(f) willfully depriving a prisoner of war or a civilian of the rights of fair and regular trial;
(g) unlawful deportation or transfer or unlawful confinement of a civilian;
(h) taking civilians as hostages.

Article 3
Violations of the Laws or Customs of War

The International Tribunal shall have the power to prosecute persons violating the laws or customs of war. Such violations shall include, but not be limited to:

(a) employment of poisonous weapons or other weapons calculated to cause unnecessary suffering;
(b) wanton destruction of cities, towns or villages, or devastation not justified by military necessity;
(c) attack, or bombardment, by whatever means, of undefended towns, villages, dwellings, or buildings;

(d) seizure of, destruction or willful damage done to institutions dedicated to religion, charity and education, the arts and sciences, historic monuments and works of art and science;
(e) plunder of public or private property.

[Articles 4–6 omitted]

Article 7
Individual Criminal Responsibility

1. A person who planned, instigated, ordered, committed or otherwise aided and abetted in the planning, preparation or execution of a crime referred to in articles 2 to 5 of the present Statute, shall be individually responsible for the crime.

2. The official position of any accused person, whether as Head of State or Government or as a responsible Government official, shall not relieve such person of criminal responsibility nor mitigate punishment.

3. The fact that any of the acts referred to in articles 2 to 5 of the present Statute was committed by a subordinate does not relieve his superior of criminal responsibility if he knew or had reason to know that the subordinate was about to commit such acts or had done so and the superior failed to take the necessary and reasonable measures to prevent such acts or to punish the perpetrators thereof.

4. The fact that an accused person acted pursuant to an order of a Government or of a superior shall not relieve him of criminal responsibility, but may be considered in mitigation of punishment if the International Tribunal determines that justice so requires.

STRUCTURE

Because the two main ad hoc courts established by the Security Council have exactly the same structural arrangements, the following discussion will also apply to the International Criminal Tribunal for Rwanda (ICTR). The ICTY and the ICTR were ad hoc, set up as a temporary arrangement to carry out specific tasks. The ad hoc status of the ICTY and ICTR contrasts with that of the International Criminal Court (ICC) and the International Court of Justice (ICJ), which are permanent institutions whose jurisdiction and authority stem from international agreements (treaties) accepted and ratified by states. The Security Council can refer cases to both the ICJ and the ICC, but these two courts are otherwise independent of the United Nations. The Security Council does not control their agendas.

The ICTY completed its agenda of trials in December 2015. With the arrest of the last two fugitives sought by the ICTY, Ratko Mladić and Goran Hadžić, in 2011 the Security Council extended the life of the ICTY until 2017. Hadžić died in custody. Mladić's verdict was finally delivered in late November 2017. He was found guilty of genocide and received a sentence of life, The appeal will be heard by the Mechanism for International Tribunals (MICT, or Mechanism—see later discussion) set up to deal with ongoing matters after the court officially closes. As of January 1, 2018, the MICT had one other case on appeal from the ICTY.

The courts had three divisions: Chambers (Trials and Appeals), Office of the Prosecutor, and a Registry. The Chambers division of each court consisted of 16 permanent judges elected by the UN General Assembly from lists prepared by the Security Council. Table 22.1 provides a quick summary and comparison of the ad hoc ICTY and ICTR, and the permanent ICC. The seat of the ICTY is The Hague, Netherlands; that of the ICTR is Arusha, Tanzania. Because of the heavy caseloads and the length of trials, the Security Council also authorized 12 judges *ad litem* (ad hoc judges) for the ICTY and 9 judges *ad litem* for the ICTR. Permanent judges were elected to four-year terms and could stand for reelection. Judges *ad litem* also served four-year terms but could not stand for reelection. No two permanent judges on a trial panel could be of the same nationality. In overall membership, the personnel of the courts had to reflect the major legal systems of the world.

Each court had three Trial Chambers divided into two sections. Trials did not involve juries. A three-judge panel presided over each trial. Each trial panel must have a minimum of two permanent judges. The Appeals Chamber consisted of seven permanent Judges, five of whom are permanent judges of the ICTY and two of whom are permanent judges of the ICTR. These seven judges also constituted the Appeals Chamber of the ICTR. Each appeal is heard and decided by a bench of five judges of the Appeals Chamber. In theory this was done to ensure the development of consistent practice and precedent between the two courts. The Appeals Chamber sits at The Hague.

THE APPEALS CHAMBER

The Appeals Chamber marked an important addition to the ICTY/ICTR process. The Nuremberg and Tokyo Charters did not have a formal mechanism to hear appeals of sentences. Article 26 of the Nuremberg Charter specified that "the judgment of the Tribunal as to the guilt or the innocence of any Defendant shall give the reasons on which it is based and shall be final and not subject to review." Nonetheless, as noted in the discussion of World War II cases, a number of the sentences were subject to political review. Article 29 stated, "In case of guilt, sentences shall be carried out in accordance with the orders of the Control Council for Germany, which may at any time reduce or otherwise alter the sentences, but may not increase the severity thereof." The lack of any type of appeals mechanism was one reason many characterized the Nuremberg and Tokyo trials as "victor's justice."

The language for the appeals process is virtually identical for the ICTY and the ICTR. Either the Prosecutor or a person convicted may request an appeal on two grounds: an error on a question of law that would invalidate the decision; or an error of fact that produced a miscarriage of justice. The principles apply to verdicts of guilty as well as to verdicts of innocent. An appeals panel may reverse an acquittal and instate a verdict of guilty. As part of its role, the Appeals Chamber has made rulings on issues it considers of "general significance" to the unification of application law.

OFFICE OF THE PROSECUTOR AND THE REGISTRY

The Office of the Prosecutor (OTP) was responsible for investigating and prosecuting the crimes that fall within the jurisdiction of the Tribunal. Initially, the Prosecutor for the ICTY also served as the prosecutor for the ICTR. As the case load of both Tribunals increased, the Security Council authorized a separate prosecutor for the ICTR in August 2003. The office consisted of two primary divisions, the Prosecution Division and the Investigations Division. Other sections deal with appeals, international law questions, and evidence.

The Registry provides administrative support for the OTP and Chambers. These support services include translation and interpretation, finance, personnel, security, building maintenance, and relations with the host States. It also encompassed two specialized legal support units, one for the judges and one for the Tribunal as a whole.

MECHANISM FOR INTERNATIONAL TRIBUNALS

Anticipating the closure of the ad hoc courts, the UN Security Council established the Mechanism for International Criminal Tribunals (MICT or Mechanism), through SC Resolution 1966 (2010). Formally referred to as the International Residual Mechanism for Criminal Tribunals, the MICT has a mandate to assume and continue the jurisdiction, rights, obligations, and essential functions of the ICTY and ICTR. Among the more important tasks, the MICT has the responsibility for continuing witness protection, and for the tracking, arrest, and prosecution of the eight remaining fugitives still wanted by the ICTR.

Under Article 6(3) of its Statute, the MICT will retain jurisdiction over those individuals considered to be the most responsible for committing the gravest crimes. Of the eight fugitives, the MICT Prosecutor has maintained jurisdiction over three and requested that when apprehended, the other five be referred to Rwandan courts. Unlike national judicial systems, the MICT has no police force and no powers of arrest. It must rely on the cooperation of national governments to

Table 22.1 Selected International Courts at a Glance

Court	Number of Judges	Election	Term of Office	Seat
ICTY	16 permanent 12 *ad litem* (temporary increase to 16 in 2008)	Elected by the UN General Assembly	Permanent: 4 years (can be re-elected) *Ad litem*: 4 years (no re-election)	The Hague (Netherlands)
ICTR	16 permanent 9 *ad litem* (maximum)	Elected by the UN General Assembly	Permanent: 4 years (can be re-elected) *Ad litem*: 4 years (no re-election)	Arusha (Tanzania)
ICC	18 permanent	Elected by the Assembly of States Parties	9-year terms (can be re-elected; one-third elected every 3 years)	The Hague (Netherlands)

arrest fugitives. Member states are obliged to cooperate and to comply fully with requests for assistance from the Mechanism.

The Office of the Prosecutor has a tracking team that is responsible for gathering intelligence on the whereabouts and activities of the fugitives and providing support to national law enforcement authorities in arresting them. The work of the tracking team involves major challenges. To succeed in apprehending these fugitives, the team needs extensive cooperation from the states in which the fugitives are suspected to have taken refuge. Active cooperation is crucial because the strategy of the fugitives for evading justice include identity changes and a constant mobility across a large belt of East, Central, and Southern Africa, and inaccessible areas of the Democratic Republic of the Congo.

GUILTY PLEAS

Under the Tribunal's rules, an accused can enter a plea agreement expressing his or her admission of guilt to all charges or to certain selected charges. As in domestic courts, the agreement would be negotiated between the Prosecution and the accused. The Trial Chamber does not have any input into the negotiation of a plea agreement; however, the Trial Chamber must accept the terms of any plea agreement before it can come into force. In order for a plea of guilty to be accepted, the Trial Chamber has to be satisfied that it is voluntary, informed, and unequivocal and that facts point to the accused's responsibility for the charged crime.

When the accused pleads guilty only to certain selected charges, the prosecution may withdraw the other charges and apply to the Trial Chamber to amend the indictment accordingly. Guilty pleas render a trial unnecessary and lead directly to a sentencing hearing and the imposition of a sentence. As part of the plea agreement, both parties may ask for a specific sentence. However, the Trial Chamber is not bound by the plea agreement and can use its discretion in determining the sentence. Of the 161 individuals indicted by the ICTY, 20 negotiated successful plea agreement.

PROBLEMS

At the beginning of the trials, IHL did not constitute a coherent legal code. It had not evolved in a logical or consistent way, but in bits and pieces through different experiences, which may or may not have been linked to one another. Moreover, treaties (and customary law) are often vague and incomplete, lacking specificity with respect to the elements that determine criminality. Simply making certain actions an offense under international law marks only the first step. Treaties and customary law may contain prohibitions against certain battlefield action such as deliberate attacks on civilians, but they fail to define other essential elements necessary to turn a prohibition into an enforceable rule. What specific acts under what specific circumstances fall under the prohibition. Furthermore, the relevant law may fail to define what consequences should result from specific violations or to elaborate the important procedural elements necessary for prosecution. Many treaties lack any provisions for enforcement at all, leaving it to states essentially to specify appropriate measures if they choose to do so.

The ad hoc courts established under the auspices of the United Nations, the ICTY, ICTR, had limited jurisdiction in terms of specific time frames, territoriality, and defined crimes, as well as a limited institutional life. They could not try alleged crimes that fell outside of their constitutive charters. Even though it is a permanent court, the ICC also must operate within the terms of the Rome Statute, the treaty that defines its competence with regard to substantive law. Even more interesting, neither the authorizing resolutions for the ad hoc international courts nor the Rome Statute of the ICC contain a scale of penalties. They grant authorization to try certain crimes committed under certain circumstances, but then do not deal with appropriate punishment for those found guilty.

Questions of cost form an area of major concern. Enforcement requires expenditures of resources, both tangible in the form of manpower, matériél, and money, and intangible in terms of reputation and public support. For governments, immediate self-interest will tend to override arguments based upon the good of the international community. International justice is expensive. Rhetorical support for peace, nondiscrimination, and other human rights values comes easily; but, rhetoric and reality often clash when circumstances require intervention to address a major breach of "community" obligations such as the ongoing situation in South Sudan. For example, consider the length of time it took the Security Council to deal with the situations in the former Yugoslavia and Rwanda. A response necessitates a major commitment of resources to a problem that does not necessarily directly affect the self-interest of states outside the immediate area. This explains the reluctance of states to engage in Bosnia and Rwanda in a timely fashion. A strong reaction by States to these breaches presupposes the existence of a community interest to stop them. However, when a situation may require direct action to address a breach, the community response often remains potential rather than real.

Adhering to the ideal of fair trials also has a hefty price tag. Consider first the costs of maintaining the basic structure (overhead): in terms of salaries for judges, prosecutors, support staff, and facilities apart from the cost of trials. To use the ICTY as an example, in addition to the 16 permanent and 12 *ad litem* judges, the bulk of the fixed cost comes from salaries and maintenance of 1,200 staff. Now, add the costs of individual trials to the ongoing fixed costs. The first trial in the ICTY, that of Duško Tadić, a lowly foot soldier, cost $20 million dollars.

In addition to the cost and length of individual trials, include the length of time the entire process has taken. The trial of Radovan Karadžić began on October 26, 2009. The defense case commenced on October 16, 2012, and closed on May 1, 2014. The judgement of the Trial Chamber was delivered on March 24, 2016. Fifty-six of those convicted had already served their sentences before the ICTY closed. The MICT will conduct two retrials and two appeals. Granted, much of the delay in the early years of both Tribunals occurred because judges, conservative by training and experience, proceeded very cautiously because they had no firm guidelines. Later cases did advance more expeditiously because they drew upon the groundwork laid by the early cautious and careful approach. Yet others, like the *Milošević* case called into question the utility of the entire enterprise. Table 22.2

Table 22.2   ICTY: Disposition of Cases

Indicted	161
Ongoing Proceedings[a]	2
Concluded Proceedings	154
Sentenced	83
Plea Agreements	20
Acquitted	19
Referred to National Jurisdiction	13
Deceased	
before trial	17
after trial	8

[a] 1 trial (Mladić), 1 case on appeal (6 individuals)

summarizes the record of the court. We will explore these issues more fully in the next several chapters.

References

Genocide Watch. 2008. "Genocides, Politicides, and Other Mass Murder since 1945, with Stages in 2008." http://www.genocidewatch.org/images/GenocidesandPoliticidessince1945withstagesin2008.pdf.

Glaurdic, Josip. 2011. *The Hour of Europe: Western Powers and the Breakup of Yugoslavia*. New Haven, CT: Yale University Press.

Schabas, William A. 2006. *The UN International Criminal Tribunals*. Cambridge: Cambridge University Press.

Taulbee, James Larry. 2009. *International Criminal Law: A Guide to the Issues*. Santa Barbara, CA: ABC-CLIO.

23

Duško Tadić Trial

INTRODUCTION: THE BOSNIAN WARS

In 1989, Radovan Karadžić founded the Serbian Democratic Party (Srpska Demokratska Stranka, or SDS) in Bosnia and Herzegovina. The SDS wanted to unite all ethnic Serbs in Bosnia into a single community. The Bosnian Serb community would work to remain part of Serbia in a Serbian-dominated Yugoslavia if Bosnia or Croatia decided to break away from the federal Yugoslav government in Belgrade. Slobodan Milošević, the president of Serbia, supported Karadžić's efforts. In June 1991, Slovenia and Croatia unilaterally declared their independence from the Yugoslav Federation. Their decision to secede initiated the Balkan Wars (Yugoslav Wars) that would dominate the region for the next four years. Macedonia followed soon after, declaring its independence in September 1991.

As a response to these announcements of secession, Karadžić and the SDS joined with other Serbian parties in Bosnia-Herzegovina to establish a Serb Legislative Assembly separate from the national Bosnian Parliament. Several majority Serb districts in Bosnia and Croatia declared their autonomy and pledged their continued allegiance to the Serb-dominated federal government in Belgrade. This led to armed conflict breaking out between Serbs and non-Serbs. Karadžić rejected proposals that Bosnia-Herzegovina follow the three other republics by declaring its independence. In a referendum held in November 1991, most Bosnian Serbs voted to remain part of Yugoslavia. In the aftermath of the Bosnian declaration of independence from Yugoslavia on April 6, 1992, Karadžić declared the Serb sections of Bosnia independent from the central Bosnian government under the name Republica Srpska. Backed by Milošević, he then began a vicious campaign of "ethnic cleansing" against the Muslims of Bosnia-Herzegovina—the Bosniaks.

Bosnia also suffered an invasion from Croatia. While Karadžić and Milošević had a vision of uniting all Serbs in a larger Serbia, the newly elected president of Croatia, Franjo Tuđman (Tudjman) had a vision of uniting all Croatians in a greater Croatia. Tuđman backed the formation of the Croatian Republic of Herzeg-Bosnia in northwestern Bosnia. The leaders of Herzeg-Bosnia proclaimed borders that encompassed about 30 percent of the country, but they never achieved effective control over the territory. At one point, Bosniak and Croatian forces fought as allies against the Serbs. Tensions increased and open hostilities between the two former allies began in early 1993. The Washington Agreement in March 1994 effectively ended the conflict between Bosniaks and Croats. Herzeg-Bosnia ceased to exist at the end of August 1996.

DUŠKO TADIĆ

Duško ("Dule") Tadić became the first individual indicted and tried by the International Criminal Tribunal for the Former Yugoslavia (ICTY). His trial also marked the first by an international court since the Nuremberg and Tokyo trials after World War II. He was charged with war crimes and of committing atrocities at the Serb-run Omarska concentration camp in Bosnia-Herzegovina in 1992.

A Bosnian Serb, Tadić was born in Kozarac. After attending college in Belgrade, he lived in several different places and had a number of different jobs before returning to Kozarac in 1989 where he taught karate and operated a pub. Testimony at his trial revealed that Tadić owed substantial sums of money to Muslim friends because he had borrowed heavily from them to finance his pub. He joined the SDS in August 1990. When Slovenia and Croatia seceded from the federal Yugoslav union, he banned Muslims from his pub. Trial testimony also suggested that he had become a member of a local Serb paramilitary militia.

At this time, Kozarac was 90 percent Muslim (Bosniak), one of several predominantly Muslim towns in the Prijedor region. The region had major importance for the Serbs because it connected the Serbian-dominated region of Bosnia with a Serb majority area in Croatia. For Serbs, claiming the region meant eliminating the Muslim Bosniak population ("ethnic cleansing"), which comprised over 40 percent of approximately 110,000 total residents. In mid-May, the Bosnian Serb Army (Vojska Republike Srpske, or VRS) forces began its assault on Kozarac. The first artillery barrage resulted in the death of 800 civilians. The Bosnian Serbs then expelled the town's non-Serb population in an ethnic cleansing campaign that included beatings, robberies, rape, and large-scale mass murder. The residents were removed to concentration camps located at Omarska, Keraterm, and Trnopolje. Tadić participated in this forced transfer by identifying prominent leaders of the Muslim community. Omarska, the most brutal of the camps, became known as the "death camp." By one estimate 90 percent of the town's leaders were killed before they arrived at the camps and at least 50 percent of the town's Muslim population was killed during the operation (Scharf 1997, 95).

Even though Tadić had no official position at the Omarska camp, witnesses testified that he visited on a regular basis. Beatings and mutilation were common, frequently leading to death. On one occasion, he reportedly supervised a torture in which an inmate was ordered to bite off the testicles of a fellow prisoner. He presumably tortured and killed Emir Karabasić, who had been his friend. Once the ethnic cleansing process in Kozarac was complete in August 1992, he was elected president of the local council of the SDS. Ironically, after the "ethnic cleansing" operation, his pub had very little business. Tadić became a traffic policeman.

Tadić immigrated to Munich Germany in the fall of 1993. The real reasons he left Bosnia for Germany still remain somewhat clouded in mystery. Tadić's lawyer said that he left because he did not wish to be drafted into the Bosnian Serb Army. Others have suggested that he quarreled with Serbian officials over the division of confiscated Muslim property, or that he could no longer earn a decent living because the war had destroyed the local economy (Scharf 1997, 96). Many Muslim refugees from Bosnia had also immigrated to Germany and that proved to be his undoing. Someone recognized him and the information spread quickly among the refugee community.

The chief federal prosecutor's office in Germany had opened investigations against a number of suspected war criminals from the former Yugoslavia. Germany, as a state party to the 1949 Geneva Convention, had passed laws that permitted the arrest and trial of individuals accused of war crimes and genocide even if the crimes occurred in territory outside of Germany and the accused was not a German citizen. On February 12, 1994, as he left his brother's apartment, German police arrested him on suspicion of "murder, aiding and abetting genocide, and causing grievous bodily harm" (Scharf 1997, 97). At the request of the ICTY prosecutor, Germany transferred Tadić to the jurisdiction of the court in April 1995.

INTERNATIONAL TRIBUNAL FOR THE PROSECUTION OF PERSONS RESPONSIBLE FOR SERIOUS VIOLATIONS OF INTERNATIONAL HUMANITARIAN LAW COMMITTED IN THE TERRITORY OF THE FORMER YUGOSLAVIA SINCE 1991

The Charter for the ICTY provided the basic outline and specified important parameters such as jurisdiction. The actual operation of the Court required a more detailed set of rules and procedures.

DOCUMENT: RULES OF PROCEDURE AND EVIDENCE

When: Originally adopted February 11, 1994; revised July 8, 2015
Where: The Hague, Netherlands
Source: ICTY [IT/32/Rev. 50]. Online at http://www.icty.org/x/file/Legal%20Library/Rules_procedure_evidence/IT032Rev50_en.pdf.
Significance: The Rules of Procedure and Evidence stand at the heart of the trial process. A coherent set of rules ensures that each trial panel applies the same standards to each case. In the case of the ICTY, because the tribunal represented an innovation, the rules were revised and amended fifty times to cover situations that had not been anticipated at the beginning of the process. The document has ten major divisions that specify the official languages of the Court, the organization, its relationship with other courts, the rights of suspects,

procedures for pre-trial panels, rules for actual trials, and the appeals process. For the sake of brevity, the following comprises two different excerpts. The first comes from the Table of Contents of Part 6: "Proceedings before Trial Chambers" (page numbers omitted). The second is a sample of the actual rules in Part 6. The words *bis*, *ter*, and *quarter* after the rule number simply mean 2, 3, and 4. Thus, Rule 81 *bis* would be Rule 81.2.

PART 6
PROCEEDINGS BEFORE TRIAL CHAMBERS
Section 1 General Provisions

Rule 74 Amicus Curiae
Rule 74 *bis* Medical Examination of the Accused
Rule 75 Measures for the Protection of Victims and Witnesses
Rule 75 *bis* Requests for Assistance of the Tribunal in Obtaining Testimony
Rule 75 *ter* Transfer of Persons for the Purpose of Testimony in Proceedings Not Pending Before the Tribunal
Rule 76 Solemn Declaration by Interpreters and Translators
Rule 77 Contempt of the Tribunal
Rule 77 *bis* Payment of Fines
Rule 78 Open Sessions
Rule 79 Closed Sessions
Rule 80 Control of Proceedings
Rule 81 Records of Proceedings and Evidence
Rule 81 *bis* Proceedings by Video-Conference Link

[Section 2 omitted]

Section 3 Rules of Evidence

Rule 89 General Provisions
Rule 90 Testimony of Witnesses
Rule 90 *bis* Transfer of a Detained Witness
Rule 91 False Testimony under Solemn Declaration
Rule 92 Confessions
Rule 92 *bis* Admission of Written Statements and Transcripts in Lieu of Oral Testimony
Rule 92 *ter* Other Admission of Written Statements and Transcripts
Rule 92 *quater* Unavailable Persons
Rule 92 *quinquies* Admission of Statements and Transcripts of Persons Subjected to Interference
Rule 93 Evidence of Consistent Pattern of Conduct
Rule 94 Judicial Notice

Rule 94 *bis* Testimony of Expert Witnesses
Rule 94 *ter* [Deleted]
Rule 95 Exclusion of Certain Evidence
Rule 96 Evidence in Cases of Sexual Assault
Rule 97 Lawyer-Client Privilege
Rule 98 Power of Chambers to Order Production of Additional Evidence
[Sections 4 and 5 omitted]

> [*bis* = 2, *ter* = 3, *quater* = 4, *quinquies* = 5; these are later additions/amendments to the rules. So Rule 92 *bis* translates as Rule 92.2.]

Rule 90
Testimony of Witnesses

(Adopted 11 Feb 1994, amended 30 Jan 1995, amended 25 July 1997, amended 17 Nov 1999, amended 1 Dec 2000, amended 13 Dec 2000)

(A) Every witness shall, before giving evidence, make the following solemn declaration: "I solemnly declare that I will speak the truth, the whole truth and nothing but the truth."

(B) A child who, in the opinion of the Chamber, does not understand the nature of a solemn declaration, may be permitted to testify without that formality, if the Chamber is of the opinion that the child is sufficiently mature to be able to report the facts of which the child had knowledge and understands the duty to tell the truth. A judgement, however, cannot be based on such testimony alone. (Amended 30 Jan 1995)

(C) A witness, other than an expert, who has not yet testified shall not be present when the testimony of another witness is given. However, a witness who has heard the testimony of another witness shall not for that reason alone be disqualified from testifying.

(D) Notwithstanding paragraph (C), upon order of the Chamber, an investigator in charge of a party's investigation shall not be precluded from being called as a witness on the ground that he or she has been present in the courtroom during the proceedings. (Amended 25 July 1997, amended 1 Dec 2000, amended 13 Dec 2000)

(E) A witness may object to making any statement which might tend to incriminate the witness. The Chamber may, however, compel the witness to answer the question. Testimony compelled in this way shall not be used as evidence in a subsequent prosecution against the witness for any offence other than false testimony. (Amended 30 Jan 1995, amended 1 Dec 2000, amended 13 Dec 2000)

(F) The Trial Chamber shall exercise control over the mode and order of interrogating witnesses and presenting evidence so as to

(i) make the interrogation and presentation effective for the ascertainment of the truth; and

(ii) avoid needless consumption of time.
(Amended 10 July 1998)

(G) The Trial Chamber may refuse to hear a witness whose name does not appear on the list of witnesses compiled pursuant to Rules 73 *bis* (C) and 73 *ter* (C). (Amended 12 Apr 2001)

(H) (i) Cross-examination shall be limited to the subject-matter of the evidence-in-chief and matters affecting the credibility of the witness and, where the witness is able to give evidence relevant to the case for the cross-examining party, to the subject-matter of that case.
 (ii) In the cross-examination of a witness who is able to give evidence relevant to the case for the cross-examining party, counsel shall put to that witness the nature of the case of the party for whom that counsel appears which is in contradiction of the evidence given by the witness.
 (iii) The Trial Chamber may, in the exercise of its discretion, permit enquiry into additional matters.

WHAT IS THE PURPOSE OF A TRIAL?

The procedures of a trial are designed *to establish the facts* associated with a particular violation of the law and *to determine the appropriate law* applicable to the facts. The Tadić trial provides a very good example of both purposes:

- First, the prosecution had to establish the existence of a widespread pattern of systematic abuse (ethnic cleansing) against the non-Serb population (question of fact).
- Second, the prosecution had to establish that the pattern met the requirements for an "armed conflict" (question of fact and law). Before opening statements on the first day of the trial, the court stated:

    The Trial Chamber has determined that it does wish to hear testimony regarding the character of the conflict . . . [T]he Trial Chamber determined that it was necessary for the Prosecutor to offer evidence, that the crimes charged in the indictment were committed in the context of an armed conflict. We consider that that is a burden that the Prosecutor must bear. (May 7, 1996, p. 6)

- Third, the evidence had to establish that Tadić had actually committed the specific crimes (question of fact).
- Fourth, the evidence had to show that the crimes were committed in connection with the pattern of widespread, systematic abuse. This required proving *intent* and opportunity. (question of fact); and,
- Fifth, the Trial Chamber had to determine if the conflict met the requirement for an *international* armed conflict (question of fact). If it did not, the charges relating to grave breaches of the Geneva Conventions did not apply (question of law).

TRIAL SUMMARY #15: *PROSECUTOR V. DUŠKO TADIĆ (AKA "DULE")*

Court: International Criminal Tribunal for the Former Yugoslavia
Defendant: Duško Tadić
Where: The Hague, Netherlands
When: April 1996–December 1996. May 7, 1997 (Trial Judgement)
Source: Trial Chamber II: Case No. IT-94-1. Online at http://www.icty.org/case/tadic/4.
Charges: The amended indictment charged him with 12 counts of crimes against humanity, 12 counts of grave breaches of the 1949 Geneva Conventions, and 10 counts of violations of the laws and customs of war. Rape, beatings, and killings of civilians, both inside and outside Omarska, were among the specific crimes alleged.
See Second Amended Indictment, December 14, 1995. http://www.icty.org/x/cases/tadic/ind/en/tad-2ai951214e.pdf.
Defense: Alibi (was not there); innocent bystander (did not participate); inapplicability of the law (no armed conflict); character witnesses; and on appeal, the legitimacy of the court.
Verdict: Charges on counts declared inapplicable; not guilty on 20 counts; guilty on 11counts of crimes against humanity and violations of the laws and customs of war; three counts withdrawn. See later Discussion for Appeals Court decisions.
Sentence: 20 years
Significance: Conducting the first trial by an international court since the Nuremberg and Tokyo trials, the judges faced significant challenges. As a very low-level participant, Tadić would not have been a target of prosecution later. He became the first person tried because he happened to be available. The trial assumed a greater importance than it might otherwise have had because it forced the court to deal with many unresolved issues that could have formed major roadblocks in future trials. Decisions reached by the Appeals Chamber added important case-law decisions to international criminal law. In this sense, Tadić became much more important than his low status within the overall structure of Bosnian Serb politics warranted. Like Nuremberg and Tokyo, the ICTY was set up to prosecute the planners and leaders, not the lowly foot soldiers.

DOCUMENT: OPENING STATEMENT BY PRESIDING JUDGE GABRIELLE KIRK MCDONALD

This is the beginning of the first trial before the International Criminal Tribunal for the former Yugoslavia; an International Tribunal specially created by the United Nations to try persons charged with serious violations of international humanitarian law in the former Yugoslavia.

. . .

In conducting the trial, the Judges will be guided by the Rules of Procedure and Evidence that the Tribunal has adopted. As you lawyers know, we have approximately 125 Rules of Procedure and Evidence, but we only have 10 rules of evidence that will guide the conduct of the trial and the receipt of evidence, compared with the dozens of often-times hypertechnical rules of other legal systems. We have no rule of hearsay, for example, and Rule 89(c) of our Rules of Procedure and Evidence provides that *a Chamber may admit any relevant evidence which it deems to have probative value*, and Rule 89(B) of our Rules of Evidence requires that the Trial Chamber apply the rules of evidence which will best favour a fair determination of the matter before it and are consonant with the spirit of the Statute and the general principles of law. In this context, we Judges, will be tryers of fact and we will apply the law to our findings. (May 7, 1996, pp. 9–10, emphasis added)

TESTIMONY

The trial had 125 witnesses and produced 6,000 pages of testimony. Needless to say, the following comprises only a very small thumbnail of the proceedings. Hakija Elezovic offered some of the most convincing testimony for the Prosecution concerning Tadić's actions at the camp (July 30, 1996, pp. 4372–4391). Miss Brenda Hollis represents the Prosecution.

MISS HOLLIS: Thank you. Sir, would you please state your name?
A. Hakija Elezovic.
Q. What is your nationality or ethnic group?
A. Muslim.

. . .

Q. How long did you live in Elezovici?
A. My whole life, up until now.
Q. What was the nationality or ethnic group of the inhabitants of Elezovici?
A. The population of Elezovici was Muslim.

. . .

Q. How far was it from Kozarac?
A. Six kilometres.

. . .

Q. If we were to talk about an average, monthly average, how often would you go to Kozarac in a month?
A. I cannot quite say. Sometimes I would not go at all, sometimes five or six times.
Q. Why would you go there?
A. There was an office there, there was a market and then my wife also had her family in Kozarusa and so—

. . .

Q. Did you know Dule Tadic?
A. I knew him from sight, but up until the conflict I did not know him really. I just know him from the sight.
Q. How long had you known him by sight?
A. Maybe five or six years.
Q. When you went to Kozarac was he someone you would see frequently, occasionally, or seldom?
A. Not every time I went, but I would see him

. . .

Q. Sir, at this time I would ask you to look around the courtroom and see if you see Dule Tadic from Kozarac in the courtroom, and if he is, I would ask you to point to him?
A. I see him.
Q. Would you tell us also where he is seated?
A. On the left-hand side between the two policemen.
MISS HOLLIS: Your Honour, I would ask a correct identification of the accused?
THE PRESIDING JUDGE: Yes. The record will reflect that the witness properly identified the accused.

. . .

MISS HOLLIS: Sir, you indicated that at the beginning of the attack on Kozarac you had two sons, Salih and Samir.

. . .

Q. Did your sons have any weapons?
A. No, nobody.

. . .

Q. Did Salih later go to Kamicani to see if his girlfriend and her family were all right?
A. Yes.
Q. Was Salih then captured and taken to Omarska camp?
A. Yes.

. . .

Q. When did the cleansing in the Trnopolje area begin?
A. July 9th, around 5 o'clock in the afternoon.

Q. That was your particular area?
A. That was the area up until Rajici and Matici and Elezovici and Trnjani.
Q. Had the other areas already been cleansed by that time?
A. Yes.
Q. Sir, on 9th July were you and your children helping Serb neighbours in their field before the Serbs soldiers came?
A. Yes.
Q. On that day did the soldiers come to your home and force you and your son Samir to join a column that was going down the road toward Trnopolje camp?
A. Yes.
Q. How large a column was that?
A. I cannot quite know, but I believe it was around 300 people.
Q. What were the gender and age groups of the people in that column?
A. From 16 to 70, men.

. . .

Q. Were you walking in this column with your son Samir?
A. Yes.
Q. What happened as you walked in this column to Trnopolje camp?
A. Just before the camp, there was a hamlet, Reljici, and first they brought out Esad Mujgic and then my son Samir, Edhem Elezovic and Amir and Halil, the two sons, and then they shot them, about three metres away from me.
Q. Sir, did you see them when they shot your son and these other men?
A. Yes.
Q. Did you see who it was who shot your son?
A. Yes.
Q. Who was that?
A. Minja from Zmijanac and some others that I do not know.

. . .

Q. Did you have an opportunity to go to your son after he had been shot?
A. No, because we moved on another five or six steps and then stopped.
Q. What was being done to the other people in the column when these men had been pulled out and shot?
A. Nothing—they were picking out other people, a lot of people were killed there, about 30 at that time.
Q. So other people were taken out of the column and killed along the route?
A. Yes, they were killed.

. . .

Q. When you arrived at Trnopolje camp, were you put on to buses and taken to Omarska camp and then from there sent on to Keraterm?
A. Yes.

Q. How long were you held in Keraterm?
A. About 10 days, not longer. I do not know if it was even that long.

...

Q. While you were at Keraterm were you ever interrogated?
A. Yes.

...

Q. When you were taken in for interrogation, who did that interrogation at Keraterm?
A. [Dragan] Radakovic, the Director of the National Park, Kozarac National Park.
Q. Was there anyone else present?
A. Dule Tadic was his bodyguard.
Q. What happened during that interrogation?
A. Well, they interrogated me, then mostly about my son, and that I was responsible for his leaving the army, for deserting, and they began to beat me. Dule began to—first he kicked me with his foot and I fell. Then he went around the table and continued to beat me on the back and on the chest.
Q. You said that Dule first kicked you with his foot and you fell? Where did he kick you?
A. From the chair. Up here in the chest.
Q. When he kicked you in the chest, how did he kick you, was it a regular kick or was it a different kind of kick?
A. That master's kick.
Q. What do you mean by that, "a master's kick"?
A. Well, he was not—he did not just kick me, he sort of fooled around then and, I mean, he waited for me to relax a little bit and then he hit me.
Q. When he kicked you was he facing you straight on or did he kick you from the side with his body to the side?
A. Then when I fell down he came round, because he was on the other side of the table, so he went around the table to approach me and continued hitting me.
Q. When you say he was hitting you, what was he hitting you with?
A. With his feet.
Q. Did he continue to kick you the same way throughout this beating?
A. Well, one would say that, yes, with his feet.
Q. Had you ever seen this kind of kicking before, this kind of kicking and fighting?
A. I have seen it in films and such like.
Q. What kind of films were these where you saw this kind of kicking?
A. Well, karate, judo.
Q. Sir, how long did this beating last with Dule Tadic kicking you?
A. Well, it could be about a couple of minutes, and the interrogation altogether lasted for about half an hour.

Q. Was Mr. Radakovic joining in on this beating of you?
A. Radakovic was in the room. He interrogated me.
Q. Did he also beat you?
A. No, he did not. He simply grinned and laughed as this one was beating me.
Q. You said that when they were interrogating you and talking to you, they were talking mostly about your son. That was your son Salih?
A. Yes, Salih.

. . .

Q. Did they say anything about you meeting your son or being reunited with your son?
A. Yes, Radakovic said, "Sentenced to death" and he said, "You will have an opportunity to see him in Omarska," that I was going to Omarska.
Q. During this incident when Dule Tadic was beating you, in total throughout this incident, how long did you look at Dule Tadic?
A. Well, all the time.
Q. Were you able to see him clearly?
A. Yes.
Q. What was he wearing on that occasion?
A. He had a police uniform on then.
Q. Did he have any weapons on his person?
A. A pistol.

. . .

Q. What injuries did you suffer from that beating?
A. My ribs were broken.
Q. Did you suffer any other injuries in addition to your ribs being broken?
A. Kidneys, and I have headaches.
Q. Did you have any difficulty breathing after that interrogation and beating?
A. Yes.

. . .

Q. It was the next day then that you were taken to Omarska camp?
A. Yes.

. . .

A. They took me in for interrogation. When I came back from the interrogation for the second time, they did not take me in. The second time they took me to beat me again.

Q. Where did they take you to do that?
A. From the white house, there was tall grass there. There were some holes, and there were about 10, up to 10, soldiers beating. There was already a heap of dead and that is where I saw my son being beaten. I knew those five or six people who were there. Dule was the first to meet me. He started with his foot and said, "Now you have come to the right place," and began to beat me and my son was crying, "Let my old man go," and then he got after my son, and when I started standing up somebody struck me on the neck and I fell again. I received a very severe blow and then I was unconscious for quite some time. When I came to, and they were already loading the dead, and I must have been unconscious for an hour or two. There were very many dead. There was my son and Sivac, the veterinarian, what is his name, Sivac, I have forgotten his name, but I know he was the veterinarian. They were already lying one on top of the other. Then I recognised Redo and then a football player. They were dead already. They were very many dead there. The truck was full of dead.

. . .

Q. Sir, if we could go back for a moment? You said that they brought you to the white house, an area where there was tall grass. Was that to the side of the white house, behind the white house? Where was that located?
A. Behind the white house, right where that bathroom was, on the side where the bathroom was.
Q. As you came around to the back of the white house, what did you see?
A. I saw them beating people, a group of those, all soldiers, and Dule with them in camouflage, in camouflage clothes, military uniform, he had a baton, and fighting. They were not firing off their rifles. They were simply beating people.

. . .

Q. Then Dule Tadic began to beat you as well, is that correct?
A. Yes.
Q. When he was beating you, how was he beating you?
A. With the foot in the stomach.
Q. These feet to the stomach, was this the same sort of kick that he had used in Keraterm camp?
A. Why, yes, they were similar, those kicks. He really knew how to use his feet.
Q. During this incident when you saw Dule Tadic behind the white house, do you have any idea how long it was you were actually able to look at him?
A. Well, it was not long, five or six minutes. When my son said to let me go, not to beat me, he left me and then got after my son with a pistol and then my son fell. After that I was struck very badly. There was a severe blow and I lost consciousness.

WHY TADIĆ?

As the first case to go to trial, the Tadić verdict became the first to be reviewed by the Appeals Chamber. The appeal covered many issues of importance to other trials. Many of these involved technical matters beyond the scope of this discussion. The most important issue for the entire set of trials in the ICTY involved the challenge by Tadić's defense team to the legitimacy of the Court and its jurisdiction over the charges against the defendant. On appeal, the Appeals Chamber upheld the Trial Chamber's dismissal of the defendant's challenge to the jurisdiction of the Tribunal. But, it did so for reasons that differed in important ways from those advanced by the Trial Chamber. The reasoning of the Appeals Chamber also reinstated and affirmed several charges dropped by the Trial Chamber.

Most of the counts in the indictment concerned events alleged to have taken place at the camp at Omarska, where large numbers of Bosnian Muslims and Croats were detained by Serb forces. The charges dealt with accusations of rape, unlawful killing, torture, and cruel treatment. Using Articles 2, 3, and 5 of the Statute of the Tribunal, the indictment had charged the defendant with a grave breach of willfully causing great suffering; or, alternatively, of specifically engaging in cruel treatment as specified in Article 3. Arguing from the precedent set by Nuremberg, the Defense had maintained that the Tribunal lacked subject-matter jurisdiction over these charges because none of the acts alleged in the indictment had taken place in the course of an international armed conflict. The Trial Chamber had agreed with the Defense in the original verdict.

The Prosecutor countered with the argument that the Security Council had treated the entire situation in the former Yugoslavia as an international armed conflict. Resolutions had continuously admonished the parties to observe the Geneva Conventions. A number of resolutions specifically mentioned *grave breaches*. Clearly the conflict in Bosnia in the summer of 1992 involved the federal Yugoslav army to an extent that the conflict had to be regarded as an international conflict. Moreover, so far as crimes against humanity were concerned, the Prosecutor maintained that Article 5 of the Statute expressly conferred jurisdiction over crimes against humanity committed during an internal armed conflict.

The Appeals Chamber found that at the relevant time and place (May–December 1992) in Prijedor, an *international armed conflict* did exist. As a result, victims were legally classed as *protected persons* according to the 1949 Fourth Geneva Convention specifically referenced in Article 2 of the Statute of the ICTY. Consequently, the Appeals Chamber reversed the Trial Chamber's verdict and found the appellant guilty on Counts 8, 9, 12, 15, and 32 of the Indictment that charged him with grave breaches of the Geneva Conventions. In reversing the decision of the Trial Chamber, the Appeals Chamber held that:

> an armed conflict exists whenever there is a resort to armed force between States or protracted armed violence between governmental authorities and organized armed groups or between such groups within a State. International humanitarian law applies from the initiation of such armed conflicts and extends beyond the cessation of hostilities until a general conclusion of peace is reached; or, in the case of internal conflicts, a peaceful settlement is achieved. Until that moment, international

humanitarian law continues to apply in the whole territory of the warring States or, in the case of internal conflicts, the whole territory under the control of a party, whether or not actual combat takes place there. (Appeals, para. 70)

Although Tadić had been acquitted on grave breaches charges, the same crimes had also qualified as crimes against humanity and/or violations of the laws or customs of war, on which the trial chamber had pronounced him guilty.

The only new crime, of which the Appeals Chamber found Tadić guilty, was the killing of five Muslim men in the village of Jakšići. The Appeals Chamber ruled that the Trial Chamber erred when it decided that, on the evidence presented, it could not be satisfied beyond reasonable doubt that Tadić had played any part in the killing of the five men. As a result the Appeals Chamber found the appellant guilty on Counts 29, 30, and 31 of the Indictment—murder qualified as grave breaches of the Geneva Convention, violation of the laws or customs of war and crime against humanity.

On the basis of the judgement of the Appeals Chamber, in November 1999, Tadić received a sentence of twenty-five years' imprisonment. The Appeals Chamber ordered that Tadić should serve a minimum of ten years, calculated from the date of the first sentencing judgement of July 14, 1997. He was transferred to Germany to serve his sentence. The ICTY ordered his early release on July 18, 2008.

References

Borger, Julian. 2016. *The Butcher's Trail: How the Search for Balkan War Criminals Became the World's Most Successful Manhunt.* New York: Other Press.

Maas, Peter. 1996. *Love Thy Neighbor: A Story of War.* New York: Vintage.

Scharf, Michael. 1997. *Balkan Justice: The Story behind the First International War Crimes Trial since Nuremberg.* Durham, NC: Carolina Academic Press.

24

Slobodan Milošević

Slobodan Milošević served as president of Serbia between 1989 and 1997, and then of the remnants of Yugoslavia between 1997 and 2000. He came to power in Serbia, blaming the "ethnic others" for all of the nation's crises. Milošević used historical tragedies to imply the same could happen to the Serbian nation again from contemporary threats by the "Ustaše" Croats and "Turk" Bosniaks. The Ustaše were members of a fascist terrorist organization dedicated to achieving an independent and ethnically "pure" Croatia. During World War II, the Ustaše had cooperated with the German Nazis in organizing a genocidal campaign against Serbs, Jews, and the Romani. The "Turk" referenced the Ottoman Empire, which had ruled the entire Balkan area for four centuries before becoming part of the Austro-Hungarian Empire in the late nineteenth century.

Milošević advocated "Serbian unity" as the only solution to these threats. In a fiery speech in 1989, Milošević declared that he would never allow anyone to hurt Serbs as long as he was their leader. Both Milošević and his speech became famous overnight. Thereafter, he served as the symbolic leader of Serbs in all parts of Yugoslavia. He emerged as a zealous promoter of a Greater Serbia, a long-time aspiration of many Serbian nationalists. The possibility of a greater Serbia, long feared by many non-Serbs in Yugoslavia, fueled the ascension of his Croatian counterpart, Franjo Tuđman, whose equally impassioned nationalism increased instability and mistrust in Croatia. By 1990, the idea of "Brotherhood and Unity" had crumbled under the weight of nationalistic hysteria. Had Tuđman not died in 1999, he might also have been indicted by the ICTY.

By June 1991, Milošević's growing influence upset Yugoslavia's delicate balance. Slovenia seceded, gaining independence after a "Ten Day War." The Croatian War soon followed (1991–1992). Violence in Croatia's Krajina region, with a significant ethnic-Serb population, continued through 1995. Meanwhile, as ethnic tensions escalated, Bosnia's political situation grew progressively volatile. Convinced that remaining in Serb-dominated "rump Yugoslavia" would be disastrous to peaceful multiethnic coexistence, Bosnian-Croats and Bosniaks voted for an independent Bosnia on March 1, 1992.

Milošević appeared to have but one aim in mind: to keep the country together under Serbian domination at all costs. Toward that end, he encouraged Serbian minorities in Croatia and Bosnia to free themselves from "foreign"—that is, Croatian and Bosniak—rule. To make their defense possible, Milošević provided weapons to the supposedly threatened Serbian minorities within those two newly independent states and incited them to wage ethnic war.

Single-mindedly against separation from Serbia, Bosnian-Serbs declared an independent Bosnian-Serb Republic under President Radovan Karadžić (Republika Srpska). Immediately, Serbian paramilitary groups began "ethnic cleansing"—burning homes, raping, forcibly deporting civilians to concentration camps, and killing all non-Serbs in Eastern Bosnia. Meanwhile the Yugoslav National Army (JNA, for *Jugoslovenska narodna armija*) surrounded Sarajevo, beginning the city's nearly four-year siege. Within a month, Serb forces controlled 70 percent of Bosnia.

In April 1992, the international community recognized Bosnia's independence. As a result, Milošević withdrew JNA forces in early May 1992, leaving weapons, artillery, and supplies. Bosnian-Serb JNA soldiers became the Bosnian Serb Army (Vojska Republike Srpske, or VRS) under General Ratko Mladić. Influenced by Milošević's claims of a civil war in which Serbia had no part, and the UN had no business, the JNA's official withdrawal placated Western politicians and journalists who were quick to characterize the violence as inevitable civil war.

Within an otherwise brutal and bloody conflict, arguably the worst atrocity committed at Bosnian Serb hands took place in July 1995, when Serb troops took over the UN safe haven of Srebrenica. As Dutch UN peacekeepers looked on, the VRS massacred some 8,000 Muslim boys and men in a genocidal bloodbath that was the largest such atrocity in Europe since the Holocaust.

The result saw the practice of ethnic cleansing introduced throughout the Balkans. Over succeeding years, Milošević became the prime mover of the violent dissolution of Yugoslavia along ethnic lines. While the Bosnian Serb forces under the command of generals, such as Ratko Mladić, Milenko Zivanović, and Radislav Krstić, directed the Serb war effort, Milošević was prepared to take something of a back seat in the prosecution of pan-Serb interests. Moreover, the Bosnian Serb political leader, Radislav Karadžić, now attracted most of the West's censure for the horrors committed in the name of Greater Serbia.

THE DAYTON AGREEMENT

The Dayton Agreement in December 1995 addressed the following conflicts within the former Yugoslavia:

- Croatian government and ethnic Serbs (ended 1992)
- Croat–Bosniak War between the Republic of Bosnia and Herzegovina and the self-proclaimed Croatian Republic of Herzeg-Bosnia (1994)
- Croat-Bosniak Army and Republika Srpska

The war in Croatia lasted until January 1992, when an unconditional cease-fire established an uneasy peace between the Croatian government and ethnic Serbs. In late May 1992, the UN Security Council (Resolution 757) imposed a broad range of sanctions on Serbia that included an economic and arms embargo and a no-fly zone. These sanctions did not impact the war between Croats and Bosniaks, which continued until 1994, when the Washington agreement established an awkward and shaky alliance known as the Bosniak-Croat federation. Meanwhile, fighting between Croat-Bosniak forces and Bosnian Serbs (Republika Srpska) continued, despite international efforts to establish a lasting cease-fire. The North Atlantic Treaty Organization (NATO) became involved in February 1994 when in the first-ever use of force, NATO fighters shot down four Serb planes that had violated the no-fly zone. Later, in May 1995, NATO conducted air strikes on the Serb stronghold of Pale.

In the summer of 1995, the tide began to turn against the Serbs, as Bosniak and Croat forces recaptured some of the Serb-held territory in Bosnia through a large-scale military operation code-named Operation Storm. U.S. president Bill Clinton had authorized a private company to use retired U.S. military personnel to improve and train the Croatian army. Croatian forces took Krajina with little resistance. It was the first defeat for the Serbs in four years, and it changed both the balance of power on the ground and the psychology of all the parties.

The fighting was essentially over by mid-November 1995. The leaders of Serbia (representing the Bosnian Serbs), Croatia, and Bosnia met for talks in Dayton, Ohio. The war ended officially on December 14, when Croatian, Serbian, and Bosnian officials signed the Dayton Peace Accords. Milošević represented all Serb factions at the conference. Despite the widespread suffering, the Croats emerged from the conflict entirely victorious. They preserved their independence and ensured the territorial integrity of their nation. The Peace Agreements divided Bosnia into two "entities"—the Bosniak-Croat Federation, which controlled 51% of the territory and the Bosnian Serb entity, which controlled 49%. The Dayton Agreements also established a NATO Implementation Force to enforce the cease-fire. With the signing of the Dayton Agreement, the United Nations lifted sanctions.

KOSOVO AND "THE TURKS"

As a means of enhancing his position as the defender of Serbian heritage, in 1989 Milošević sponsored a number of mass rallies led by Serb ultra-nationalists to commemorate the 600th anniversary of the Battle of Kosovo. In the battle, the Ottoman Turks annihilated the Serbian army but also suffered crippling losses themselves. Nonetheless, the victory in 1389 paved the way for the Turks to incorporate Serbia into the Ottoman Empire. In the years following, one after another, Serbian principalities became Ottoman vassals.

After the Dayton Agreement, Milošević had reconstituted the Yugoslavian state and government as a two-republic federation that included only Serbia and Montenegro. He had been forced to act because of the devastating impact of sanctions on the economy. The Dayton Accords did not address the festering problem of Kosovo, which now became a central focus for the reconstituted Yugoslavia. The problems in Kosovo primarily resulted from repressive actions taken against the majority ethnic Albanian population under the premise of protecting the rights of ethnic Serbs.

In 1989, Milošević had declared a new Serbian constitution that severely curtailed the autonomy of Kosovo. After a series peaceful protests, the ethnic Albanian majority in Kosovo proclaimed the Republic of Kosovo in July 1990. Milošević sent in the VJN, which brought the province to the verge of civil war. The elected parliament and government of Kosovo were deposed, and the ethnic Albanian media totally silenced. The only Albanian-language daily newspaper was banned, and all Albanian-language radio and television broadcasting was prohibited. "Emergency legislation" facilitated the direct takeover of all Kosovo industry and the firing not only of Albanian management but of all employees of Albanian nationality. This action deprived hundreds of thousands of workers of an income. In the autumn of 1991, teaching at the University of Pristina was suspended, with the exception of courses reserved for students from the Serb minority. All Albanian professors were expelled. Albanian-language elementary and secondary schools were closed.

Although the Serb-controlled Yugoslavian Army was sent into the province ostensibly to root out members of the rebel Kosovo Liberation Army (KLA), the military's ethnic cleansing campaign led to hundreds of civilian deaths, as hundreds of thousands of villagers fled to the mountains and forests for safety. Armed clashes between the KLA, the local Serbian paramilitary police, and the VJN led to escalating rounds of repression by Milošević's government against the Kosovars. In January 1998, Serbian special police began operations that raided villages in the Drenica Valley region. Thousands of Kosovar civilians were forcibly expelled from the province, accompanied by an orgy of looting, destruction of houses, and shelling of villages. This last action proved the tipping point for the West, leading to the second major external intervention against Milošević and, ultimately, his undoing. The massacres marked the beginning of the Kosovo War. After February 28, 1998, the fighting was officially designated an *armed conflict*.

Milošević's refusal to sign an internationally brokered peace agreement in March 1999 precipitated another NATO air campaign. It began with an intense NATO bombing of Serbian military installations, and then was extended to infrastructure targets such as electric grids in Serbia proper. In response to the bombing, Milošević took the opportunity afforded by the resulting chaos to carry out a massive campaign of "ethnic cleansing" against the Kosovar Albanian population. Ironically, as NATO carried out its controversial bombing effort intended to stop Serb aggression against the Kosovars, the Serbs intensified their measures against the very population NATO was trying to save. While Serbia ultimately surrendered because of the damage caused by the attacks, Milošević considered the cleansing operation a victory.

Forced to surrender, Milošević was ordered by the allies to desist from ordering any further attacks against the Kosovars and to evacuate all military, paramilitary, and police forces from the province. Following the Serbian retreat from Kosovo, UN peacekeepers moved in and assumed administrative control of the region. Deliberations about Kosovo's future under UN control began and continued for a number of years without a resolution to the situation. Kosovo declared its independence in 2008. By January 2018, 60 percent of UN member states (115), including the United States, had granted official recognition.

INDICTMENT AND TRANSFER

On May 27, 1999, the ICTY issued an indictment against Milošević for crimes against humanity in Kosovo. Charges of grave breaches of the Geneva Conventions, violations of the laws and customs of war in Croatia and Bosnia, and genocide in Bosnia, were added eighteen months later. The original indictment focused only on Kosovo, ignoring his role in the earlier conflict. *Heads of government*, such as Jean Kambanda, the Rwandan prime minister, had already been tried by the ICTR, but Milošević became the first *head of state* to be charged "during an on-going armed conflict with the commission of serious violations of international humanitarian law" (ICTY press release, May 27, 1999).

A faltering economy and increasing unrest led to Milošević's losing the presidential election held in September 2000 to Vojislav Koštunica. Koštunica resisted pressure to transfer Milošević to the ICTY, arguing that he should be tried in Serbia for the crimes against his own people. Following his arrest, the United States pressured the Yugoslav government to extradite Milošević to the ICTY or lose financial aid from the IMF and World Bank.

Prime Minister Zoran Đinđić called an extraordinary meeting of the government to issue a decree for extradition. Milošević's lawyers appealed to the Yugoslav Constitutional Court, which asked for time to deliberate. Pleading potential economic consequences, Đinđić ignored objections from the president and the constitutional court. He ordered the extradition of Milošević to the ICTY. On June 28, 2001, Milošević was flown by helicopter from Belgrade to a U.S. air base in Bosnia and Herzegovina, and then to The Hague.

TRIAL SUMMARY #16: *PROSECUTOR V. SLOBODAN MILOŠEVIĆ*

Preliminary Trial Notes

When his trial began in February 2002, Milošević refused to recognize the legitimacy of the Tribunal. He decided to represent himself rather than accept court-appointed counsel. The trial was controversial from the beginning. Considering the complexity of the task, many had serious doubts about the wisdom of placing such an enormous burden on the prosecution. Moreover, Milošević still enjoyed a high level of support within Serbia and the Serb area of Bosnia known as Republika Srpska. Other critics immediately voiced concerns about the extent to which he was likely to receive a fair trial from the ICTY so soon after the Kosovo intervention.

The decision by Milošević to conduct his own defense in combination with the importance of the trial generated a large number of unique "case management issues" for the Court. The decisions here illustrate how decisions on procedure may have a major impact on the evidence presented to the Court. Suljagić gives an important example:

> [T]he majority of the "crime base" witness testimony—the kind that is perhaps the most repetitive and even tiresome in terms of reporting but that provides essential legitimacy to these kinds of trials by presenting what happened to the victims of the crimes—was introduced in writing. This seriously undermined the transparency of the trial and, in turn, made it possible for Milošević to pin stereotypes on prosecution witnesses that resonated with his regional audience. (2009, 184)

Equally important, the Trial Chamber had initially decided to proceed only on the charges connected to Kosovo. The Appeals Chamber overruled that decision. The Appeals Chamber decision resulted in a case of incredible complexity. The single indictment contained sixty-six separate charges stemming from events that happened over the course of almost ten years and involved conflicts in three other states in addition to Kosovo.

TESTIMONY

Given the complexity of the case, no single piece of testimony stands out. Much of the transcript deals with quibbling over evidentiary and other procedural issues. The following exchange illustrates this (p. 37):

> **Milošević:** [Interpretation] I believe that it is inappropriate to take these statements, to admit these statements over the telephone. This is Witness number 3. We have the tapes. If Mr. Nice wishes to challenge anything that Witness number 3 said on the tapes, he can call the witness himself. Getting statements by telephone that we don't even know what they are, and on the other hand not challenging what is on the tapes, that is totally inappropriate. He can call the witness any time. Call the witness and have him testify here.
>
> **Judge [Patrick] Robinson:** You're speaking so much like a common lawyer now, Mr. Milosevic, but we do admit hearsay here.

The prosecutor called 330 witnesses. Milošević initially submitted a list of 1,631. The prosecution took two years to present its arguments in the first part of the trial, which covered the wars in Croatia, Bosnia, and Kosovo. It concluded its case on February 25, 2004, after hearing nearly 300 witnesses.

In August 2004, Milošević began his case for the defense. He dismissed all accusations of war crimes, genocide, and crimes against humanity. The procedural rules for a "fair trial" gave him the spotlight and a stage from which he attacked the credibility of the Court and proclaimed his own status as a victim of unwarranted persecution and prosecution. Playing to his Serbian constituency, Milošević presented himself as the great defender of the Serb people, and as the personification of the continued persecution of the Serbs. He assumed the role of the heroic victim struggling against overwhelming odds, thus reinforcing the illegitimacy of the prosecution to his Serbian support base.

His tactics and the rulings of the Trial Chamber made many observers lose confidence in, and respect for, the trial proceedings. A respected analyst of international trials observed that the Trial Chamber permitted Milošević to treat witnesses, prosecutors, and judges in a manner that would have earned an ordinary defense counsel a citation or jail time for contempt of court. The Court had appointed *amici curiae* or "friends of the court" to assist Milošević. But, ultimately he knew his cases better than anyone and used his position to great advantage in pursuing his own agenda.

The following summarizes the testimony of an important witness for the defense, General Radomir Gojovic, a former military prosecutor and judge who once held the position of chief of the legal staff of the Yugoslav Army (JNA) and president of the Yugoslav Military Court. In an effort to undercut the charges associated with command responsibility, his testimony focused on efforts made by the Yugoslav Army to observe and enforce principles of international humanitarian law during the Kosovo campaign. His appearance required three days, March 15, 16, and 22, 2005. To give some context and emphasize the earlier remarks about complexity and length, General Gojovic's first appearance as a witness occurs on page 37,392 of the trial transcript. In total, the transcript comprised 49,191 pages.

General Gojovic's testimony covered several issues. At one point in the morning testimony on the first day, the Court exhibited some frustration with the course of questioning. The presiding judge instructed Milošević to restrict his examination in chief to evidence that directly related to specific allegations made in the indictment. The following summary will address two primary issues: (1) evidence that military prosecutors did investigate and prosecute war crimes committed by Yugoslav forces in Kosovo during the 1999 war and (2) the specific case of the massacre at Izbica. The Izbica massacre (March 27–28, 1999), which resulted in the deliberate slaughter of at least 93 (estimates vary even in the testimony) men as well as other crimes, was among the incidents of deliberate mass murder in the Kosovo War.

Document: Evidence That the Yugoslav Military Had Investigated and Prosecuted War Crimes

Court: International Criminal Tribunal for the Former Yugoslavia
Defendant: Slobodan Milošević
When: February 12, 2002–March 14, 2006
Where: The Hague, Netherlands
Source: Trial Chamber III [IT-02-54]. Online at http://www.icty.org/case/slobodan_milosevic/4#trans.
Charges: The specific counts involved genocide, complicity in genocide, deportation, murder, persecutions on political, racial, or religious grounds, inhumane acts and forcible transfer, extermination, imprisonment, torture, willful killing, unlawful confinement, willfully causing great suffering, unlawful deportation or transfer, extensive destruction and appropriation of property not justified

by military necessity and carried out unlawfully and wantonly, cruel treatment, plunder of public or private property, attacks on civilians, destruction or willful damage done to historic monuments and institutions dedicated to education or religion, and unlawful attacks on civilian objects.

According to the indictment, during the relevant period, Milošević was the President of Federal Republic of Yugoslavia (FRY), President of the Supreme Defence Council of the FRY, and the Supreme Commander of the Yugoslav Army (VJN). Pursuant to his position, he exercised command authority over the VJN and the police forces subordinated to the VJN. In addition to his de jure powers, he also exercised extensive de facto control over numerous institutions essential to, or involved in, the conduct of the crimes alleged in the indictment. Online at http://www.icty.org/x/cases/slobodan_milosevic/cis/en/cis_milosevic_slobodan_en.pdf.

Defense: Lack of convincing evidence; actions were warranted by circumstances; violators of IHL by members of Yugoslav forces were prosecuted; the Yamashita defense: NATO action had hindered efforts to control troops in the field; credibility of witnesses

Verdict: Defendant deceased before completion of the trial

Significance: The first indictment by an international court of a head of state while still in office

March 15, 2005

Q. [Milošević] And do you happen to know what the reasons were for you to be appointed head of the legal department in the general staff of the Yugoslav army?

A. [Gojovic] Well, what I know is that General Ojdanic, who was the Chief of Staff of the Supreme Command, called me up on the telephone and told me that he would like to have a conversation with me in that connection. He came the next day. He came to court. We talked, and he said that the mobilised courts under their war obligation weren't functioning as well as they could and that he had been assigned the task, and this is what he said, "The president asked me"—the president of the republic, that is Mr. Milosevic—"asked me to find a proper solution for that work to be improved . . ."

. . .

Q. [Milošević] General Gojovic, do you know whether in the army of Yugoslavia before the NATO aggression people were educated in the sphere of international humanitarian law?

A. [Gojovic] Yes, education was done on the basis of a protocol which was signed by the defence minister and a representative of the International Red Cross.

Q. [Milošević] General Gojovic, what did every soldier in the army of Yugoslavia have to know? Let me be very specific: What did every soldier of the army of Yugoslavia have with him within the frameworks of his regular kit and equipment, which is linked to international humanitarian law?
A. [Gojovic] Well, every soldier had within his kit, once he was issued a kit, he had a Code of Conduct, rules of behaviour during conflict and wars, which stipulate his rights, how he is to behave, how he is to behave to the wounded, to POWs, with the civilian population, and other definitions.

Summary: In answers to further questions, General Gojovic maintained that Yugoslav military officers were given strict orders to enforce the principles of international humanitarian law. He provided copies of orders from the Supreme Command Staff that instructed soldiers to abide by the Geneva Conventions.

. . .

Q. [Milošević] General Gojovic, however, or should I say unfortunately, despite all the measures that were taken that you described before and after the NATO aggression, despite all the measures taken to ensure adherence to international humanitarian law, violations of humanitarian law by members of our armed forces still occurred.
A. [Gojovic] Yes, they did.

Q. [Milošević] Would it be fair to say that your key, your principal activity in this period was to monitor the work of military judicial bodies, including violations of humanitarian law and issues related to trials, et cetera?
A. [Gojovic] Yes. After the military judicial bodies were organised to work in wartime, my job was to monitor their operation, including all the proceedings, all the legal actions taken to prosecute violations and offenders.

Q. [Milošević] Very well. I suppose that even in that time minor offences were in the majority.
A. [Gojovic] Yes, yes, yes.

[**Author comment:** NOTE: *at this point the prosecution objected to the improper (leading) question. The presiding judge admonished Milošević to follow procedure:*]

> **Judge Robinson**: Mr. Milosevic, let's not play around. You know very well that the question was improper, leading, and you're perfectly capable of formulating it in a proper manner. So I expect you to do that.

[**Author comment:** OMITTED: *a discussion of the origin and function of the military courts. Recall that General Gojovic had testified earlier that "they were not functioning as well as they could. . . ."*]

Q. [Milošević] Now, tell me, at what level was it decided that the system of military courts and military prosecutors was not functioning well enough, and whose was the initiative to improve and enhance the system and to maximise its efficiency?

A. [Gojovic] I said already it was concluded at the level of the Supreme Command Staff. In my conversation with General Ojdanic, he told me that it was necessary to enhance the work of this system, that there was certain difficulties, and that President Milosevic demanded that some solution be found to deal with this problem. That's how I came to be appointed in my new position, because I had experience in all these various jobs.

[Author comment: After a rather lengthy set of Q & A that examined the reorganization and its problems in great detail the presiding judge again became impatient:]

Judge Robinson: Are you going to ask him how many prosecutions actually took place in the period between 1st January and 20th June, 1999, or even thereafter, if prosecutions started and continued after the 20th of June, 1999? Are you coming to that in the evidence?

Milošević: [Interpretation] By all means. By all means, Mr. Robinson.

Judge Robinson: Yes, then—

Milošević: [Interpretation] This is an unavoidable question.

Judge Robinson: All right. We'll let you proceed.

Q. [Milošević] Thank you, General. You spoke about the establishment and all the difficulties entailed from the point of view of your organisation, et cetera. But tell me, when you toured all these military courts and when you familiarised yourself with their work in practice, what were all the problems they had while operating in a state of war, and what was the nature of these problems and difficulties.

A. [Gojovic] There were quite a few problems involved. They mostly underlined the problem of the security of work of these military courts because they were within the area of the command posts of the units that they were in. So they were exposed to NATO attacks, and therefore they had to change their locations frequently. Then they would move and then again they would have to organise their entire work at a new location. So their safety and security was one problem. Then there were practical problems related to procedure, communicating with units, that is. Communications were down, telephone lines, that is. There were other types of communication by way of messenger, but then it was also difficult to send all documents to suspects, to other persons involved, because movement in general was difficult. So these were all the problems they encountered, and they sought explanations, advice. Also, there were a lot of investigations, and when they went to carry out on-site investigations, it was very hard. It was virtually impossible to find some units.

[Author comment: This statement set the foundation for the "Yamashita" defense—communications difficulties caused by the ongoing activities of NATO forces limited and inhibited the volume and type of information sent up the chain of command. The statute provides that a superior is criminally responsible for the acts of his subordinates "if he knew or had reason to know that the

subordinate was about to commit such acts or had done so and the superior failed to take the necessary and reasonable measures to prevent such acts or to punish the perpetrators thereof." When cross-examined about why certain atrocities were not investigated by his office, General Gojovic testified that NATO bombing effectively curtailed the ability to relay such information. He claimed that the work of the military prosecutors and courts would have been far more thorough had NATO not intervened and expelled Yugoslav forces from Kosovo. He asserted that their removal deprived the JNA of the opportunity to gather the information and evidence it would have needed for prosecution.

On cross-examination, Gojovic was asked about cooperation with various authorities concerning Kosovo. By his testimony, working with these organizations always encountered obstacles that precluded a positive outcome.]

March 16, 2005

Q. [Milošević] I wish to draw everyone's attention to tab 15. It contains a paper titled "Information." Was that the kind of information that was supplied to the Supreme Command Staff?
A. [Gojovic] Yes. That's the kind of report we received.

Q. [Milošević] It contains all the general data about formation, 1st Army, 2nd Army, 3rd Army. In the penultimate paragraph, concerning the 3rd Army, it says: "The difficulties encountered by this court in its work also exist when it comes to delivering subpoenas because of the lack of security and safety of movement in combat operations zones, the intense attacks carried out by the aggressor's air force and the covert operations by dispersed terrorists groups."
A. Yes. This is typical of the military corps and the military prosecutor's office of the Pristina Corps. [**Author comment:** *Corps responsible for the entire territory of Kosovo.*]

. . .

Q. [Milošević] On the next page, in paragraph 3, we see information about the number of cases. It says: "From the moment of establishment of military judicial organs, military prosecutors received 7.807 criminal reports, 15 filed reports for the investigation of 2.911 persons, and charged 3.928 persons. A total of 2.825 requests to start an investigation were submitted. 1.395 were implemented. Some 3.897 persons have been indicted. . . ." That is the kind of information you showed us in the form of tables.
A. [Gojovic] Yes. . . .

The questioning on pages 37,503–37,511 dealt with statistics of cases and how they should be interpreted. Milošević cited a number of separate incidents, but the Court had questions about the outcomes. Later questioning pointed up the primary problem both with the summary statistics and with General Gojovic's testimony—the lack of information concerning the specifics of incidents and data on punishment. Many of the "crimes" were petty or offenses such as AWOL, desertion, or minor infractions of military regulations. General Gojovic's testimony did confirm is that Yugoslav forces had in fact committed a large number of "grave breaches" of the Geneva Convention in Kosovo. These were charged as "crimes against life and limb" (e.g., murder, manslaughter, etc.), but the evidence in testimony demonstrated that few of these were ever investigated and charged.

Izbeca

Izbeca became the focus of questions because General Gojovic presented evidence that military prosecutors investigated and prosecuted war crimes committed by Yugoslav forces in Kosovo during the 1999 conflict. Milošević made Izbeca a focal point by trying to use this evidence to prove that he was not criminally liable for atrocities committed in Kosovo under the theory of command responsibility. In his testimony, General Gojovic admitted that the Yugoslav government knew of the massacre at Izbeca along with that confirming the shooting and execution of other Albanians without cause. On cross-examination, Prosecutor Geoffrey Nice questioned whether the Yugoslav investigation of the Izbica village gravesite was conducted only because of international outrage and NATO's use of satellite imagery suggesting a mass grave. General Gojovic strongly denied this.

A MIXED LEGACY

Building on the efforts of others whom he supplied and supported, Milošević came close to achieving his goal of a Greater Serbia. His policies resulted in hundreds of thousands dead and the dissolution of what had been the Federal Republic of Yugoslavia, and he saw the Bosnian Serbs rewarded with the permanent acquisition of large tracts of land that had formerly been majority Bosniak or Croat. The new map of Bosnia incorporated many of the military gains won by Bosnian Serb militias and regular forces through force of arms, but while the peace settlement represented a limited victory for Milošević, it stopped short of giving him total mastery over Bosnia, which remained independent. In the second conflict, NATO intervention set the stage for the eventual independence of Kosovo. If not for the two major interventions, Milošević might ultimately have succeeded in his quest for a Greater Serbia.

The trial itself leaves a mixed legacy. It graphically illustrates the tension that exists between "fairness" and the necessity for procedures that promote an expeditious trial because "justice delayed is justice denied." The ICTY erred in combining the two indictments, which worked against an expeditious proceeding. In the quest for "fairness," the Trial Chamber granted Milošević too much latitude to engage in his histrionic condemnation of the indictments and the Court itself. In Serbia, the trial reinforced the general feeling that Serbs had been singled out for persecution by the international community. For these reasons, the trial served as a roadmap of what not to do.

References

Boas, Gideon. 2007. *The Milošević Trial: Lessons for the Conduct of Complex International Criminal Proceedings*. Cambridge: Cambridge University Press.

Judah, Tim. 1997. *The Serbs, History, Myth and the Destruction of Yugoslavia*. New Haven, CT: Yale University Press.

Sell, Louis. 2002. *Slobodan Milošević and the Destruction of Yugoslavia*. Durham, NC: Duke University Press.

Suljagić, Emil. 2009. "Justice Squandered? The Trial of Slobodan Milošević." In *Prosecuting Heads of State*, edited by Ellen L. Lutz and Caitlin Reiger, 176–204. Cambridge: Cambridge University Press.

25

Radovan Karadžić

Radovan Karadžić came to prominence as one of the principal architects of the ethnic cleansing in Bosnia. As a founder of the Serbian Democratic Party (Srpska Demokratska Stranka, or SDS) in Bosnia-Herzegovina, he worked to unite all ethnic Serbs in Bosnia into a single community. The goal of the SDS was to keep the Bosnian Serb community as part of a Greater Serbia if either the Croatian or Bosnian Parliamentary Assembly voted to declare their sovereign independence from the central government in Belgrade. Slobodan Milošević, the president of Serbia, supported Karadžić's efforts. In June 1991, Slovenia and Croatia declared their independence from the Yugoslav Federation. The decision of Slovenia and Croatia to secede initiated the Balkan Wars (Yugoslav Wars) that would dominate the region for the next four years. Macedonia followed soon after in September 1991. On September 25, 1991, the UN Security Council passed Resolution 713, imposing an arms embargo on all of the former Yugoslav territories. The embargo hurt the Army of the Republic of Bosnia and Herzegovina the most. The Republic of Serbia controlled the lion's share of the Yugoslav Peoples Army's (JNA) arsenal, and the Croatian Army could smuggle weapons through its coastline.

As a response to the secession of the three states, the SDS and other Bosnian Serb parties formed a separate Serb Legislative Assembly in Bosnia-Herzegovina in October 1991. Some Serb-dominated areas declared their autonomy from Bosnia, and their allegiance to the Serb-dominated federal government in Belgrade. At a closed referendum among Bosnian Serbs held in November 1991, most voted to remain part of Yugoslavia. On January 9, 1992, the Bosnian Serb Assembly proclaimed the Republic of the Serb people of Bosnia and Herzegovina, Republika Srpska. Karadžić was elected president. The Bosnian Parliamentary Assembly (legitimately elected government) declared independence from the federal Yugoslav government on March 1, 1992. The division led to an armed conflict between Serbs and non-Serbs.

At the time, the population of Bosnia-Herzegovina was composed of 40 percent Muslims (Bosniaks), 30 percent Serb, and 18 percent Croats. Although Bosnia's Muslims formed the majority with 2 million people, the Serbian minority was better armed because it received substantial support from the neighboring VJN. Serbian militias, backed by the VJN, quickly took control of two-thirds of Bosnia. Afterward, the Bosnian Serbs launched a campaign of "ethnic cleansing" directed at the Muslim population.

Karadžić orchestrated the almost four-year-long siege of Bosnia's capital city, Sarajevo (April 1992–February 1996). Day after day, he ordered a barrage of artillery to rain on the defenseless city. From his headquarters in Pale, he ordered the systematic destruction of historic Muslim targets, such as the National Library, and the killing of unarmed civilians in open-air markets. The siege lasted three times longer than the Battle of Stalingrad and more than a year longer than the Siege of Leningrad, both of which occurred in World War II. It resulted in 13,950 deaths, of which, 40 percent were innocent civilians.

His most egregious crime was the offensive he ordered in 1995 against the six designated "safe areas" under UN protection: Sarajevo, Tuzla, Gorazde, Srebrenica, Zepa, and Bihac. In the worst of these, Karadžić's senior military officer, General Ratko Mladić, attacked the city of Srebrenica. Systematically, militias and troops from the Bosnian Serb Army (Vojska Republike Srpske, or VRS) captured as many men and boys between the ages of 10 and 65 as they could find. They then led them out of the city, killed them in the surrounding hills, and buried the bodies in mass graves. The women and children of Srebrenica were deported to areas outside the borders of Republika Srpska.

After this massacre, the position of the Bosnian Serbs began to deteriorate, as international opinion turned against them. General Sir Rupert Smith, Deputy Supreme Allied Commander Europe (NATO) started a campaign aimed at bringing those responsible for the genocide to justice. On August 4, 1995, Karadžić announced he was removing Mladić from command of the VRS, and personally taking command. Popular pressure forced him to overturn this order a few days later. The International Criminal Tribunal for the Former Yugoslavia (ICTY) indicted Karadžić and Mladić on July 24, 1995. The indictment had sixteen counts of genocide, crimes against humanity, and war crimes. These included extermination, murder, persecutions on political, racial, and religious grounds, forcible transfer because of religious or national identity, murder, unlawfully inflicting terror upon civilians, and taking hostages.

On November 21, 1995, the war came to an end when Milošević, Bosnian president Alija Izetbegović and Croatian president Franjo Tuđman signed the Dayton Accords in the United States. President Bill Clinton had excluded Karadžić from participating in the negotiations on the grounds that he was under indictment by the ICTY. After the agreement, as an indicted war criminal Karadžić was banned from standing for Parliament and pressured into relinquishing his government and party positions. He was succeeded as president by Biljana Plavšić, who would also be indicted, tried, and convicted by the ICTY.

Karadžić went into hiding and remained a fugitive from 1996 until his arrest in Belgrade in July 2008. He was working as an alternative medicine practitioner in Belgrade, using a very heavy disguise. Transferred to ICTY custody at The Hague, at his initial arraignment, like Milošević, Karadžić, informed the court that he intended to represent himself. At a second court appearance in late August 2008, he refused to enter a plea. Finally, in March 2009, the Trial Chamber entered a plea of not guilty on his behalf after he refused to enter a plea to new charges brought against him in a third amended indictment.

THE TRIBULATIONS OF TRIALS

Cooperation of the Accused

The trial began on October 26, 2009, with opening statements from the prosecution. Claiming that he had not had enough time to prepare his defense, Karadžić declared that he would boycott the trial and he failed to appear. In the absence of the accused or anyone to defend him, the presiding Trial Judge suspended the case for 24 hours. The prosecution began its opening statement the next day. On November 5, 2009, the court forcibly imposed a lawyer on Karadžić and postponed his trial until March 1, 2010. On November 26, 2009, however, Karadžić challenged the legal validity and legitimacy of the Tribunal. The Tribunal rejected the challenge and the trial duly resumed on March 1, 2010, when Karadžić decided to attend to present his opening statement.

A month later, on April 1, 2010, Karadžić again told the Tribunal that he would represent himself, and once more refused to recognize the charges or the legitimacy of the Court. He denied all charges against him. By these constant delaying tactics, Karadžić hindered the progress of the trial. The capture of Ratko Mladić on May 26, 2011, did not help his case. Mladić was asked to provide corroborating evidence against Karadžić. He refused to testify, denouncing the Court as "satanic."

TRIAL SUMMARY #17: PROSECUTOR V. RADOVAN KARADŽIĆ

Proving Individual Liability in Cases Involving Genocide and Crimes against Humanity

The ICTY struggled early on with the problem of how to deal with establishing individual liability for actions when crimes involve a large number of individuals at various levels in a hierarchy. In the *Tadić* case, the ICTY Appeals Chamber asserted that recognition of *group criminality* is essential for the enforcement of international criminal law because these crimes do not result from the criminal propensity of a single individual (Judgement §191). Some at the top gave orders, others took actions that enabled the implementation of the orders (provided transportation, weapons, etc.), and those at the low end actually committed the physical acts that define the crimes. The further up an individual stands in the hierarchy of responsibility in an civilian organization or in the chain of command in a military force, the more difficult it becomes to build the links that clearly define accountability. The questions relate to finding a methodology that would permit assigning a relevant measure of liability for each participant in the resulting carnage.

The Nuremberg trials used the idea of conspiracy and the tactic of indicting whole organizations as criminal enterprises. Both proved unsatisfactory. In the

Tadić trial, judges struggled with the task because none of the witnesses could positively testify to seeing Tadić commit many of the offenses charged in the indictment. They settled on the doctrine of *joint criminal enterprise* (JCE). JCE encompasses three different types of liability. For each charge, the prosecution must establish three distinct elements:

1. a plurality of persons;
2. who acted according to a common plan or purpose that involved commission of a crime provided for in the ICTY Statute; and
3. evidence of actual participation of the accused in the common design (Judgement §227).

The rationale has raised a great deal of controversy, but because of a lack of any compelling alternative formulas, the ICTY continued to use it. To jump ahead, the judges of the International Criminal Court have not embraced "joint criminal responsibility" as a useful concept.

DOCUMENT: *PROSECUTOR V. RADOVAN KARADŽIĆ*

When:	October 26, 2009–March 24, 2016
Where:	The Hague, Netherlands
Court:	International Criminal Tribunal for the Former Yugoslavia
Defendant:	Radovan Karadžić
Source:	Case No. IT-95-5-I. Online at http://www.icty.org/case/karadzic/4.
Charges:	In the first indictment, Part I (Counts 1 to 9) included a crime of genocide, crimes against humanity, and crimes that were perpetrated against the civilian population and against places of worship throughout the territory of the Republic of Bosnia and Herzegovina.
	Part II (Counts 10 to 12) involved crimes relating to the sniping campaign against civilians in Sarajevo.
	Part III (Counts 13 to 16) concerned crimes relating to the taking of UN peacekeepers as hostages.
	http://www.icty.org/x/cases/mladic/ind/en/kar-ii950724e.pdf.
	The Third Amended Indictment (October 19, 2009) reduced the Counts to 11. Online at
	http://www.icty.org/x/cases/karadzic/ind/en/markedup_indictment_091019.pdf.
Defense:	He blamed Muslims' actions; atrocities were "staged" by the Muslims themselves; he cited the nature of the civil war, which required actions in self-defense. With respect to Srebrenica, he claimed that he was not aware of any executions. He blamed General Ratko Mladić. Karadžić argued that he was a "tolerant man" who has done "everything within human power to avoid the war and to reduce the human suffering." In his opening statement, he asserted, "Instead of being accused, I should have been rewarded for all the good things I have done."

Verdict: Guilty on ten of eleven counts including one count of genocide; forty years

Significance: The Karadžić trial marked one of the most important prosecutions for war crimes since the conclusion of the trials stemming from World War II. As president of Republika Srpska, Karadžić played a central role in the ethnic cleansing in Bosnia. His convictions made him the most senior political figure to be convicted of war crimes and genocide stemming from the conflict in the former Yugoslavia during the 1990s.

TESTIMONY

Without inclusion of the formal written statements submitted to the Court by victims, the transcript of the oral testimony in the trial comprises 48,161 pages. The Final Judgement runs to 2,590 pages. The following is a small except from the oral testimony. The first witness is Ahmit Zulić, a Muslim survivor of a Serbian detention camp who also testified that the death squads made victims dig their own graves. The oral testimony often refers to a long written statement, which had been submitted to the Court. The oral testimony only covers what the prosecution thought were points of emphasis.

April 13, 2010

Q. Mr. Zulic, we will get to Betonirka and discuss that in a few moments, but I now want to turn to the attacks on villages and settlements in the Sanski Most municipality. . . . Mr. Zulic, one of the attacks you describe is the attack on the Mahala settlement. Approximately how many Muslim households were in Mahala?
A. I really don't know, but there were Serbian houses too in Mahala. In any case there were over 500 houses in all.

Q. What was the majority of the population there, their ethnicity?
A. It was majority Muslim.

Q. In your statement, you say that the attack commenced on the 28th of May, 1992. Were you able to see this attack?
A. From the place where I was born and where I lived, I could see shells flying in and exploding. And, of course, you could see houses burning at night.

Q. And who did attack the settlement?
A. The occupational Serb army, I mean the JNA, the Yugoslav People's Army, and Serbian paramilitaries of all kinds: There were Seselj's men, Chetniks, there were some sort of White Eagles, there were some that called themselves SOS. I can't remember them all. I'm sure I'm missing a few. . . .

Q. Do you know of anyone killed during the attack?
A. Muslims, yes, they were killed but not during the attack, after the attack. Five or six people were killed in just one house. Don't ask me about the exact

number. I know there were killed three women, the daughter of Ivo Uzar, Nafija Nalic, two Vojnikovic brothers were killed in that house as well because they were in the basement. I know that because the mother of the Vojnikovic brothers came, brought a bloodied little chain, and said they were dead. But the perpetrators had already left and came to the exercise ground and announced that everyone must come out. (pp. 1,017–1,018)

[pp. 1,019–1,027 omitted]

Q. You stated that during your detention in Betonirka you were beaten. How often did this happen?
A. I know—well, three nights—only on three nights was I not beaten when Tonci was on duty. He didn't touch anybody. That's a fact.

Q. Where were you beaten—where were you taken?
A. There was a building over here behind these garages, the ones I indicated, and that was an office belonging to the Betonirka firm. That's where they took us and that's where they beat us. That was in the evening. During the day, they would take us to the police station.

Q. Who beat you at these buildings? First of all, who beat you at the building behind the Betonirka garages?
A. Anybody who came first, the guards, children coming back from school, people going home from the cafe. So this began at 10.00 at night until it was over, and I know the kind of language they spoke so that if the children came by they would sort of train karate beating us. We had to do push-ups, for example, and then two men would kick us in one part of our body and the other would use a baton to hit up over the head with it until you become unconscious. Once you lose consciousness then something else happens which I don't want to say in open session, in public session, but if we go into private session I can tell you what happened to us.

Q. You said that on some occasion you lost consciousness. What other injuries did you receive as a result of the beatings?
A. Well, I had fractures, broken ribs, six or seven vertebras were affected. I had a fracture on my arm. They made me make the sign of the cross which I refused to do, and so when I was doing push-ups, they stepped on my hands so my fingers were broken.

Q. Did you receive any medical care for the injuries you suffered?
A. No. And the wound on my back went septic and the doctors used a razor blade to treat it at Manjaca. (pp. 1,028–1,029)

[pp. 1,029–1,033 omitted]

Q. Mr. Zulic, how often were you interrogated and/or beaten in Manjaca?

A. To be honest, I was rarely beaten up, only one sent [as interpreted]. I don't even count the occasional hitting. [W]hen I allowed the Red Cross delegation to examine me that had arrived that day from Geneva, after that they beat me nearly to death along with two other men.

Q. You said that you were nearly beat to death. What injuries did you receive as a result of this beating?
A. Well, I had horrific injuries that you can see on me today, that I can feel to this day. And if I showed you—if I wanted to show you I would have to take my clothes off.

Q. I will ask you to describe a little later the injuries that you have. But just getting back to this beating that occurred as a result of you allowing the Red Cross to examine you, what happened to you that night after you were severely beaten?
A. Somebody pulled me into the building, into the stable. I really don't know who it was. I was in terrible pain. There was water in my lungs.

Q. What happened the following morning?
A. The following morning, one paramedic came in on the sly and gave me some medicine and told me to take it, and, of course, I could see when they were taking out those people—whether you were able to stand up or not, you had to stand up and get out when it was time. So I could see the bodies being taken out: Esad Filipovic and Omer Bender. . . .

Q. And you said that you saw the bodies being taken out. Were these two men—had these two men died?
A. They died. They died after being beaten up. (pp. 1,034–1,035)

SECOND WITNESS

This witness was permitted to testify under conditions that guaranteed anonymity for fear of retribution. The prosecutor (Mr. Julian Nicholls) read the following summary of events to the Court based upon the written statement of the witness. At the beginning of March 1993, the witness and his family were forced from their home by Bosnian Serb forces. On July 13, the witness was hiding in some woods with other refugees. Bosnian Serb soldiers with megaphones called on the people in the woods to surrender. The excerpt below comes from an oral summary of his testimony presented to the Court by the prosecutor.

April 21, 2010

Statement
That afternoon at around 1500 hours, he and many others decided to surrender to Serb soldiers who were calling them. These prisoners, approximately a thousand of them, over a thousand of them, according to the witness's estimate, were lined

up in rows in a large group in a meadow in Sandici next to the Bratunac-Konjevic Polje road. There were also some women, girls, and boys present amongst the prisoners at Sandici meadow. About a dozen boys under 15 and some women and girls were permitted to get onto buses carrying Muslim women and children from Srebrenica which were passing by on the Bratunac-Konjevic Polje road taking these people from Potocari. That afternoon, General Mladić came to Sandici meadow and he addressed the prisoners, promising them that they would be exchanged. And the prisoners applauded General Mladić when he said that. Later that evening, a large number of trucks and buses arrived at Sandici. The prisoners boarded those buses and trucks and were taken away to Bratunac.

He spent the night, the witness spent the night, 13 to 14 July, in Bratunac inside the truck he'd been placed on, parked outside buildings of Vihor garages. During the night some prisoners were taken off of these parked trucks. Soldiers would shout out for prisoners from certain villages, and those who answered were taken off the trucks. The witness could hear sounds of beating, screams, shots being fired, and these prisoners were not seen again and were not returned to the trucks. The witness himself did not see any prisoners being shot from inside of his truck, but this is what he heard around him.

The next day, 14 July, the trucks and buses left Bratunac in a long convoy, 20 to 30 vehicles the witness saw, and headed north towards Zvornik via Konjevic Polje. In Divic, a village just south of Zvornik, the witness saw a white UN APC. The convoy of vehicles continued to Karakaj, north of Zvornik, and then turned left in the general direction of Tuzla, the witness hoped, and the others, that they were being taken to Tuzla for an exchange. However, instead this convoy of trucks and buses went to Orahovac and stopped at the elementary school there. The UN APC was parked there in the schoolyard, and the witness realised it had actually been captured by Bosnian Serb soldiers.

The witness and hundreds and hundreds of other Muslim men, along with four young children aged approximately 10 to 14, placed in the gym of the elementary school at Orahovac and kept there as the gym kept filling up with prisoners. He and the other prisoners were forced to leave some of their clothing in a large pile on the way to the gym. The witness was told to take off his jacket and leave it there. Other men were told to take off their shirts—

[**Author comment:** *Take note of the following exchange between Karadžić and the Court. It occurs over and over again in the transcript.*]

THE ACCUSED: Objection, Excellency.

JUDGE [O-GON] KWON: Mr. Karadzic, yes.

THE ACCUSED: Yes, I would object, really. Of course, if—if—[Interpretation] In any case, if you want to hear this for dramatic reasons, the details of this to be presented, that's fine, but it will take away a lot of my time, and this is also a form of cumulative testimony in view of the fact that in the previous—

JUDGE KWON: Mr. Karadzic. This is unacceptable. This is a summary of the witness's evidence on the part of the Prosecution for the benefit of you and the public, and the Chamber as well. This is not part of evidence. You will be given ample opportunity to cross-examine this witness, so I would like you not to interrupt this, giving the summary of the evidence by the Prosecution. You can cross-examine the witness later on. Mr. Nicholls, please go on.

MR. NICHOLLS: Thank you.

The gym was packed and the witness and the other prisoners had to sit closely packed together as it became full. It was very hot that—on 14 July, and the prisoners were given some water but not nearly enough water for everybody, and they were very thirsty. From the time of his detention in Sandici meadow and up until his eventual escape, the witness was given some water on different occasions but no food. And the witness observed that none of the other prisoners were given food and none of the ill or wounded were given medical care. Also, the witness observed that at no time were the prisoners registered, listed, or counted by their captors.

They remained in the Orahovac school for a few hours and sometimes the guards would fire shots into the walls and ceiling to keep the prisoners quiet. Some officers arrived at the school and the prisoners were ordered to stand up in rows and face one end of the gym, and it was about this time that one of the prisoners objected and said that these men should not be killed. Guards took this prisoner outside and a shot was fired that the witness heard, and the man did not come back. Then another prisoner was taken out and again a shot was heard. Again, the prisoner did not come back.

Once the officers left, the soldiers began taking prisoners in groups through a small room next to the gym where they were given a cup of water by a female soldier, blindfolded, taken outside and placed in TAM trucks. And the witness estimates that approximately 30 prisoners could fit in the back of one of these TAM trucks.

Prisoners were told that they were being taken to a camp in Bijeljina as they got on the trucks. However, the trucks drove just a very short distance to a field in Orahovac and the prisoners were told then to get off the trucks. The men were lined up in rows and shot. The witness managed to survive by feigning death as he lay under the body of another victim. And the witness observed that approximately every 10 to 15 minutes a new truck full of prisoners would arrive, and those prisoners would be killed in the same manner.

These killings continued for hours. After nightfall, a loader truck arrived with its lights on, and as it continued, the witness lay still and heard some of the executioners speaking and calling to one another, and they called their leader by name. The witness recognised the first name and the distinctive voice of this leader of the executioners as a long-time co-worker who he knew was from the village of Orahovac. The leader told the other soldiers to collect ammunition and go to a nearby field to continue killing people. The soldiers then left and continued killing prisoners at a nearby field.

Later that night while the soldiers were distracted, the witness was able to escape into the woods. As he ran away, he got turned around at one point and found himself back at the killing site, and he saw that most of the field was covered in bodies. . . . After several very difficult days of—as he describes it, of moving and hiding, he managed to reach safety in Muslim-held territory. (pp. 1,287–1,292)

TIMELY JUSTICE AND THE REQUIREMENT OF "FAIR TRIALS"

The Milošević and Karadžić trials both illustrate the tension between the requirements of efficient and expeditious procedures and the imperative that trials be "fair." Given that the Courts were traversing new grounds, they tended to err on the side of "fairness." Given the importance of the trial, the Court made many concessions to ensure a perception of fairness. While the example in the testimony suggests that the Court kept a tight rein on Karadžić, in fact during his cross-examination of witnesses, it permitted him to engage in bullying tactics that occasionally bordered on intimidation before intervening. In normal circumstances, the continued conduct after warning would have merited sanctions or a contempt of court citation.

Even though Karadžić had elected to act as his own counsel, the Court appointed Peter Robinson, a respected defense attorney, to assist him in preparation of his case. The Court also paid for three case managers and two researchers. As additional resources, Karadžić had access to a network of volunteer on-call international lawyers and academics. For his defense, Karadžić called 238 witnesses.

He had promised a point by point destruction of the prosecution's case. This did not happen. Instead, after the first weeks of the trial, most of his cross-examination involved reading statements to witnesses and then asking them to confirm the information. The method had been used in other trials as a procedure to speed up lengthy and complex cases. In this case, however, observers thought that it served a different purpose. It provided a way to limit the possibility that Karadžić, as an amateur in the art of cross-examination, would ask questions that might damage his own case. Even with this safeguard in place, a number of Bosnian Serb army officers proved more useful for the prosecution than for the defense. In telling their side of the story, they all displayed an obvious indifference concerning the deaths of large numbers of Muslim civilians during the Sarajevo Siege.

The judges took more than a year to deliberate. Karadžić was convicted of genocide for the Srebrenica massacre. Proving genocide requires that the Prosecution must prove that the accused acted on a very narrowly defined *intent*. Genocidal acts must be taken "with intent to destroy, in whole, or in part." The Convention does include harmful actions other than that of simple killing, but this phrase places an important limiting condition in terms of the purposes of the destructive acts. Thus, a second genocide charge that involved seven Bosnian towns was reduced to "extermination."

The Court found him complicit in the campaign of sniping and shelling Sarajevo. While the Judges agreed that he did not know of the plans in advance, he became culpable by implication when he did not act to stop the slaughter after he did learn of it. He was found guilty of persecution, extermination, deportation, forcible transfer, and murder in connection with a campaign to drive Bosnian Muslims and Croats out of villages claimed by Serb forces during war (1992 to 1995); and, he was convicted of leading the seizure of UN employees as hostages, to obstruct NATO from carrying out airstrikes on behalf of besieged Bosnian Muslim civilians.

THE APPEALS PROCESS

In most domestic legal systems, the appeals process normally considers only questions of law, not those of fact unless evidence of perjury or other errors have come to light after the conclusion of the trial. In addition, in domestic law, an acquittal ends a case. Only convictions are subject to appeal. The international process has some different wrinkles. An interesting feature of the international process is that prosecutors may appeal any decision of a trial including an acquittal on a charge. After the completion of the prosecution case in June 2012, Karadžić moved for a judgement of acquittal on all counts of the indictment. After a hearing, the Trial Chamber found that there was "no evidence, even taken at its highest, which could be capable of supporting a conviction for genocide in the municipalities as charged under Article 4(3) of the Statute." The Trial Chamber then entered a Judgement of Acquittal on Count 1 of the Indictment, which charged Karadžić with genocide in the Municipalities. The Prosecution immediately appealed the decision of the Trial Court. The prosecution brief alleged the Court erred "in law and in fact" including their rejection of "genocidal intent." The Appeals Chamber reversed the Trial Chamber's acquittal of Karadžić for genocide in the Municipalities under Count 1 of the Indictment; and reinstated the charges against him. (Rule 98 *bis* Appeals Judgement summary in the case of Radovan Karadžić, July 11, 2013).

Appeals Chambers have frequently reminded prosecutors and defense counsels that an appeal does not provide an opportunity to re-argue a case. On appeal, the parties must limit their arguments to matters that fall within the scope of Article 25 of the Statute. In the *Kupreškić* case the ICTY Appeals Chamber stated that "the general rule is that the Appeals Chamber will not entertain arguments that do not allege legal errors invalidating the judgement, or factual errors occasioning a miscarriage of justice." With respect to an appeal that alleges an error of law, the Appeals Chamber has the authority to reverse or revise the decision of a Trial Chamber only if the error would invalidate the decision. Not every error of law justifies a reversal or alteration of a decision (Schabas 2006, 444).

In the Karadžić verdict, recall that the Trial Chamber still reduced the charge to "extermination" before finding Karadžić guilty. The appeal brief focuses on errors of law but also disputes facts, particularly in Section III that deals with the Municipalities charges. In the original trial, Karadžić, like Milošević, had acted as his own legal counsel based on the argument that he knew the facts much better than anyone else. He entrusted the appeal to the attorney, Peter Robinson, who had assisted him during the original trial because appeals depend more on issues of law than issues of fact. The following summarizes the initial filing of Mr. Robinson and his team. The Prosecution also filed a brief. Each side has filed a rebuttal to the respective initial briefs; and both sides have filed a set of responses to the rebuttals. The Appeal Judgement from the MICT is expected sometime in early 2019.

DOCUMENT: RADOVAN KARADŽIĆ'S APPEAL BRIEF

When: December 23, 2016
Where: The Hague, Netherlands
Source: The Mechanism for International Criminal Tribunals [MICT-13-55-A 2].
Online at http://www.unmict.org/en/cases/mict-13-55.
Counsel: Peter Robinson, Kate Gibson
Significance: The following presents the main objections to Karadžić's conviction. The Table of Contents summarizes the points raised by the defense.

TABLE OF CONTENTS

I. INTRODUCTION

II. THE TRIAL WAS UNFAIR

1. The Trial Chamber violated President Karadzic's right to self-representation by requiring him to be questioned by counsel when testifying

2. The Trial Chamber erred in conducting a site visit in President Karadzic's absence

3–5. The Trial Chamber erred in convicting President Karadzic on Counts Four, Seven, and Eleven where the Indictment was defective

6. The Trial Chamber's failure to limit the scope of the trial and remedy the Prosecution's disclosure violations made the trial unfair

7. The Trial Chamber erred in taking judicial notice of adjudicated facts

8–9. The Trial Chamber erred in refusing to enable President Karadzic to interview Prosecution Rule 92 *bis* witnesses

10. The Trial Chamber erred in refusing to call Prosecution Rule 92 *bis* witness Ferid Spahic for cross-examination

11–12. The Trial Chamber erred in excluding Defence Rule 92 *bis* evidence

13. The Trial Chamber erred in refusing to admit written evidence from Pero Rendic and Branko Basara

14. The Trial Chamber erred in refusing to admit the written evidence of Borivoje Jakovljevic

15. The Trial Chamber erred in refusing to admit the written evidence of deceased witness Rajko Koprivica

16. The excessive number of adjudicated facts and Rule 92 *bis* evidence violated the presumption of innocence and shifted the burden of proof

17. The Trial Chamber erred in delaying disclosure of the identities and statements of Prosecution witnesses

18. The Trial Chamber erred in denying protective measures for Defence witnesses and granting protective measures for Prosecution witnesses

19. The Trial Chamber erred in refusing to subpoena four Defence witnesses

20. The Trial Chamber erred in refusing to compel General Mladic to answer President Karadzic's questions

[Numbers 21–27 omitted]

III. THE MUNICIPALITIES

28. The Trial Chamber erred in finding that there was a common plan to permanently remove Muslims and Croats from Serb territory to create a homogeneous entity

29. There are cogent reasons to hold that for JCE III liability, the extended crime must be more than a possibility

30. The Trial Chamber erred when convicting President Karadzic of persecution by forcible transfer of prisoners—a crime not charged in the indictment

31. The Trial Chamber erred when convicting President Karadzic of scheduled incidents based solely on untested evidence

IV. SARAJEVO

33. The Trial Chamber misapplied principles of the law of armed conflict in its analysis of the shelling of Sarajevo

34. The Trial Chamber erred when concluding that the VRS fired the shell that landed on the Markale market on 5 February 1994

36–37. The Trial Chamber erred when finding that President Karadzic shared the common purpose of spreading terror among the civilian population of Sarajevo and in relying on a meeting that never occurred

V. SREBRENICA

38–39. The Trial Chamber erred when finding that President Karadzic shared the common purpose of removing the Bosnian Muslims from Srebrenica and when relying on Directive 7

40. The Trial Chamber erred when concluding that President Karadzic agreed to the killing of Bosnian Muslim males from Srebrenica and shared the common purpose of eliminating them

41. The Trial Chamber erred when concluding that President Karadzic had the *mens rea* for genocide

42–43. The Trial Chamber erred in finding President Karadzic responsible as a superior for 13 July killings

VI. HOSTAGE TAKING

44–45. The Trial Chamber erred in convicting President Karadzic of hostage taking.

46. The Trial Chamber erred in finding that there is an absolute prohibition of reprisals against protected persons

VII. SENTENCING

47–50. The Trial Chamber erred in declining to find mitigating circumstances when sentencing President Karadzic

The appeal turns on nuances of international law and criminal procedure that go beyond the purposes of this discussion. Nonetheless, for future reference, the decision here will form one of the most important precedents for future prosecutions.

References

Broz, Svetlana, Laurie Kain Hart, and Ellen Elias-Bursac. 2005. *Good People in an Evil Time: Portraits of Complicity and Resistance in the Bosnian War*. 2nd ed. New York: Other Press.

Rieff, David. 1995. *Slaughterhouse: Bosnia and the Failure of the West*. London: Vintage.

Schabas, William A. 2006. *The UN International Criminal Tribunals: The Former Yugoslavia, Rwanda and Sierra Leone*. Cambridge: Cambridge University Press.

Silber, Laura, and Allan Little. 1997. *Yugoslavia: Death of a Nation*. New York: Penguin Books.

26

Trial of Radislav Krstić

BOSNIAN SERB ARMY

The most powerful of the parties in the Bosnian War of 1992–1995, the Bosnian Serb Army was also the militia of the ruling Serbian Democratic Party (SDS), led by Radovan Karadžić. Officially known as Vojska Republike Srpske (VRS), the Bosnian Serb Army was formally constituted in May 1992. At the same time, the Federal Republic of Yugoslavia replaced the Yugoslav Peoples' Army (JNA) with a new Army of Yugoslavia. The VRS was created from 80,000 former JNA troops of Bosnian origin who had remained in Bosnia and Herzegovina after the JNA had officially left the republic. The departing JNA also left the VRS with large quantities of armaments and ammunition, numerous military installations, and military industries. Led by General Ratko Mladić, former JNA officers provided the high command of the VRS. Mladić had formerly commanded the First Krajina Corps and served during the earlier JNA campaign in Croatia.

Beginning in April 1992, the VRS carried out a ruthless and extremely violent blitzkrieg against its Bosnian Muslim (Bosniak) enemies, taking 70 percent of the territory of Bosnia and Herzegovina. This campaign included the "ethnic cleansing" of the Bosniak population from all Serb-controlled territories. Due to geography, the VRS could not take Sarajevo, the capital of Bosnia, without incurring large casualties. In May 1992, it began a long siege effort. Beyond Bosniak-controlled Sarajevo and a small triangular area of territory in central Bosnia, the Serbs then faced serious opposition only from the Croatian Council of Defense (Hrvatsko vijeće obrane, or HVO), in Herzegovina.

RADISLAV KRSTIĆ

From October 1994 until July 12, 1995, Radislav Krstić was the deputy commander and later chief of staff of the Drina Corps of the Army of Republika Srpska. Prior to the breakup of Yugoslavia, Krstić had served as a commissioned officer in the JNA. After the secession of Bosnia from Yugoslavia in April 1992, Krstić elected to return to his place of birth. He joined the VRS, where he was given the rank of lieutenant colonel. After seeing action in a number of engagements, and an accompanying series of promotions, in August 1994, Krstić became chief of staff and deputy commander of the Drina Corps. On December 29, 1994, Krstić stepped on a landmine and was seriously wounded; losing the lower part of his right leg. After a period of recuperation and treatment, he returned to active service in the middle of May 1995. He received a promotion to the rank of major general in June 1995 and assumed command of the Drina Corps on July 13, 1995.

The Drina Corps was one of six geographically based corps of the Army of the Republika Srpska (VRS) during the 1992–1995 Bosnian War. Elements of the Drina Corps were principally responsible for the Srebrenica Massacre (July 11–13, 1995), in which as many as 8,000 Bosniak men and boys were systematically slaughtered. Numbering some 15,000 men at its peak deployment, the Drina Corps was created in November 1992, under the command of General Milenko Zivanović; who commanded the unit until July 13,1995 when Radislav Krstić took charge.

SREBRENICA

In April 1993, in an effort to halt ethnic cleansing, the UN Security Council had declared Srebrenica to be a "safe haven," where persecuted civilian minorities could safely seek refuge. The city was then secured by peacekeeping troops under the United Nations Protection Force (UNPROFOR). In July 1995, the UNPROFOR force consisted of 1,170 Dutch troops. Despite its new status, Srebrenica was never properly defended by UNPROFOR and constantly suffered extreme privation as the Serbs tested the UN resolves by blocking aid convoys. Of over 30,000 UN troops requested for Bosnian Muslim "safe areas," only 7,600 were actually deployed. Only 750 Dutch troops were deployed at Srebrenica. The UN troops were lightly armed and operated under a stringent mandate (rules of engagement) that made them powerless to take any action of enforcement against either of the conflicting sides. By 1995, after almost three years of resistance, Srebrenica had become a symbol of Bosniak resistance, further increasing the city's importance.

On July 9, General Ratko Mladić, overall commander of the VRS, arrived in the area with orders that the town of Srebrenica must be taken. The Drina Wolves from the 1st Battalion of the Zvornik Brigade were the first VRS soldiers to enter the town of Srebrenica on July 10. After the area was cleared and more forces arrived, Krstić and his staff moved into the town of Srebrenica itself. Krstić visited nearby Potocari, the location of the base housing the Dutch soldiers of UNPROFOR. Because he operated under the overall command of Mladić and Zivanović, the full extent of his responsibility for the ensuing massacre is somewhat unclear. Nonetheless, when the Srebrenica operation began, Krstić held responsibility for the planning and execution of the campaign, and he was closely involved in the Bosnian Serb attacks at the height of the assault.

On July 12 and 13, women, children, and the elderly sheltered in the UN base were put onto buses and deported *en masse*. The men were then systematically hunted down in the hills surrounding the city and slaughtered. As second-in-command of Serbian forces responsible for the fall of Srebrenica, Krstić saw his troops massacre an estimated 8,000 Bosniak men and boys in Europe's worst atrocity since the Holocaust. During a period of several weeks, in September and early October 1995, Bosnian Serb forces dug up a number of the primary mass graves containing the bodies of executed Bosnian Muslim men and reburied them in secondary graves in still more remote locations. The Srebrenica Massacre became the worst single war crime of the entire Bosnian conflict. It shocked the international community. The UN secretary-general, Boutros Boutros-Ghali, labeled the killings as Europe's worst massacre since World War II.

Krstić remained a senior officer for the duration of the war. He led the attack that resulted in the capture of another UN safe haven, Zepa, on August 1, 1995. On November 21, 1995, he left his post as commander of the Drina Corps to attend the National Defense School in Belgrade. For crimes committed during the Srebrenica campaign, the ICTY issued an indictment and arrest warrant for Krstić on October 30, 1998. The charges included genocide, complicity to commit genocide, extermination, and two counts of murder, and persecution. Up to this point, Krstić had led an open life in Republika Srpska and had been given command of the 5th Corps of the VRS in April 1998. On December 2, 1998, however, he was arrested by soldiers of the United Nations Stabilization Force for Bosnia-Herzegovina (SFOR). He was transferred for trial to The Hague the next day.

TRIAL SUMMARY #18: *PROSECUTOR V. RADISLAV KRSTIĆ*

Defense Strategy

In his defense, Krstić denied all complicity and involvement in the Srebrenica Massacre. He acknowledged that war crimes had been committed by the VRS but denied that he had issued orders for the actions for which he had been charged. He placed full responsibility with Mladić. He claimed that he did not participate in planning, organizing, or ordering any killing or deportations. He denied knowing anything about such things until placed on trial. He pleaded not guilty to all charges. The strategy of denial did not work. On August 2, 2001, the Trial Chamber found Krstić guilty on all counts and sentenced him to forty-six years' imprisonment. He became the first person convicted of genocide by the Tribunal, and only the third person ever to have been convicted under the 1948 UN Convention on the Prevention and Punishment of the Crime of Genocide.

DOCUMENT: *PROSECUTOR V. RADISLAV KRSTIĆ*

Court:	International Criminal Tribunal for the Former Yugoslavia
Defendant:	Radislav Krstić
Where:	The Hague, Netherlands
When:	December 7, 1998–August 2, 2001
Source:	IT-98-33. Online at http://www.icty.org/case/krstic/4.
Charges:	Genocide, Complicity to commit genocide, Crimes Against Humanity (Murder, Persecutions, Deportation, and Inhumane Acts), and Violations of the Laws or Customs of War, as set forth in http://www.icty.org/x/cases/krstic/ind/en/krs-1ai991027e.pdf.

Verdict: Guilty on all counts; forty-six years
Significance: Krstić was not the first man convicted of genocide. That distinction belonged to Jean-Paul Akayesu, convicted by the ICTR. He, however, was the first to be convicted of genocide by the ICTY.

TESTIMONY

The following testimony deals with the events in Srebrenica. The witness is Nesib Mandzic, who prior to the war worked in a secondary school as a teacher in Srebrenica.

March 21, 2000

Q. Mr. Mandzic, let's move ahead in time to the 11th of July, 1995. You were still in the town of Srebrenica. Can you tell the Judges what you saw and heard on that day?
A. If we are talking about the urban area of Srebrenica, from that area more than half of the population had been expelled, forced out due to the military activities of the VRS, who, as early as the 10th of July, started setting Bosniak houses on fire in the Petrica Street. They were still firing from infantry weapons and so on. On the 11th of July, after 11.00 a.m., the situation got further complicated, because the VRS opened fire from their artillery, targeting the population itself and opening fire on the area where the population had gathered on the 10th of July, late in the afternoon.

I was very close to the area, some 70 metres as the crow flies, on the other side of the street. I was standing next to a building, and I could hear very well the sound of shells, artillery shells coming in Immediately after that, I would actually see the shell fall on the group of between 5,000, and 10,000 refugees who were staying there, expecting some kind of response from the UNPROFOR forces. They somehow felt safer in the vicinity of UNPROFOR. Immediately after this shell had fallen, I happened to see a terrible scene. I saw a column of smoke rising from the spot where the people had gathered. I heard screams, moans. There were some wounded people there.

. . .

Q. Let's move on in time, Mr. Mandzic. The population started to move towards Potocari. Can you tell the Judges when that happened and why it happened?
A. The population was forced to move. This happened on the 11th of July, around 4.00 p.m. The residents of the town started to move towards Potocari. They were actually forced to leave the last part of the safe area, because the VRS had continued with its offensive activities. So the population was actually being pushed from the area. They couldn't go back. They couldn't go back to the enclave itself, because everybody could see Bosniak houses on fire at that time. So in view of the situation, in view of the fear and feeling of helplessness,

residents started to move towards Potocari, which was the last safe haven in the area, that is, the command of the Dutch battalion.

Q. Mr. Mandzic, are you aware as to whether or not any senior member of the population, or members of the population, took a decision that the population would move to Potocari from Srebrenica?
A. It was no higher representative who would be inviting people to head for Potocari. It was all civilian population and they all thought about Potocari. The majority of the civilians thought about Potocari, because the major part of the enclave had already been physically taken by the troops of the VRS and there was nowhere else to go. We could only withdraw by a couple of kilometres further on towards the Dutch compound at Potocari. So the passage of the civilian population through the area, even those areas that were inhabited by Bosniaks before the war, but they had been taken by the armed forces of the Republika Srpska, so it was impossible to go through those places. Both the Serb artillery and infantry fire were targeting the population directly, and it seemed that their objective was to kill as many civilians as possible, to sow as much panic, to sow as much chaos amongst them.

And I can also corroborate by saying the following: On the 11th of July, I happened to be in the column of the civilian population on the road to Potocari. At that time the Serb artillery fired at us. From the neighbouring hills we could clearly see that there were—they could see that there were tens of thousands of refugees who were on their way to Potocari, to the Dutch battalion. But they were so aggressive that they simply opened direct fire on this stream of refugees which was several kilometres long....

Q. Let's move to the evening of the 11th of 12 July, 1995. Where do you find yourself?
A. I found myself at Potocari, or to be more accurate, within the compound of the 11 of March Factory. [UN Compound] ...

Q. Can you tell the Judges the scene on the evening of the 11th of July in and around the UN compound at Potocari?
A. Yes, indeed. The scene was hair-raising. Something about 25,000 of those expellees....
were crowding in a very small, in a very tight space. They tried to find some accommodation in some ancient factory.

Q. Mr. Mandzic, if you could stop there. There's a mistake in the transcript and then you said the scene was hair-raising and then you said, "Something about 25,000 of those...." Twenty-five thousand of whom?
A. The expellees, the expelled refugees, Bosniak people who had been expelled from the largest part of the enclave, because only a minor part of the enclave was surviving, and that was Potocari.

Q. Please continue with your testimony.
A. At that very small space of perhaps less than one kilometre square, there were some 25.000 expelled. Most of them were women with small children,

elderly and emaciated people. We were all without food or water or medicines or clothing or footwear, accommodation, or anything. We expected that the International Community would give us protection, fearing the worst from the Bosnian Serb army, and indeed I do remember that 11th of July, sometime around 2100, the Bosnian Serb army launched an operation. As far as I can remember, they opened artillery fire at this crowd, this multitude of people forced into that space.

Q. Did you see the artillery firing?
A. Well, they fired over my head, over the heads of 25,000 people.

Q. Do you know roughly how far away they were, the VRS artillery, when they were firing at this huge multitude of people?
A. Some 300 to 500 meters. From different 3 places, so I say it was 300 meters was the closest and 500 meters was perhaps the site furthest away.

Q. How did the population react to this artillery fire?
A. We all tried to find some shelter, but there was none, so we simply threw ourselves down on the asphalt, somewhere in the street, that is, on the road from Potocari to Bratunac, because they couldn't find any shelter whatsoever. So panic again started, screaming, and so—

Q. Do you know of any deaths or injuries that were caused by that artillery.
A. As soon as this artillery fire stopped, the Dutch battalion called me, and so that night I could not really hear if there had been any wounded, because that night, between the 11th and the 12th, I spent in the camp of the Dutch soldiers.

March 22, 2000

Q. Now, the movement of the population, do you recall what time the movement of the population that was still in the UN compound finished on the 13th of July?
A. Yes. Sometime around 1900 on the 13th of July, the Dutch soldiers' camp, where there were still some 5.000 people, but it was practically empty, the army of Republika Srpska ordered all the expellees, all the expelled, to come out of the camp so after 1900 there was only a small group of severely wounded, and a group of Bosniaks who had been working for UNPROFOR or MSF as their local staff were left in the camp.

Q. Now, since these were individuals that had been in the compound rather than outside the compound, were you able to observe more closely what was actually happening with these individuals that were being expelled?
A. Yes.

Q. Can you tell the Judges what you saw taking place?
A. I can, yes. On the 12th of July and on the 13th of July too, I saw and I watched women and small children board buses, trucks, and the scene which I described, women crying, children screaming, those women tearing their hair off, in pain because their next of kin had been separated from them. I could see that they

were evacuating or, rather, deporting women and children. And in the same manner they evacuated or, rather, deported men from the Dutch Battalion compound, where there were some 5,000 people. One could invariably see one or two soldiers who would announce, "Now, this group. That group goes now. One hundred, 200, 300, move," and so on and so forth.

Q. Now, you say that you saw men being deported, and by the manner of your evidence, are you saying that the men were being separated?
A. Yes. I watched from a distance of some 50 to 100 metres away how only women with small children boarded the buses, with children up—from infants from up to 12, 13 years of age. I saw those women screaming, moaning, crying, tearing their hair off. On that day, the 13th of July, on the 12th of July, the same scene repeated over and over again. Everybody reacted in the same way. And I could see that male individuals, as of the age of 12 or 13, had been separated by force from their next of kin, from their families.

Q. Who was carrying out the separation of the men from their families?
A. Well, soldiers of the VRS.

Q. Now, speaking of these VRS soldiers, did you observe the uniforms and the insignia of these soldiers?
A. Yes, I did. On the first day, on the 11th of July, and on the following day, on the 12th of July, as I was coming back from Bratunac on my way to Potocari, I could observe hundreds of soldiers standing next to the road, wearing uniforms, brand-new uniforms, I might say. Some of them were wearing the insignia of the VRS. Some didn't have any insignia at all. But they did have new military clothing. I could also hear various dialects, very just accents which did not resemble the dialect, the Ijekavski dialect, which is used by Bosnian Serbs in the region of Podrinje in Eastern Bosnia.

THE APPEAL

Krstić's legal team appealed the judgement, as did the prosecution. The prosecution based its appeal on two grounds: the Trial Chamber's conclusion on impermissible cumulative convictions (a complex technicality) and the sentence imposed by the Trial Chamber. It requested the imposition of a life sentence with a minimum of thirty years' imprisonment. The defense based its appeal on four grounds. First, it contested the conviction for genocide, alleging both factual and legal errors. It claimed that the court misconstrued the legal definition of genocide and erred in applying the definition to several cases. Second, it appealed on the basis of various disclosure practices of the prosecution (a procedural issue), which allegedly deprived Krstić of a fair trial. Third, the defense contended that the Trial Chamber made a number of other factual and legal errors. Fourth, it appealed the sentence handed down to Krstić, alleging that the Trial Chamber failed to take into account the sentencing practice in the former Yugoslavia and gave insufficient weight to the mitigating circumstances.

The principal issue here focuses on the Appeals Chamber discussion of Genocide. In the following discussion, one must keep firmly in mind that the key element in the legal definition of genocide is *intent*. In the summary of its judgement, the Appeals Chamber unanimously found that ". . . Bosnia Serb forces carried out genocide against the Bosnian Muslims." The judgement, the Appeals Chamber noted:

> Among the grievous crimes this Tribunal has the duty to punish, the crime of genocide is singled out for special condemnation and opprobrium. The crime is horrific in its scope; its perpetrators identify entire human groups for extinction. Those who devise and implement genocide seek to deprive humanity of the manifold richness its nationalities, races, ethnicities and religions provide. This is a crime against all of humankind, its harm being felt not only by the group targeted for destruction, but by all of humanity.
>
> *The gravity of genocide is reflected in the stringent requirements which must be satisfied before this conviction is imposed. These requirements—the demanding proof of specific intent and the showing that the group was targeted for destruction in its entirety or in substantial part—guard against a danger that convictions for this crime will be imposed lightly.* Where these requirements are satisfied, however, the law must not shy away from referring to the crime committed by its proper name. By seeking to eliminate a part of the Bosnian Muslims, the Bosnian Serb forces committed genocide. [emphasis added]
>
> They targeted for extinction the forty thousand Bosnian Muslims living in Srebrenica, a group which was emblematic of the Bosnian Muslims in general. They stripped all the male Muslim prisoners, military and civilian, elderly and young, of their personal belongings and identification, and deliberately and methodically killed them solely on the basis of their identity. The Bosnian Serb forces were aware, when they embarked on this genocidal venture, that the harm they caused would continue to plague the Bosnian Muslims. The Appeals Chamber states unequivocally that the law condemns, in appropriate terms, the deep and lasting injury inflicted, and calls the massacre at Srebrenica by its proper name: genocide. Those responsible will bear this stigma, and it will serve as a warning to those who may in future contemplate the commission of such a heinous act.
>
> In concluding that some members of the VRS Main Staff intended to destroy the Bosnian Muslims of Srebrenica, the Trial Chamber did not depart from the legal requirements for genocide. The Defence appeal on this issue is dismissed. (http://www.icty.org/x/cases/krstic/acjug/en/krs-aj040419e.pdf, pp. 6–7)

The issue, however, was, did the prosecution establish beyond doubt that Krstić had demonstrated the necessary intent to sustain a charge of genocide? In appeals that involve allegations of errors of fact, the standard adopted by Appeals Chambers has been that of "reasonableness" (Schabas 2006, 445). In review, the Appeals Chamber found:

> The case against Radislav Krstić was one based on circumstantial evidence, and the finding of the Trial Chamber was largely based upon a combination of circumstantial facts. In convicting Mr Krstić as a participant in a joint criminal enterprise to commit genocide, the Trial Chamber relied upon evidence establishing his knowledge of the intention on the part of General Mladić and other members of the VRS Main Staff to execute the Bosnian Muslims of Srebrenica, his knowledge of the use of personnel and resources of the Drina Corps to carry out that intention given his command position, and upon evidence that Radislav Krstić supervised the participation of his subordinates in carrying out those executions. . . .
>
> The Appeals Chamber is of the view *that all that the evidence can establish is that Mr Krstić was aware of the intent to commit genocide on the part of some members*

of the Main Staff, and with that knowledge, he did nothing to prevent the use of Drina Corps personnel and resources to facilitate those killings. This knowledge on his part alone cannot support an inference of genocidal intent. Genocide is one of the worst crimes known to humankind, and its gravity is reflected in the stringent requirement of specific intent. Convictions for genocide can be entered only where that intent has been unequivocally established. There was a demonstrable failure by the Trial Chamber to supply adequate proof that Radislav Krstić possessed genocidal intent. *Mr Krstić, therefore, is not guilty of genocide as a principal perpetrator.* (p. 12, emphasis added)

Based upon this reasoning, the Appeals Chamber concluded that "Radislav Krstić's responsibility is properly characterized as that of aiding and abetting genocide."

The Appeals Chamber continued to explain its reasoning by arguing "that an individual who aids and abets a specific intent offense may be held responsible if he assists the commission of the crime knowing the intent behind the crime. . . . The conviction for aiding and abetting genocide upon proof that the defendant knew about the principal perpetrator's genocidal intent is permitted by the Statute and case-law of the Tribunal. The same approach is followed by many domestic jurisdictions, both common and civil law" (pp. 13–14).

The disposition of the other issues had little impact on the decision of the Appeals Chamber to reduce Krstić's sentence to thirty-five years with credit for time served. The modification in charges changed the nature of his liability from that of a direct planner and participant to that of an "aider and abettor."

References

Brkic, Courtney Angela. 2004. *The Stone Fields: An Epitaph for the Living.* New York: Farrar, Straus, and Giroux.

Pontus, Thierry. 2005. *J'étais médecin dans Srebrenica assiégée: Au prélude du grand massacre* (I was a doctor during the Srebrenica siege: Prelude to the great massacre). French ed. Paris: L'Harmattan, 2005.

Rohde, David. [1997] 2012. *Endgame: The Betrayal and Fall of Srebrenica, Europe's Worst Massacre since World War II.* New York: Penguin Books.

Schabas, William A. 2006. *The UN International Criminal Tribunals: The Former Yugoslavia, Rwanda and Sierra Leone.* Cambridge: Cambridge University Press.

27

Croatia, Operation Storm, and Ante Gotovina

CROATIA

Julian Borger, who covered the Balkan Wars for *The Guardian* (Manchester, UK), observed that for Franjo Tuđman, the president of Croatia, "the very idea of Croatian war criminals was an oxymoron" (2016, 101). For Tuđman, those who fought for Croatian independence from the Serb-dominated Yugoslavia were heroes. The war criminals were the Serbs and all others who opposed Croatia. The Croats were victims, not perpetrators. Tuđman and his successors resisted efforts to bring Croats accused of war crimes before the ICTY. Borger also notes that when the Croatian government finally succumbed to Western pressure and permitted the extradition of Dario Kordić, one of the principals involved in the Lašva Valley massacres, along with nine others associated with the Hrvatsko vijeće obrane (HVO), a large crowd of supporters gathered at the airport to wish them well.

Document: Operation Storm: Croatia's Triumph, Serbia's Grief

Differing perceptions of Operation Storm have long been a bitterly divisive factor in relations between Croatia and Serbia.

Zagreb views Storm as a military triumph that liberated its territory from Serb aggression—the crowning victory of what Croatia calls its "Homeland War" for independence from 1991–95. "It was professionally and superbly conducted," Sinisa Kralj, a retired Croatian artillery officer who fought during Storm, told BIRN. "We were defending our country. The civilians who died—well, in every war a lot of civilians get killed," he said. He insisted that he saw no brutal abuses of Serbs during the operation. Croatian prime minister Zoran Milanovic has also described the war as "just, defensive and human."

But for Serbian prime minister Aleksandar Vucic, Operation Storm was "the biggest [example of] ethnic cleansing since World War II." While Croatia will celebrate the 20th anniversary this week, Serbia will solemnly commemorate the victims. "We just want to mourn the expelled and killed Serbs and no one can stop us from crying for them and lighting a candle," Vucic said.

These two rival viewpoints are almost impossible to reconcile, said Belgrade-based sociologist Jovo Bakic.

Source: Marija Ristic, Ivana Nikolic, and Sven Milekic. "Operation Storm: Croatia's Triumph, Serbia's Grief." Balkan Transitional Justice. August 2, 2015. Used by permission of BIRN. Online at http://www.balkaninsight.com/en/article/operation-storm-croatia-s-triumph-serbia-s-grief-07-31-2015.

BALKAN TRANSITIONAL JUSTICE

Of course, if reversed, this version of the Croat narrative then becomes the Serb lament as well—the criminals were Croats (and Bosniaks) and Serbs were the victims. Just as Milošević pursued the idea of a Greater Serbia, Tuđman pursued the idea of a Greater Croatia. Both did so at the expense of the Muslim populations in their own respective countries as well as the Bosniaks. Demonized and marginalized by both visions, the Muslim population, wherever it resided, became the ultimate victim. Like Milošević, Tuđman would have faced prosecution if he had not died of stomach cancer in 1999. A great deal of evidence indicated that Tuđman had personally helped plan and direct the "ethnic cleansing" of Serbs and Muslims in Croatian-held territory in Bosnia.

In Belgrade, many regard Radovan Karadjić, Željko Ražnatović (Arkan), and Ratko Mladić as heroes unjustly accused and persecuted by forces that had no basis for intervention and no authority to pass judgement on events. Shops sell coffee mugs emblazoned with their pictures. One finds a "culture of victimization" that does not acknowledge that the actions of Serbian forces, either local or JNA, were improper in any respect. Serbs see themselves as the main victims in the breakup of Yugoslavia. They resent that tens of thousands of Serbs were expelled from Croatia in 1995 in the Croatians' own "ethnic cleansing" campaign, which also included forced deportation. These complaints should not be dismissed lightly. People react to the perception of personal consequences to themselves and their neighbors regardless of what precipitated the events that led to the eventual outcome.

CROATIA AND THE ICTY

Tihomir Blaškić

Unlike Milošević, Tuđman looked to the West for support. His goal was having Croatia accepted as a member of the European Union and the NATO alliance. These aspirations provided the incentive that finally pushed him to cooperate with the ICTY. The first Croat to surrender was Tihomir Blaškić, who had commanded the Central Bosnia Operative Zone of the HVO. The initial indictment joined Blaškić's case with that of Dario Kordić and Mario Čerkez and several others.

Although Blaškić surrendered, the others still remained at large. To expedite the process, the Prosecutor decided to sever his indictment from the original and proceed to trial [IT-95-14]. Blaškić was sentenced to forty-five years' imprisonment after being found guilty of committing, ordering, planning, or otherwise aiding and abetting various crimes against the Bosnian Muslim population in central Bosnia and Herzegovina (Lašva Valley). Close to the entire Muslim population had been driven from their homes and systematically slaughtered. As in other instances, the shock to survivors came from the fact that long-time neighbors helped.

On appeal, the ICTY Appeals Chamber dismissed sixteen of nineteen counts in the initial indictment, most notably the claims that Blaškić had command responsibility for the massacre in Ahmići and the charge that Ahmići was not a legitimate military target. The appeals panel reaffirmed less serious charges, including responsibility for the inhumane treatment of POWs. It reduced Blaškić's prison sentence to nine years. His defense applied for an early release because he had already served eight years and four months in detention. This request was granted in late July 2004 (see ICTY, "Tihomir Blaškić Granted Early Release," Press Release, July 29, 2004). Exactly one year later, ICTY prosecutor Carla Del Ponte filed a motion for new trial, citing new evidence. The Appeals Chamber dismissed this motion on November 23, 2006.

Kordić and the Nine (The Lašva Valley Ten)

The disposition of the cases against Kordić and his co-defendants illustrates the pitfalls of international prosecution. The events giving rise to these prosecutions also took place during the conflict between the Croatian Defense Council (HVO) and the Bosnian Muslim Army in the Lašva Valley region. Of the original ten accused, only four were found guilty. Two of the ten had the charges dropped before trial and four were acquitted. Kordić received a twenty-five-year sentence, and the other three received sentences ranging from six to eighteen years.

As did the later Gotovina trial, these hearings illustrated how deeply Tuđman was involved in the planning, organization, and active direction of the HVO. The Appeals Chamber Judgement in the *Kordić* case (IT-95-14/2-A) stated that the "Appeals Chamber is satisfied that 'Croatia exercised overall control over the HVO' and 'provided leadership, coordination and organisation of the HVO and that there was an international armed conflict between Croatia and Bosnia and Herzegovina'" (Appeals Judgement, Summary).

But, even though testimony in this trial and the Gotovina trial identified Tuđman as a key member of the relevant "joint criminal enterprises" (JCE), the full extent of his involvement in the ethnic cleansing did not emerge until the ICTY trial of Jadranko Prlić, et al. (IT-04-74). Prlić served as president of Herceg-Bosna. Just as the Serbs had declared their ambitions with Republika Srpska, Croats had declared a Croatian Community of Herceg-Bosna in November 1991. In August 1993, the Croatian Community of Herceg-Bosna declared itself the Croatian Republic of Herceg-Bosna. Herceg-Bosna was formally abolished in

August 1996. The Trial Judgement in the *Prlić* case issued on May 29, 2013, stated that:

> As early as December 1991, the leadership of the Croatian Community of Herceg-Bosna (which included Mate Boban, president of the Croatian Community (and later Republic) of Herceg-Bosna) and Croatian leaders (including Franjo Tuđman, the president of Croatia) deemed that in order to achieve the ultimate goal, namely the establishment of a Croatian territorial entity as previously described, it was necessary to modify the ethnic composition of the territories claimed to be part of the Croatian Community of Herceg-Bosna. From at least the end of October 1992, Prlić, Stojić, Petković and Praljak were aware that achieving this goal went against the peace talks conducted in Geneva and would entail moving Muslim populations out of the territory of Herceg-Bosna. (Prlić, Case Information Sheet, p. 6)

In late November 2017, the Appeals Chamber affirmed the verdicts of the Trial Chamber. Prlić received a sentence of 25 years. His codefendants received lesser punishment: Bruno Stojić (20 years), Slobodan Praljak (20 years), Milivoj Petković (20 years), Valentin Ćorić (16 years), and Berislav Pušić (10 years).

The relatively minimal sentence given to Blaškić, combined with the dismissal of cases, and acquittals in the Lašva Valley Ten proceedings confirmed the belief of Serbs that the ICTY and the international community had singled them out as scapegoats for all the troubles and atrocities in the former Yugoslavia, while excusing others or giving them a mere slap on the wrist for doing the same things. Despite the fact that later a Trial Chamber acquitted the head of Yugoslav State Security, Jovica Sanišić, and his deputy, Franko Simatović [IT-03-6], and the Appeals Chamber reversed the conviction of General Momĉilo Perišić, chief of staff of the Yugoslav Army [IT-04-81], for Serbs, the outcome of the *Gotovina, et al.* case etched the perception of bias in stone.

ANTE GOTOVINA, IVAN ČERMAK, AND MLADEN MARKAČ

Ante Gotovina began his military career by enlisting in the French Foreign Legion (FFL) at age 17. During his enlistment, he participated in a number of French operations in Africa. After the FFL, he worked for a variety of French private security companies before returning to Croatia in 1991 when the Croatian War of Independence had just started. He enlisted in the Croatian National Guard (ZNG), the first organized military body in Croatia. Upon Croatia's declaration of independence from Yugoslavia, it would become the Croatian Army (HV).

Gotovina rapidly established himself as an excellent leader. Unlike most other Croatian soldiers, he had combat experience. He served a short term with the Croatian Defense Council (HVO), before becoming Commander of the Split Military District. As the Commander of the Split military district, he organized several successful key military operations that thwarted and reversed the gains made by the Bosnian Serb general Ratko Mladić. He commanded Operation Storm ("Oluja"), August 4–6, 1995, in which forces under his command rolled back Serbian advances. The Serbian retreat ended only because President Franjo Tuđman honored the Dayton Agreement to cease hostilities.

While Tuđman had finally cooperated by giving up Blaškić and the Lašva Valley Ten, Croatian authorities deliberately and repeatedly frustrated attempts to arrest Gotovina. The reluctance to provide assistance and often active resistance had its price. The prosecutor, Carla Del Ponte, highlighted Croatian resistance in every public appearance, particularly in reports to the United Nations. Talks scheduled for March 2005 concerning the possible admission of Croatia into the European Union were cancelled. Investigators eventually found Gotovina in Tenerife, Canary Islands. With the help of local police, he was arrested and taken to The Hague in December 2007.

Indictment

The initial indictment against Ante Gotovina was confirmed in June 2001. It asserted that as commander, Gotovina possessed effective control over all units, elements, and members of the HV that comprised or were attached to the Split Military District and such other forces as were subordinated to his command and operated and/or were present in the southern portion of the Krajina region during Operation Storm. Ante Gotovina was considered a Croatian war hero—the man who had finally driven the Serbians out of Croatia after three years of occupation. This signaled the beginning of the end game of the Yugoslav war.

An indictment against Ivan Čermak and Mladen Markač was confirmed in February 2004. On July 14, 2006, the Trial Chamber granted the prosecution's consolidated motion to amend the indictment and join the two sets of indictments. All three accused appealed the decision. On October 25, 2006, the Appeals Chamber affirmed the Trial Chamber's decision, making the joinder indictment the operative indictment for the case. The amended joinder indictment alleged that, on August 4, 1995, Croatia launched a military offensive known as Operation Storm (or "Oluja"), with the objective of retaking the Krajina region of the country. On August 7, 1995, the Croatian government announced that the operation had been successfully completed. Follow-up actions continued until the middle of November in 1995.

Ivan Čermak served as assistant minister of defence in the Croatian government from 1991 to 1993. From early August 1995, he commanded the Knin Garrison. From October 1990, eight months before Croatia declared independence (June 25, 1991) from Yugoslavia. Knin was the main stronghold for the Serbs in the region. It became the capital city of the internationally unrecognized Republic of Serbian Krajina in 1991. Serbs held the town until Croatian forces captured it during Operation Storm on August 5, 1995. The indictment states that "in his combined capacities, Ivan CERMAK participated in various structures of power and responsibility and possessed effective control over members of the HV units or elements who comprised or were attached to, or operated in the Knin Garrison, and also over civilian police who operated in the Garrison area and areas adjacent to it."

From February 1994, Mladen Markač commanded the Special Police of the Ministry of the Interior of the Republic of Croatia. This position gave him overall authority and responsibility for the operation and functioning of the Special Police. As commander, he "participated in various structures of power and responsibility and possessed effective control over all members of the Special Police who were involved in Operation Storm and the continuing related operations and/or actions in that region."

In the indictment, the "Factual Description of the Joint Criminal Enterprise" alleges that:

> From at least July 1995 to 30 September 1995, Ante GOTOVINA, Ivan CERMAK and Mladen MARKAC, along with other persons described below, participated in a joint criminal enterprise, the common purpose being the permanent removal of the Serb population from the Krajina region by force, fear or threat of force, persecution, forced displacement, transfer and deportation, appropriation and destruction of property or other means. These constituted or involved the commission of crimes punishable under Articles 3 and 5 of the Tribunal Statute, as further described herein. In addition to the crimes which were set out above as part of the joint criminal enterprise, it was foreseeable that the crimes of murder, inhumane acts and cruel treatment were a possible consequence in the execution of the enterprise. (pp. 2–3, May 17, 2007)

Trial and Verdicts

The Trial Chamber Judgement asserted that Franjo Tuđman, the main political and military leader in Croatia before, during, and after the Indictment period, was the key member of the joint criminal enterprise. It found that Tuđman intended to repopulate the Krajina with Croats and ensured that his ideas were transformed into policy and action through his powerful position as president and supreme commander of the armed forces. Tuđman and high-ranking military officials discussed how the military forces should be used to ensure that not only the Serb Krajina army but also the Serb civilian population would leave the Krajina. The Trial Chamber found that high-ranking Croatian military officials, including Tuđman, used the Croatian military forces and the Special Police to commit the crimes within the objective of the joint criminal enterprise. The Croatian military forces included the Croatian army and military police, as well as Bosnian Croatian army, units which had been subordinated to Croatian army commanders.

TRIAL SUMMARY #19: APPEAL OF ANTE GOTOVINA AND MLADEN MARKAČ

The Trial Chamber found Gotovina guilty on eight of nine charges and imposed a sentence of twenty-four years. Markač was also found guilty on eight of nine charges and sentenced to eighteen years. Čermak was acquitted on all charges. Gotovina and Markač appealed. A majority (3–2) of the Appeals Chamber reversed the convictions of both men on all counts. Curiously, the majority refused to enter convictions on alternate grounds such as aiding and abetting. They argued that this would effectively have amounted to a retrial and would exceed the proper scope of appellate review.

The Appeals Chamber found that the Trial Chamber had insufficiently explained why it had come to a factual conclusion. The failure to provide a reasoned opinion was an error of law, which gave the Appeals Chamber the right to undertake a de novo review of the record without giving any deference to the findings of the Trial Chamber. This permitted the Appeals Chambers to substitute their findings for those of the Trial Chambers without applying the standard of review normally applicable to errors of fact. A Trial Chamber's judgement is overturned only if no reasonable trier of fact could have come to same conclusion. The Appeals Chambers' novel use of de novo review in cases where the error is the failure to provide a reasoned opinion based on a Trial Chamber's factual mistake is unsupported by the case law of either the ICTY or the ICTR.

DOCUMENT: SUMMARY OF APPEALS JUDGMENT

Court: International Criminal Tribunal for the Former Yugoslavia Appeals Chamber: Judge Theodor Meron, Presiding Judge Carmel Agius, Judge Patrick Robinson, Judge Mehmet Güney, Judge Fausto Pocar

Defendants: Ante Gotovina, Mladen Markač

Where: The Hague, Netherlands

When: Trial: March 12, 2004–April 15, 2011
Appeal Judgement, November 16, 2012

Source: IT-06-90-A. Online at http://www.icty.org/case/gotovina.

Charges: Crimes Against Humanity (Murder, Persecutions, Deportation, and Inhumane Acts), and Violations of the Laws or Customs of War.
The accused "orchestrated [a] campaign to drive the Serbs from the Krajina region began before the major military operation commenced on 4 August 1995, largely by the use of propaganda, disinformation and psychological warfare. . . . As the operation went forward, Croatian forces shelled civilian areas, entered civilian Serb settlements at night, and threatened those civilians who had not already fled, with gunfire and other intimidation. . . . Croatian forces engaged in looting Serb owned or inhabited civilian property almost at the beginning, starting on the second day. Large-scale looting was carried out on a systematic basis, involving both homes and businesses. . . . The ethnic cleansing operation included the organised and systematic plunder and destruction of Serb owned or inhabited property. This conduct was not sporadic or limited, but part and parcel of the whole campaign, intended to drive any remaining Serbs from the area and/or to prevent or discourage those who had fled from returning. Some who were attempting to flee were rounded up, loaded into vehicles and transported to detention facilities and "collection centres," to better ensure that they did not return to their settlements." (Indictment, pp. 8-9)

Verdict: On a 3–2 decision in both cases, the Appeals Chamber reversed the convictions of Gotovina and Markač on all counts.

Significance: Gotovina appears to be the first case in which an ICTY Appeals Chamber held that a *de novo* (from the new) review was appropriate when a legal error resulted in a failure to provide a reasoned opinion. ICTY cases contain many assertions that an appeals chamber will not conduct a trial *de novo*. In a very critical and bitter statement, Judges Carmel Agius and Fausto Pocar dissented and expressed their disagreement in unusually harsh terms, stating that certain elements of the judgement were "confusing, inconsistent, unclear, artificial and defective." Judge Pocar characterized the decision as contradicting "any sense of justice."

November 16, 2012

The Appeals Chamber recalls that the Trial Chamber concluded that the Appellants were members of a JCE whose common purpose was to permanently remove Serb civilians from the Krajina by force or threat of force. The Trial Chamber's conclusion that a JCE existed was based on its overall assessment of several mutually-reinforcing findings. The Appeals Chamber, Judge Agius and Judge Pocar dissenting, considers that the touchstone of the Trial Chamber's analysis concerning the existence of a JCE was its conclusion that unlawful artillery attacks targeted civilians and civilian objects in the Four Towns, and that these unlawful attacks caused the deportation of large numbers of civilians from the Krajina region.

The Trial Chamber's finding that the artillery attacks on the Four Towns were unlawful was heavily premised on its analysis of individual impact sites within the Four Towns, which I will refer to as the "Impact Analysis." This Impact Analysis was in turn based on the Trial Chamber's finding a 200 metre range of error for artillery projectiles fired at the Four Towns, which I will refer to as the "200 Metre Standard." Based on this range of error, the Trial Chamber found that all impact sites located more than 200 metres from a target it deemed legitimate served as evidence of an unlawful artillery attack. In identifying legitimate targets, the Trial Chamber took into account, in part, its finding that the HV could not identify targets of opportunity, such as moving police or military vehicles, in the Four Towns.

The Appeals Chamber unanimously holds that the Trial Chamber erred in deriving the 200 Metre Standard. The Trial Judgement contains no indication that any evidence considered by the Trial Chamber suggested a 200 metre margin of error, and it is devoid of any specific reasoning as to how the Trial Chamber derived this margin of error. The Trial Chamber considered evidence from expert witnesses who testified as to factors, such as wind speed and air temperature, that could cause variations in the accuracy of the weapons used by the HV against the Four Towns, and the Trial Chamber explicitly noted that it had not received sufficient evidence to make findings about these factors with respect to each of the Four Towns. In its Impact Analysis, however, the Trial Chamber applied the 200 Metre Standard uniformly to all impact sites in each of the Four Towns.

In these circumstances, the Appeals Chamber is unanimous in finding that the Trial Chamber erred in adopting a margin of error that was not linked to the evidence it received.

With respect to targets of opportunity in the Four Towns, the Appeals Chamber holds that the Trial Chamber did not err in determining that the HV had no ability to strike targets of opportunity in the towns of Benkovac, Gračac, and Obrovac. However, the Appeals Chamber notes that the Trial Chamber was presented with, and did not clearly discount, evidence of targets of opportunity in the town of Knin. In this context, the Appeals Chamber, Judge Agius and Judge Pocar dissenting, holds that the Trial Chamber erred in concluding that attacks on Knin were not aimed at targets of opportunity.

The Appeals Chamber, Judge Agius and Judge Pocar dissenting, recalls that, while the Trial Chamber considered a number of factors in assessing whether particular shells were aimed at lawful military targets, the distance between a given impact site and the nearest identified artillery target was the cornerstone and organising principle of the Trial Chamber's Impact Analysis. The Appeals Chamber, Judge Agius and Judge Pocar dissenting, holds that the Trial Chamber's errors with respect to the 200 Metre Standard and targets of opportunity are sufficiently serious that the conclusions of the Impact Analysis cannot be sustained. Although the Trial Chamber considered additional evidence in finding that the attacks on the Four Towns were unlawful, the Appeals Chamber, Judge Agius and Judge Pocar dissenting, holds that, absent the Impact Analysis, this remaining evidence is insufficient to support a finding that the artillery attacks on the Four Towns were unlawful.

In view of the foregoing, the Appeals Chamber, Judge Agius and Judge Pocar dissenting, finds that no reasonable trial chamber could conclude beyond reasonable doubt that the Four Towns were subject to unlawful artillery attacks. Accordingly, the Appeals Chamber, Judge Agius and Judge Pocar dissenting, grants Mr. Gotovina's First Ground of Appeal, in part, and Mr. Markač's Second Ground of Appeal, in part, and reverses the Trial Chamber's finding that the artillery attacks on the Four Towns were unlawful.

With respect to liability via JCE, the Appeals Chamber observes that the Trial Chamber's conclusion that a JCE existed was based on its overall assessment of several mutually-reinforcing findings, but the Appeals Chamber, Judge Agius and Judge Pocar dissenting, considers that the Trial Chamber's findings on the JCE's core common purpose of forcibly removing Serb civilians from the Krajina rested primarily on the existence of unlawful artillery attacks against civilians and civilian objects in the Four Towns. While the Trial Chamber also considered evidence concerning the planning and aftermath of the artillery attacks to support its finding that a JCE existed, it explicitly considered this evidence in light of its conclusion that the attacks on the Four Towns were unlawful. Furthermore, the Trial Chamber did not find that either of the Appellants was directly implicated in Croatia's adoption of discriminatory policies.

In these circumstances, having reversed the Trial Chamber's finding that artillery attacks on the Four Towns were unlawful, the Appeals Chamber, Judge Agius and Judge Pocar dissenting, considers that no reasonable trial chamber could conclude that the only reasonable interpretation of the circumstantial evidence on the record was the existence of a JCE with the common purpose of permanently removing the Serb population from the Krajina by force or threat of force.

ISSUES FOR THE FUTURE

This case resulted in the most controversial decision of the ICTY. As pointed out earlier, the decision had enormous political consequences apart from the questions relating to the jurisprudence of the Court. The decision shocked the international community. On the basis of this analysis, by a 3–2 vote, the panel, voided the convictions of both men on all counts.

Rather than discuss the rather arcane and convoluted technical discussion at the center of the debate, the analysis will focus on the general issues raised by the dissenting opinions. Recall that appeals in the ICTY usually turn only on two possibilities: (1) *errors of law*—violations of proper procedure (fairness) or interpretation or application of a specific rule (substantive); or on (2) the absence of a reasoned opinion. If any reasonable panel could have made the relevant finding on the strength of the record as presented, the Appeals Chamber normally will defer to the Trial Chamber with regard to findings of fact. This is a matter of both procedural economy (time) and respect for the integrity of the very exhaustive fact-finding process in the Trial Court Simply, the appellate process should not amount to a retrial, that is, an examination of the entire case from the beginning.

The most significant critique of the Judgement centered on the allegation that, not only did the majority on the appeal panel disregard the unanimous evaluation of the facts by the Trial Chamber, they also did not take into consideration the totality of the evidence. To use an old observation, the majority "failed to see the forest because of all the trees." They took what they collectively considered one error concerning the accuracy of artillery and turned it into a fatal flaw for the entire case. This ignored the vast body of other evidence that justified the Trial Court's Judgement.

The Trial Chamber had conducted an "impact analysis" to determine if the use of artillery in the campaign against the four towns was indiscriminate. It compared impacts with the location of nearby clearly identified military objectives to assess if, given the accepted margin of error of artillery weapons used by the HV at the time, the shelling was actually directed at lawful targets. For that purpose, the Trial Chamber established a 200-meter threshold. All impacts situated within 200 meters of an identified military objective were considered lawful, while all those falling beyond considered indiscriminate and unlawful. The Trial Chamber also took into consideration the fact that mobile targets, such as enemy vehicles, could also be legitimately shelled. The Trial Chamber concluded that in the absence of evidence of "targets of opportunity," all shell impacts in the four towns situated beyond the 200-meter limit would constitute an indiscriminate attack.

The Appeals Chamber unanimously rejected the 200-meter standard. All judges agreed that no evidence on the record, including testimony from several artillery experts, could reasonably lead to the conclusion that 200 meters was an appropriate estimate. Consensus, however, ended there. The majority drew the conclusion that the Trial Chamber erred in finding that the artillery attacks were unlawful. But, it then took this finding to conclude that absent unlawful artillery attacks on the Serb civilian population, no evidence of a joint criminal enterprise (JCE) had been presented.

Moreover, from a technical viewpoint, the Appeals Chamber did not adhere to the Statute of the Tribunal. The rule of appellate review pursuant to Article 25 of the Statute of the Tribunal requires that if the Appellate Chamber determines the standard applied by the Trial Chamber is in error, it has a duty to provide the correct legal standard. Although it was required to do so, the Appeals Chamber Judgement did not offer any alternative rationale to the 200-meter standard used by the Trial Chamber.

The strangest argument came from the presiding judge, Theodor Meron, who wrote a separate opinion in support of the majority finding. His reasoning in the opinion would seem to void the conclusion the majority reached. He argued that the Appeals Chamber's authority should not serve "as a licence for wholesale reconstruction or revision of approaches adopted or decisions taken by a trial chamber." This would seem an appropriate sentiment that applied with special force after a large number of other cases had gone through the appeal process. Yet, Judge Meron's own opinion represents exactly what he condemned—a "wholesale reconstruction" of the case.

POLITICS AND THE LAW

To return to a point made earlier, the ICTY trials have an enormous impact on public opinion in Croatia and Serbia. In Zagreb (Croatia), the crowds cheered the verdict. In Belgrade, the press and politicians expressed great anger, characterizing the revised verdict as a total whitewash of Croatia's actions during the 1991–1995 war of independence. This trial confirmed a view that the ICTY was nothing more than a sham set up to punish Serbs while ignoring the actions of their enemies.

References

Borger, Julian. 2016. *The Butcher's Trail: How the Search for Balkan War Criminals Became the World's Most Successful Manhunt.* New York: Other Press.

Bosco, David. 2014. *Rough Justice: The International Criminal Court in a World of Power Politics.* New York: Oxford University Press.

Job, Cvijeto. 2002. *Yugoslavia's Ruin: The Bloody Lessons of Nationalism.* Lanham, MD: Rowman and Littlefield.

Scheffer, David. 2012. *All the Missing Souls: A Personal History of the War Crimes Tribunals.* Princeton, NJ: Princeton University Press.

28

Rwanda: The Genocide

At first glance, the circumstances of the Rwanda case seem quite different from those of the Holocaust. Yet Philip Gourevitch observed, "The government, and an astounding number of its subjects, imagined that by exterminating the Tutsi people they could make the world a better place, and the mass killing had followed" (1998, 6). By substituting Jew for Tutsi in the quote, the observation could just as well as have been written about Nazi Germany. Nonetheless, Rwanda stands alone in that, unlike other instances of mass murder and atrocity, the state actively enlisted and urged large numbers of the *civilian population* to take an active part. In the short space of three months, primarily by machete and club, the genocidal crusade killed approximately 1 million Tutsis, political opponents of the regime, and others unfortunate enough to be caught up in the events. Gérard Prunier has calculated that during that time the killing rate "was at least five times that of the Nazi death camps" (1994, 261). René Lemarchand states that the genocide claimed twice as many victims in one month as the Bosnian civil war (1992–1995) did in two years (2009, 483). *The killings wiped out one-tenth of Rwanda's total population.* A member of the Rwandan Patriotic Front (RPF) Army that finally quelled the violence stated that "When we captured Kigali we thought we would face criminals in the state; instead we faced a criminal population." At one point, more than 90,000 individuals had been arrested and were awaiting some disposition of their status.

SETTING THE STAGE: THE COLONIAL LEGACY

The conflict grew out the practice of the Belgian colonial governors and the struggle for control of the postcolonial independent state. The sparks did not come from "ancient hatreds and rivalries." As with the hatred between Serbs and Croats, the roots of this conflict are in the period after Belgium took control of the territory during World War I (1916). Scholars have argued that traditions are something we invent. The historian Ernest Renan simply stated that nationalism means "getting history wrong." A cynical French epigram defines a nation as "a group of people united by a common error about their ancestry and a common hatred of their neighbors." These quotes apply with special force to the evolution of "ethnic identity" in Rwanda and its twin, Burundi. The hatred that came to characterize the division between Hutu and Tutsi was in large part created and manipulated by individuals who took advantage of the situation fashioned by its Belgian colonizers.

The colonial legacy made racism an integral part of an institutional structure that defined the essential structure of social relations. Rwanda has three main ethnic groups: Hutu, Tutsi, and Twa. During Belgian colonial rule, the Catholic Church played an equal part with the colonial governors in clearly favoring the minority Tutsis over the majority Hutus. Pierre Ryckmans served in Ruanda-Urundi from the time Belgium first took control until 1928. His biographer observed that Ryckmans always tended to emphasize the preeminence of the Tutsi reinforcing the major cleavage existing in the country. Ryckmans wrote:

> The Batutsi [Tutsi] were meant to reign. Their fine presence is in itself enough to give them a great prestige vis-á-vis the inferior races which surround. . . . It is not surprising that those good Bahutu [Hutu], less intelligent, more simple, more spontaneous, more trusting, have let themselves be enslaved without ever daring to revolt. (Quoted in Prunier 1994, 11)

That attitude would have devastating consequences for the future.

In the period leading up to independence as a sovereign state in 1962, Hutu leaders, using appeals to ethnicity, mobilized their communities to back their personal drive to control political power in the new state by demonizing the Tutsis. The violence resulted in an estimated 20,000 deaths. This established a pattern that produced periodic episodes of mass murder in both Rwanda and Burundi over the next thirty years. Resentment, fear, and the prospect of personal gain, not nationalism, were the principal motivations. Firmly held but mistaken ideas about the past fueled the common resentment and fear. In the 1994 Rwandan genocide, the Hutu-dominated government overtly promoted misinformation to incite the populace to commit the genocide. Alison Des Forges noted that: "Organizers . . . who had themselves grown up with these distortions of history, skillfully exploited misconceptions about who the Tutsi were, where they had come from, and what they had done in the past. From these elements, they fueled the fear and hatred that made genocide imaginable" (1991, 31).

During the 1950s, Tutsi control over Rwanda began to erode as the United Nations supervised decolonization. Hutus were successful in exploiting the decolonization process to gain power throughout Rwanda. When Rwanda revolted against Belgium and secured its independence in 1961, the class roles were reversed, and the Hutus held the positions of power. The first elected president Grégoire Kayibanda, an ethnic Hutu, used these ethnic tensions to enhance his own power. Radical Hutus began depicting the Tutsi as outsiders who had invaded Rwanda. Some Hutu radicals called for the Tutsi to be "sent back to Abyssinia," a reference to their supposed homeland. This early concept evolved into an ideology that became known as Hutu Power. Hutu Power sought to recreate an ethnically pure "pre-invasion Rwanda."

PRELUDE TO GENOCIDE

The countdown to the genocide in 1994 actually began in July 1973 when General Juvénal Habyarimana, also a Hutu, engineered a bloodless coup, deposing Kayibanda and ending the First Republic. In 1975, Habyarimana outlawed all political parties except the one he created, the Mouvement Révolutionaire National pour le Développement (MRND). The coup altered very little for Tutsis. Policies continued to discriminate against them. Quotas designed to intentionally disadvantage Tutsis were applied to jobs in universities and government services. The principal difficulties came from the very narrow economic base of the economy. Peasant subsistence agriculture contributes little. Cash crops of coffee and tea, tin mining, and foreign aid formed the three essential sectors.

During the 1980s, fluctuations in commodity prices affected both the cash crops and tin, actually causing the closure of mining operations. By the end of the 1980s, foreign aid underwrote about 60 percent of the government's annual budget. As incomes dwindled in the private sector, competition to gain or maintain access for shares of the third source, skimming foreign aid, became more intense. Since access to this resource depended upon having influence at the highest levels of the government, positions were jealously and ruthlessly protected. As Habyarimana continued to favor a smaller and smaller group of supporters, Hutu groups, slighted by the nation's leader, cooperated with Tutsis to weaken his leadership.

As the 1980s ended, a combination of climatic hazards (excessive rain, landslides, hail, and drought), fungal diseases, and parasitic attacks combined with government cutbacks in rural assistance produced a major famine that caused a mass exodus to Burundi and Tanzania. The 1989 State budget decreased nearly 40 percent largely with the "social" ministries taking the greatest cuts.

REFUGEES AND THE RWANDAN PATRIOTIC FRONT

Economic conditions, as well as the periodic outbreaks of persecution and violence in both Rwanda and Burundi had produced a large number of refugees (Banyarwanda) who had fled to adjacent states. Of course, many settled permanently in their new homes. In particular, the large Rwandan Tutsi refugee population in Uganda played a pivotal role, in the struggles that erupted internally in that country and also in the events surrounding the 1994 genocide and its aftermath in Rwanda. In Uganda, during 1982 the Milton Obote government suddenly unleashed a campaign of active harassment and persecution against the Tutsi. Many joined the guerilla movement of Yoweri Museveni (National Resistance Army, NRA) that succeeded in removing Obote from power in 1986.

After their participation in his successful insurgent campaign, in fall 1989, Ugandan president Museveni had dismissed Rwandans from the NRA because of mounting jealousy and fear on the part of Ugandans. Fred Rwigyema, former deputy minister for defense and Paul Kagame, deputy chief of intelligence both lost their posts as did many other Rwandan officers. At this point, a return to Rwanda seemed an attractive alternative because it seemed that the Habyarimana regime no longer enjoyed widespread legitimacy and support outside its northwestern base.

There had always been a significant number of exiles who believed that one day they would return to Rwanda. In 1987, their political arm, the Rwandan Alliance for National Unity (RANU) changed its name to the Rwandan Patriotic Front (RPF) signaling a more serious effort to organize a resistance. Many young RPA (action wing of RPF) militants had managed to survive the purge of the Ugandan army or infiltrate its ranks. The southwestern Kigezi district of Uganda became the staging area. According to official Ugandan reports, when the time came for action, three thousand Banyarwandan soldiers "deserted," taking their weapons with them. Major-General Fred Rwigyema led the invasion force of approximately 2,500. He was killed on the second day of action. Major Paul Kagame was still in the United States, having been sent there for advanced training.

The loss of Rwigyema was a major blow. Equally important the RPF had not made preparations for a long campaign, and support from local sources never materialized. But, the most important factor was the arrival of French troops. To gain French military support, Habyarimana had staged a fake attack on Kigali, raising fears that the RPF had widespread support. Habyarimana counted on the French desire to maintain influence in the area (contra the British). The French would remain, ostensibly to protect French citizens, until the genocide. The French support included ignoring the ongoing reprisals against Tutsi by the regime, while highlighting RPF/RPA "atrocities." By the end of November, the RPF had retreated back into Uganda. Paul Kagame had returned and assumed command. Organizing his version of the "long march," he led a retreat back into Uganda to regroup. The retreat did not mark the end of resistance, but the start of a "protracted war" that would play a major role in setting the stage for genocide.

The problems for the RPF came not from defeat but from the frustrations of victory that brought home the realities of Rwanda domestic politics. Hutu peasants showed no appreciation for being "liberated" by Tutsi forces—they ran away. As the RPF forces advanced, the numbers of the displaced multiplied. At the end of their 1993 offensive when they had doubled the area under their control, the number of displaced had risen to an estimated 950,000. The struggle in Rwanda turned out to be very different from that of the NRA in Uganda. The RPF did not introduce an alternate government structure, and after a time, made no efforts to reach out to mobilize the peasants as resources. The Habyarimana regime had successfully played on the fear that the goal of the RPF was a return to the old days of Tutsi domination and oppression. The RPF began to engage in actions that mimicked their extremist opponents.

THE SITUATION IN RWANDA

In 1990, journalist Hassan Ngeze created the Hutu Ten Commandments that outlined the basic principles of Hutu Power ideology. The Commandments called for absolute Hutu control of Rwanda's public institutions and public life, complete segregation between Hutus and Tutsis, and complete exclusion of Tutsis from public institutions and public life. Hutu Power ideology idealized all things Hutu, while demonizing Tutsis as outsiders bent on restoring an dictatorial Tutsi-dominated monarchy.

The media became central to the plan. Hutu hardliners sponsored a newspaper named *Kangura* (Wake It Up!) that had as its principal mission the demonization of the Tutsi. The paper published the Hutu Ten Commandments. The eighth commandment became a mantra: "Hutus must stop having mercy on the Tutsi." As part of liberalization, Radio Rwanda, the state-run radio network was joined on air by a supposedly privately owned station, Radio–Télévision Libre des Mille Collines (RTLM, FM 106). The name meant one thousand hills free radio and television, based on Rwanda's nickname—the land of one thousand hills. It began broadcasting on July 8, 1993. RTLM actually was the voice of the radical Hutu Party CDR (Coalition pour la Défense de la République) founded in March 1992. The radio station and newspaper continually repeated the Hutu Ten Commandments in an attempt to mobilize the population

Document: Hutu Ten Commandments

When: December 1990
Where: Published in *Kangura No. 6*, Kigali, Rwanda
Source: Online at http://www.uwosh.edu/faculty_staff/henson/188/rwanda_kangura_ten.html
Significance: This document was widely circulated and promoted in the media in both Rwanda and Burundi. It was the principal statement of the Hutu Power movement.

1. Every Hutu must know that the Tutsi woman, wherever she may be, is working for the Tutsi ethnic cause. In consequence, any Hutu is a traitor who:
   —Acquires a Tutsi wife;
   —Acquires a Tutsi concubine;
   —Acquires a Tutsi secretary or protégée.
2. Every Hutu must know that our Hutu daughters are more worthy and more conscientious as women, as wives and as mothers. Aren't they lovely, excellent secretaries, and more honest!
3. Hutu women, be vigilant and make sure that your husbands, brothers and sons see reason.
4. All Hutus must know that all Tutsis are dishonest in business. Their only goal is ethnic superiority. We have learned this from experience. In consequence, any Hutu is a traitor who:
   —Forms a business alliance with a Tutsi
   —Invests his own funds or public funds in a Tutsi enterprise
   —Borrows money from or loans money to a Tutsi
   —Grants favors to Tutsis (import licenses, bank loans, land for construction, public markets . . .)
5. Strategic positions such as politics, administration, economics, the military and security must be restricted to the Hutu.
6. A Hutu majority must prevail throughout the educational system (pupils, scholars, teachers).

7. The Rwandan Army must be exclusively Hutu. The war of October 1990 has taught us that. No soldier may marry a Tutsi woman.
8. Hutu must stop having mercy on the Tutsi.
9. Hutu wherever they be must stand united, in solidarity, and concerned with the fate of their Hutu brothers. Hutu within and without Rwanda must constantly search for friends and allies to the Hutu Cause, beginning with their Bantu brothers.

Hutu must constantly counter Tutsi propaganda.

Hutu must stand firm and vigilant against their common enemy: the Tutsi.

10. The Social Revolution of 1959, the Referendum of 1961 and the Hutu Ideology must be taught to Hutu of every age. Every Hutu must spread the word wherever he goes. Any Hutu who persecutes his brother Hutu for spreading and teaching this ideology is a traitor.

PREPARATION

Preparation for the genocide had four related components: central direction, the media, local authorities, and the recruitment and "training" of local militias (Interahamwe and Impuzamugambi). While some controversy exists over the exact nature of the communication networks, clearly the mechanisms for orchestrating local massacres on cue were in place by the time of the October 1990 invasion. The process became more refined over time. Over the next three years, four massacres took place, each timed to follow a critical time in the war or the negotiations and justify continuation of the status quo (estimated 3,000 total deaths). The crucial questions involve the quantum jump from localized massacres to wholesale slaughter of an entire people.

How do ordinary peasants become willing participants in killings that serve only elite interests? The answers are rooted in four basic factors that define Rwandan culture and society: traditional obedience to authority, illiteracy and superstition, trivialization of the tasks, and promise of rewards. The first two contribute to the process by which the enemy Tutsi became demonized and dehumanized. The combination of the second two explains the willingness to move from belief to overt action. The authoritarian tradition meant that people believed what they were told; illiteracy and parochialism meant they had little or no access to information that might have countered the content of the message from above even if they did have alternative sources. Using the language of rural work placed the tasks in an appropriate context. The actual killing would be done in special "collective work sessions (*umuganda*)." The work became "bush-clearing" and "pulling the roots of noxious weeds."

At the beginning of the bloodbath, on orders from the central government, local authorities organized killing squads. Jean Hatzfeld had the opportunity to interview Hutus who had played a part in the massacres. One participant stated: "The first day, a messenger from the municipal judge went house to house summoning us to a meeting right away. There the judge announced that the reason for the meeting was the killing of every Tutsi without exception" (2003, 11). Another said: "The judge told us that from now on we were to do nothing but kill Tutsis. Well, we understood, that was a final plan" (13). Still another stated: "The intimidators made the plans and whipped up enthusiasm; the shopkeepers paid and provided transportation; the farmers prowled and pillaged" (13). Another perpetrator said: "We no longer saw a human being when we turned up a Tutsi in the swamps. I mean a person like us, sharing similar thoughts and feelings. . . . [S]avagery took over the mind" (47). Another said: "They had become people to throw away, so to speak. They no longer were what they had been . . ." (47). The point is that genocide and other forms of mass atrocity do not happen spontaneously.

Add the simple fact that someone had to get the land and livestock after the owners were gone. The nature of the activities encouraged random killings, banditry, and pillage that often had more to do with personal motives than with the ethnic divide. In a number of instances, poor versus rich more that Hutu versus Tutsi better characterized the nature of the killing. This becomes hard to sort out because in the minds of many Hutu, the rich, if not Tutsi, had become "Tutsified" and thus justifiable targets: "People whose children had to walk barefoot to school killed those who could buy shoes for theirs" (Prunier 1994, 250).

The origin of the Interahamwe (those who work/fight together) and the lesser well known Impuzamugambi (those who have the same goal) yields a familiar story. The organizations started as youth arms of the MRND, Habyarimana's reformed and renamed party, and the CDR. They found ready recruits among disaffected students, the unemployed, delinquents, petty criminals, and those with real or imagined grievances. Beginning in 1992, they were taught to kill (and kill quickly) and some were given training in the use of explosives. The Interahamwe had committees in every one of Rwanda's 148 communes. Over time the youth groups evolved first into vigilante bands and then into death squads who spearheaded the final solution. Given the origins of the recruits, despite training, discipline was often poor. Toward the end of the war, the groups became nothing more than bands of armed self-serving thugs as controlling administrative structures, such as they were, broke down. When the genocide began on April 6, 1994, the militias had enlisted 50,000 members.

THE SPARK

When Paul Kagame returned from America, he reorganized the RPF and began an intensive guerrilla campaign. By mid-1992, the war had taken its toll on the economy. After some exploratory talk in Paris between several opposition parties and the RPF in May and June 1992, the RPF agreed to a cease-fire on July 12, 1992. Formal peace negotiations began in August in Arusha, Uganda. The Arusha process, characterized by many stops and starts, was finally signed in August 1993. It was never implemented because the domestic political situation unraveled to the point where the prime minister could not pull together a coalition government to carry out the necessary tasks for transition. President Habyarimana most probably signed his own death warrant with the signing of Arusha.

The RPF wanted the French military withdrawn and a neutral international monitoring force to oversee the transition. Security Resolution 872 (October 5,

1993) established the UN Assistance Mission for Rwanda (UNAMIR) with a mandate to assist in ensuring the security of the capital city of Kigali and to monitor the security situation during the final period of the transitional Government's mandate leading up to elections. The UN contingent arrived in November. The French left the next month, after an RPF battalion had been established in Kigali. The violence began in April 1994. Instead of moving to contain it, after the death of ten Belgian peacekeepers sent to guard the prime minister, Agathe Uwilingiyimana, the United Nations instead chose to pull out, leaving only a shadow force of 270. The UNAMIR commander, General Roméo Dallaire, had harsh words for European countries (France and Belgium) who sent troops to evacuate their own citizens and other Europeans but refused to provide protection for locals. The question that will always remain unanswered is: Could early intervention by UNAMIR, acting on received intelligence, have stopped the genocide by forestalling the initial actions in Kigali?

THE GENOCIDE BEGINS

President Habyarimana had flown to Dar-es-Salaam for a meeting with the presidents of Tanzania, Burundi, and Uganda about regional concerns. During the course of the meeting, he received a strong message about the necessity of implementing the Arusha Accords from his peers. Because the Rwandan plane was newer, more comfortable, and faster, President Cyprien Ntaryamira (Burundi) asked for a ride back to Kigali. Several of Habyarimana's closest advisors, and two Burundi government ministers were also on the flight. On April 6, 1994, as the aircraft approached Kigali airport, all lights at the airport suddenly went out and two ground-to-air missiles were launched. The aircraft received a direct hit, crashing and killing all on board. Belgian peacekeepers RTLM broadcast news of the president's death within a half hour of the crash. Radio Rwanda remained neutral, broadcasting only information bulletins. RTML began calling for blood in earnest.

The Interahamwe and Impuzamugambi militias mobilized quickly as did the Presidential Guard. Within an hour, the Interahamwe had already set up roadblocks and detachments of police and soldiers working from prepared lists began a campaign of rounding up and eliminating moderate Hutus who held positions of power. Anyone who had supported or been involved with the negotiation or promotion of the Arusha Accords topped the lists. The prime minister and the principal negotiator of the Arusha Accords were among the first killed, along with other "enemies": the president of the Constitutional Court, civil rights activists, journalists, and the leadership of all opposition parties. In the cities, searches went systematically street by street, house by house. Tutsi were killed simply because they were Tutsi, but to be Hutu did not guarantee your safety. Professionals and others with education were killed even if they were Hutu because they were seen as potential opponents. Brazenly, several mass killings took place as peacekeepers had to stand by and watch.

With the death of Habyarimana, Colonel Théoneste Bagosora took charge. The minister of defense, Augustin Bizimana, and two members of the general staff,

Col. Aloys Ntiwiragabo and Col. Gratien Kabiligi were abroad. The chief of staff had died with Habyarimana. When sixteen high-ranking officers convened just after the crash to decide on a course of action, although he was just a retired officer, Bagosora insisted on chairing the meeting. Alison Des Forges claimed that although Bagosora ran the meeting he lacked strong support among those present and was not able to persuade the group to support his first choice for chief of staff nor to have them accept the proposition that the army should take charge rather than another civilian government. Subsequently, General Dallaire and the Senior UN representative, Jacques-Roger Booh-Booh, both emphasized to Bagosora the necessity of a civilian government.

Outvoting Bagosora was one thing—gaining effective control was another. The Presidential Guard, with the best trained and best armed soldiers in the Rwandan armed forces (Forces Armées Rwandaise [FAR]), stood outside the normal command structure. Its commander had died with Habyarimana in the crash. Bagosora reportedly took direct control of this unit and also had the loyalty of the commanders of the reconnaissance and paracommando battalions, the other two strongest units in the Rwandan army. Together he could count on 2,000 elite troops stationed in and around Kigali while the forces of his rivals were stationed across the country. When the killings continued, RPF troops came out of their CND headquarters and engaged the Presidential Guard. With the RPF in the field, those opposed to Bagosora had the possibility of cooperating with them to restore order and they explored this possibility through the good offices of Dallaire. The senior officers opposed to Bagosora instead looked to the international community for support. Such support never materialized. While they hesitated, Bagosora acted preemptively.

The efficiency of the operation testifies to the amount of advanced planning that had taken place. It also emphasizes a very chilling and disconcerting point made at the beginning of this chapter—this genocide could not have happened without the moral support and approval of a large segment of the population that enabled recruitment and support of a very large number of killers. The killing—those doing the actual killing were not government officials, but ordinary peasants. Prunier estimates that 80 percent of the victims were killed in the six weeks between the onset on April 6 and the third week of May. This would mean that the daily killing rate was at least five times that of the Nazi death camps. Malvern describes the process in one sentence: "The genocide spread and in some places it settled into a routine" (2006, 206).

THE RPF ADVANCE

The RPF restarted their campaign on April 8, 1994. RPF troops actually reached the outskirts of Kigali on April 11, but the battle for control of the city lasted three months. While stalled at Kigali, RPF troops rapidly moved to eliminate resistance in other parts of the country. The problem stemmed from the fact that the war existed somewhat apart from the genocide. The RPF did not have sufficient manpower to deal with both. As the civil war progressed, the RPF had actually established safe zones for Tutsis within Kigali. They finally took the city on July 4th. This produced an anomalous situation given that the genocide continued in full force in the countryside. More than a million refugees crossed over into

Zaire within a week. Within three months, 10 percent of the population had been killed, and another 30 percent had fled the country.

Using the reverse logic of Hutu Power, RPF forces began a program of retaliation as they advanced. In their drive for military victory and a halt to the genocide, the RPF also killed noncombatants in numerous summary executions and in massacres. Although the subject of substantial speculation, the number killed in deliberate RPF massacres of civilians remained poorly documented. Killing did not stop with the formal end of the war. As the magnitude of the slaughter promoted by the *génocidaires* became more widely known, the push to discredit the RPF through *tu quoque* (you did it too!) arguments quickly lost steam. The RPF faced the problem of putting back together a country looted by members of the previous regime as they left, and that still had to live with the fact that genocide had become so intertwined with everyday life that it could be used at every turn to secure an economic advantage, to settle an old grudge, or to cover one's tracks. To add to the problems, there were 700,000 Tutsis who had returned from the diaspora, and nearly 300,000 children without parents.

The struggle continued in the refugee camps with Hutu Power still exercising influence. Where assistance had been lacking before to deal with the genocide, countries and humanitarian NGOs now literally could not respond fast enough to provide humanitarian aid to the camps. The horrendous conditions in the camps tended to override previous events—the focus on the sufferings of the present took precedence over addressing the horrors of the immediate past. Attacks on Tutsis in eastern Zaire (Democratic Republic of the Congo) began, as did sporadic raids across the border as the FAR regrouped in exile. The camps remained under the political control of those who had planned the genocide.

THE WHIMS OF INTERNATIONAL RESPONSE

The lack of timely and appropriate response by the international community forms one of the more shameful incidents of the late twentieth century. Actions by the French government actually aided and then protected those responsible for the genocide. Other governments took action to evacuate their own citizens but refused help otherwise. Faced with an opportunity to act decisively at the onset, the United Nations instead withdrew most of its troops and then refused to permit the remainder to take any action as they watched the genocide occur.

THE INTERNATIONAL CRIMINAL TRIBUNAL FOR RWANDA

The UN Security Council did authorize the International Criminal Tribunal for Rwanda (ICTR) in November 1994, designed to try the high-ranking architects and organizers. As an exercise in international atonement, it fell far short of addressing the question of what was really needed. The genocide had decimated the judicial system. Prime Minister Faustin Twagiramungu had estimated that 30,000 individuals would be put on trial. The number of detainees would pass the 100,000 mark by 1997. The ICTR had a list of 400, but no means to enforce the warrants. In its twenty-year existence, the tribunal managed to try seventy-five cases.

References

Des Forges, Alison. 1999. *Leave None to Tell the Story*. New York: Human Rights Watch.

Gourevitch, Philip. 1998. *We Wish to Inform You That Tomorrow We Will Be Killed with Our Families: Stories from Rwanda*. New York: Picador.

Hatzfeld, Jean. 2003. *Machete Season*. Translated by Linda Coverdale. New York: Picador.

Lemarchand, René. 2009. "The 1994 Rwanda Genocide." In *Century of Genocide: Critical Essays and Eyewitness Accounts*, 3rd ed., edited by Samuel Totten and William S. Parsons, 404–422. New York & London: Routledge.

Malvern, Linda. 2006. *Conspiracy to Murder: The Rwandan Genocide*. Rev. ed. London: Verso.

Prunier, Gérard. 1994. *The Rwanda Crisis: History of a Genocide*. New York: Columbia University Press.

29

The International Criminal Tribunal for Rwanda: Jean-Paul Akayesu

Unlike the fighting in Yugoslavia, the violence in Rwanda attracted attention, although the United Nations was slow to act in ways other than expressing concern. The Security Council condemned the violence by calling for those involved "to respect fully international humanitarian law" (S/RES/912). On July 1, 1994, the UN Security Council asked the Secretary-General to appoint a commission to accumulate evidence of war crimes in Rwanda. After copious supporting material on the massacres had been secured, on November 8, 1994, the Security Council, acting on its authority under Chapter VII of the Charter, adopted the Statute of the International Tribunal for Rwanda (S/Res/953).

The biggest obstacles came from the new Rwandan regime. By happenstance, Rwanda was serving a two-year elected term on the Security Council at the time the violence began. Initially the new Rwandan government pressed for an international tribunal modeled on the ICTY. As negotiations wore on, Rwanda became increasingly negative toward the idea. According to UN personnel, the negativity stemmed from several factors:

- the realization that the tribunal could not possibly undertake the prosecution of the thousands of detainees then in Rwandan prisons,
- the severe limitation put on the temporal jurisdiction of the court (only 1994),
- the decision not to locate the tribunal in Kigali,
- the lack of an independent Appeals Chamber (would share with ICTY), and
- the prohibition on capital punishment.

In the end, Rwanda voted against the Security Council resolution approving the establishment of the court. Despite the negative vote, unlike the former Yugoslav Republics, the Rwandan government cooperated with the ICTR in finding and arresting those indicted by the Prosecutor.

As discussed in chapter 22, the structure of the ICTR paralleled that of the ICTY. The two courts shared an Appeals Chamber. However, because they represent responses to quite different factual situations, the two Statutes embody very different concerns. Rwanda was primarily an internal conflict, so a different body of law applied (but not a different set of criminal acts). Paragraph 3 of the Preamble to the resolution authorizing the Tribunal specifically voiced the concern that "genocide and other systematic, widespread and flagrant violations of international humanitarian law had been committed in Rwanda." The Statute authorized the court to try those responsible for acts of genocide, and other serious violations of international law within the territory of Rwanda or Rwandan citizens who performed these acts in adjacent states from January 1, 1994, through December 31, 1994. As a result, almost all of the cases before the ICTR have involved charges of genocide. In contrast, very few indictments by the ICTY included the charge. Moreover, the crimes of those accused were well documented and their then current locations known.

The Rwandan government had a strong interest in trying to limit both the temporal jurisdiction (time frame) and the subject matter jurisdiction (types of crimes). First, it did not wish the Court to waste time and resources on trials for lesser crimes that could be punished by domestic courts. Second, it wished to ensure that the focus stayed on the Hutu *génocidaires*. As discussed in the narrative in chapter 28, RPF troops had also engaged in actions that could be prosecutable under the statute of the court. The Security Council, however, resisted the lobbying effort. It included "crimes against humanity" along with genocide, but with a slightly different definition. Article 5 of the ICTY Statute defines crimes against humanity as an attack "in an armed conflict, whether international or internal in character, and directed against any civilian population." Article 3 of the ICTR Statute defines the crime as involving "widespread or systematic attack against any civilian population on national, political, ethnic, racial or religious grounds." In application, there is no significant difference between the two even though the ICTR definition may seem more inclusive. The Security Council also resisted the Rwandan government's effort to backdate the relevant time frame to 1990, which would have included the four incidents of mass murder prior to the 1994 genocide (chapter 28).

Article 4 of the ICTR Statute groups together violations in common Article 3 of the Geneva Conventions and Article 4 of Geneva Protocol Additional II (chapter 19). It includes violence to the life, health, or physical well-being of individuals as well as murder, rape, pillage, cruel treatment, acts of terrorism, and other outrages on personal dignity. The interesting element of these specifications is that while the ICTY was authorized to apply only provisions of customary law regarding the criminal responsibility of individuals, the Security Council permitted the ICTR to utilize provisions of Protocol Additional II, much of which had not been acknowledged as part of customary law.

THE POLITICS OF PLACES

Selecting a home base for the trials generated a debate. Some member states preferred the Hague, but others argued for an "African seat" that would be in close proximity to witnesses, evidence, and the locations where the crimes had occurred. The situation in Rwanda precluded holding the trials at any location in the country.

Table 29.1 The ICTR Indictments for Genocide and Other Serious Violations of International Humanitarian Law Committed in 1994

Concluded Proceedings for Accused	85
Transferred to a State to serve sentence	23
Awaiting transfer to a State to serve their sentence	10
Have served their sentence	23
Died before or while serving their sentence	6
Acquitted and released	14
Indictments withdrawn	2
Died before judgement	2
Transferred to other jurisdictions:	
Rwanda	3
France	2
Fugitive Cases Transferred to Other Jurisdictions	**8**
Fugitive cases under Rwandan jurisdiction	5
Fugitive cases under MICT jurisdiction	3

Source: http://unictr.unmict.org/sites/unictr.org/files/publications/ictr-key-figures-en.pdf.

Bringing the leaders of the previous regime to trial in any venue inside Rwanda would have involved serious security risks. Moreover, having the Court in Rwanda could have made requesting the surrender of Tutsis accused of violations problematic. The final choice was Arusha, Tanzania—close by, but in neutral territory. Table 29.1 summarizes the caseload and verdicts of the court.

ESTABLISHING GENOCIDE

Article 2 of the Convention on the Prevention and Punishment of the Crime of Genocide (1948) defines genocide as "any of the following acts committed with *intent to destroy, in whole or in part, a national, ethnical, racial or religious group*, as such: killing members of the group; causing serious bodily or mental harm to members of the group; deliberately inflicting on the group conditions of life calculated to bring about its physical destruction in whole or in part; imposing measures intended to prevent births within the group; [and] forcibly transferring children of the group to another group" (emphasis added). In the first cases heard by the International Criminal Tribunal for Rwanda (ICTR), judges had great difficulty in characterizing actions as genocide because they could not find any ethnic, language, religious, or racial distinctions that would separate Hutu from Tutsi. Interestingly, this included dominant physical characteristics. Based on testimony of experts, the Court first concluded that class, not ethnicity, formed the critical element. Note that the legal definition of genocide does not include class as a category. In the end, in order to establish the necessary criteria, the Court had to use the self-identification mandated on required identification cards that had been instituted under Belgian colonial rule in order to establish the ethnic/racial difference mandated in the definition.

Normally, *intent* is the most difficult element to determine. To establish genocide, there must be a proven intent on the part of perpetrators to commit acts that were meant to aid in destroying physically, a national, ethnical, racial, or religious group. Cultural destruction does not suffice nor does an intention to disperse a group. This special intent is what makes the crime of genocide unique. Importantly, the victims of genocide are deliberately targeted because of their real or perceived membership of one of the four groups protected under the Convention (which excludes political groups). This means that the target of destruction must be the group, as such, and not just against particular members as individuals. People take advantage of the chaos to commit criminal acts that have nothing to do with "genocide." Looking at Bosnia and Rwanda, some people killed Bosniaks or Tutsis for person hatred of the person or, as with Tadić, for personal gain. Genocide can also be committed against only a part of the group, as long as that part is identifiable (including within a geographically limited area) and "substantial."

DOCUMENT: ANALYSIS FRAMEWORK TO DETERMINE IF GENOCIDE HAS OCCURRED

When: Established in July 2004 (Security Council Resolution 1366), the Office of the Special Adviser on the Prevention of Genocide was created to serve the UN Secretary-General as an early warning mechanism.

Source: Office of the UN Special Adviser on the Prevention of Genocide (OSAPG). Online at http://www.un.org/ar/preventgenocide/adviser/pdf/osapg_analysis_framework.pdf

Significance: The mandate of the office is to collect existing information, particularly from within the UN system, act as an early warning mechanism, and make recommendations to the Security Council through the Secretary General.

Elements of the Framework

The Analysis Framework comprises eight categories of factors that the OSAPG uses to determine whether there may be a risk of genocide in a given situation. The eight categories of factors are not ranked, and the absence of information relating to one or more categories does not necessarily indicate the absence of a risk of genocide; what is significant is the cumulative effect of the factors. Where these factors are effectively addressed, no longer exist or are no longer relevant, the risk of genocide is assumed to decrease.

[The following lists only the categories. Each of the categories has an extensive list of factors to be evaluated. Space does not permit me to reproduce the entire document.]

1. Inter-group relations, including a record of discrimination and/or other human rights violations committed against a group
2. Circumstances that affect the capacity to prevent genocide

3. Presence of illegal arms and armed elements
4. Motivation of leading actors in the State/region; acts which serve to encourage divisions between national, racial, ethnic, and religious groups
5. Circumstances that facilitate perpetration of genocide (dynamic factors)
6. Genocidal acts
7. Evidence of intent "to destroy in whole or in part . . ."
8. Triggering factors

In Rwanda, the responsibility for crimes could not be determined only by looking at rank in the military or official position in the government. The reality was a situation where many of those most to blame were not necessarily part of a formal military or civilian chain of command. Many were local officials. One of the first people indicted and convicted, Jean-Paul Akayesu served as mayor (*bourgmestre*) of the Taba commune. The Republic of Rwanda is divided into eleven prefectures. These eleven prefectures are further divided into communes. In Rwanda, the *bourgmestre* is the most powerful figure in the commune. As mayor, Akayesu had the duty to maintain public order within his commune, subject to the authority of the prefect. He had exclusive control over the communal police, as well as any other police officers put at the disposition of the commune. He was responsible for the enforcement of laws and regulations and the administration of justice, also subject only to the authority of the prefect.

The authority of a mayor in the area extends significantly beyond the formal limits conferred upon him by law. In Rwanda, the mayor exercised a considerable degree of informal authority. He occupied the role of a "father figure" within the commune. As a communal leader he was respected, widely considered to be a man of high morals, intelligence, and integrity. A family man, Akayesu was the father of five children. His connection with the genocide came through his affiliation with the Democratic Republican Movement (Mouvement Démocratique Républicain, or MDR), a Hutu political party. After joining in 1991, he rose through the party ranks and eventually became the local branch president.

Between April 7, 1994, and the end of June 1994, hundreds of civilians sought refuge at the communal headquarters. The majority of the displaced civilians were Tutsi. Initially, Akayesu insulated the Taba commune from the mass killing after the genocide began on April 6, 1994. He refused to let Interahamwe militia operate there and struggled with them to protect the local Tutsi population. On April 18, however, a meeting of mayors with leaders of Rwanda's Interim Government saw a fundamental change take place—both in Taba and in Akayesu himself. Conscious that his political and social future depended on joining those carrying out the genocide, Akayesu began collaborating directly with the extremists, and from this point started to incite his citizens to join in the killing.

During this time, female displaced civilians were regularly taken by armed local militia or communal police and subjected to sexual violence, and/or beaten on or near the bureau communal premises. Displaced civilians were also murdered frequently on or near the bureau communal premises. These acts of sexual violence were generally accompanied by explicit threats of death or bodily harm. The female displaced civilians lived in constant fear and their physical and psychological health deteriorated as a result of the sexual violence and beatings and killings.

TRIAL SUMMARY #20: *PROSECUTOR V. JEAN-PAUL AKAYESU*

The indictment alleged that Akayesu knew that these acts of sexual violence, beatings, and murders were being committed, and was at times present during their commission. Further, he facilitated the commission of the sexual violence, beatings, and murders by allowing them to occur on or near the bureau communal premises. By virtue of his presence during the commission of these crimes, he encouraged these activities. In addition to these general charges, the indictment detailed a number of specific incidents which included ordering several murders. The Court determined that his actions amounted to direct participation in genocide. Akayesu was the first person to be convicted of the crime of genocide in an international tribunal.

In the aftermath of the conquest of Rwanda in July 1994 by the forces of the Tutsi-led Rwandan Patriotic Front (RPF), Akayesu fled the country. He first went to Zaire (now the Democratic Republic of the Congo), then to Lusaka in Zambia. He was arrested on October 10, 1995. Zambia became the first African nation to extradite an alleged *génocidaire* to the International Criminal Tribunal for Rwanda (ICTR). He was formally indicted on February 13, 1996, and transferred to ICTR jurisdiction in mid-May 1996.

DOCUMENT: *PROSECUTOR V. JEAN-PAUL AKAYESU*

When: January 9, 1997–September 2, 1998
Where: Arusha, Tanzania
Court: International Criminal Court for Rwanda
Defendant: Jean-Paul Akayesu
Source: ICTR-96-4-T. Online at http://unictr.unmict.org/en/cases/ictr-96-4.
Charges: Fifteen counts of genocide, crimes against humanity, including rape
Defense: Pled not guilty on all counts. His primary defense was that he had played no part in the killings and that he had been powerless to stop them. His essential position was that at the time of the genocide he had not been in a position of authority. His attorneys argued that Akayesu was being made a scapegoat for the crimes of the people of Taba.
Verdict: Guilty on nine of fifteen counts; life imprisonment. Judgement affirmed by the Appeals Chamber.
Significance: The first person convicted of genocide by an international court.

TESTIMONY

The witness testified under the pseudonym, Poppa Poppa. She was a Tutsi woman married to a Hutu man. The testimony does not detail the crimes committed directly in the genocide but does illustrate the central role that the Interahamwe and Akayesu played. She is a witness for the Defense.

November 4, 1997

Q: In 1994, April, were you considered to be a Hutu or a Tutsi?
A: I was a Tutsi.

Q: At that time were you married?
A: Yes, I was married.

Q: And your husband, was he considered to be a Hutu or a Tutsi?
A: He is a Hutu.

...

Q: Do you know a person by the name of Gene [*sic*, Jean] Paul Akayesu?
A: I know him.

Q: And how did you know him?
A: I knew him when he was a teacher and I also knew him when he was the burgomaster of Taba commune.

Q: Did you know any members of his family?
A: I only know his wife.

Q: Do you know whether or not your husband knew Jean-Paul Akayesu?
A: They knew each other because they would share a glass of beer at the bar, which was within the commune.

Q: In April of 1994 do you recall the day that the killings began in Taba?
A: I remember that the killings started on the 19th of April.

Q: At that time were you able to move around the commune?
A: Yes, I could move. I was not worried.

Q: Why were you not worried?
A: I was not worried because when killings started it was said that they were looking for intellectuals.

Q: At this time, where was your husband?
A: He was working at Byumba.

Q: Do you know whether or not the fact that your husband was a Hutu, whether or not that would have allowed you to walk around or feel safe?
A: Later on I continued to walk about because I was married to a Hutu.

Q: At any point in time, following April 19th, was your home ever attacked?
A: Yes, we were attacked.

Q: Do you recall approximately when this happened?
A: Yes, I remember.

Q: Can you please tell us?
A: It was on the 28th.

Q: Of what month?
A: April.

Q: Can you tell us what happened?
A: They came to attack me at 2 a.m. I opened the door . . . and . . . they took me out of the house, out of the piece of land.

Q: First of all, who came to your house. . . .
A: An Interahamwe who was called Bongo, another one who was called Ugirimana, another one called Mugemana: I was unable to know the name of the fourth person.

Q: What happened . . . ?
A: We stayed on the piece of land at the house and I was waiting for day to break. . . . [I]n the morning that we reached the bureau communal.

Q: During this time what were these people saying to you? What did they want?
A: They told me they wanted to kill me because I was Tutsi.

Q: Did you respond to them?
A: I told them that I was not Tutsi.

Q: What happened at this time?
A: I told them I had money and I told them that they should go up to the bureau communal where I was going to distribute the money to them.

Q: Then what happened?
A: Since I knew the bureau communal, when we arrived there I met Akayesu.

Q: Where were these Interahamwes at this time?
A: I left them at the entrance to the bureau communal.

Q: Explain how that happened. Did they stay? Were they waiting for you or to run away? What happened?
A: They waited for me. I told them I was going to look for Akayesu, so he should distribute to them money and they believed me. They kept hoping.

Q: Did Akayesu have your money?
A: I was the one who had the money.

Q: You told us that after you left the Interahamwe you met Akayesu. Can you tell us what happened at this time, please?
A: I told him that the people had attacked me. He asked me which ethnic group I belonged to, whether I was Tutsi. I told him I was Hutu. He replied to me that I had to return home and that if they came to see me again I should come to the bureau communal.

Q Did you ever discuss an issue about an identity card?
A: When we tackled this issue I told him that I had misplaced my ID.

Q: Are you originally from Taba?
A: I am not a native of Taba: I come from another prefecture.

...

Q: After having this discussion with Akayesu, what did you do?
A: I went to the house. I went home.

Q: At this time were you staying in your home or were you walking around as you were before?
A: On that day I was afraid and I had to hide in a field of french beans, which was below the house.

Q: How long did you remain in hiding?
A: I stayed there for two days.

Q: After these two days, what did you do?
A: After these two days I returned home.

Q: What happened then?
A: Since the Interahamwes were moving about everywhere, at some time in point I met one of the Interahamwes who was called Nyirinkindi.

Q: What happened at this time?
A: He told me it was no longer necessary for me to hide.

Q: Did he give a reason?
A: Yes, because I no longer hid.

...

[Author comment: The following testimony is a summary of testimony made by the Court in the Judgement.]

Witness JJ testified that this happened to her—that she was stripped of her clothing and raped in front of other people. At the request of the Prosecutor and with great embarrassment, she explicitly specified that the rapist, a young man armed with an axe and a long knife, penetrated her. . . . She stated that on this occasion she was raped twice. Subsequently, she told the Chamber, on a day when it was raining, she was taken by force from near the bureau communal into the cultural center within the compound of the bureau communal, in a group of approximately fifteen girls and women. In the cultural center, according to Witness JJ, they were raped. She was raped twice by one man. Then another man came to where she was lying and he also raped her. A third man then raped her, she said, at which point she described herself as feeling near dead. Witness JJ testified that she was at a later time dragged back to the cultural center in a group of approximately ten girls and women and they were raped. She was raped again, two times. Witness JJ testified that she could not count the total number of times she was raped. She said, "each time you encountered attackers they would rape you,"—in the forest, in the sorghum fields. Witness JJ related to the Chamber the experience of finding her sister before she died, having been raped and cut with a machete. (Akayesu, Judgement, para. 421).

NOTABLE FIRSTS

The trial of Jean Paul Akayesu established many "firsts" in international criminal law. It resulted in the first adversarial conviction for genocide under international law since that crime's inception fifty years prior. It also established a number of extremely important jurisprudential precedents concerning individual criminal responsibility in non-international armed conflicts and proving the constitutive elements of the crime of genocide. Finally, the case was the first to recognize the concept of genocidal rape. Rape has long been considered a war crime by the international community but was only rarely punished. Rape was a common war crime in the Rwandan Civil War (as it was in Bosnia). Genocidal rape is done with the intent to shame and terrorize a group and destroy the cohesion of the community.

Rape was used as a weapon of genocide by the Hutu ethnic majority of Rwanda against the Tutsi ethnic minority during the Rwandan Genocide. Common estimates of 250,000 to 500,000 of mostly Tutsi women and girls were raped in a systematic fashion and often in a public or group setting. Hutu women who resisted the genocide or were married to Tutsi men were also targeted, as were some men.

Frequently, Tutsi women were held as sexual slaves and raped many times a day. Approximately five weeks after the start of the genocide in mid-May 1994, a centralized command went out from the government to begin murdering Tutsi women in addition to the men, increasing the frequency of deaths amongst rape victims. The mostly Tutsi Rwandan Patriotic Army that won the civil war, ending the genocide, also raped and enslaved some Tutsi women who had been taken by the Hutu. Rape victims who remained alive at the end of the civil war suffered economic deprivation, extreme psychological trauma, physical mutilations, and permanent health problems, including an extremely high rate of HIV/AIDS. Rape victims were also often ostracized by their families and communities. Several thousand children were born from the genocidal rape victims.

DEFENDING ACCUSATIONS OF GENOCIDE

Because of the special requirements for proving genocide, the last part of the discussion will focus on the defense. The prosecutor had to prove not only that Akayesu committed, encouraged, or aided and abetted in, the acts charged in the indictment, but that he did so with *genocidal intent*. The defense conceded that genocide had occurred in Rwanda and massacres of Tutsis had taken place in Taba commune. It argued, however, that despite his position, Akayesu, had no means to prevent them. He was outnumbered by the Interahamwe. He had only ten communal policemen at his command. Once the massacres had become widespread, he had very little authority and lacked the means to stop the killings. The defense claimed that it would be totally unreasonable for the Court to require Akayesu to act as a hero, that is, to risk his life in a futile cause. With regard to the charges for acts of sexual violence, the defense strategy was to deny that acts of sexual violence were committed, at least at the Bureau Communal. During his testimony the Akayesu emphatically denied that any rapes had taken place at the Bureau Communal, even when he was not there.

The defense argued that the prosecutor admitted that Akayesu had opposed massacres before April 18, 1994. How then could prosecutor assert that Akayesu was a "genocidal ideologue." One does not adopt the ideology of genocide overnight. Hence, the defense that Akayesu could not be convicted of genocide. In closing, the defense argued that the Akayesu was a "scapegoat," who found himself on trial only because he was a Hutu and a mayor at the time of the massacres.

DECISION

The trial judges found that, in his role as mayor, Jean-Paul Akayesu did have the responsibility for maintaining public order and executing the law in the municipality of Taba and that, in this function, he had effective authority over the police. His criminal responsibility was based on his direct participation in acts of genocide and on his position as hierarchical superior. Article 6, section 3, of the statute setting up the ICTR states that a superior can be responsible if he knew or had reason to know that a subordinate was about to commit criminal acts or had done so, and that the superior had failed to take the necessary measures to prevent such acts or punish the perpetrators.

References

Nowrojee, Binaifer. 1996. *Shattered Lives: Sexual Violence during the Rwandan Genocide and Its Aftermath*. New York: Human Rights Watch.

Shaw, Martin. 2003. *War and Genocide: Organized Killing in Modern Society*. Cambridge: Polity.

Van Schaack, Beth. 2008. "Engendering Genocide: The Akayesu Case before the International Criminal Tribunal for Rwanda." Santa Clara Law Digital Commons. http://digitalcommons.law.scu.edu/cgi/viewcontent.cgi?article=1626&context=facpubs.

30

Prosecutor v. Théoneste Bagosora, et al.
(The Military Trial I)

THÉONESTE BAGOSORA

During the period of the 1994 Rwandan Genocide, Colonel Théoneste Bagosora served as Rwandan defense minister. A Hutu, Bagosora came from the Giciye commune of the Gisenyi prefecture, an area in which Rwandan president Juvénal Habyarimana was born. Because of his origin, he gained favor with the Akazu (the so-called Little Hut), the inner circle of Habyarimana's associates, dominated by the president's wife, Agathe Habyarimana.

Bagosora spent his entire career in the Rwandan army, the Forces Armées Rwandaises (FAR). The FAR consisted of the Armée Rwandaise (AR) and the Gendarmerie Nationale (GN). In 1964, he graduated from Kigali's Officers' School (École des officiers). He was later appointed second-in-command of the Military College (École supérieure militaire). He received promotion to the rank of colonel, with command over the important Kanombe military camp. He remained there until June 1992, when he was appointed as director of the cabinet (*directeur du cabinet*) in Rwanda's Ministry of Defense. Despite his official retirement from the military on September 23, 1993, he retained this position until fleeing the country in July 1994.

Bagosora was considered to be the mastermind of the genocide. Reportedly, by 1990, he had developed a plan to exterminate Rwanda's Tutsis. In December 1991, President Habyarimana set up a military commission whose task was to find a reply to the question: "What must be done to defeat the enemy in military, propaganda and political terms?" Bagosora was appointed to coordinate an appropriate response. The report he submitted reflected an incitement to hatred and a call to senior military officers that encouraged and facilitated ethnic violence.

Even though he was present at the negotiations in Arusha, he was a vehement opponent of the Arusha Accords of 1993. He wanted nothing to do with the Rwandan Patriotic Front (RPF) or any plan of shared governance with Tutsis. Sounding much like Adolf Hitler, who warned the Jews on January 30, 1939, that if

Germany's treatment of them resulted in a war being waged against Germany they would face total annihilation, Bagosora publicly stated that the Tutsis would be wiped out if the RPF continued its fight against Rwanda or if the provisions of the Arusha Accords setting up a shared division of power were implemented.

As early as 1992, Bagosora reportedly had the Rwandan army's general staff draw up lists of all those who were thought to be associated with the RPF. Ultimately, such lists were used by the military and the Interahamwe militias to locate, capture, and kill Tutsis and moderate Hutus during the period of the genocide. Beginning in early 1993, Bagosora is known to have had weapons distributed to the militias and other extremist Hutus.

In the confusion in the aftermath of the Habyarimana's assassination, Bagosora assumed effective control of the country. Most accounts consider Bagosora the individual most responsible for coordinating the genocide of Rwanda's Tutsi population. He allegedly gave the order on April 7, 1994, for the military to begin the killing and issued the order that roadblocks be set up across Rwanda to capture and kill fleeing Tutsis and moderate Hutus. With the end of the genocide and the victory of the RPF in July 1994, Bagosora disappeared, taking flight to Zaire (now the Democratic Republic of Congo), after which he moved to Yaoundé, Cameroon. He lived there from July 1995 until his arrest on March 9, 1996.

Bagosora's case was joined with those of, other top-ranking military officials: Brigadier General Gratien Kabiligi, former chief of military operations in the FAR, Lieutenant Colonel Anatole Nsengiyumva, former military commander of Gisenyi Military Camp, and Major Aloys Ntabakuze, former commander of the Kanombe Paracommando Battalion, Kigali. The joint proceedings became known as the "Military Trial 1."

GRATIEN KABILIGI

During the period of the genocide, Gratien Kabiligi served as chief of military operations within the High Command of the Rwandan Army. He had the responsibility of planning, coordinating, and ensuring the execution of military operations throughout the territory of Rwanda. In his capacity as chief of military operations, he had under his control the units of the sectors of Byumba, Ruhengeri, Mutara, and Kigali, as well as the elite units such as the Presidential Guard, the ParaCommando Battalion, and the Reconnaissance Battalion.

ALOYS NTABAKUZE

During the events referred to in this indictment, Aloys Ntabakuze exercised the functions of Commander of the ParaCommando Battalion in the Rwandan Army. He served in the Presidential Guard before being promoted to the position of Commander of the ParaCommando Battalion in the Rwandan Army in 1992. In his capacity as Commander of the ParaCommando Battalion of the Rwandan Army, he had direct control of the units.

ANATOLE NSENGIYUMVA

During the events listed in the indictment, Anatole Nsengiyumva served as commander of military operations for Gisenyi sector. Before that appointment in June 1993, he was chief of military intelligence within the High Command of the Rwandan Army. In his capacity as commander of military operations for the Gisenyi sector, he had authority over the MRND militia (the Interahamwe), and the CDR militia (the Impuzamugambi).

TRIAL SUMMARY #21: *PROSECUTOR V. THÉONESTE BAGOSORA, GRATIEN KABILIGI, ALOYS NTABAKUZE, AND ANATOLE NSENGIYUMVA*

The International Criminal Tribunal for Rwanda (ICTR) had long been interested in Bagosora and had indicted him soon after its inception in 1994. Upon being located and arrested in Cameroon, Bagosora was transferred to the UN prison quarters in Arusha on January 23, 1997, to face thirteen counts of eleven different international crimes relating to genocide, crimes against humanity, and war crimes. At his first appearance before the Tribunal, he entered a plea of not guilty.

As the first trial involving charges of genocide, the Prosecution took up an enormous amount of the Tribunal's time in preparation. It was only on April 2, 2002, that the prosecution began its case. The trial concluded on June 1, 2007. On December 18, 2008, the ICTR found Bagosora, Ntabakuze, and Nsengiyumva guilty of genocide, crimes against humanity, and war crimes. Bagosora was convicted of ten counts of eight different crimes, including genocide, murder, extermination, rape, persecution, other inhumane acts, two counts of violence to life, and outrages upon personal dignity.

From late 1990 until July 1994, Gratien Kabiligi, Aloys Ntabakuze, Théoneste Bagosora, Augustin Ndindiliyimana, Augustin Bizimungu, Aloys Ntiwiragabo, Protais Mpiranya, François-Xavier Nzuwonemeye, Anatole Nsengiyumva, Augustin Bizimana, and Tharcisse Renzaho conspired among themselves and with others to work out a plan with the intent to exterminate the civilian Tutsi population and eliminate members of the opposition, so that they could remain in power. The components of this plan consisted of, among other things, recourse to hatred and ethnic violence, the training of and distribution of weapons to militiamen as well as the preparation of lists of people to be eliminated. In executing the plan, they organized, ordered, and participated in the massacres perpetrated against the Tutsi population and of moderate Hutus. Bagosura was one of the principal planners and directors of the genocide.

DOCUMENT: **ICTR-98-41-T**

When: April 2, 2002–December 18, 2008
Where: Arusha, Tanzania
Court: International Criminal Court for Rwanda

Defendants: Théoneste Bagosora, Gratien Kabiligi, Aloys Ntabakuze, and Anatole Nsengiyumva
Source: http://unictr.unmict.org/sites/unictr.org/files/case-documents/ictr-98-41/trial-judgements/en/081218.pdf.
Charges: Conspiracy to Commit Genocide, Genocide, Complicity in Genocide, Direct a Public Incitement to Commit Genocide, Crimes Against Humanity, and Violations of Article 3 Common to the Geneva Conventions and Additional Protocol II, offenses stipulated in Articles 2, 3, and 4 in the Statute of the Tribunal.
Defense: The "civilian violence" was the result of a war initiated by the RPF. Denied that a genocide occurred; denied having any part in the killing. Bagosora testified that he was "powerless" to stop it. Challenged the "fairness" of the proceedings.
Verdict: Kabiligi, acquitted, December 18, 2008. Appeals Chamber: Bagosora, guilty, 35 years; Nsengiyumva, guilty, 15 years; Ntabakuze, guilty, 35 years.
Significance: As a founder and sponsor of Hutu Power, Bagosora was one of the individuals most responsible for the genocide. This trial clearly established the full extent of planning for the genocide at the highest level of the Rwandan military.

TESTIMONY

As in the ICTY trials, much of the testimony is highly edited to protect the identities of witnesses. The following comes from transcripts that have been carefully edited for public perusal. Establishing what took place in the genocide was an easy task. Establishing the intent and connection to the genocide proved more difficult. The following details the motives for the genocide.

Witness ZF (June 18, 2003)

> **Q.** Witness, these high-ranking officers that you have mentioned, why did they want you to become an *Interahamwe*?
> **A.** They wanted me to become an Interahamwe because—that we form a group, which would assist Habyarimana to fight against those opposed to him—that is, to Habyarimana—particularly the *Inyenzi-Inkotanyi*, particularly the Tutsi; in other words, the Tutsi.
>
> **Q.** Do you know what the objectives of the *Interahamwe* movement were at the time you became a member?
> **A.** Of course, I had to know what their objectives were because I was an *Interahamwe* myself. We had to pool our efforts to fight against the Tutsi and kill them subsequently.
>
> **Q.** To the best of your recollection, did the *Interahamwe* movement have any relationship with any political organisation during the time you were an Interahamwe?

A. When I was an *Interahamwe* we were part of a political party. We were the Interahamwes of the MRND party.

Q. My question is: did you have—did the *Interahamwe* have any relationship with any other political organisations in Gisenyi at the time?
A. Yes; yes, the *Interahamwe* had relations with some other political parties; for instance, the *Impuzamugambi*, which was of the CDR party.

Q. And what were the objectives of the *Impuzamugambi,* if you know?
A. As the name—as its name suggests, *Impuzamugambi* were people who had the same objectives as ourselves; namely, to exterminate the Tutsi.
...

Witness HU (September 2, 2003)

The questioner is Mr. Rashid Rashid for the Prosecution.

Q. Thank you. Did anything else happen that day in your locality?
A. Yes, another event took place. At around 11 o'clock, we saw a person being chased. And those people pursuing the person wanted to apprehend the person. They managed to stop him, catch him and killed him, about 20 metres from the mosque.

Q. And how many people did you see passing, pursuing this one person?
A. About 10 people were pursuing the victim.

Q. And were they civilians?
A. Yes, they were civilians who were members of the MRND Party, who were known as the *Interahamwe*.

Q. How did you recognise them as the *Interahamwe*?
A. I was able to identify those people because after they had killed that person, they came to the mosque and I noticed that I knew some of them because I used to see them during events following party rallies.

Q. How do you know that that individual was killed?
A. Those who were with me said the group that was chasing that victim, that person, had just killed him, and I thought it was necessary for me to go and check. And I noticed that he had received a machete wound on the neck—sorry, on the throat.

Q. At which point did you go over to view this person?
A. It was virtually immediately. This was while those who were chasing the victims were still there. And so I went there to check on what had happened.
...

Q. And was this individual suffering from any other wounds?
A. Yes, the person had wounds all over, but the attackers dwelled more on the lower part of the back of the head.

Q. And did you personally know this person that was killed?
A. Yes, I knew the person by sight because he lived in the area, but I didn't know his name.

Q. And would you happen to know his ethnic group?
A. That person was Tutsi.

Q. And what did you do after you went over to the spot where this person was, what did you do after that?
A. After that incident I noticed that massacres had actually started. And we tried to look for means to defend ourselves in the event we were also attacked.

Q. And the ten persons that had been pursuing this individual, where were they?
A. They had already left, they left but they weren't too far.

Q. When you say that you realised that the massacres had begun and you took steps to arm yourselves in case of an attack, what kind of arms did you gather?
A. Some were able to obtain traditional weapons, spears, machetes, bows and arrows, but above all, we used stones.

Q. And when you say some, who are you referring to?
A. I am talking about some of the people who were with us, just some, not everyone.

Q. And would these be the people that were at the mosque?
A. Yes, these were people who were at the mosque, all of those who lived close to the mosque and who were able to go back to their homes and pick up those traditional weapons.

Q. And were you subsequently attacked?
A. Yes, we were subsequently attacked. Shortly after the Interahamwe killed that person, they came back. They were led by a representative of the CDR party who went by the name Bizimana. Bizimana told us that he was looking for some Tutsis who were hiding in the mosque. He wanted that they be surrendered to him so that they be killed. We refused, we told him that this was not possible and that no one would be given to him, handed over to him.

Q. When Bizimana was saying these words, were you present?
A. I was present.

Q. And who was Bizimana with?
A. Bizimana was with some of the people whose names I do not remember. But they were part of the group; that is the group—that group of people that chased that person and killed him close to the mosque.

Q. And what was your response to his request?
A. We told him that we were not going to give him anyone so that he goes to kill them.

Q. Did Bizimana respond to your statement?
A. He said that, in view of the fact that we were not willing—or we refused to respond to his request that they were going to attack the mosque and even burn it.

...

Q. Witness, where had you met this man Bizimana before?
A. I knew him. I knew him as an official, a responsible of the CDR party.

Q. And do you know whether Bizimana had any other names, or was known by any other names?
A. I don't know his other name, but he had a nickname; he was called Gikoko.

Q. Witness, could you please spell that nickname for us?
A. G-I-K-O-K-O.

Q. After your exchange—
MR. PRESIDENT:
Does that nickname mean anything in your language?
THE WITNESS:
A. The word Gikoko refers to someone who has no pity.

THE PROBLEM OF PUNISHMENT

Let the punishment fit the crime. In considering the cases in the ICTR and ICTY, what could that possibly mean? Still, the question of what "fit" means generates considerable debate even in domestic legal systems. For example, the sentence of a dishonorable discharge without jail time, given to Sgt. Bowe Bergdahl (November 2017) for desertion and misbehavior before the enemy, raised a firestorm of criticism for being much too lenient. Bagosora originally was sentenced to life imprisonment. His trial was the most important heard before the Tribunal. It was especially significant in that it addressed such points as how the genocide was planned and carried out at the highest levels of the Rwandan military, as well as the relationship between the army and extremist Hutu politicians.

On December 14, 2011, the Appeals Chamber reduced Bagosora's life sentence to thirty-five years and Nsengiyumva's to fifteen years. Crediting time already served, the Appeals Chamber ordered the immediate release of Nsengiyumva. In a separate opinion, the Appeals Chamber also reduced Ntabakuze's life sentence to thirty-five years. On these issues, the Appeals Chamber was badly split. In the *Bagosora/Nsengiyumva* case, Judges Theodor Meron and Patrick Robinson appended a joint dissenting opinion; Judge Mehmet Güney appended a partially dissenting opinion; Judge Fausto Pocar appended a dissenting opinion; and Judges Pocar and Liu Daqun appended a joint dissenting opinion. Still, observers have asked a hard question: *Why are persons convicted of extraordinary crimes seemingly given such ordinary sentences?*

Often, disagreements flow from assumptions about the purpose of punishment. There are three important views. Is the purpose of punishment retribution, protection of society, or rehabilitation? These purposes are not necessarily mutually exclusive. Sentencing can embody one or more of the rationales. All involve an idea of proportionality, but they have generated an extended debate about what values should be placed upon the scales of justice. In cases of mass atrocities, how is it possible to make the punishment proportionate to the seriousness of the crime? Retribution ultimately relies upon the deterrent effect: you do the crime, you do the time; if you do a crime again, you will do the time again or in the case of serious crimes, you will not be given the opportunity to do the crime again (protection of society).

Rehabilitation focuses upon the chastening effect of conviction/incarceration as an opportunity for education. Deterrence is very difficult to measure. The sentences handed out at the Nuremberg and Tokyo Tribunals did not act as deterrents to future perpetrators of mass atrocities. Even, the establishment of the ICTY, with specific jurisdiction over the former Yugoslavia, did not deter the commission of massive crimes well after the Tribunal came into existence, most notoriously, the Srebrenica massacres. Yet, as with all of the rationales here, failures stand out; successes may remain hidden. Still the debate goes on. In considering the nature of the crimes at the international level, is rehabilitation then a reasonable expectation?

In the *Kambanda* case (ICTR-97-23), the ICTR Trial Chamber saw retribution and deterrence as the appropriate standards. They stated that the penalties imposed on accused persons found guilty by the Tribunal should be directed, on the one hand, at retribution of the said accused, who must see their crimes punished. But, on the other hand, sentences should aim also at deterrence by showing those contemplating such acts that the international community was ready to punish serious violations of international humanitarian law and human rights.

There is also an important difference between the purposes of international criminal law and the greatest proportion of domestic law. First, international crimes are distinctive because they are perpetrated during times of societal disintegration. This often involves the weakening of community norms prohibiting violence. Second, enforcement at the domestic level tends to focus upon those who actually carry out the acts, although prosecutors often do use some forms of joint liability (e.g., conspiracy). Normally the person who commits the act is regarded as the primary perpetrator, while those who plan, instigate, or abet in planning or instigation are regarded as secondary perpetrators.

For international criminal law, while those who commit specific acts fall within its domain, the principal focus is on those high-level individuals who plan, organize, or order the events that define the broader context. The assumption is that planners and organizers bear a far greater burden of guilt than the person in the street at a low level who commits a specific act in carrying out the broader plan. This perspective emphasizes the group nature of the crimes. Some members of the group may participate in the sense of overt criminal acts, but the activities of others in terms of planning, instigating, or ordering form an essential component in facilitating the activities of the actual perpetrators. In one sense, this flips a traditional distinction between primary and secondary participation found in domestic criminal law.

NATURE OF SENTENCES

The problem comes from the fact that in reviewing the sentences handed down they do not seem to follow the pattern that planners and organizers were punished more severely. While some Trial Chambers did survey past ICTR sentences, no formal obligation existed that mandated imposition of sentences consistent with earlier cases. The Appeals Chamber seemed to treat each case *de novo* without any consideration of its past actions. This means that the same sentence could be ordered for defendants with very different levels of involvement, or two similarly liable perpetrators could receive different sentences. The different sentences of Laurent Semanza and Jean-Paul Akayesu, who both served as mayors of local communes, illustrate this inconsistency. Each defendant pleaded not guilty but was convicted of genocide. Semanza was found to have ordered the massacre of hundreds of Tutsi refugees at a church. Both genocide convictions involved ordering or being present at killings, failing to prevent or punish widespread killings, and encouraging sexual violence against Tutsis. Both defendants were also convicted of (multiple) murders, extermination, torture, and rape, all as crimes against humanity. The influence of both men in their community was viewed as an aggravating factor. Akayesu received a life sentence, while Semanza was sentenced to 35 years. Bagosora as the principal planner and instigator also received only a 35-year sentence.

References

Barnett, Michael. 2002. *Eyewitness to a Genocide: The United Nations and Rwanda*. Ithaca, NY: Cornell University Press.

Dallaire, Roméo. 2003. *Shake Hands with the Devil: The Failure of Humanity in Rwanda*. New York: Avalon.

D'Ascoli, Silvia. 2011. *Sentencing in International Criminal Law: The UN Ad Hoc Tribunals and Future Perspectives for the ICC*. Oxford, UK: Hart Publishing.

Smith, James M., ed. 2004. *A Time to Remember. Rwanda: Ten Years after Genocide*. Retford, UK: The Aegis Institute.

31

Prosecutor v. Jean-Bosco Barayagwiza, Ferdinand Nahimana, and Hassan Ngeze

THE MEDIA TRIAL

This case also became known as the "Radio Machete" trial. It gained a great deal of attention because of the issue of free speech and its limits. Many countries have struggled with the questions of how to define "hate speech" and the point(s) at which hate speech can be considered impermissible. The International Covenant on Civil and Political Rights (ICCPR), one of the basic documents in what has become known as the "International Bill of Rights," states in Article 19 that "Everyone shall have the right to hold opinions without interference." But, Article 19 also states that the exercise of the right "carries with it special duties and responsibilities." Restrictions may be lawfully placed on speech to protect the "rights or reputations of others," and for "the protection of national security, of public order, or of public health or morals." The difficulty in regulation stems from the additional problem that, without a precise definition, "protection" could easily translate into prohibition. How do you differentiate between speech that merely expresses an opinion and that which actively displays genocidal intent?

The ICTR "Media" trial involved the editor of the newspaper *Kangura* and two principals in the radio station RTLM (Radio-Télévision Libre des Mille Collines). The three were accused of incitement to genocide through editorials and broadcasts. The court found that incitement: "implies a desire on the part of the perpetrator to create by his actions a particular state of mind necessary to commit such a crime in the minds of the person(s) he is so engaging" (Judgement, para. 1012).

A large number of Rwandans could not read and write. People received most of their information from radio broadcasts. In March 1992, Radio Rwanda was first used in directly promoting the killing of Tutsi in a place called Bugesera, south of the national capital. On March 3, 1992, the radio repeatedly broadcast a message supposedly sent by a human rights group based in Nairobi that claimed Hutus in Bugesera would be attacked by Tutsis. Local officials built on the radio announcement to convince Hutus that they needed to protect themselves by attacking first.

Led by soldiers from a nearby military base, members of the Interahamwe, and local Hutu civilians attacked and killed hundreds of Tutsi (Thompson 2007, 42).

Until 1993, Rwanda had only one national station, the government-owned Radio Rwanda. The government then gave a license to Ferdinand Nahimana and Jean-Bosco Barayagwiza to start RTLM. It denied licenses to other applicants who might have offered competing viewpoints. The radio station began operations on July 8, 1993, in Kigali, the Rwandan capital. RTLM introduced talk radio to Rwanda. The station was the country's first and only privately owned alternative to government programming. Its "popularity had as much to do with its lack of competition as with the programming choices its directors made.... In a country where secrets were legion and half-truths told, it seemed that Radio Milles Collines was ... willing to tell its listeners what was really happening" (Temple-Raston 2005, 2–3). Hassan Ngeze served as the editor of *Kangura* magazine, which ran vicious anti-Tutsi propaganda pieces that commentators often read or discussed on the air.

Although the station was supposedly independent, it received clandestine support from the Habyarimana government. It utilized transmitting equipment owned by Radio Rwanda, the official state-operated radio station. RTLM quickly became very popular, particularly among Hutu youths, who were drawn to the station by its popular music selections and other youth-oriented programming. Interspersed with that programming was virulent anti-Tutsi rhetoric and propaganda that demonized the minority group as subhuman and "cockroaches." The station was said to have had a major impact on members of the Interahamwe, a militia group which played a major role in the Rwandan Genocide.

RTLM worked closely with the virulently anti-Tutsi newspaper, *Kangura*. The editor, Hassan Ngeze, also was a major shareholder in RTLM. Although some members of the international community, including the United States, contemplated jamming RTLM's signals or destroying its transmitting towers, none took any action because they feared that such action would be interpreted as abrogating free speech and expression. Meanwhile, anti-Tutsi hate speech and propaganda intensified. After the assassination of Habyarimana in April 1994, RTLM took a central role in promoting the genocide of Tutsis and moderate Hutus by actively encouraging Hutus to murder Tutsis. The station also broadcast the location of Tutsis and sympathetic Hutus as the genocide unfolded.

The three men named in the indictment were charged with being responsible for the venomous broadcasts of what Rwandans called "Radio Hate." They became the first journalists accused of such serious crimes since 1946, when the Nazi editor Julius Streicher was sentenced to hang at Nuremberg for calling for the murder of Jews. In the eighty-page indictment, the prosecutor charged the three with inciting fellow Hutus to commit genocide. The indictment alleged that the programming on RTLM promoted ethnic stereotyping in a manner that encouraged contempt and hatred for the Tutsi population. RTLM broadcasts called on listeners to seek out and take up arms against the enemy identified as the Rwandan Patriotic Front (RPF), the *Inkotanyi* (nickname for the RPF), the *Inyenzi* ("cockroaches"), and their accomplices. RTLM broadcasts equated all of these with the Tutsi ethnic group. After April 6, 1994, the virulence and the intensity of RTLM broadcasts propagating ethnic hatred and calling for violence increased. These broadcasts called explicitly for the extermination of the Tutsi ethnic group. One witness in the trial said that RTLM "spread petrol throughout the country little by little, so that one day it would be able to set fire to the whole country."

Nahimana was described as the founder and director of RTLM. Barayagwiza was his second in command. They represented RTLM externally in official capacities. Internally, they controlled the financial operations of the company and held supervisory responsibility for all activities of RTLM, taking remedial action when they considered it necessary to do so. Nahimana also played an active role in determining the content of RTLM broadcasts, writing editorials, and giving journalists texts to read. On several RTLM broadcasts, Ngeze called for the extermination of the Tutsi and Hutu political opponents

JEAN-BOSCO BARAYAGWIZA

Jean-Bosco Barayagwiza was a lawyer by training who studied in the Soviet Union. He held the office of director of political affairs in Rwanda's Foreign Ministry. He was a cofounder, with Ferdinand Nahimana, of the organization which in turn established the anti-Tutsi radio station RTLM. Barayagwiza's political party, the Coalition pour la Défense de la République (CDR), was established in February 1992. He and two other extreme anti-Tutsi Hutu ideologues: Jean Shyirambere Barahinura and the founder-owner of the radical newspaper *Kangura*, Hassan Ngeze, were the primary sponsors. The party was exclusively and narrowly defined as Hutu. A person with even one Tutsi grandparent was denied membership. The party sponsored a youth militia movement, the Impuzamugambi ("those with a single purpose"), expressly for the purpose of harassing, assaulting, and, ultimately, murdering Tutsis.

The CDR was fervently opposed to President Juvénal Habyarimana's rapprochement with the RPF during 1993 and early 1994 and was in the forefront of those undermining his authority after the signing of the Arusha Peace Accords on August 4, 1993. After Habyarimana's assassination, the CDR entered into a coalition with the hastily formed interim government formed to deal with the emergency claimed to have been instigated by the Tutsis.

A LESSON IN LEGAL PROCEDURE

As Rwanda was progressively overrun by troops of the RPF during June and July 1994, Barayagwiza, along with most other high-ranking *génocidaires*, fled the country. Upon the request of the new, post-genocide Rwandan government, he was arrested in Yaoundé, Cameroon, in late March 1996. After spending 330 days in jail without being informed of the charges against him, he was transferred to the jurisdiction of the ICTR in Arusha, Tanzania, in mid-November 1997. The delay violated ICTR standing orders, which stipulated that charges must be made within 90 days of an arrest. He pled not guilty to all counts on February 23, 1998. In legal matters, procedural requirements play an important role in ensuring equal treatment of suspects. His attorneys, citing the violation of the rules governing the ICTR, filed a motion for release. The Appeals Chamber agreed:

> [T]he Appeals Chamber found that the facts of the case justified recourse to the abuse of process doctrine. This led the Appeals Chamber to conclude that the right of the Appellant to be informed promptly of the charges against him, his right to see his writ of habeas corpus resolved in a timely manner and the Prosecutor's duty to prosecute the case diligently had all been breached.
>
> The Appeals Chamber found the abuse so egregious and the violations so numerous that it concluded that releasing the Appellant and dismissing the charges against him was the only possible remedy. The Appeals Chamber further found that the dismissal and release had to be *with prejudice* to the Prosecutor. It concluded that "as troubling as this disposition may be to some, the Appeals Chamber believes *that to proceed with the Appellant's trial when such violations have been committed, would cause irreparable damage to the integrity of the judicial process.* Moreover, we find that it is the only effective remedy for the cumulative breaches of the accused's rights. Finally, this disposition may very well deter the commission of such serious violations in the future." The Appeals Chamber ordered the Appellant's immediate release and directed the Registrar to make the necessary arrangements to deliver the Appellant to the authorities of Cameroon immediately. (emphasis added)
>
> (*The Prosecutor v. Jean-Bosco Barayagwiza*, "Decision" ICTR-97-19-AR72, November 2, 1999)

The Prosecutor appealed the decision. On March 31, 2000, the ICTR Appeals Chamber reversed its earlier decision, and directed that Barayagwiza stand trial. His case was then consolidated into the case against the two other media executives charged with involvement in the genocide.

FERDINAND NAHIMANA

Ferdinand Nahimana earned a doctorate in History from the University of Paris. He had an appointment as Director of the Rwandan Information Office. Between 1979 and 1994, Nahimana allegedly wrote and published articles extolling the superiority of the northern Hutus and encouraging the population to rise up against the Tutsis and moderate Hutus. Known as an ideologue within the inner circle of President Habyarimana, he was a co-founder of the CDR. He was also member of "Hutu Power."

After being dismissed in 1993 from the Rwandan National Radio due to his hate-filled rantings, he took part, as a member of the "Action Committee," in the creation of the Radio Télévision Libre des Milles Collines (RTLM), becoming its director. Due to his biased radio programs, he was accused of being one of the ideologues who helped orchestrate the genocide. He gathered around him an editorial team that directly encouraged, over the air, the assassination of Tutsis and Hutus who were in opposition.

From April 1993 to July 31, 1994, approximately, Ferdinand Nahimana is said to have planned, directed, and supported such radio programs. According to the ICTR indictment, "he was aware of the programs and the effect that these programs had on the population." Between January and July 1994, Nahimana reportedly organized meetings with members of the *Mouvement Révolutionaire National pour le Développement* (MNRD), and the Interahamwe in the Ruhengeri Prefecture to discuss the elimination of the Tutsis and moderate Hutus. When the RPF took Kigali, Nahimana left the country. He finally was arrested in Cameroon in March 1996.

HASSAN NGEZE

Hassan Ngeze was the owner, founder, and editor of the *Kangura* newsletter, which was published from 1990 to 1995 and widely circulated across Rwanda. Like the programming of RTLM, *Kangura* produced hate-filled messages, characterizing Tutsis as enemies who wanted to subvert the democratic system and seize power for themselves. Additionally, Ngeze was also a founding member of the CDR. He was alleged to have participated in distributing firearms, supervising roadblocks, and ordering massacres in the Gisenyi Prefecture. The indictment charged that "as an influential militiamen in Gisenyi . . . Ngeze exercised authority over the Interahamwe (MRND) and *Impuzamugambi* (CDR) militiamen" (para. 4.3). Ngeze fled Rwanda in June 1994 as the country fell to the RPF. He was arrested in Mombasa, Kenya, on July 18, 1997.

TRIAL SUMMARY #22: *PROSECUTOR V. JEAN-BOSCO BARAYAGWIZA, FERDINAND NAHIMANA, AND HASSAN NGEZE*

This prosecution raised many issues that continue to be controversial in countries that value "free speech" as a constitutional right. In the United States, standards govern "irresponsible" speech, such as "shouting fire in a crowded theater" and "hate" speech that encourages action against a specific person or group. Note that in defining "hate" speech, the important element is active encouragement of a specific course of action, not speech that is simply "hateful" in describing the group or individual. In considering these issues, remember that RTLM was a sole source. No competing radio station had similar programming that either glorified Tutsi heritage or actively advocated the suppression of Hutus.

DOCUMENT: "JUDGEMENT AND SENTENCE," DECEMBER 3, 2003
(PARAS. 392–398; 408–409)

When:	October 23, 2000–December 3, 2003
Where:	Arusha, Tanzania
Court:	International Criminal Court for Rwanda
Defendants:	Jean-Bosco Barayagwiza, Ferdinand Nahimana, and Hassan Ngeze
Source:	ICTR-99-52-T. Online at http://unictr.unmict.org/sites/unictr.org/files/case-documents/ictr-98-41/trial-judgements/en/081218.pdf and http://unictr.unmict.org/en/cases/ictr-99-52. See also *Ferdinand Nahimana, Jean-Bosco Barayagwiza, and Hassan Ngeze*

	(Appellants) v. The Prosecutor, ICTR-99-52-A, November 28, 2007. Online at http://www.un.org/en/preventgenocide/rwanda/pdf/NAHIMANA%20ET%20AL%20-%20APPEALS%20JUDGEMENT.pdf.
Charges:	Barayagwiza, nine counts: conspiracy to commit genocide, genocide, direct and public incitement to commit genocide, complicity in genocide, crimes against humanity (persecution, extermination, and murder), and two counts of serious violations of Article 3 common to the Geneva Conventions and of Additional Protocol II; Nahimana seven counts: conspiracy to commit genocide, genocide, direct and public incitement to commit genocide, complicity in genocide, and crimes against humanity (persecution, extermination, and murder); Ngeze, seven counts: conspiracy to commit genocide, genocide, direct and public incitement to commit genocide, complicity in genocide, and crimes against humanity (persecution, extermination, and murder)
Defense:	Barayagwiza refused to participate in the trial, claiming that the judges were not impartial. Nahimana was "a man of words and he manipulated words to suit the circumstances." He denied responsibility for broadcasts after April 6, 1994, and denied that he held any position of authority. Ngeze wavered back and forth in his testimony on fundamental issues, as well as virtually every detail of his evidence. He often claimed that he did not know or could not remember.
Verdict:	Barayagwiza guilty, 35 years' imprisonment, reduced to 32 years on appeal; Nahimana, guilty, life imprisonment reduced to 30 years; Ngeze, guilty, life imprisonment, reduced to 35 years.
Significance:	The first conviction of news media executives as complicit in mass murder since 1946, when the Nuremberg Tribunal sentenced the Nazi publisher Julius Streicher to hang.

TESTIMONY

The RTLM broadcasts are excerpted from the testimony of Jean-Pierre Chrétien (University of Paris) who was called as an expert witness. Professor Chrétien had supervised Nahimana's doctoral dissertation (1986). Because Professor Chrétien's testimony (July 1–5, 2002) runs to several hundred pages, the excerpts are from the examples the Trial Chamber found most compelling concerning the role of RTLM.

RTLM broadcasts continued after 6 April to define the enemy as the Tutsi, at times explicitly. In a broadcast on 15 May 1994, for example, the RTLM Editor-in-Chief Gaspard Gahigi said:

> The war we are waging, especially since its early days in 1990, was said to concern people who wanted to institute "democracy." . . . We have said time and again that it was a lie. . . . these days, they trumpet, they say the Tutsi are being

exterminated, they are being decimated by the Hutu, and other things. I would like to tell you, dear listeners of RTLM, that the war we are waging is actually between these two ethnic groups, the Hutu and the Tutsi.

Similarly, in an RTLM broadcast on 29 May 1994 of an exchange between residents and soldiers, a resident said:

> [O]ne who does not have papers should remain there or even leave his (her) head there. However, in reality, I think that the check should be necessary because everybody should have his (her) papers with him (her) certifying that he (she) is really Rwandan and is really a son of "Sebahinzi" that he is not an enemy, or an accomplice or an *Inkotanyi*. I think that all those who remain in this country, we know each other. We are all sons of the "same man. . . ."

Using the term "Son of Sebahinzi," a reference to the Hutu as the real Rwandans, the broadcast in effect equated an enemy, or an accomplice or an "Inkotanyi" with anyone who was not a Hutu. In an RTLM broadcast on 30 May 1994, Kantano Habimana equated Inkotanyi with Tutsi, referring to the enemy several times first as Inkotanyi and then as Tutsi:

> If everybody, if all the 90% of Rwandans, rise like one man and turn on the same thing called *Inkotanyi*, only on the thing called *Inkonyi*, they will chase it away until it disappears and it will never dream of returning to Rwanda. If they continue killing themselves like this, they will disappear. Look, the day all these young people receive guns in all the communes, everyone wants a gun, all of them are Hutu, how will the Tutsi, who make up 10% of the population, find enough young people, even if they called on the refugees, to match those who form 90% of the population.
>
> How are the *Inkotanyi* going to carry this war through? If all the Hutu children were to stand up like one man and say we do not want any more descendants of Gatutsi in this country, what would they do? I hope they understand the advice that even foreigners are giving them.

In an RTLM broadcast on 4 June 1994 Kantano Habimana more graphically equaled *Inkotanyi* with Tutsi, describing the physical characteristics of the ethnic group as a guide to selecting targets of violence. He said:

> One hundred thousand young men must be recruited rapidly. They should all stand up so that we kill the *Inkotanyi* and exterminate them, all the easier that . . . the reason we will exterminate them is that they belong to one ethnic group. Look at the person's height and his physical appearance. Just look at his small nose and then break it. Then we will go on to Kibungo, Rusurno, Ruhengeri, Byumba, everywhere. We will rest after liberating our county.

The call for extermination of the *Inkotanyi* was explicitly equated with extermination of the Tutsi in an RTLM broadcast on 13 May 1994 by Kantano Habimana:

> I suspect that among those people, those *Inkotanvi*, there hides a "devil of a bullcalf that will exterminate the herd of cattle with which it was born." . . . Someone must have signed the contract to exterminate the *Inkotanyi*, to make them disappear for good . . . to wipe them from human memory . . . to exterminate the Tutsi from the surface of the earth . . . to make them disappear for good.

. . .

Some RTLM broadcasts linked the war to what were perceived and portrayed as inherent ethnic traits of the Tutsi. In a broadcast on May 31, 1994, for example, Kantano Habimana said:

> The contempt, the arrogance, the feeling of being unsurpassable have always been the hallmark of the Tutsis. They have always considered themselves more intelligent and sharper compared to the Hutus. It's this arrogance and contempt which have caused so much suffering to the *Inyenzi-Inkotanvi* and their fellow Tutsis, who have been decimated. And now the *Inyenzi-Inkotanyi* are also being decimated, so much so that it's difficult to understand how those crazy people reason.

In an interview of a Simbomana by Gaspard Gahigi, broadcast on RTLM on June 20, 1994, the cunning, predatory nature of the Tutsi and the innocent, vulnerable nature of the Hutu were discussed:

> Simbomana: Thus therefore the trickery, you have known for a long time that the Tutsi are very cunning, they are a people who always smile, who always wink. It is a smile which delights us, the members of our family, he smiles at you but is thinking of other things. The Hutus, we are innocent people who think that everything is good and that no one will do us any harm. As for the Tutsi, if he smiles at you or winks at you it is to achieve a goal. And it is why, their trickery made the Hutu unable to see further and to know that behind this trickery there was something else that the Tutsi wanted. The first thing to do from today, and even when we will triumph, is that we know, from today, every Tutsi trickery.
>
> Gahigi: I would remind our listeners that at present you say that it is the wickedness and the trickery of the Tutsi that has complicated this war. Therefore for us to deal with this problem, this trickery and this wickedness must be released so that people know it. And that it is this trickery which puts the population into confusion. And then that these Tutsi extremists forming the *Inyenzi* front have lied to the population.

THE POWER OF THE MEDIA IN A CLOSED ENVIRONMENT

The Trial Chamber thoroughly documented the role of Rwandan hate media in the killing:

> The newspaper and the radio explicitly and repeatedly, in fact relentlessly, targeted the Tutsi population for destruction. Demonizing the Tutsi as having inherently evil qualities, equating the ethnic group with "the enemy" and portraying its women as seductive enemy agents, the media called for the extermination of the Tutsi ethnic group as a response to the political threat that they associated with Tutsi ethnicity. (ICTR 2003, para. 72)

In some cases, authorities picked up radio messages and used them to mobilize local people more effectively. Thus, when theradio claimed that supporters of the RPF had hidden weapons in or near churches, local authorities staged incidents in which they "discovered" planted weapons to give credence to the reports of secret preparations for attacks against Hutu.

To re-emphasize a point made earlier in chapter 28, Jean Hatzfeld reported that one of his interviewees said:

Killing is very discouraging if you must decide to do so yourself . . . but if you are obeying orders from the authorities, if you are adequately conditioned, if you feel pushed and pulled, if you see that the carnage will have absolutely no adverse effects in future, you feel comforted and revitalized. You do it without shame. . . . We envisaged this relief with no reluctance whatsoever . . . we were efficiently conditioned by radio broadcasts and advice we heard. (Hatzfeld 2003, 85)

A FINAL NOTE ON THE ICTR

The three accused lodged an appeal against the Trial Judgement on various grounds of errors of fact and law. The appeal was heard in January 2007 with the verdict rendered in late November 2007. In its judgement, the Appeals Chamber reversed several parts of the Trial Judgement. It acquitted all three of conspiracy to commit genocide, and all genocide charges relating to their involvement with RTLM and Kangura.

The reasoning of the Chamber dealt with several important elements. First, Nahimana and Ngeze had argued that the Trial Chamber had erred in that it included Hutu opponents who could not be part of the Tutsi protected group. The Chamber found that the perception of the offenders as to identity was a valid factor in determining whether or not particular individuals belonged to a group; but, in this instance, they held that no evidence existed to show that the accused had such perceptions.

Second, the Appeals Chamber reversed Nahimana's conviction for genocide because, although the founder of RTLM, he had not played an active role after April 6, 1994. Moreover, no evidence existed that indicated that he had ordered any on air personality to incite the murder of Tutsis. Barayagwiza, originally convicted for "superior responsibility," also had his conviction reversed on the grounds that the evidence was insufficient to establish that he had effective control over journalists and others after April 6.

Perhaps the most important part of the decision related to the charge of "direct and public incitement" to commit genocide. The Trial Chamber's had taken a rather broad and somewhat confused position on the relationship between "hate speech," freedom of speech, and incitement to genocide. The decision had generated some considerable commentary. For example, Diane Orentlicher argued that the Trial Chamber had broadened the standard considerably beyond what the Convention (and the Court's Statute) required:

> Speech made punishable by the convention is limited to words that advocate the commission of genocide by the speaker's intended audience. However pernicious, propaganda that instead seeks to induce racial, religious, or national hatred is beyond the reach of the convention's provision on "direct and public incitement to commit genocide."

The Appeals Chamber discussed the difference between instigation as an "inchoate (embryonic) crime" and direct and public incitement at some length. It did not agree that the Trial Chamber had blurred the distinction between hate speech and public direct incitement. It agreed with the Trial Chamber that cultural context and the nuances of the local language could be analyzed with an eye toward what the audience might have read into certain words and phrases. Nahimana's original conviction for "instigation" was overturned because evidence did not establish sufficient personal involvement. His conviction for "superior responsibility" was upheld. With respect to Ngeze, the Chamber decided that some articles published in 1994 did constitute direct and public incitement to commit genocide and affirmed that conviction.

References

Chrétien, Jean-Pierre. 2000. *Rwanda, les médias du genocide.* New revised and expanded ed. Paris: Karthala.

Hatzfeld, Jean. 2003. *Machete Season.* Translated by Linda Coverdale. New York: Picador.

Orentlicher, Diane F. 2006. "Criminalizing Hate Speech in the Crucible of Trial: *Prosecutor v. Nahimana.*" *American University International Law Review* 21(4): 557–596.

Temple-Raston, Dina. 2005. *Justice on the Grass: Three Rwandan Journalists, Their Trial for War Crimes, and a Nation's Quest for Redemption.* New York: Free Press.

Thompson, Allan, ed. 2007. *The Media and the Rwanda Genocide.* London: Pluto Press.

32

The Special Court for Sierra Leone: The Charles Taylor Trial

BACKGROUND: LIBERIA AND SIERRA LEONE

Although endowed with abundant natural resources (particularly diamonds), Sierra Leone ranks as one of the poorest countries in the world. Since gaining independence from Great Britain in 1961, the country has had a history of political instability. The events that led to the establishment of the Special Court for Sierra Leone began in the late 1980s. In large part, the roots of the violence stemmed from attempts to control the diamond fields and consequently the enormous proceeds from their sale. The Liberian president, Charles Taylor, played a prominent role in the conflict.

LIBERIA

Founded in 1822 as a settlement of the American Colonization Society (ACS), Liberia is Africa's oldest independent republic. The ACS believed that African Americans would face better chances for freedom in Africa than in the United States. Liberia declared its independence in 1847 with a constitution based on that of the United States. Interestingly, Great Britain, not the United States was the first country to extend international recognition. The United States did not grant recognition until 1862, during the first year of the Civil War.

In the 1970s, Liberia began having economic problems that caused a great deal of unrest. Given the atmosphere of instability, a group of soldiers led by Samuel Doe staged a coup in April 1980. The new regime promised a more equitable distribution of wealth and power. Instead, it enriched its members at the nation's expense by developing an extensive system of patronage. A disproportionate number of desirable political and military positions went to Doe's ethnic group.

Toward the end of the 1980s, discontent in Liberia once again manifested itself in the appearance of several regional rebel groups. In December 1989, these groups joined together under a former military officer, Charles Ghankay Taylor, the leader of the National Patriotic Front of Liberia (NPFL), in a guerrilla war against Doe from neighboring Côte d'Ivoire (Ivory Coast). The United States and the West declined to intervene in the conflict, although Doe received support from the Economic Community of West African States (ECOWAS), which sent a peacekeeping force, ECOMOG (Economic Community of West African States Monitoring Group), to Liberia in August 1990. In September 1990, rebels captured and killed Doe, precipitating a seven-year civil war among the rebel factions. ECOMOG set up an interim government in Monrovia in October 1990. Taylor proclaimed himself president a month later, setting up a separate government and capital in Gbarnga. Over the next six years, the NPFL gained control of a large portion of the country, but their tactics raised accusations of a wanton disregard for human rights.

Following a peace agreement that ended the war in August 1996, Taylor was elected president in the 1997 election with close to 75 percent of the vote, but Liberians became outraged with his heavy-handed rule. The discontent erupted into a second Liberian civil war between 1999 and 2003. Taylor was forced to resign and flee into exile in 2003. In 2005, free and fair elections were held in Liberia. Since then the country has experienced relative political stability. However, the country remains still remains impoverished. Eighty percent of its population has annual incomes below the international poverty line.

SIERRA LEONE AND LIBERIA

Beginning in 1990, Taylor provided money, arms, and training support to Foday Sankoh to form the Revolutionary United Front (RUF) in Sierra Leone. In return, Taylor received diamonds from Sierra Leone. The RUF launched its first campaign into eastern Sierra Leone from Liberia in late March 1991. In the months following, over 100,000 refugees fled the conflict into Guinea. The government of Sierra Leone was unable to mount an effective counterattack.

The RUF funded their insurgency through the illegal mining and exporting of Sierra Leone's diamonds. After accusing Taylor of enriching himself through arms-for-diamonds trading with the RUF, the United Nations imposed a worldwide ban on the trade of rough Sierra Leone diamonds in July 2000. The United Nations also imposed travel sanctions on Taylor and banned the trade of weapons and diamonds with Liberia. The United Nations extended the sanctions in May 2003, citing the government's "active support" of various rebel groups destabilizing West Africa. It also added a ban on timber sales because tropical hardwoods were another main source of Liberia's income. The following month, the UN Special Court for Sierra Leone (SCSL) indicted Taylor for his role in the Sierra Leone conflict, a move applauded by many but condemned by others who feared that the indictment would increase factional fighting in Liberia.

The RUF's signature tactic was terror through physical mutilation. An estimated 20,000 civilians suffered amputation of arms, legs, ears, and other body parts from machetes and axes. Fighting continued in the ensuing months, with the RUF gaining control of the diamond mines. The Sierra Leone Army was totally ineffective. A military coup in April 1992 unseated the government, but those who staged the coup seemed no more equipped to deal with the challenge presented by the RUF than their predecessors. In desperation the new government contracted the private military firm, Executive Outcomes (South Africa). In approximately six weeks, the situation changed dramatically with the RUF reduced to existence in border enclaves.

Under the auspices of the United Nations, Sierra Leone president Ahmad Tejan Kabbah and RUF leader Foday Sankoh negotiated the Lomé Peace Accord in July 1999. The agreement made Sankoh vice president and gave other RUF members positions in the government. It called for an international peacekeeping force under the auspices of the United Nations—the United Nations Mission in Sierra Leone (UNAMISL). Almost immediately, however, the RUF began to violate the agreement, most notably by holding hundreds of UNAMSIL personnel hostage and capturing their arms and ammunition during the first half of 2000. In May 2000, the situation deteriorated to the point that British troops intervened to evacuate foreign nationals and establish order.

Still, not until January 2002 did the fighting end. In June 2000, President Kabbah wrote to UN secretary-general Kofi Annan requesting the United Nations to authorize a court to deal with crimes during the conflict. In August 2000, the UN Security Council adopted Resolution 1315 requesting the secretary-general to start negotiations with the Sierra Leone government to create a Special Court. On January 16, 2002, the United Nations and government of Sierra Leone signed an agreement establishing the Court. The Court has authority to try those who bear the greatest responsibility for serious violations of international humanitarian law and Sierra Leone law committed in the territory of Sierra Leone since November 30, 1996.

Document: Statute of the Special Court for Sierra Leone

When: August 14, 2000
Where: United Nations, New York City, New York
Source: Security Council Resolution 1315 (2000). Online at http://www.rscsl.org/Documents/scsl-statute.pdf.
Significance: The Special Court for Sierra Leone was the first international court to be funded by voluntary contributions. It was the first international tribunal to try and convict persons for the use of child soldiers (AFRC trial), for forced marriage (and other inhumane acts) as a crime against humanity (RUF trial), and for attacks directed against UN peacekeepers (RUF trial). In 2013, it became the first of the ad hoc courts to complete its mandate and transition to a residual mechanism.

Having been established by an Agreement between the United Nations and the Government of Sierra Leone pursuant to Security Council resolution 1315 (2000) of 14 August 2000, the Special Court for Sierra Leone (hereinafter "the Special Court") shall function in accordance with the provisions of the present Statute.

Article 1
Competence of the Special Court

1. The Special Court shall, except as provided in subparagraph (2), have the power to prosecute persons who bear the greatest responsibility for serious violations of international humanitarian law and Sierra Leonean law committed in the territory of Sierra Leone since 30 November 1996, including those leaders who, in committing such crimes, have threatened the establishment of and implementation of the peace process in Sierra Leone.
2. Any transgressions by peacekeepers and related personnel present in Sierra Leone pursuant to the Status of Mission Agreement in force between the United Nations and the Government of Sierra Leone or agreements between Sierra Leone and other Governments or regional organizations, or, in the absence of such agreement, provided that the peacekeeping operations were undertaken with the consent of the Government of Sierra Leone, shall be within the primary jurisdiction of the sending State.
3. In the event the sending State is unwilling or unable genuinely to carry out an investigation or prosecution, the Court may, if authorized by the Security Council on the proposal of any State, exercise jurisdiction over such persons.

Article 2
Crimes against Humanity

The Special Court shall have the power to prosecute persons who committed the following crimes as part of a widespread or systematic attack against any civilian population:

a. Murder;
b. Extermination;
c. Enslavement;
d. Deportation;
e. Imprisonment;
f. Torture;
g. Rape, sexual slavery, enforced prostitution, forced pregnancy and any other form of sexual violence;
h. Persecution on political, racial, ethnic or religious grounds;
i. Other inhumane acts.

Article 3
Violations of Article 3 Common to the Geneva Conventions and of Additional Protocol II

The Special Court shall have the power to prosecute persons who committed or ordered the commission of serious violations of article 3 common to the Geneva Conventions of 12 August 1949 for the Protection of War Victims, and of Additional Protocol II thereto of 8 June 1977. These violations shall include:

a. Violence to life, health and physical or mental well-being of persons, in particular murder as well as cruel treatment such as torture, mutilation or any form of corporal punishment;
b. Collective punishments;
c. Taking of hostages;
d. Acts of terrorism;
e. Outrages upon personal dignity, in particular humiliating and degrading treatment, rape, enforced prostitution and any form of indecent assault;
f. Pillage;
g. The passing of sentences and the carrying out of executions without previous judgement pronounced by a regularly constituted court, affording all the judicial guarantees which are recognized as indispensable by civilized peoples;
h. Threats to commit any of the foregoing acts.

Article 4
Other Serious Violations of International Humanitarian Law

The Special Court shall have the power to prosecute persons who committed the following serious violations of international humanitarian law:

a. Intentionally directing attacks against the civilian population as such or against individual civilians not taking direct part in hostilities;
b. Intentionally directing attacks against personnel, installations, material, units or vehicles involved in a humanitarian assistance or peacekeeping mission in accordance with the Charter of the United Nations, as long as they are entitled to the protection given to civilians or civilian objects under the international law of armed conflict;
c. *Conscripting or enlisting children under the age of 15 years into armed forces or groups or using them to participate actively in hostilities.* [emphasis added]

Article 5
Crimes under Sierra Leonean Law

The Special Court shall have the power to prosecute persons who have committed the following crimes under Sierra Leonean law:

a. Offences relating to the abuse of girls under the Prevention of Cruelty to Children Act, 1926 (Cap. 31):
   i. Abusing a girl under 13 years of age, contrary to section 6;
   ii. Abusing a girl between 13 and 14 years of age, contrary to section 7;
   iii. Abduction of a girl for immoral purposes, contrary to section 12.
b. Offences relating to the wanton destruction of property under the Malicious Damage Act, 1861:
   i. Setting fire to dwelling-houses, any person being therein, contrary to section 2;

ii. Setting fire to public buildings, contrary to sections 5 and 6;
iii. Setting fire to other buildings, contrary to section 6.

[Article 6 Individual Criminal Responsibility omitted]

Article 7
Jurisdiction over Persons of 15 Years of Age

1. The Special Court shall have no jurisdiction over any person who was under the age of 15 at the time of the alleged commission of the crime. Should any person who was at the time of the alleged commission of the crime between 15 and 18 years of age come before the Court, he or she shall be treated with dignity and a sense of worth, taking into account his or her young age and the desirability of promoting his or her rehabilitation, reintegration into and assumption of a constructive role in society, and in accordance with international human rights standards, in particular the rights of the child.
2. In the disposition of a case against a juvenile offender, the Special Court shall order any of the following: care guidance and supervision orders, community service orders, counselling, foster care, correctional, educational and vocational training programmes, approved schools and, as appropriate, any programmes of disarmament, demobilization and reintegration or programmes of child protection agencies.

[Article 8 Concurrent Jurisdiction and Article 9 Double Jeopardy omitted]

Article 10
Amnesty

An amnesty granted to any person falling within the jurisdiction of the Special Court in respect of the crimes referred to in articles 2 to 4 of the present Statute shall not be a bar to prosecution.

[Articles 11–25 omitted]

THE STATUTE

The Statute has a number of interesting features. First, it does not empower the court to issue indictments for genocide. Neither Secretary-General Kofi Annan nor the members of the Security Council thought that any of the circumstances of the conflicts fit the rather narrow definition. Second, the Lomé Peace Agreement had included an amnesty provision for the members and leadership of the RUF. In his letter, President Kabbah argued that the RUF had reneged on its obligations under the agreement. In particular, the RUF had taken UN peacekeepers as hostages. Article 10 of the Statute reflects the preamble to SC Resolution 1315 authorizing the court which says "the United Nations holds the understanding that the amnesty provisions of the [Lomé] Agreement shall not apply to international crimes of genocide, crimes against humanity, war crimes and other serious violations of international humanitarian law."

Table 32.1 SCSL at a Glance

Court	Judges	Selection Process	Tenure	Seat
SCSL	11 permanent	Trial: 4 appointed by UN secretary-general: 2 by the government of SL	3-year terms	Freetown, Sierra Leone
		Appeals: 3 appointed by UN secretary-general, 2 by government of Sierra Leone		

Third, funding for the Court would be through voluntary contributions, not through the regular UN budget. Fourth, the Court is a "hybrid" in that it has judges from Sierra Leone as well as drawing on the broader international community. Table 32.1 summarizes the hybrid structure. Fifth, neither the ICTY nor the ICTR had any provisions concerning the minimum age for prosecution, nor specifications for treatment of those considered minors. One of the most distressing parts of the conflict in Sierra Leone was the large-scale participation of "child soldiers." The legal code of Sierra Leone sets the age of criminal responsibility at the age of seven. The compromise was to set the minimum age at fifteen but also to require that some of the judges have experience in juvenile justice (Article 13(2)). Finally, Article 4(c) does provide punishment for conscription or otherwise using children under fifteen to conduct hostilities.

CHARLES TAYLOR INDICTMENT

Taylor lived in exile in Nigeria from 2003 to 2006, all the while saying he hoped to return to his home country. One month after he left for Nigeria, a UN investigation charged Taylor with stealing or illegally diverting at least $100 million during his years in office. In March 2006, Taylor was arrested as he tried to escape Nigeria. He was flown to Sierra Leone, where the UN-backed Special Court for Sierra Leone charged him with 11 counts of crimes against humanity and war atrocities, including leading and financing a rebel army that murdered, mutilated, raped, and abused tens of thousands of civilians. He pleaded not guilty to all 11 charges and said he could not afford defense attorneys.

TRIAL SUMMARY #23: *PROSECUTOR V. CHARLES GHANKAY TAYLOR*

In June 2006, Taylor was extradited to The Hague, Netherlands, for trial, as officials feared tension over the case in Sierra Leone would lead to renewed violence. After several delays, the trial began in January 2008 as Taylor became the first former African ruler to stand trial for war crimes. He was convicted on April 26, 2012, on all 11 counts, but on reduced charges of "aiding and abetting," rather than leading, rebel militia groups in the specified atrocities and crimes against humanity.

DOCUMENT: *PROSECUTOR V. CHARLES GHANKAY TAYLOR*

Court: Special Court for Sierra Leone
Defendant: Charles Ghankay Taylor

Where:	The Hague, Netherlands. This court was supposed to hold all of its proceedings in Sierra Leone, to allow victims of the alleged crimes to see justice at work. Taylor's case was moved to The Netherlands in case the hearings sparked fresh instability in Sierra Leone.
When:	June 4, 2007–April 26, 2012
Source:	SCSL-2002—1-PT. Trial Judgement of May 18, 2012. Online at http://www.scsldocs.org/documents/view/6662-11.
Charges:	Terrorism (Common Article 3), unlawful killings, sexual violence, outrages on personal dignity (Common Article 3), physical violence, other inhumane activity, recruitment and use of child soldiers, abductions, and forced labor
Defense:	Denied any connection to war crimes committed during the conflicts; lacking means to support the alleged activities; was a force to settle the disputes, not part of the problem; much of evidence is open to question with regard to credibility; prosecution is "selective and vindictive."
Verdict:	Guilty on all counts, but on "aiding and abetting" rather than direct participation. Sentence, 50 years, upheld on appeal.
Significance:	The final Judgement comprises almost 2,500 pages. The indictment and conviction broke new ground in that it included the recruitment and use of child soldiers. Taylor was the first sitting African head of state to be indicted.

TESTIMONY

Most of the testimony is sealed because of the potential danger to victims who testified. The following is an excerpt from the original trial judgement, which evaluated the evidence. Samuel "Sam" Bockarie (nickname Mosquito), whose name appears often, was a leading member of the Revolutionary United Front in Sierra Leone. Bockarie became infamous during the Sierra Leone Civil War for his brutal tactics. Indicted by the SCSL, he could have given very damaging testimony about Taylor's involvement. Bockarie was killed in suspicious circumstances that were officially reported as a shootout with Liberian forces trying to arrest him.

Prosecution Witness Joseph Marzah

Witness Joseph ("Zigzag") Marzah, an NPFL soldier, testified that after 1991, ULIMO occupied Lofa County in Liberia blocking the supply road between Liberia and Sierra Leone. As a result, Taylor instructed Marzah to "penetrate through" with arms and ammunition. Taylor gave Marzah $USD 1,600 and a Nissan pickup. Marzah pretended to be a businessman selling kola nuts and established relationships with a couple of Guinean customs officers who, after being given a balawal a bag of kola nuts, assisted him in transporting the kola nuts bags as far as Kissidugu. Marzah testified that ammunition from Charles Taylor, like rockets, was hidden in the bags. In Kissidugu, Tiagen Wantee and a Mandi friend collected the kola nuts bags and brought them to the Liberian Embassy in Conakry.

...

According to [bodyguards] Shabado, Ray and others, Bockarie and Eddie Kanneh returned from Liberia to Sierra Leone and briefed the attendees on their travels and about the materiel they had brought. They said that they went to Charles Taylor in Liberia and proceeded to Burkina Faso, returning to Sierra Leone with "a lot of ammunition and arms."

[**Author comment:** *The defense challenged Marzah's testimony on numerous grounds including drug use, payments from the Prosecution, and the evidence that he was senior enough to have the type of contact with Taylor that he claimed. In one of the more startling pieces of testimony, Marzah alleged that he, Taylor, and Benjamin Yeaten were all in the same poro society (a traditional West African secret religious society) and that Taylor himself had eaten human hearts with him on multiple occasions. Marzah also told the Court that Taylor had ordered his fighters to eat their enemies, including UN peacekeepers, as a means of terrorizing the population.*]

Prosecution Witness TFI-367
TFI-367 was the only witness who testified that he was with Sankoh when Sankoh took diamonds to the Accused during this period. The Trial Chamber noted that his evidence was corroborated by Witnesses TFI-168 and TFI-567, both of whom testified that Sankoh told them that diamonds were brought to the Accused. Witness TPI-567 testified that he saw Bockarie give Sankoh plenty of diamonds captured from civilians and that at a meeting called by Sankoh, Sankoh said that he had given some of the diamonds looted from Kono to the Accused in exchange for arms and ammunition.

Witness TFI-367, who was stationed in Kono, testified that he heard from Rambo that Bockarie went to see Charles Taylor, "Father," in Monrovia for arms and ammunition, and that when Bockarie returned [Issa] Sesay would come to Kono and they will attack Koidu Town. When Bockarie went to Liberia Sesay was left in charge of Buedu. Two to three days after a radio message announced Bockarie's return, Sesay returned to Kono with ammunition and a strong manpower which included his bodyguards and some officers. This was new ammunition that they used in order to capture Koidu Town.

Prosecution Witness Isaac Mongor
(a former commander in the Revolutionary United Front)

Witness Isaac Mongor, an RUF commander testified that in 1996, while the RUF was still in the bush, they learned that elections were going to be held in Sierra

Leone. Foday Sankoh called the RUF Commanders to his base at Zogoda in Kenema District and expressed concern that while fighting was still going on between the NPRC Government and the RUF, the former had decided to hold national elections without involving the latter. Sankoh told the RUF Commanders that since the Government did not acknowledge the RUF, the latter should carry out an offensive to stop the elections.

Mongor attended this meeting in Zogoda along with several other RUF commanders including Mohamed Tarawalli, Issa Sesay, Augustine Gbao, CO Rocky (Emmanuel Williams), Rambo (Boston Flomo) and Jungle (Daniel Tamba). While Mongor was there, an RUF radio operator named Z_Man told Sankoh that Charles Taylor wanted to speak with him on the radio set. Mongor joined Sankoh and both went to the thatched hut where the radio was located. Mongor stood just in front of the radio room within earshot as Sankoh spoke to Taylor.

During the radio conversation, which lasted 20 to 25 minutes, Mongor overheard Sankoh explain to Taylor that the RUF had been cut off by ULIMO and were not getting supplies from Liberia anymore; that the NPRC Government had decided to carry on with the elections; that Sankoh had summoned his commanders to instruct them to carry out an offensive to disrupt the elections; and that the offensive entailed a plan to instil terror in the voters by amputating the hands of captured civilians who had participated or were going to participate in the voting and asking them to "take their hands off the election." Mongor overheard Taylor responding that "the plan was not a bad one." After the radio conversation, Sankoh told the RUF commanders that he had discussed the planned offensive with Taylor who considered it "not a bad plan at all." Two days later, the RUF launched "Operation Stop Election."

Mongor states that the meeting of the RUF Commanders took place two days after the radio communication between Sankoh and Taylor.

At the meeting, each commander was assigned an area to attack. Mongor was to attack Masingbi; Mohamed Tarawalli and Superman were to attack Magburaka and Makeni, while RUF Rambo and Mosquito were to attack Kenema Town.

Mongor testified that Operation Stop Election was not successful in Masingbi as his fighters were unable to overrun the SLA and Kamajors or to capture or amputate any civilians taking part in the elections there.

However, he heard that Mohamed Tarawalli and Superman successfully carried out the operation in Magburaka where RUF Commanders captured civilians, amputated their hands and carved RUF on their chests with razor blades.

The Defence cross-examined Mongor at length as to why he failed to mention the alleged conversation between Taylor and Sankoh regarding "Operation Stop Election" in his 4 September 2006 statement to the Prosecution investigators, and instead waited until February 2008, just before his testimony, to do so. Mongor stated that he did mention the information to the investigators in 2006 but that they failed to record it.

APPEAL

Both the prosecution and the defense filed Appeals Briefs. The prosecution's grounds of appeal included the Trial Chamber's failure to find Taylor liable for ordering and instigating the commission of crimes, the Chamber's failure to find him liable for crimes committed in certain locations in five districts on the ground that they fell outside the scope of the indictment, and the Chamber's sentencing decision which was an error in fact and in law. The defense appealed the finding of guilt and sentence on forty-two grounds that alleged both errors in law and in fact.

While not accepting some very minor parts of the Trial Chamber's decision, the Appeals Chamber affirmed the decision and sentence of the Trial Chamber. Of considerable interest is the concurring opinion of Judges Shireen Avis Fisher and Renate Winter. Setting the stage for this requires a rather quick lesson in the formation of customary law. The United States, Great Britain, and Canada base their legal systems on customary law. The question becomes: What does that mean beyond the fact that within domestic court systems, precedent (cases decided previously) becomes an important factor in many cases? In the contemporary era, that is the principal role of custom because formal legislation has totally replaced custom as a "source" of new law in most common law states.

Current-day issues involve questions of *international law*. The language in indictments throughout this book has used the terminology "the laws and customs" of war. Because no international legislature exists, *customary practice*, that is evidence that a very large number of states have clear accepted a particular prohibition by their behaviors, may still apply to a particular action. The question addressed in the following involves how a party would mount a "principled" challenge to a customary law or practice with which they disagree. The issue is the nature of the defense challenge to the definition of "aiding and abetting." It is a form of the *tu quoque* argument—others are doing it and enough people are doing it that a new standard has emerged that would permit this as a matter of international customary law. The opinions of the two judges on the Appeals Panel address this reasoning:

> The essential elements of aiding and abetting liability as properly applied in this case establish the boundaries which protect against over-criminalization. As with all forms of criminal participation, it is up to the Trial Chamber to test the facts it finds against the essential elements, mindful of the limitations, the burden of proof, and the presumption of innocence. This is the routine task of judges, and there is nothing different in the way judges interpret and apply the elements of aiding and abetting from the way they interpret and apply the elements of any other mode of liability or substantive crime. The Appeals Chamber unanimously determined that the Trial Chamber committed no error in performing this task in the present case.
>
> . . .
>
> The Defense argues that the essential elements of aiding and abetting as applied and relied on by the Trial Chamber are insufficient and require additional or different elements or analysis because the concept of aiding and abetting is so broad that it

would in fact encompass actions that are today carried out by a great many States in relation to their assistance to rebel groups or to governments that are well known to be engaging in crimes of varying degrees of frequency. . . . Such assistance, the Defense argues, is going on in many other countries that are supported in some cases by the very sponsors of this Court. *By this argument, the Defense purposely confuses customary law-making with international law-breaking.*

Furthermore, suggesting that the Judges of this Court would be open to the argument that we should change the law or fashion our decisions in the interests of officials of States that provide support for this or any international criminal court is an affront to international criminal law and the judges who serve it. The Defense has interjected a political and highly inappropriate conceit into these proceedings, which has no place in courts of law and which has found no place in the Judgment of this Court. The Judges of this Court, like our colleagues in our sister Tribunals, are sworn to act independently without fear or favour, affection or ill-will and to serve honestly, faithfully, impartially and conscientiously. To suggest otherwise wrongfully casts a cloud on the integrity of judges in international criminal courts generally and the rule of law which we are sworn to uphold, and encourages unfounded speculation and loss of confidence in the decisionmaking process as well as in the decisions themselves.

I wish to make clear that this line of argument is absolutely repudiated. . . .

Reasonable minds may differ on the law. I am convinced that the customary law on the elements of aiding and abetting are as stated by the Trial Chamber and that application of the law to the facts in this particular case was properly and fairly calculated. (emphasis added)

The Judges essentially said: *because others are violating the law established to protect human rights does not give another person leave to do the same.* One cannot change laws that violate certain principles just because others have done so. A simple analogy: Given the large number of murders that occur within the United States within a year, would you argue that the repeated "occurrence" over time should change the law on murder because it has become an accepted practice? The logic seems very straightforward here.

THE RESIDUAL SPECIAL COURT

The Residual Special Court was established pursuant to an agreement signed between the United Nations and the government of Sierra Leone on August 11, 2010. It was ratified by Parliament on December 15, 2011, and signed into law on February 1, 2012. The agreement stipulates that the RSCSL shall have its principal seat in Freetown but shall carry out its functions at an interim seat in The Netherlands with a sub-office in Freetown for witness and victim protection and support. The RSCSL, like the SCSL, is funded by voluntary contributions from the international community, but the agreement permits it to seek alternative means of funding. The RSCSL has an oversight committee to assist in obtaining adequate funds and to provide advice and policy direction on non-judicial aspects of the Court.

References
Campbell, Greg. 2012. *Blood Diamonds: Tracing the Deadly Path of the World's Most Precious Stones.* Rev. ed. New York: Basic Books.

Gberie, Lansana. 2005. *A Dirty War in West Africa: The RUF and the Destruction of Sierra Leone*. Bloomington: Indiana University Press.

Higbie, James, and Bernard S. Moigula. 2017. *Sierra Leone: Inside the War: History and Narratives*. Bangkok: Orchid Press.

Mitton, Kieran. 2015. *Rebels in a Rotten State: Understanding Atrocity in the Sierra Leone Civil War*. Oxford: Oxford University Press.

Waugh, Colin M. 2011. *Charles Taylor and Liberia: Ambition and Atrocity in Africa's Lone Star State*. London: Zed.

33

The International Criminal Court

POLITICS AND PROMISE

When negotiation began for the current International Criminal Court (ICC), the idea of a permanent court that would hear cases of international criminal law had been widely discussed by scholars for over a century. Serious debate began after the conclusion of World War I. In 1937, the League of Nations sponsored two international treaties: the Prevention and Repression of Terrorism, and the Creation of an International Criminal Court. The charter for the creation of an international criminal court required the ratification of the Prevention and Repression of Terrorism Treaty. Neither convention, however, obtained sufficient support for ratification.

After World War II, efforts to construct the present International Criminal Court followed two separate tracks: (1) an initiative to draft an international criminal code; and (2) planning for an independent international criminal court. Although these two enterprises would seem inextricably entwined, the politics of development meant that they followed very different paths.

In November 1947, the General Assembly charged the International Law Commission (ILC) with two tasks.

1. to formulate the principles of international law recognized in the Charter and Judgement of the Nuremberg Tribunal; and, with careful attention to these principles,
2. to prepare a draft code of offenses against the peace and security of mankind.

The creation of the court was tied to other negotiations then in progress. During the preparatory work, which produced the Genocide Convention, representatives from the United States pushed hard for inclusion of language authorizing the creation of an international tribunal.

Delegates from the Soviet Union, among others, expressed major reservations. Unlike the International Court of Justice, where jurisdiction was limited to disputes between countries, the International Criminal Court envisioned a court that would have jurisdiction over individuals for specific crimes not otherwise punishable in national courts. Article VI of the Genocide Convention emerged as a compromise, providing for trial "by a competent tribunal of the State in the territory of which the act was committed, or by such international penal tribunal as may have jurisdiction with respect to those Contracting Parties which shall have accepted its jurisdiction."

At this time, another issue arose. The General Assembly noted that while the ILC's draft code listed aggression as the first offense, the General Assembly had already entrusted a Special Committee with the task of preparing a report on a draft definition of aggression. The Assembly decided to postpone consideration of the ILC draft code until the Special Committee had submitted its report. That decision effectively ended active consideration of the issues for the next twenty-five years. Not until 1981 did the General Assembly invite the ILC to resume its work on the draft code. Another fifteen years passed before the Commission finally produced a second draft code (1996).

It took the events in the former Yugoslavia and Rwanda to move the issue forward in an expeditious manner. In late 1992, the General Assembly requested the ILC to undertake the "elaboration of a draft statute for an international criminal court." Subsequently, in 1993 and 1994, the Security Council authorized the ad hoc International Criminal tribunals for the former Yugoslavia (ICTY) and for Rwanda (ICTR). The ILC moved promptly on the ICC assignment, issuing its report in 1994. Because of continuing division over the desirability of establishing a permanent court, the General Assembly then established an ad hoc committee to study the issue further. Two years later the General Assembly finally authorized a Preparatory Committee to create a statute for consideration by a diplomatic conference of interested states. Early in 1998, the Preparatory Committee submitted the text of a statute that would establish a permanent international criminal court. The Conference of Plenipotentiaries (those officially authorized to sign for a state) met in Rome from June 15–17, 1998.

At the conference, states voted to establish a permanent court by an overwhelming majority: 120–7 with 21 abstentions. The Rome Statute entered into force on July 1, 2002 (60 ratifications). Of the five permanent members of the UN Security Council, only Britain and France have ratified the Statute. The Russian Federation has signed it (September 2000), China has not signed it, and the United States has "withdrawn" its signature. Table 33.1 gives a breakdown of court membership by geographic region.

Table 33.1 Members of the ICC by Geographic Region

Region/Country	Number of States[a]
Africa	32
North Africa/Middle East	2
Americas	28
Asia/Pacific Islands	19
Europe	42
Total	123

[a] As of January 1, 2018.

From the Middle East and North Africa group, only Jordan and Tunisia have ratified the Statute. The nascent "state" of Palestine has also ratified but has not been included in the official member count in the table because of its uncertain status. Exploring the politics of the long-standing and continuing struggle of Palestine for international recognition would require a separate chapter not a paragraph. India and Pakistan also remain non-members as do many other states in Asia.

DOCUMENT: ROME STATUTE OF THE INTERNATIONAL CRIMINAL COURT

When: Opened for signature July 17, 1998; entered into force July 1, 2002
Where: Rome, Italy
States Parties: 123 (as of January 1, 2018)
Source: United Nations Diplomatic Conference of Plenipotentiaries on the Establishment of an International Criminal Court, A/CONF.183/9. Online at http://www.un.org/law/icc/index.html.
Significance: An international criminal court was seen as the missing link in the international legal system. The International Court of Justice at The Hague handles only cases between States, not the prosecution of individuals. Without an international criminal court for dealing with individual responsibility as an enforcement mechanism, acts of genocide and massive violations of human rights often went unpunished.

[The Table of Contents is not part of the original text. It is reproduced here in part as a guide to the document. Some articles have been omitted.]

Table of Contents

Preamble

Part I Establishment of the Court
Article 1 The Court
Article 2 Relationship of the Court with the United Nations

Part II Jurisdiction, Admissibility and Applicable Law
Article 5 Crimes within the Jurisdiction of the Court
Article 6 Genocide
Article 7 Crimes against Humanity
Article 8 War Crimes
*Article 8*bis* Crime of Aggression
Articles 9, 10 Elements of Crimes
Article 11 Jurisdiction *ratione temporis* [temporal jurisdiction]
Article 12 Preconditions to the Exercise of Jurisdiction
Article 13 Exercise of Jurisdiction
Article 14 Referral of a Situation by a State Party
Article 15 Prosecutor
*Article 15*bis* Exercise of Jurisdiction over the Crime of Aggression (State Referral, *proprio motu*)

*Article 15ter Exercise of Jurisdiction over the Crime of Aggression (Security Council Referral)
Article 16 Deferral of Investigation and Prosecution
Article 17 Issues of Admissibility
Article 19 Challenges to the Jurisdiction of the Court or the Admissibility of a Case
Article 20 *Ne bis in idem* [no double jeopardy]
Article 21 Applicable Law

Part III General Principles of Criminal Law
Article 22 *Nullum crimen sine lege* [no crime without law]
Article 23 *Nulla poena sine lege* [no punishment without law]
Article 24 Non-retroactivity *ratione personae* [no retroactive prosecutions]
Article 25 Individual Criminal Responsibility
Article 26 Exclusion of Jurisdiction over Persons under Eighteen
Article 27 Irrelevance of Official Capacity
Article 28 Responsibility of Commanders and Other Superiors
Article 29 Non-applicability of Statute of Limitations
Article 30 Mental Element
Article 31 Grounds for Excluding Criminal Responsibility
Article 32 Mistake of Fact or Mistake of Law
Article 33 Superior Orders and Prescription of Law

Part IV Composition and Administration of the Court

Part V Investigation and Prosecution
Article 53 Initiation of an Investigation
Article 54 Duties and Powers of the Prosecutor with Respect to Investigations
Article 55 Rights of Persons during an Investigation
Article 56 Role of the Pre-Trial Chamber in Relation to a Unique Investigative Opportunity
Article 57 Functions and Powers of the Pre-Trial Chamber
Article 58 Issuance by the Pre-Trial Chamber of a Warrant of Arrest or a Summons to Appear
Article 59 Arrest Proceedings in the Custodial State
Article 60 Initial Proceedings before the Court
Article 61 Confirmation of the Charges before Trial

Part VI The Trial

Part VII Penalties
Article 77 Applicable Penalties
Article 78 Determination of the Sentence

Part VIII Appeal and Revision

Part IX International Cooperation and Judicial Assistance
Article 86 General Obligation to Cooperate
Article 87 Requests for Cooperation: General Provisions
Article 88 Availability of Procedures under National Law

Article 89 Surrender of Persons to the Court
Article 90 Competing Requests

Part X Enforcement
Article 103 Role of States in Enforcement of Sentences of Imprisonment

Part XI Assembly of States Parties

Part XII Financing

Part XIII Final Clauses
Article 119 Settlement of Disputes
Article 120 Reservations
Article 121 Amendments

[Articles 122–128 omitted]

* Added after Kampala Review Conference 2010; activated at New York Review Conference, December 2017.

A NOTE ON OTHER COURTS

The ICTY and ICTR established a precedent, but a problem quickly emerged. Many other situations had evolved where advocates pressed for courts as a mechanism to deal with the issues. In particular, Cambodia and East Timor stood at the top of the list. On the other hand, Kofi Annan, the secretary-general of the United Nations resisted pressure to set up additional ad hoc courts. His position was based on several considerations. The post–Cold War era of cooperation among the great powers on the Security Council had passed. Wealthier nations that had borne the greatest part of the considerable costs of the two operating tribunals had become averse to any institution that would increase their financial obligations. Equally important, the establishment of the International Criminal Court (ICC) provided a permanent forum that presumably would address these issues in the future.

STRUCTURE AND JURISDICTION

The International Criminal Court sits at The Hague and operates as an independent international organization. In accordance with Article 2 of the Rome Statute, the Negotiated Relationship Agreement between the International Criminal Court and the United Nations governs the relationship. The Assembly of States Parties forms the management oversight and legislative body for the court. The Assembly has a permanent Secretariat and a Bureau (interim oversight) to manage the everyday operations of the court. The court consists of eighteen judges elected for nine-year terms. The terms are staggered. Six judges will be elected every three years. To establish the election cycle, in the first election six judges were elected for terms of three years, six for six years, and six for nine years. Judges may be re-elected (table 33.2). The judges constitute a forum of international experts who represent the world's principal legal systems. Judges must be nationals of States Parties to the Statute. The Court became a functioning entity in February 2003 when the Assembly of States Parties elected the first eighteen judges of the Court.

The election process itself contains an interesting requirement because the Rome Statute specifies two different sets of qualifications that define eligible candidates. One list consists of candidates with established competence in criminal law and procedures, who have relevant experience in criminal proceedings as a judge, prosecutor, advocate, or other similar capacity. The second list consists of candidates with established competence in relevant areas of international law, such as international humanitarian law and the law of human rights, and extensive experience in a professional legal capacity which is of relevance to the judicial work of the Court (Article 36(5)).

The Court is divided into three functional chambers or divisions: pre-trial, trial, and appellate. The Pre-Trial Chamber serves the function of a grand jury. It issues the indictments and arrest warrants. The Appeals Division is composed of the president of the Court and four other judges. The Trial Division consists of the second vice president and five other judges; and the Pre-Trial Division is headed by the first vice president and six other judges. The other important official is the prosecutor, who heads the Office of the Prosecutor and who also is elected for a nine-year term.

The ICC was designed to complement national justice systems, not to replace them. It is the court of last resort. This means that the ICC has *in personam* jurisdiction (over individuals) accused of the crimes in the Statute only in cases where "a state is *unwilling or unable* to carry out the investigation or prosecution" (Article 17(1)(a)) (emphasis added). Two further limitations on jurisdiction exist as well. Article 5 establishes the grant of subject matter jurisdiction as: "limited to the most serious crimes of concern to the international community as a whole"—genocide, crimes against humanity, war crimes, and aggression. Rather than referencing the relevant treaties, the drafters of the Rome Statute included the definitions of the crimes within the Court's jurisdiction in the body of the treaty. Concerted attempts to include drug trafficking and "terrorism" in the list failed. The court may only seize cases where the events (or portions of the events) have occurred after July 1, 2002 (temporal jurisdiction) when the Rome Statute entered into effect. Double jeopardy applies as well. The court may not try individuals if they have already been tried in another court unless the trial was considered a sham designed to absolve the person of any guilt (Article 20). Table 33.2 gives a concise overview of the structure of the Court.

Table 33.2 The International Criminal Court

Court	Judges	Type of appointment	Term of service	Seat
ICC	18 elected	Elected by the Assembly of States Parties	9-year terms (can be re-elected; one-third elected every 3 years)	The Hague (Netherlands}

HOW DO CASES COME TO THE COURT?

Cases may come to the ICC by four different methods: Articles 11–21 of the Statute establish the bases of authority.

- by recommendation of a State Party;
- by recommendation of the Security Council;
- by the Chief Prosecutor acting *proprio motu* (on his/her own authority); or
- by recommendation of a non-member state if it explicitly accepts the jurisdiction of the Court and agrees to cooperate fully (Article 12(3)).

In the case of a referral from a State Party, Article 12(2) provides that state referral must satisfy one of two conditions:

(1) the crime must have been committed on the *territory* of the requesting state or within other "territorial" jurisdiction such as an aircraft or vessel registered in the state and/or,

(2) by a *national* of the requesting state. Territory and nationality are the universally accepted principles of exercising jurisdiction in international law.

The first several cases illustrate the procedure. The president of the Democratic Republic of the Congo (DRC) requested an investigation into events that occurred within the DRC after the Statute of the Court entered into force. The investigation resulted in the Court issuing indictments for four individuals. The UN Security Council formally referred the situation in Darfur (Sudan) to the Court in 2005. A UN referral has broader scope in that it may encompass acts committed in the territory of states that are not party to the Statute and also acts committed by nationals of states not party to the Statute.

ARTICLE 16: DEFERRAL OF INVESTIGATION AND PROSECUTION

The ICC stands as separate international organization. This status has good and bad features. The separation was meant to ensure the Court would operate independently without being affected by the whims of politics in the General Assembly and Security Council. The downside is that the United Nations does not serve as the enforcement body for decisions nor does the Court have an "international" police force at its command. It must rely upon member states to surrender those indicted.

Article 16 (Deferral of Investigation or Prosecution) of the Rome Statute does give the Security Council of the United Nations one important power, which played an important role in the early years of the Court.

> No investigation or prosecution may be commenced or proceeded with under this Statute for a period of 12 months after the Security Council, in a resolution adopted under Chapter VII of the Charter of the United Nations, has requested the Court to that effect; that request may be renewed by the Council under the same conditions.

ARTICLE 9: ELEMENTS OF CRIMES

As it evolved after World War II, one of the persistent criticisms of international criminal law was that it lacked specificity. The discussions of the ad hoc international courts stressed the early difficulties faced by judges who often had to develop guidelines and standards as they proceeded. In order to implement the Rome Statute, Article 9 of the Rome Statute authorized the Assembly of States Parties to develop a comprehensive elaboration of Articles 6 (Genocide), 7 (Crimes against Humanity), and 8 (War Crimes). The text of Article 9 (Elements of Crimes) states:

1. Elements of Crimes shall assist the Court in the interpretation and application of articles 6, 7 and 8. They shall be adopted by a two-thirds majority of the members of the Assembly of States Parties.

2. Amendments to the Elements of Crimes may be proposed by:

    (a) Any State Party;

    (b) The judges acting by an absolute majority;

    (c) The Prosecutor.

    Such amendments shall be adopted by a two-thirds majority of the members of the Assembly of States Parties.

3. The Elements of Crimes and amendments thereto shall be consistent with this Statute.

DOCUMENT: ELEMENTS OF CRIMES: CRIMES AGAINST HUMANITY

When: September 3–10, 2002

Where: New York, New York

Source: Official Records of the Assembly of States Parties to the Rome Statute of the International Criminal Court, Report of the First Session, New York, September 3–10, 2002. Online at https://www.icc-cpi.int/resourcelibrary/official-journal/elements-of-crimes.aspx#article7.

Significance: Elements of crimes and rules of evidence and procedure are the essential foundations of any criminal justice system. They provide the normative guidelines that establish the link between specific actions and crimes, and the systematic standards necessary for obtaining acceptable proof. A simple example from domestic law provides an easy illustration. Killing is a crime, but intent and circumstances determine the extent of the perpetrator's liability for the act or acts that caused the death. Was the death due to an act of self-defense, involuntary manslaughter, voluntary manslaughter, second-degree murder, or first-degree murder? Each of these charges has a definite set of criteria, the "elements" that define the acts.

For example, the state of California charged Michael Jackson's doctor with involuntary manslaughter after the singer's death.

The state based its criminal charges on the fact that the doctor continued to prescribe multiple sedative drugs for Jackson under circumstances when the doctor should have known a combination could have been lethal. Prescribing drugs generally is a lawful activity. To prove involuntary manslaughter, the state only needed to show that the doctor acted recklessly or carelessly. The State did not have to prove that the doctor intended to kill.

In contrast, voluntary manslaughter involves the killing of a human being in circumstances where the offender had no prior intent to kill, but acted during the heat of passion, under circumstances that would cause a reasonable person to become emotionally or mentally disturbed to the point that they cannot reasonably control their emotions.

ARTICLE 7: CRIMES AGAINST HUMANITY

In the Rome Statute, Article 7(1) lists ten categories of offenses. Article 7(2) gives definitions for terms used in each of the sections of Article 7(1). The following is an excerpt from the Elements of Crimes that gives specific guidance for framing indictments for the ten crimes listed in the Statute. Because of the nature of the crimes, the specifications do not need to be quite as detailed as for those defining the crime in domestic law. The excerpt deals with Articles 7(1), 7(1)(a), and 7(1)(b).

The format of the document requires some explanation. English and French are the official working languages of the Court. All public documents including transcripts will be issued in both languages. Translation between the two languages is not an exact science. To lessen the problem of quibbles over precise meaning where one language may seem to offer a more lenient or more harsh interpretation, this document includes footnotes that specify acceptable alternative constructions and interpretations, as well as explanations and elaborations of certain ideas.

Within the document, specific footnotes will denote acceptable alternative constructions and phrases that can be used to characterize certain acts. For illustration and ease of access and understanding, the appropriate explanations will appear right after the footnote number rather than at the end of the document. To illustrate the difficulties inherent in translation, the full document has 75 clarifying footnotes.

Article 7
Crimes against Humanity

Introduction

1. Since article 7 pertains to international criminal law, its provisions, consistent with article 22, must be strictly construed, taking into account

that crimes against humanity as defined in article 7 are among the most serious crimes of concern to the international community as a whole, warrant and entail individual criminal responsibility, and require conduct which is impermissible under generally applicable international law, as recognized by the principal legal systems of the world.
2. The last two elements for each crime against humanity describe the *context* in which the conduct must take place. These elements clarify the requisite participation in and knowledge of a widespread or systematic attack against a civilian population. However, the last element should not be interpreted as requiring proof that the perpetrator had knowledge of all characteristics of the attack or the precise details of the plan or policy of the State or organization. In the case of an emerging widespread or systematic attack against a civilian population, the intent clause of the last element indicates that this mental element is satisfied if the perpetrator intended to further such an attack. [emphasis added]
3. "Attack directed against a civilian population" in these context elements is understood to mean a course of conduct involving the multiple commission of acts referred to in article 7, paragraph 1, of the Statute against any civilian population, pursuant to or in furtherance of a State or organizational policy to commit such attack. The acts need not constitute a military attack. It is understood that "policy to commit such attack" requires that the State or organization actively promote or encourage such an attack against a civilian population.[6]

> 6. A policy which has a civilian population as the object of the attack would be implemented by State or organizational action. Such a policy may, in exceptional circumstances, be implemented by a deliberate failure to take action, which is consciously aimed at encouraging such attack. The existence of such a policy cannot be inferred solely from the absence of governmental or organizational action.]

Article 7(1)(a)
Crime against Humanity of Murder

Elements

1. The perpetrator killed[7] one or more persons.
    > 7. The term "killed" is interchangeable with the term "caused death." This footnote applies to all elements which use either of these concepts.
2. The conduct was committed as part of a widespread or systematic attack directed against a civilian population.
3. The perpetrator knew that the conduct was part of or intended the conduct to be part of a widespread or systematic attack against a civilian population.

Article 7(1)(b)
Crime against Humanity of Extermination

Elements

1. The perpetrator killed[8] one or more persons, including by inflicting conditions of life calculated to bring about the destruction of part of a population[9]
    8. The conduct could be committed by different methods of killing, either directly or indirectly.
    9. The infliction of such conditions could include the deprivation of access to food and medicine.
2. The conduct constituted, or took place as part of[10] a mass killing of members of a civilian population.
    10. The term "as part of" would include the initial conduct in a mass killing.
3. The conduct was committed as part of a widespread or systematic attack directed against a civilian population.
4. The perpetrator knew that the conduct was part of or intended the conduct to be part of a widespread or systematic attack directed against a civilian population.

THE UNITED STATES AND THE ICC

The policy of the United States toward the ICC can be summed up simply. The United States will back the Court only if guarantees exist that will ensure that no American will ever face prosecution before it. The fear of an independent court does not rest upon unreasonable concerns. In the past, there have been attempts to secure warrants of arrest for violations of international humanitarian law for President George W. Bush (Iraq and Afghanistan), President Bill Clinton (for the bombing of Serbia), former secretary of state Henry Kissinger (Angola), and former secretary of defense Donald Rumsfeld (Iraq and Afghanistan).

When the Court began operation in 2002, using Article 16 of the Rome Statute as the justification, the United States threatened to veto all future Security Council resolutions concerning peacekeeping and other collective security operation unless the Security Council passed a resolution granting participating soldiers immunity from the jurisdiction of the ICC. The blackmail worked in the short run, but at the cost of angering American allies and many other states by placing ongoing UN peacekeeping operations at risk. In addition, the Congress passed, and President George W. Bush signed, the American Servicemembers' Protection Act of 2002 (22 U.S.C. 7401 §§2001–2015). The law prohibited any agency of the U.S. government from cooperating with the Court, prohibited military assistance to States Parties to the Statute, and authorized the use of force to "free" any U.S. citizen detained or imprisoned by any action of the ICC.

This was followed by "Article 98" Bilateral Immunity Agreements (BIAs) with various countries. The BIAs precluded bilateral partners from surrendering U.S.

nationals to the ICC. Under Article 98 of the Rome Statute, the ICC is prohibited from proceeding with the surrender of an individual to the Court, unless the Court has first obtained the cooperation of the sending state for surrender. The Court cannot compel a state to violate an international agreement it has made.

Over time the U.S. position became impossible to sustain diplomatically. The BIAs in practice never had that much impact. Many were with states like India, which had not joined the Court. The threat to withdraw military assistance proved hollow because the United States often was not the sole source of supply. Countries that did not sign could obtain aid elsewhere. In November 2006, President Bush waived the penalties for states that had refused to sign a BIA. Moreover, practically, U.S. tactics in opposition never proved much of an obstacle for Court activities. John Bellinger, a former legal adviser to Secretary of State Condoleezza Rice (2005–2009), observed:

> In its second term, the Bush administration pursued a more pragmatic approach toward the ICC, first agreeing to the U.N. Security Council's March 2005 referral of the Darfur atrocities to the court for investigation and later offering support to the ICC prosecutor. The president waived the statutory restrictions on foreign assistance to ICC members, and last fall Secretary of State Condoleezza Rice even threatened to veto efforts by some Security Council members, including China and France, to defer the ICC's arrest warrant for Sudanese President Omar Hassan al-Bashir, earning plaudits from human rights groups. (*Washington Post*, August 10, 2009)

As a candidate, President Barack Obama stated that his administration would cooperate with the Court on Darfur and other cases. He promised to consult with military and legal advisers before making a decision on whether to propose joining the Court. The consultations on joining the Court through ratification of the Rome Statute were quickly halted because gaining the necessary two-thirds vote in the Senate for ratification appeared impossible.

The Obama administration's approach to the Court was defined by a policy statement in the National Security Strategy for 2010. The United States would assist and cooperate on all cases deemed to be within U.S. national interest. The United States would send observer delegations to the Assembly of States Parties and U.S. officials would meet directly with the staff and leaders of the ICC. The Obama administration lent support for the Darfur investigation, voted for a Security Council resolution to refer Libya to the ICC, and repealed legislation that placed sanctions on countries that did not conclude bilateral immunity agreements with the United States. The most notable incident of cooperation was the transfer of Bosco Ntaganda to the Court after he entered the U.S. embassy in Kigali, Rwanda, in March 2013. The Pre-Trial Chamber of the Court had issued an arrest warrant for Ntaganda for war crimes committed in the Democratic Republic of the Congo.

The administration of President Donald Trump returned to a policy of total noncooperation and opposition. Given the priority of other foreign policy issues, the full extent of the change in direction was not evident at the time this book went to press. Given the current political climate, the odds are heavily against the United States joining the Court at any time in the near future.

OTHER CRISES: THE POLITICS OF PROSECUTION

The other major crisis that threatened to undercut much of what the Court had accomplished occurred in July 2008 when the prosecutor issued an arrest warrant for Omar al-Bashir, the president of Sudan, on charges of crimes against humanity in Darfur. The African Union demanded that the Security Council invoke Article 16 to defer the execution of the warrant. At the time, for a large number of African countries, the indictment verified their perception that the Court had unfairly focused on Africa. Yoweri Museveni, the president of Uganda, called the ICC "a bunch of useless people." Paul Kagame of Rwanda said the Court was never about "justice but politics disguised as international justice." President Uhuru Kenyatta of Kenya, once indicted by the ICC, castigated the Court as a "tool of global power politics and not the justice it was built to dispense" (Kuwonu 2017).

Dissatisfaction with the Court lies in the perception that the ICC has ignored crimes committed by Western states, has disproportionally targeted Africans, and has not respected the politics and sovereignty of African countries. In the short history of the Court, two sitting African heads of state have been indicted. Charges against Uhuru Kenyatta, the Kenyan president, and his deputy William Ruto were later shelved (witnesses disappeared). Omar al-Bashir, the Sudanese president, remains under indictment and Laurent Gbagbo, former president of Côte d'Ivoire, is currently on trial. Nine out of the ten cases currently before the court involve African countries. Critics of the ICC point out that both Sudan and Libya were referred to the Court by the UN Security Council, where three of the five veto-wielding countries (China, Russia, and the United States) are not even members of the Court. While the Security Council was quick to have leaders of the two countries indicted, the critics have observed that efforts to refer countries like Syria have been thwarted by some of these same countries (Kuwonu 2017).

Article 127 states that a State Party may withdraw "by written notification addressed to the Secretary-General of the United Nations." The withdrawal will "take effect one year after the date of receipt of the notification, unless the notification specifies a later date." After giving its appropriate written notice. Burundi became the first State Party to withdraw in October 2017. The Gambia, Kenya, and South Africa have made similar threats. President Pierre Nkurunziza and other officials of the government in Burundi have been accused of committing crimes against humanity that include execution and torture. A UN Commission of Inquiry has urged the ICC to open a prosecution. Withdrawal does not automatically bar continued investigation and potential charges for crimes that occurred while Burundi was a member state.

DEFERRED ISSUE: THE CRIME OF AGGRESSION

Since the devastation caused by World War I, states have attempted to define aggression as the illegal resort to the use of force. The idea of holding individual leaders responsible began with the attempt to prosecute Kaiser Wilhelm after World War I. Although, the attempt to hold the Kaiser personally responsible for the start of World War I failed, the League of Nations spent a lot of energy developing a definition of aggression, as did the United Nations after World War II. The prosecution of the major political and military leaders at the Nuremberg and Tokyo war crimes tribunals provided the initial underpinnings for a criminal tribunal that could, on an individual basis, prosecute government officials who planned and unleased attacks on other states. As discussed earlier, this did not become a reality until states established the ICC over fifty years later. Because of the politically divisive nature of the subject, delegations at the Rome Conference did not wish to have a fight over defining aggression that might delay the creation of the Court. As a result, the Rome Statute envisioned the creation of ICC jurisdiction over the crime of aggression, but only at a future point when the crime would be defined and the conditions for its operation would be elaborated.

At the ICC Review Conference, held in 2010 at Kampala, Uganda, the States Parties reached major decisions toward incorporating aggression into the Statute. They developed definitions for "act of aggression" and "crime of aggression" and made the jurisdiction potentially available even in the absence of a referral from the Security Council. Because of a number of issues concerning the exact process for incorporation as well as some practical political issues, the States Parties also decided to defer activation until the Review Conference in December 2017. New Articles 8*bis* (8(2)), 15*bis* (1(2)), and 15*ter* (15(3)) defined the crime and the parameters of the Court's jurisdiction over the acts described.

DOCUMENT: JURISDICTION OVER THE CRIME OF AGGRESSION

When: Assembly of States Parties
June 2010 (Kampala, Uganda); December 2017 (New York)
Source: Revised Rome Statute of the International Criminal Court. United Nations, Treaty Series, vol. 2187, No. 38544. Online at https://www.icc-cpi.int/NR/rdonlyres/ADD16852-AEE9-4757-ABE7-9CDC7CF02886/283503/RomeStatutEng1.pdf.
Status: Thirty ratifications required for activation of jurisdiction
Significance: Since the end of World War I, states have sought a means to punish the illegal resort to force. The decision to incorporate the crime into the Rome Statute of the ICC marked a major step forward.

Article 8*bis*
Crime of Aggression

1. For the purpose of this Statute, "crime of aggression" means the planning, preparation, initiation or execution, by a person in a position effectively to exercise control over or to direct the political or military action of a State, of an act of aggression which, by its character, gravity and scale, constitutes a manifest violation of the Charter of the United Nations.
2. For the purpose of paragraph 1, "act of aggression" means the use of armed force by a State against the sovereignty, territorial integrity or

political independence of another State, or in any other manner inconsistent with the Charter of the United Nations. Any of the following acts, regardless of a declaration of war, shall, in accordance with United Nations General Assembly resolution 3314 (XXIX) of 14 December 1974, qualify as an act of aggression:

(a) The invasion or attack by the armed forces of a State of the territory of another State, or any military occupation, however temporary, resulting from such invasion or attack, or any annexation by the use of force of the territory of another State or part thereof;
(b) Bombardment by the armed forces of a State against the territory of another State or the use of any weapons by a State against the territory of another State;
(c) The blockade of the ports or coasts of a State by the armed forces of another State;
(d) An attack by the armed forces of a State on the land, sea or air forces, or marine and air fleets of another State;
(e) The use of armed forces of one State which are within the territory of another State with the agreement of the receiving State, in contravention of the conditions provided for in the agreement or any extension of their presence in such territory beyond the termination of the agreement;
(f) The action of a State in allowing its territory, which it has placed at the disposal of another State, to be used by that other State for perpetrating an act of aggression against a third State;
(g) The sending by or on behalf of a State of armed bands, groups, irregulars or mercenaries, which carry out acts of armed force against another State of such gravity as to amount to the acts listed above, or its substantial involvement

Article 15*bis*
Exercise of Jurisdiction over the Crime of Aggression
(State Referral, *proprio motu*)

1. The Court may exercise jurisdiction over the crime of aggression in accordance with article 13, paragraphs (a) and (c), subject to the provisions of this article.
2. The Court may exercise jurisdiction only with respect to crimes of aggression committed one year after the ratification or acceptance of the amendments by thirty States Parties.
3. The Court shall exercise jurisdiction over the crime of aggression in accordance with this article, subject to a decision to be taken after 1 January 2017 by the same majority of States Parties as is required for the adoption of an amendment to the Statute.
4. The Court may, in accordance with article 12, exercise jurisdiction over a crime of aggression, arising from an act of aggression committed by a State Party, unless that State Party has previously declared that it

does not accept such jurisdiction by lodging a declaration with the Registrar. The withdrawal of such a declaration may be effected at any time and shall be considered by the State Party within three years.
5. *In respect of a State that is not a party to this Statute, the Court shall not exercise its jurisdiction over the crime of aggression when committed by that State's nationals or on its territory.*
6. Where the Prosecutor concludes that there is a reasonable basis to proceed with an investigation in respect of a crime of aggression, he or she shall first ascertain whether the Security Council has made a determination of an act of aggression committed by the State concerned. The Prosecutor shall notify the Secretary-General of the United Nations of the situation before the Court, including any relevant information and documents.
7. Where the Security Council has made such a determination, the Prosecutor may proceed with the investigation in respect of a crime of aggression.
8. Where no such determination is made within six months after the date of notification, the Prosecutor may proceed with the investigation in respect of a crime of aggression, provided that the Pre-Trial Division has authorized the commencement of the investigation in respect of a crime of aggression in accordance with the procedure contained in article 15, and the Security Council has not decided otherwise in accordance with article 16.
9. A determination of an act of aggression by an organ outside the Court shall be without prejudice to the Court's own findings under this Statute.
10. This article is without prejudice to the provisions relating to the exercise of jurisdiction with respect to other crimes referred to in article 5.

Article 15ter
Exercise of Jurisdiction over the Crime of Aggression (Security Council Referral)

1. The Court may exercise jurisdiction over the crime of aggression in accordance with article 13, paragraph (b), subject to the provisions of this article.
2. The Court may exercise jurisdiction only with respect to crimes of aggression committed one year after the ratification or acceptance of the amendments by thirty States Parties.
3. The Court shall exercise jurisdiction over the crime of aggression in accordance with this article, subject to a decision to be taken after 1 January 2017 by the same majority of States Parties as is required for the adoption of an amendment to the Statute.
4. A determination of an act of aggression by an organ outside the Court shall be without prejudice to the Court's own findings under this Statute.
5. This article is without prejudice to the provisions relating to the exercise of jurisdiction with respect to other crimes referred to in article 5.

ACTIVATION

In December 2017, the 2017 Review Conference was held in New York City. After ten days of intense diplomatic negations, the conference approved a resolution to activate the crime of aggression. The negotiations focused on the scope of the Court's jurisdiction once the crime was formally incorporated into the Statute. A split had emerged among states. Would the jurisdiction apply to all ICC member states now that the threshold of thirty ratifications had been met, or only to those that had formally accepted the Court's jurisdiction over the crime. The final resolution limits the Court's jurisdiction to those ICC member states that have ratified the amendment to the Rome Statute. This decision embodies a general rule of treaty making that stipulates that only those states which formally agree to a treaty are bound by its terms. In this instance, it reflected a consensus that a decision to amend the original treaty by a minority of member states could not have a binding effect on those states that chose not to give their consent to the proposed amendments. The new amendment will enter into force on July 17, 2018, the date of the 20th anniversary of the ICC's founding treaty.

Because jurisdiction over aggression does not extend to all member states, the Crime of Aggression has a unique jurisdictional regime, which cannot be triggered in the same manner as other crimes of the Rome Statute (genocide, crimes against humanity, and war crimes). The unique feature stems from the exceptions generated by member states not consenting to the addition of the new crime. The Court may exercise jurisdiction over the crime in three ways:

1. An ICC member state refers a situation to the Court.
2. The prosecutor initiates an investigation *proprio motu*.
3. UN Security Council refers the situation to the Court

First, in the case of a state referral (Article 15*bis*), the Court can only exercise jurisdiction if the amendments have entered into force for at least one of the ICC member states, either victim or aggressor, involved. The Prosecutor must then determine if a reasonable basis to proceed exists. If an investigation yields a positive answer, the Prosecutor must notify the UN Secretary-General of the situation. The Security Council has the authority to determine, whether an act of aggression has been committed. The Prosecutor must allow the Security Council six months to make a determination. If no such determination is made, the Prosecutor may still proceed with investigation but only with authorization of the Pre-Trial Division judges.

Second, in the case of the Prosecutor initiating an investigation *proprio motu* (Article 15*bis*), the same conditions apply as in the case of Article 15*bis* state referrals. Third, in the case of a UN Security Council referral (Article 15*ter*), if the UN Security Council refers a situation, the Prosecutor has the authority to investigate any of the four core crimes, including the crime of aggression, committed in any territory by any state's national. In this situation, the Court is able to exercise jurisdiction over crimes of aggression involving ICC member states, regardless of their individual ratification status or "opt-out" status, and non-ICC member states alike.

DOCUMENT: ELEMENTS OF CRIMES: AGGRESSION

When:	December 2017
Where:	New York City
Source:	International Criminal Court. Online at https://www.icc-cpi.int/resource-library/Documents/ElementsOfCrimesEng.pdf.
Status:	34 States Parties; will become effective on July 17, 2018
Significance:	Since the Nuremberg and Tokyo Trials, this stands as the only successful effort to create international laws that would enable prosecution of individuals for committing the crime of aggression.

Elements of Crimes
Article 8bis

Introduction

1. It is understood that any of the acts referred to in article 8*bis*, paragraph 2, qualify as an act of aggression.
2. There is no requirement to prove that the perpetrator has made a legal evaluation as to whether the use of armed force was inconsistent with the Charter of the United Nations.
3. The term "manifest" is an objective qualification.
4. There is no requirement to prove that the perpetrator has made a legal evaluation as to the "manifest" nature of the violation of the Charter of the United Nations.

Elements

1. The perpetrator planned, prepared, initiated or executed an act of aggression.
2. The perpetrator was a person in a position effectively to exercise control over or to direct the political or military action of the State which committed the act of aggression.
3. The act of aggression—the use of armed force by a State against the sovereignty, territorial integrity or political independence of another State, or in any other manner inconsistent with the Charter of the United Nations—was committed.
4. The perpetrator was aware of the factual circumstances that established that such a use of armed force was inconsistent with the Charter of the United Nations.
5. The act of aggression, by its character, gravity and scale, constituted a manifest violation of the Charter of the United Nations.
6. The perpetrator was aware of the factual circumstances that established such a manifest violation of the Charter of the United Nations.

Whether the incorporation of jurisdiction over the crime of aggression into the ICC mandate ultimately serves to deter aggression or to punish those who initiate it remains to be seen. For now, despite the success in moving forward in terms of the articles approved, considerable uncertainties remain concerning procedural and substantive aspects of how the crime of aggression at the ICC will actually operate.

References

Kuwonu, Franck. 2017. "ICC: Beyond the Threats of Withdrawal: African Countries in Dilemma over Whether to Leave or Support the International Criminal Court." *African Renewal* (May–July). http://www.un.org/africarenewal/magazine/may-july-2017/icc-beyond-threats-withdrawal.

Murphy, Sean D. 2012. "The Crime of Aggression at the ICC." George Washington University Law School, Legal Studies Research Paper No. 2012-50. http://ssrn.com/abstract=2083091.

Roach, Steven. 2006. *Politicizing the International Criminal Court: The Convergence of Politics, Ethics, and Law.* Lanham, MD: Rowman and Littlefield.

Schabas, William A. 2011. *An Introduction to the International Criminal Court.* 4th ed. Cambridge: Cambridge University Press.

Taulbee, James L. 2000. "A Call to Arms Declined: The United States and the International Criminal Court." *Emory International Law Review* 14 (Spring): 105–156.

34

Prosecutor v. Thomas Lubanga Dyilo

DEMOCRATIC REPUBLIC OF THE CONGO

In 1960, the Belgian Congo gained its independence as a newly minted sovereign state, the Republic of the Congo (Léopoldville). Since then, the area has been continually engulfed by war. Shortly after gaining independence, the new government faced a mutiny by its army and an announcement of secession by the governing authorities in Katanga province. The Belgian military intervened to protect the remaining Belgian residents. The announcement of secession triggered a bloody civil war. For the second time in its short history, the United Nations sent in a peacekeeping force, Organisation des Nations Unies au Congo (ONUC), which proved totally ineffective in restoring order in the country. Because of its total lack of effectiveness, other than a second United Nations Emergency Force (UNEF) deployed in 1973 after the Yom Kippur War, ONUC would be the last "peacekeeping" mission of any type authorized by the UN Security Council until 1988.

A series of coups resulted in Joseph Mobutu (later Mobutu Sese Seko) taking power in 1965. Mobutu renamed the country Zaire and the capital city, Kinshasa. A staunch Cold War ally of the United States, Mobutu allowed Zaire to become a staging ground for military operations against Soviet-backed Angola. In return, the United States helped stabilize Mobutu's regime. U.S. aid helped to suppress antigovernment movements. After the Cold War ended in the early 1990s, Zaire and Mobutu were no longer important to the United States. When Rwanda invaded Zaire in 1997 in pursuit of Hutu guerillas, anti-Mobutu forces used the opportunity to rebel. They captured the capital of Kinshasa (the former Leopoldville) and forced Mobuto to flee. The rebels then installed Laurent-Désiré Kabila as president. One of Kabila's first official acts was to rename Zaire the Democratic Republic of Congo (DRC).

Between 1997 and 1998, the country enjoyed almost a year without conflict, In 1998, a rift developed between Kabila and his former allies, igniting another civil war that would claim his life in 2001. In February 2000, the UN Security Council authorized the deployment of a peacekeeping mission (Mission de l'Organisation des Nations Unies en République démocratique du Congo, or MONUC) in the DRC. Although usually described as a civil war, the fighting in the DRC between 1998 and 2003 looked more like a world war. Gérard Prunier, an eminent analyst of African wars, labeled it a "continental catastrophe." In the new conflict, nearly 4 million people died and another 2 million became refugees. The country was flooded with troops from Angola, Namibia, Rwanda, Uganda, and Zimbabwe.

The war also brought Thomas Lubanga Dyilo to the attention of the ICC. Lubanga was a military commander and "Minister of Defense" in the pro-Uganda Rassemblement Congolais pour la Démocratie (Congolese Rally for Democracy-Liberation Movement, RCD-ML). In July 2001, he founded another rebel group, the Union des Patriotes Congolais (Union of Congolese Patriots, UPC). In September 2002, he became President of the UPC and founded its military wing, the Patriotic Force for the Liberation of the Congo (FPLC), staffed in part by child soldiers. Lubanga's base consisted primarily of Hema (Hima), an ethnic group located in the eastern DRC (the Ituri region) as well as parts of Uganda. With the help of the Ugandan army, the UPC seized control of Bunia, the capital of the Ituri region, in 2002.

The ongoing conflict pitted the Hemas against the Lendu, a rival ethnic group. During this struggle, Lubanga's group was implicated in a number of alleged massacres and atrocities, including rape, mutilation, murder, and ethnic cleansing. In the Mongbwalu region, the FPLC reportedly killed some 800 civilians between November 2002 and June 2003. During February and March 2003, FPLC forces were accused of having purposely destroyed 26 villages, resulting in the deaths of at least 350 civilians, and the displacement of another 60,000. At the same time, Lubanga stood accused of having employed as many as 3,000 children as soldiers, some as young as eight years old. The UPC and FPLC allegedly forced local civilians to support the war effort by donating anything they had, including their young children. In February 2005, nine UN peacekeepers from Bangladesh were murdered in Ituri. Lubanga's forces were suspected of having participated in the killings.

In the ever-changing politics of the Congo, the UPC was forced out of Bunia in March 2003 by its former ally, the Ugandan Army. Tension between the UPC and Uganda arose in late 2002 when the UPC demanded the immediate withdrawal of all remaining Ugandan troops from the DRC. The tension widened into a split in January 2003, when the UPC formed an alliance with the Rwandan-backed Rally for Congolese Democracy-Goma (RCD-G). In March 2003, many in the UPC who opposed Lubanga's decision defected to another military coalition sponsored by Uganda—Parti pour l'unité et la sauvegarde de l'intégrité du Congo (Party for Unity and Safeguarding of the Integrity of Congo, or PUSIC). The UPC refused to sign the Ituri Cessation of Hostilities Agreement reached between rival governments and political, ethnic, and militia groups in May 2004.

REFERRAL AND ARREST

The DRC ratified the Rome Statute in April 2002. In March 2004, the Congolese government, now under the leadership of Laurent Kabila's son, Joseph, referred the situation (events falling within the Court's jurisdiction) to the Court. After undertaking a preliminary investigation to determine if the referral met the necessary requirements for trial, the prosecutor filed an application for an arrest warrant with the Pre-Trial Chamber. The Pre-Trial Chamber issued the warrant on February 10, 2006. Congolese authorities already had Lubanga in custody. He had been arrested in March 2005, following an investigation into the killing of nine Bangladeshi UN peacekeepers in Ituri. Congolese authorities surrendered Lubanga to the Court on March 17, 2007. He became the first person brought to trial by the ICC. His trial began on January 26, 2009.

WARRANT OF ARREST

The Rome Statute avoids using the word "indictment." Nonetheless, the term is still commonly used to describe the arrest warrant and the document that sets out the charges. Article 58 sets the parameters.

ARTICLE 58

1. At any time after the initiation of an investigation, the Pre-Trial Chamber shall, on the application of the Prosecutor, issue a warrant of arrest of a person if, having examined the application and the evidence or other information submitted by the Prosecutor, it is satisfied that:

    (a) There are reasonable grounds to believe that the person has committed a crime within the jurisdiction of the Court; and

    (b) The arrest of the person appears necessary:
    - (i) To ensure the person's appearance at trial;
    - (ii) To ensure that the person does not obstruct or endanger the investigation or the court proceedings; or
    - (iii) Where applicable, to prevent the person from continuing with the commission of that crime or a related crime which is within the jurisdiction of the Court and which arises out of the same circumstances.

2. The application of the Prosecutor shall contain:
    (a) The name of the person and any other relevant identifying information;
    (b) A specific reference to the crimes within the jurisdiction of the Court which the person is alleged to have committed;
    (c) A concise statement of the facts which are alleged to constitute those crimes;
    (d) A summary of the evidence and any other information which establish reasonable grounds to believe that the person committed those crimes; and
    (e) The reason why the Prosecutor believes that the arrest of the person is necessary.

3. The warrant of arrest shall contain:
    (a) The name of the person and any other relevant identifying information;
    (b) A specific reference to the crimes within the jurisdiction of the Court for which the person's arrest is sought; and

(c) A concise statement of the facts which are alleged to constitute those crimes.
4. The warrant of arrest shall remain in effect until otherwise ordered by the Court.

WARRANT FOR THOMAS LUBANGA DYILO

The warrant for arrest started the process, but many other hurdles remained. The next document, the "warrant of arrest" details the charges against Lubanga.

DOCUMENT: WARRANT OF ARREST, SITUATION IN THE DEMOCRATIC REPUBLIC OF THE CONGO IN THE CASE OF THE *PROSECUTOR V. THOMAS LUBANGA DYILO*

When: February 10, 2006
Where: The Hague, Netherlands
Source: ICC-01/04-01/06. Pre-Trial Chamber I, International Criminal Court. Online at https://www.icc-cpi.int/CourtRecords/CR2006_02234.PDF
Significance: First arrest warrant issued by the ICC

PRE-TRIAL CHAMBER I of the International Criminal Court ("the Court");

HAVING EXAMINED the Prosecution's Application for a warrant of arrest for Mr Thomas Lubanga Dyilo filed on 13 January 2006;

HAVING EXAMINED the evidence and other information submitted by the Prosecution;

NOTING articles 19(1) and 58(1) of the Rome Statute;

HAVING FOUND that, on the basis of the evidence and information provided by the Prosecution, the case against Mr Thomas Lubanga Dyilo falls within the jurisdiction of the Court and is admissible;

HAVING FOUND that there are reasonable grounds to believe that a protracted armed conflict took place in Ituri from July 2002 until the end of 2003 at least;

HAVING FOUND that there are reasonable grounds to believe that from July 2002 to December 2003 members of the FPLC carried out repeated acts of enlistment into the FPLC of children under the age of fifteen who were trained in the FPLC training camps of Bule, Centrale, Mandro, Rwampara, Bogoro, Sota and Irumu;

HAVING FOUND that there are reasonable grounds to believe that from July 2002 to December 2003 members of the FPLC carried out repeated acts of conscription into the FPLC of children under the age of fifteen who were trained in the FPLC training camps of Bule, Centrale, Mandro, Rwampara, Bogoro, Sota and Irumu;

HAVING FOUND that there are reasonable grounds to believe that, during the relevant period, members of the FPLC repeatedly used children under the age of fifteen to participate actively in hostilities in Libi and Mbau in October 2002, in Largu at the beginning of 2003, in Lipri and Bogoro in February and March 2003, in Bunia in May 2003 and in Djugu and Mongwalu in June 2003;

HAVING FOUND that there are reasonable grounds to believe that the alleged UPC/FPLC's policy/practice of enlisting into the FPLC, conscripting into the FPLC and using to participate actively in hostilities children under the age of fifteen was implemented in the context of and in association with the ongoing conflict in Ituri;

HAVING FOUND that there are also reasonable grounds to believe that Mr Thomas Lubanga Dyilo has been President of the UPC since its foundation on 15 September 2000, that in early or mid-September 2002 Mr Thomas Lubanga Dyilo founded the FPLC as the military wing of the UPC and that he immediately became its Commander-in-Chief and remained in that position until the end of 2003 at least;

HAVING FOUND that there are reasonable grounds to believe that Mr Thomas Lubanga Dyilo
  (i) exercised de facto authority which corresponded to his positions as President of the UPC and Commander-in-Chief of the FPLC,
  (ii) that he had ultimate control over the adoption and implementation of the policies/practices of the UPC/FPLC—a hierarchically organised armed group—between July 2002 and December 2003, including the enlistment into the FPLC, the conscription into the FPLC and the use to participate actively in hostilities of children under the age of fifteen, and
  (iii) that he was aware of his unique role within the UPC/FPLC and actively used that role;

HAVING FOUND that for the above reasons there are reasonable grounds to believe that Mr Thomas Lubanga Dyilo is criminally responsible under article 25(3) (a) of the Statute for:
  (i) the war crime of enlisting children under the age of fifteen punishable under article 8(2)(b)(xxvi) or article 8(2)(e)(vii) of the Statute;
  (ii) the war crime of conscription of children under the age of fifteen punishable under article 8(2)(b)(xxvi) or article 8(2)(e)(vii) of the Statute; and
  (iii) the war crime of using children under the age of fifteen to participate actively in hostilities punishable under article 8(2)(b)(xxvi) or article 8(2)(e)(vii) of the Statute;

HAVING FOUND that, under article 58(1)(b) of the Statute, the arrest of Mr Thomas Lubanga Dyilo appears necessary at this stage to ensure his appearance at trial and to ensure that he does not obstruct or endanger the investigation or the court proceedings;

FOR THESE REASONS,
HEREBY ISSUES:
A WARRANT OF ARREST for Mr. THOMAS LUBANGA DYILO

LEGAL ISSUES PRIOR TO THE TRIAL

Any new enterprise will have glitches and hiccups. Article 61(1) of the Rome Statute is an innovation in the procedure of international criminal courts. After arrest, the Pre-Trial Chamber must hold a hearing to confirm the charges. Although nothing akin to this requirement was formally part of the Statute of any prior court, in the absence of defendants in its early years, the ICTY judges did engage in ex parte hearings to rule on sufficiency of evidence. An ex parte hearing occurs *without the presence of the defendant*. While interesting, the exercise, as an ad hoc procedure in an ad hoc court, still differs from the Article 61(1) mandate. In form, the requirement resembles a preliminary hearing, which is held in domestic common law proceedings to confirm the prosecution has a *prima facie* case. The point is to establish the basis of the charges and that the evidence against the defendant is sufficient and credible enough to go forward with a trial. The presumed purpose of a preliminary hearing is to protect defendants against trivial, abusive, or unfounded prosecutions. Because the prosecutor must support each charge with sufficient evidence, the hearing provides an opportunity for the defendant to become fully aware of the nature and validity of the evidence the prosecution has to support the charges (Schabas 2016, 288).

At Lubanga's confirmation hearing in January 2007, the defense challenged the prosecution case on both the factual vagueness of the arrest warrant and the lack of specificity in articulating the points of law on which several of the charges rested. Although it confirmed the charges, the Pre-Trial Chamber asserted it could "only regret that the prosecution did not see fit to plead with greater specificity the context in which the crimes with which Thomas Lubanga Dyilo is charged occurred" (Decision on the confirmation of charges, para. 153). The Count also found that "the Prosecution is under no obligation to articulate in the Document Containing the Charges its legal understanding of the various modes of liability and the alleged crimes" (para. 151).

A second contentious issue arose as well over the nature of the conflict. The prosecutor had originally included charges of using child soldiers in both an internal conflict and an international conflict. The provisions relating to child soldiers in the two bodies of law do not materially differ; but, subsequently the prosecutor amended the charges by eliminating those related to an international conflict. The Pre-Trial Chamber sought to reinstate the charges relating to an international conflict, raising the question of the authority of the Chamber to add charges. In a practical sense, this was a non-issue. The Pre-Trial Chamber has no control over the Prosecutor after the confirmation hearing. The prosecutor cannot be forced to investigate and prove charges just because the Pre-Trial Chamber added them.

THE FIRST STAY OF TRIAL PROCEEDINGS

A more serious problem involving the issue of "fairness" surfaced just before the trial was to begin in June 2008. The Trial Chamber indefinitely stayed the proceedings, finding that "the trial process ha[d] been ruptured to such a degree that it . . . [was] impossible to piece together the constituent elements of a fair trial" (https://www.icc-cpi.int/Pages/record.aspx?docNo=ICC-01/04-01/06-1401). The judges issued the stay order because the prosecution was unable to make available to the Defense more than 200 documents that might have contained evidence that would have mitigated guilt, undermined the credibility of prosecution evidence, or otherwise shown the innocence of the accused. The prosecution materials were obtained on the condition of confidentiality from a number of information providers, including the United Nations. Under Article 54(3)(e) of the Rome Statute, the prosecution can agree to receive documents or information on a confidential basis solely for the purpose of generating new evidence that could then be used at trial. If the prosecution wants to use the information obtained under confidentiality at trial, it must first obtain the permission of the information provider.

In their decision to halt the proceedings, the ICC judges called into question the use of Article 54(3)(e) by the prosecution. According to the judges, the general approach of the prosecution was to use the Article to obtain a wide range of materials under the cloak of confidentiality, and then to identify from those materials evidence to be used at trial. This then required that the prosecution must seek consent from those who provided information for each piece of evidence they wished to use or disclose. This procedure resulted in a cumbersome, time-consuming, and ultimately, unworkable system. In the view of the Trial Chamber, the prosecution's tactic embodied the exact opposite of the proper use of the provision. The original intent was to permit the prosecution to receive confidential information or documents on an exceptional basis, not as a matter of routine practice.

The Trial Chamber maintained that, in accordance with Article 67(2) of the Statute, the disclosure of exculpatory evidence in the possession of the prosecution is *a fundamental aspect of the right of an accused to a fair trial.* At the time of the decision to stay the proceedings, there was no agreement with the United Nations to allow disclosure of confidential documents to the Trial Chamber or the defense. Therefore, the Trial Chamber halted the trial proceedings because it deemed the possibility of a fair trial to be in jeopardy. The Appeals Chamber affirmed the Trial Chamber's decision to suspend the trial, but not its order to release Lubanga. In all probability Lubanga's release would have ended any possibility of the trial continuing because, once released, the Court would have had great difficulty in regaining custody. After extended negotiations, the providers agreed to disclosure with careful editing. This permitted the stay to be lifted and the trial to continue. The episode highlighted a fundamental conflict in the ICC rules between the lead evidence provision and the obligation of the prosecution for disclosure.

The conflict between disclosure and confidentiality had also been possible in the ad hoc tribunals because their statutes contained parallel requirements. But, none of the statutes or rules of any of the Courts give clear guidance on how this conflict should be resolved or provide remedies to rectify the situation. For the ad hoc Tribunals, the circumstances under which the prosecution obtained evidence made the issue much less important. Very few trials had to address the problem. The problem arose as well in the *Germain Katanga* Case (ICC-01/04-01/07) that had begun in November 2009. The ICC Appeals Chamber decision in that case did establish criteria for dealing with the conflict between the two principles. Trial Chambers should try to balance confidentiality with "the right to know the source of the evidence" on a case by case basis.

THE SECOND STAY OF TRIAL PROCEEDINGS

Defense alleged that various intermediaries working for the prosecution had bribed and coached prosecution witnesses and fabricated evidence. On May 12, 2009, the Trial Chamber ordered that two prosecution intermediaries (321 and 316) be called to testify and that the identity of a third intermediary (143) be disclosed to the defense (https://www.icc-cpi.int/pages/record.aspx?uri=906146). Intermediaries worked as agents of prosecution investigators in the DRC. They helped investigators identify individuals who would testify against Lubanga. The prosecution indicated that the individuals would appear after necessary protection measures were in place. Protection measures were proposed by the Victim and Witness Unit (VWU) and initially agreed upon with intermediary 143. They were due to be implemented in early July.

On July 6, the Chamber was informed that the protection package put forward by VWU could no longer be implemented. Intermediary 143 had since rejected the package and requested that certain adjustments be made. The adjustments would include a significant financial payment. After hearing submissions on the issue, the Chamber ruled on July 6 that disclosure should go ahead. The identity would be revealed only to members of the defense team present in Court, the accused, and their long-term resource person in the field. On the same day, the Office of the Prosecutor indicated its intent to appeal the decision and refused to undertake disclosure.

On July 8, 2010, the judges halted proceedings again, citing abuse of the court's process by the prosecution. The immediate cause of the stay was the prosecution's "unequivocal refusal to implement the repeated orders" for the disclosure of the identity of intermediary 143 to the Defense. The Chamber was extremely concerned by the position of the Office of the Prosecutor (OTP) that the OTP had a right to decide whether or not to comply with a Court order relating to protection measures ("Redacted Decision," 2010).

The Trial Chamber ruled that Article 68 did not give the prosecution license or discretion to disregard judicial orders necessary to ensure a fair and impartial trial. It concluded that it was not in a position to permit further evidence to be heard without taking measures to safeguard the right of the accused to a fair trial. The stay would remain in place as long as the circumstances regarded by the Court as an abuse of process endured. The Appeals Chamber reversed the

Trial Chamber's order. The Appeals Chamber ruled that the Trial Chamber had made an error by resorting to the stay immediately without first imposing sanctions on the prosecution to bring about compliance. Alternative measures such as imposing a fine on the Office of the Prosecutor could still ensure a fair trial but entail fewer potential costs in terms of other goals of international criminal justice.

Subsequent decisions in the Trial Chambers have taken notice of this point and have been more sensitive to balancing all of the legitimate interests at stake. This reflects a realization that an absolutist approach toward ensuring the rights of a defendant to "fairness" can work against the achievement of other goals of the Court such as *successfully punishing international crimes, offering relief to victims, and compiling an accurate historical record.*

TRIAL SUMMARY #24: *PROSECUTOR V. THOMAS LUBANGA DYILO*

Thomas Lubanga Dyilo became the first person convicted by the ICC. The course of the trial reflects the awareness that critics and supporters alike were observing very closely. As with the trial of Slobodan Milošević, the Court may have been overly sensitive to challenges of procedures by the defense. Nonetheless, the Appeals Chamber upheld the verdict.

Document: XI. Individual Criminal Responsibility of Thomas Lubanga (Article 25(3)(a) of the Statute

When:	January 26, 2009–March 14, 2012
Where:	The Hague, Netherlands
Court:	International Criminal Court
Defendant:	Thomas Lubanga Dyilo
Source:	ICC-01/04-01/06. International Criminal Court. Judgement Pursuant to Article 74 of the Statute. April 5, 2012. Online at https://www.icc-cpi.int/Pages/record.aspx?docNo=ICC-01/04-01/06-2842.
Charge(s):	See Arrest Warrant
Defense:	Witnesses lied and were encouraged to lie; Prosecution distorted the facts
Verdict:	Guilty; fourteen years with the time spent in custody reduced by the time in custody before and during the trial. The Appeals Chamber upheld the decision and sentence (December 1, 2014).
Significance:	As the first case before the Court, the Judges were under a great deal of pressure to "get it right." They faced the fundamental political necessity of establishing the credibility of the Court as an important player without appearing to violate standards of a "fair trial." The conviction came ten years after the formation of the Court.

TESTIMONY

The testimony here is taken from the summaries in the judgement. For security reasons, the original transcripts are not readily accessible and the public documents are heavily edited to protect the identity of the witnesses. The *Lubanga* Judgement drew heavily on the findings from the SCSL concerning child soldiers. The following has two excerpts. The first describes the way in which the Court evaluated Lubanga's connection to the alleged crimes. The second summarizes the credible evidence concerning the use of child soldiers.

Rather than drawing on the extensive efforts of the ICTY and ICTR to establish "joint criminal enterprise" as the principal rationale for assessing liability, the ICC has relied on co-perpetration as defined in Article 25(3)(a) of the Statute. Section 923 specifies the important *mental element* (subjective element) the prosecution had to prove in order to establish liability for the alleged crimes.

The section numbering is not sequential because in the Judgement, the assessment of liability came after the evaluation of the evidence.

917. The prosecution charged Thomas Lubanga as a *co-perpetrator* under Article 25(3)(a) of the Statute, and the Pre-Trial Chamber confirmed the charges on this basis. . . .

> 3. In accordance with this Statute, a person shall be criminally responsible and liable for punishment for a crime within the jurisdiction of the Court if that person:
>   (a) Commits such a crime, whether as an individual, *jointly with another* or through another person, regardless of whether that other person is criminally responsible; [emphasis in original]

. . .

923. In the Decision on the Confirmation of Charges, the Pre-Trial Chamber set out what it described as the *objective* elements of co-perpetration as follows:

> (i) the "existence of an agreement or common plan between two or more persons"; and
> (ii) the "co-ordinated essential contribution made by each co-perpetrator resulting in the realisation of the objective elements of the crime."

As regards the *subjective* elements of co-perpetration, it stated that "[t]he Chamber [. . .] requires above all that the suspect fulfil the subjective elements of the crime with which he or she is charged [. . .]." These subjective elements are said to be:

> (i) "the suspect and the other co-perpetrators [. . .] must all be *mutually aware* of the risk that implementing their common plan may result in the realisation of the objective elements of the crime"; and
> (ii) *the suspect must be aware* of the "factual circumstances enabling him or her to jointly control the crime" [emphasis added].

. . .

932. The Pre-Trial Chamber further observed, with respect to the existence of an armed conflict, that "the Elements of Crimes require only that '[t]he

perpetrator was aware of factual circumstances that established the existence of an armed conflict', without going as far as to require that he or she conclude[s], on the basis of a legal assessment of the said circumstances, that there was an armed conflict."

933. The Pre-Trial Chamber considered that an element of "joint control over the crime" is that the suspect was aware of "the factual circumstances enabling him to jointly control the crime." It found "this requires the suspect to be aware

(i) that his or her role is essential to the implementation of the common plan, and hence in the commission of the crime, and
(ii) that he or she can—by reason of the essential nature of his or her task—frustrate the implementation of the common plan, and hence the commission of the crime, by refusing to perform the task assigned to him or her."

Child Soldiers
6. Overall Conclusions as Regards Conscription, Enlistment and Use of Children under the Age of 15 within the UPC/FPLC

909. It is alleged that the accused conscripted and enlisted children under the age of 15 years into the armed forces of the UPC/FPLC and that he used them to participate actively in hostilities between 1 September 2002 and 13 August 2003.

910. The Chamber has already set out its conclusion that the UPC/FPLC was an armed group.

a) Conscription and Enlistment in the UPC/FPLC

911. The Chamber finds that between 1 September 2002 and 13 August 2003, the armed wing of the UPC/FPLC was responsible for the widespread recruitment of young people, including children under the age of 15, on an enforced as well as a "voluntary" basis. The evidence of witnesses P-00055, P-0014 and P-0017, coupled with the documentary evidence establishes that during this period certain UPC/FPLC leaders, including Thomas Lubanga, Chief [Yves] Kahwa [Panga Mandro], and Bosco Ntaganda, and Hema elders such as Eloy Mafuta, were particularly active in the mobilisation drives and recruitment campaigns that were directed at persuading Hema families to send their children to serve in the UPC/FPLC army.

912. P-0014, P-0016, P-0017, P-0024, P-0030, P-0038, P-0041, P-0046 and P-0055 testified credibly and reliably that children under 15 were "voluntarily" or forcibly recruited into the UPC/FPLC and sent to either the headquarters of the UPC/FPLC in Bunia or its training camps, including at Rwampara, Mandro, and Mongbwalu. Video evidence introduced during the testimony of P-0030 clearly shows recruits under the age of 15 in the camp at Rwampara. The letter of 12 February 2003, (EVD-OTP-00518) further corroborates other evidence that there were children under the age of 15 within the ranks of the UPC.

913. The evidence of P-0016, P-0014 and P-0017 demonstrates that children in the camps endured a harsh training regime and they were subjected to a variety

of severe punishments. The evidence of P-0055, P-0017 and P-0038 establishes that children, mainly girls, were used for domestic work for the UPC commanders. The Chamber heard evidence from witnesses P-0046, P-0016, P-0055 and P-0038 that girl soldiers were subjected to sexual violence and rape. P-0046 and P-0038 specifically referred to girls under the age of 15 who were subjected to sexual violence by UPC commanders. As discussed above, in the view of the Majority, sexual violence does not form part of the charges against the accused, and the Chamber has not made any findings of fact on the issue, particularly as to whether responsibility is to be attributed to the accused.

914. In all the circumstances, the evidence has established beyond reasonable doubt that children under the age of 15 were conscripted and enlisted into the UPC/FPLC forces between 1 September 2002 and 13 August 2003.

b) Use of Children under 15 to Participate Actively in Hostilities

915. The testimony of P-0002, P-0016, P-0017, P-0024, P-0030, P-0038, P-0046, P-0055, D-0019 and D-0037 and the documentary evidence has demonstrated that children under the age of 15 were within the ranks of the UPC/FPLC between 1 September 2002 and 13 August 2003. The evidence of P-0038, P-0016, P-0012, P-0046, P-0014, D-0019 and D-0037 proves that children were deployed as soldiers in Bunia, Tchomia, Kasenyi, Bogoro and elsewhere, and they took part in fighting, including at Kobu, Songolo and Mongbwalu. The evidence of witnesses P-0016 and P-0024 establishes that the UPC used children under the age of 15 as military guards. The evidence of P-0017 reveals that a special "Kadogo Unit" was formed, which was comprised principally of children under the age of 15. The evidence of P-0014, P-0017, D-0019, P-0038 and P-041, as well as the video footage EVD-OTP-00572, demonstrates that commanders in the UPC/FPLC frequently used children under the age of 15 as bodyguards. The accounts of P-0030, P-0055, P-0016 and P-0041, along with the video evidence, clearly prove that children under the age of 15 acted as bodyguards or served within the presidential guard of Mr Lubanga.

916. In all the circumstances, the evidence has established beyond reasonable doubt that children under the age of 15 were conscripted, enlisted and used by the UPC/FPLC to participate actively in hostilities between 1 September 2002 and 13 August 2003.

CONTROVERSY

The trial was not without its critics. A number of international human rights organizations complained that the indictment had not gone far enough and did not cover ethnic cleansing, mass murder, rape, etc. Nevertheless, Lubanga's trial and conviction were important firsts for the newly created ICC and arguably set precedents for future war crime trials.

The trial also had one additional first. Article 75(1) mandates that:

> The Court shall establish principles relating to reparations to, or in respect of, victims, including restitution, compensation and rehabilitation. On this basis, in its decision the Court may, either upon request or on its own motion in exceptional

circumstances, determine the scope and extent of any damage, loss and injury to, or in respect of, victims and will state the principles on which it is acting.

In anticipation of this requirement, the Assembly of States parties established the Trust Fund for Victims (TFV) (Article 79) in 2004. The TFV has a twofold mandate: (i) to implement Court-Ordered reparations and (ii) to provide physical, psychological, and material support to victims and their families. This initiative had no precedent in other international criminal courts. In particular, the Statute provides that victims can participate and present their views and concerns at appropriate stages of ICC's proceedings and seek reparation before the Court, including through the TFV. While breaking new ground, the drafters of the Statute provided little detail on how these rights should be implemented. The reparations regime would be developed through the ICC's jurisprudence, regulations, strategies, and policy development.

As the first trial in the ICC, the *Lubanga* case provided the opportunity to elaborate the principles and procedures of reparations. In March 2015, the Appeals Chamber rendered its judgement on the principles and procedures of reparation. As the first, the judgement has great significance for international criminal justice, since it establishes a liability regime for reparations that is grounded in the principle of accountability of the convicted person toward victims and the obligation to repair harm. The idea of providing remedies for harm done complements the desire to punish. As a first effort, future proceedings will help refine the approach.

References

Autesserre, Séverine. 2010. *The Trouble with the Congo: Local Violence and the Failure of International Peacekeeping*. Cambridge: Cambridge University Press.

McCarthy, Conor. 2012. *Reparations and Victim Support in the International Criminal Court*. Cambridge: Cambridge University Press.

Prunier, Gérard. 2009. *Africa's World War: Congo, the Rwandan Genocide, and the Making of a Continental Catastrophe*. Oxford: Oxford University Press.

"Redacted Decision on the Prosecution's Urgent Request for Variation of the Time-Limit to Disclose the Identity of Intermediary 143 or Alternatively to Stay Proceedings Pending Further Consultations with the VWU." 2010. *The Prosecutor v. Thomas Lubanga Dyilo,* ICC-01/04-01/06-2517-Red, https://www.icc-cpi.int/pages/record.aspx?uri=906146.

Schabas, William A. 2016. *The International Criminal Court: A Commentary on the Rome Statute*. 2nd ed. Oxford: Oxford University Press.

35

Prosecutor v. Jean-Pierre Bemba Gombo

BEMBA AND THE FIRST CONGO WAR (1996)

Jean-Pierre Bemba Gombo enjoyed a childhood of wealth and privilege. His father, Jeannot Bemba Saolona, a very successful businessman, had a close relationship with the long in power dictator, President Mobutu Sese Seko. In his early years, Bemba Gombo spent more time in Europe than in Africa. After graduating from Boboto College in Kinshasa, Bemba earned a Master's degree in commercial and consular affairs from the prestigious Catholic Institute of Higher Commercial Studies in Brussels. He then returned to the Congo to work in his father's business. One of his sisters married Mobutu's son Nzanga.

During the Rwandan genocide in 1994, an estimated 2 million refugees, mostly Hutu fled over Rwanda's western border with the Congo (then named Zaire). The refugee camps in eastern Congo served as staging bases for the exiled Interahamwe and Army for the Liberation of Rwanda (ALiR) *génocidaires*. They terrorized and robbed the local population with impunity until October 1996, when eastern Congolese Banyamulenge (Tutsi residents of the Congo) led an effort to force the Rwandans out of the Congo. This action triggered the First Congo War.

In response, Rwandan and Ugandan armies backing Laurent-Désiré Kabila invaded the Congo. The combined effort was called the Alliance of Democratic Forces for the Liberation of Congo-Zaire (Alliance des Forces Démocratiques pour la Libération du Congo-Zaïre, or AFDL). By December, they controlled eastern Congo. By May 1997, they marched into Kinshasa and overthrew Mobutu's government. Ill with cancer, Mobutu went into exile. He died in September 1997. Zaire was renamed the Democratic Republic of Congo (DRC). Kabila took over as president in September 1997. Given his close ties to Mobutu, Bemba also went into exile, fearing for his life.

THE SECOND CONGO WAR

Despite the new government, the eastern Congo continued to be an unstable war zone. Kabila then double-crossed his former backers Rwanda and Uganda by allowing the Hutu militias to regroup in eastern Congo. This resulted in another Rwandan/Ugandan joint invasion in 1998. Other neighboring countries sent troops to support Kabila. The five-year conflict pitted Congolese government forces, supported by Angola, Namibia, and Zimbabwe, against rebels and soldiers backed by Uganda and Rwanda.

In exile, Bemba managed to gain support from the Ugandan government for a guerilla operation aimed at unseating the Kabila government. In November 1998, he announced the creation of a new rebel militia, Mouvement de Liberation du Congo (MLC), with an armed wing, the Armée de Libération du Congo (LAC). The MLC/LAC had great success, establishing control over large portions of the northern provinces of Équateur, Orientale, and North Kivu.

The first war had cost Bemba. The new Kabila government had confiscated his businesses and assets in the Congo. During the second war, he rebounded. By the end of the war, he controlled most of Northeastern Congo as well as the major smuggling route between the DRC and Central African Republic (CAR). He used his position to become one of the richest individuals in Africa. He maintained a lucrative diamond and coffee smuggling ring into the CAR using its capital city of Bangui as his base. Among other enterprises, he smuggled timber cut from the Ituri forest into the CAR and collected large operation fees from European hardwood companies operating in the area.

In July 1999, Angola, the DRC, Namibia, Uganda, Rwanda, and Zimbabwe signed the Lusaka Agreement that called for a cease-fire, withdrawal of foreign groups, disarming, demobilizing, and reintegrating of combatants, release of prisoners and hostages, re-establishment of government administration, and the selection of a mediator to facilitate an all-inclusive inter-Congolese dialogue. The agreement also called for the deployment of a UN peacekeeping force, Mission de l'Organisation de Nations Unies en République Démocratique du Congo (MONUC), that would monitor the cease-fire, help investigate violations, and oversee the withdrawal and demobilization provisions of the treaty. While the United Nations did deploy a contingent of observers in November 1999, the fighting never really stopped. Given its original disastrous experience with the first peacekeeping effort in the Congo in 1960–1964, the Organisation des Nations Unies au Congo (ONUC), the United Nations then deferred sending another large contingent of peacekeepers into the Congo when there seemed to be no peace to be kept.

MOVEMENT TOWARD PEACE

In January 2001, President Kabila was assassinated by one of his bodyguards. According to Gérard Prunier, the power brokers picked Kabila's son Joseph as his father's successor because "he was young, he was inexperienced . . . and he had no tribal constituency of his own in the Congo because he had spent practically all of his life abroad" (2009, 255). The power brokers fully expected Joseph Kabila to be their puppet. They miscalculated.

Joseph Kabila moved to resolve the ongoing conflict. By the time of his father's death, the situation for many of the participants had reached a "hurting stalemate." They could not advance their interests and the costs of maintaining their position now outweighed the benefits. In late April 2001, the first serious troop deployment for MONUC began. After an unproductive October meeting among the warring factions, South Africa stepped up as mediator, proposing another conference at Sun City in February 2002. Representatives of the MLC were part of the negotiations. In a surprise move, the MLC signed a power-sharing agreement with the government. This provided a much-needed boost to move the negotiations for a settlement toward a successful agreement. The civil war officially ended with a power-sharing agreement between the government and the major rebel movements. After another round of talks hosted by South Africa, the Pretoria Agreement was signed in December 2002 by all but the Rwandan-backed factions. The Rally for Congolese Democracy–Goma (RCD-G) (see chapter 34) tried to put together an anti-government–anti-agreement coalition, but failed. RCD-G leaders did not sign the agreement until early April 2003. The agreement outlined a path that would lead to elections in 2006.

BEMBA AND THE 2006 PRESIDENTIAL ELECTION

As leader of one of the major rebel factions, Bemba was appointed as one of four vice presidents in the transition government. Along with Kabila and 35 others, he ran for president in the July 2006 election. In the initial voting he finished second behind Kabila, necessitating a runoff. Kabila won the runoff. In January 2007, Bemba won an election for a seat in the DRC Senate. An attempt on Bemba's life in March 2007 led to an outbreak of fighting near his residence. A number of people, including both soldiers and civilians, were reported killed. Bemba called for a cease-fire and took refuge in the South African embassy. On March 23, a warrant for Bemba's arrest was issued, accusing him of high treason. Although Bemba enjoyed immunity as a senator, the chief prosecutor said that he would ask Parliament to remove it.

Late in March, it was reported that Bemba planned to travel to Portugal for treatment of a broken leg. The Portuguese ambassador subsequently said on March 30 that Bemba was expected to go to Portugal for treatment but was not going into exile. On April 9, the DRC Senate approved the trip for a period of 60 days. Without the Senate's permission, he would have been subject to the automatic loss of his seat if absent from over a quarter of Senate sessions. On April 11, under the protection of MONUC forces, Bemba left the South African embassy and flew to Portugal with his family. Over the next year, Bemba made numerous public statements that expressed his intention to return to the DRC.

INDICTMENT AND ARREST

A coup led by General François Bozizé ousted Central African president Ange-Félix Patassé in March 2003. The new government brought charges against both Patassé and Bemba in September 2004. International arrest warrants were issued, but when the new government failed to have Bemba arrested, they referred the matter to the International Criminal Court (ICC). The CAR government provided the Prosecutor with documents and court records. On May 22, 2007, the ICC prosecutor Luis Moreno Ocampo decided to open an investigation into crimes committed in the Central African Republic in 2002–2003. The Court had no authority to investigate and try crimes that may have occurred prior to the date when the Rome Statute entered into force.

On May 23, 2008, a Pre-Trial Chamber of the ICC found that reasonable grounds existed to believe that Bemba bore individual criminal responsibility for war crimes and crimes against humanity committed in the Central African Republic between October 20, 2002 and March 15, 2003. It issued a sealed warrant for his arrest. Initially he was charged with five counts of war crimes (murder, rape, torture, pillaging, and outrages upon personal dignity) and three counts of crimes against humanity (murder, rape, and torture). On May 24, 2008, Belgian authorities arrested Bemba near Brussels He was surrendered to the ICC and transferred to its detention center in The Hague on July 3, 2008.

ROLE OF THE LAC

Bemba was the leader of the MLC political branch (president) and the commander-in-chief of the LAC from its creation. Throughout the period covered in the charges, he ensured a clear division between the political and military wings. While not always involved in the implementation of administrative decisions, Bemba held ultimate authority over all decision-making for both wings, and in general, decided the course of action on all important issues. Once he had made decision, it was not debatable. Bemba had authority over strategic military decisions, such as beginning military operations, issuing orders to the units in the field, such as to attack or to progress to a certain location. Bemba could, and often did, communicate orders or instructions directly to commanders in the field without going through the hierarchy, with the General Staff usually being informed and following-up afterwards, if necessary.

The LAC was comprised of approximately 20,000 soldiers. It had the same structure as the DRC military and other armies being divided into sectors, brigades, battalions, companies, and platoons. Brigades ranged from 1,500 to 2,500 men and battalions from 400 to 700. The MLC contingent deployed to the CAR was comprised of three battalions totaling around 1,500 men; Bemba controlled the transport of MLC troops to the DRC side of the Oubangui River. CAR authorities managed the crossing itself. The CAR authorities provided other support to the MLC over the course of the 2002–2003 operation, including weapons, ammunition, vehicles, fuel, food, money, and various communications equipment, such as radiotelephones (phonies), cell phones, walkie-talkies, and Thuraya devices (satellite phones).

MLC officials could communicate with the troops in the CAR, down to the battalion level, by radiotelephone from their central headquarters. Colonel Moustapha, the brigade commanders, and the battalion commanders could also use their Thurayas to directly call individuals including Bemba. Bemba could also contact Colonel Moustapha Mukiza on his mobile phone when the latter was in Bangui. In addition to remote communication, traveling either by plane or ferry, Bemba also visited the CAR on a number of occasions when he met with the MLC troops,

THE PLOT TO PREVENT THE TRIAL

Bemba's trial at The Hague began on November 22, 2010. After his arrest, Bemba had friends and members of his defense team working on an alternate plan that would ensure all of the charges against him would be dropped. Eventually the ICC learned of the scheme and arrested four men suspected of perpetrating crimes against the court: the lead defense counsel, the case manager (also a lawyer), a member of the DRC Parliament who served as deputy secretary of the MLC, and a defense witness. Each man including Bemba was charged with presenting false or forged evidence and tampering with witnesses for the prosecution.

In April 2014, the trial judges determined that the additional charges of presenting false or forged evidence and tampering with witnesses would be treated as a different case and tried separately. On March 22, 2017, Bemba received the heaviest penalty among the five individuals accused of tampering with witnesses—one year in prison and a fine of €300,000 ($324,000), which he had to pay within three months. His former lead defense counsel, Aimé Kilolo Musamba, was fined €30,000 ($32,500), also payable in three months, and handed a prison sentence of two-and-a-half years, suspended. Judges also imposed monetary penalties and suspended sentences on the other three accused. The fines will ultimately be transferred to the Trust Fund for Victims.

TRIAL SUMMARY #25: *PROSECUTOR V. JEAN-PIERRE BEMBA GOMBO*

As the last trial in this book, perhaps it is fitting that it represents all of the problems of a trial as a means of obtaining some measure of "justice" for the victims of particular incidents where no one questions that the individuals involved committed multiple violations of international humanitarian law. The Trial Chamber found Jean-Pierre Bemba Gombo guilty. The Appeals Chamber reversed the decision.

DOCUMENT: DEFINITION OF COMMAND RESPONSIBILITY

When: November 22, 2010–March 21, 2016
Where: The Hague, Netherlands
Court: International Criminal Court
Defendant: Jean-Pierre Bemba Gombo
Source: ICC-01/01-08. International Criminal Court. Online at https://www.icc-cpi.int/car/bemba.
Charge(s): Two counts of crimes against humanity (murder and rape); three counts of war crimes (murder, rape, and pillaging).
"Mr Bemba is responsible as a person effectively acting as a military commander within the meaning of Article 28(a)5 for the crimes against humanity of murder, Article 7(1)(a), and rape,

	Article 7(1)(g), and the war crimes of murder, Article 8(2)(c)(i), rape, Article 8(2)(e)(vi), and pillaging, Article 8(2)(e)(v), allegedly committed on the territory of the Central African Republic ("CAR") from on or about 26 October 2002 to 15 March 2003."
Defense:	Challenges to the credibility of witnesses; testimony that Bemba did not have command or control over the troops in the CAR, and was not aware of the crimes committed
Verdict:	Guilty; 18 years reduced by time in custody. Appeal pending.
Significance:	The first verdict of the ICC to recognize rape as a weapon of war and to employ the doctrine of *command responsibility*.

Article 28 (Rome Statute)
Responsibility of Commanders and Other Superiors

In addition to other grounds of criminal responsibility under this Statute for crimes within the jurisdiction of the Court:

(a) A military commander or person effectively acting as a military commander shall be criminally responsible for crimes within the jurisdiction of the Court committed by forces under his or her effective command and control, or effective authority and control as the case may be, as a result of his or her failure to exercise control properly over such forces, where:

   (i) That military commander or person *either knew or, owing to the circumstances at the time, should have known* that the forces were committing or about to commit such crimes; and

   (ii) That military commander or person *failed* to take all necessary and reasonable measures within his or her power to prevent or repress their commission or to submit the matter to the competent authorities for investigation and prosecution. [emphasis added]

Testimony

July 1, 2011

Q. You have already explained that Kamisi took a road 1 through Damara to Sibut, and Sengue took a different road to Bossangoa, going through Boali and Bossembélé. Do you know who decided which road they were to take? Who gave them instructions, or who gave them the orders as to where they were supposed to go?

A. Their chief was Mr Mustapha. He is the one who was the operation 6 commander. He gave them instructions, and he gave them the plan, the strategy, that they were to implement on the front.

Q. Do you know how Mustapha made his decisions? Did he make his decisions alone, that is as to where the soldiers were to go, that is the soldiers under his command?

A. For the most part, [Redacted] when he wanted to communicate with Mr Jean-Pierre Bemba, he went off by himself because he didn't want anyone to be aware of the content of their discussion. Now, as regards the orders he received during those conversations, no one had any way of knowing what they were because [Redacted] he had spoken to his superior. [Redacted]

Q. Since no one could know what the conversation was between Jean-Pierre Bemba and Mustapha, you have no way of knowing whether they were talking about commonplace topics or whether they were talking about military matters.
A. No. No, that's not the case. [Redacted] At the time, Mustapha was the operations commander of the MLC in Bangui and the supreme chief of the MLC was Mr Jean-Pierre Bemba. Now, if they had something to say to each other [Redacted] they could do so discreetly. And when he received instructions, he then forwarded those instructions to his men. That's how it happened.

Q. Did you, yourself, hear Mustapha repeat the orders to his men?
A. I'm afraid I didn't understand your question, Mr. Prosecutor. Would you be so kind as to repeat your question, please?

Q. Yes, of course. I'm sorry, perhaps I wasn't clear enough. You have just stated that, and I quote, "When he received orders, he gave them then; he relayed them to his men in his own manner." I would like to know whether you, yourself, heard or saw, whether you were a witness to a case where Mustapha repeated orders to his men. Based on the transcript, you stated, [Redacted]—this is page 48, line 25: [Redacted] "At that time, since Mustapha was the operations commander for the MLC and the chief commander was Mr Jean-Pierre Bemba of the MLC, when and if they had something to discuss [Redacted] [Redacted] they could do so discreetly. And when he received instructions, he would then relay them to his men in his own way." I am asking you to clarify this last part; that is, when he received instructions, he would relay them to his men in his own manner. Do you have a concrete example of that?
A. Well, yes. Let me tell you, [Redacted] [Lines 18–21 Redacted] So at that point in time he received instructions, telling him to go take care of the situation; and he went to Zongo, to speak to someone in Zongo, to inform him of that. Now, what do I mean by that? Well, he was giving instructions for sure, but sometimes he would ask for instructions from his own chief. You see, this was one occasion when I saw him receive instructions and then relay I the same instructions to his men under his command.

Q. Do you know what happened after that call? You said Mustapha called Kamisi to inform him of the instructions. Do you know what Kamisi did after he received that call?
A. Well, when I came back from Bossangoa, that is when I learned about that. Maybe six months, a year later, when [Redacted] I also learned about that information. In other words, Kamisi travelled overnight and arrived at 3 o'clock in the morning. It was early March and, at the time, I was in Bossangoa. They committed a lot of atrocities, rapes, looting, and people were talking about it. They were talking about it on the radio, as well. And the late President Ange-Félix Patassé had talked about it that day, the day he made a speech in Zongo. And he said,

"You are the ones who wanted this and now you've got what you asked for." That's what I can tell you.

...

Q. You mentioned 700 men in the Sege battalion. The reference is the real-time French transcript, page 34, line 15 and in English it's page 32, line 17. You stated a few moments ago, Witness, and this is on page 50, line 25 to 27 in the French version, "It was towards the beginning of the month of March. At that time I was in Bossangoa. They committed a lot of atrocities, in particular, rapes and looting, and it was talked about on the radio a lot, regularly." Other than the radio, did any other individuals talk to you about these atrocities? And now I'm referring to the sources you mentioned, that is [Redacted] Did they also refer to these atrocities?

A. [Redacted] I remember at that time he was in Mongoumba. He gave me some information as well but he said that the rapes had not been massive. But he added that the acts that had been committed by the soldiers there were absolutely horrible. And when I, [Redacted] I stopped there and I went to a restaurant and I asked some people a few questions, and those people told me that that was true; that is, the information I had heard was true.

A Short Summary from the Trial Judgement (pp. 278–282)

MLC soldiers allegedly targeted civilians, without regard to age, gender, profession, or social status, in and around schools, homes, fields, and roads. . . . [W]itnesses testified that the troops first confirmed, by the absence of retaliatory fire and by using scouts, that General Bozizé's rebels had already departed an area. The MLC soldiers then "mop[ped] it up" searching "house-to house" for remaining rebels, pillaging goods, raping civilians, and intimidating and killing civilians who resisted As for the motivations behind the soldiers' conduct, there is evidence that MLC soldiers sought to punish civilians in the CAR, for example, for MLC losses or as suspected enemies or enemy sympathisers.

Further, as they did not receive adequate payment and rations from their superiors some MLC soldiers applied the so-called and unofficial "Article 15," a term which predates the 2002–2003 CAR Operation and means that soldiers were to do what was necessary in order to "make ends meet." Many witnesses testified that, when applying "Article 15," MLC soldiers in the CAR secured—including by acts of murder, rape, and pillaging—compensation, in cash and kind, from the civilian population. Indeed, MLC soldiers, sometimes after telling their victims that they were hungry, personally used pillaged goods. They slaughtered the livestock, prepared and ate food items, and burned shutters, doors, and furniture as firewood. In addition, MLC soldiers traded pillaged items for other goods, such as alcohol, and forced civilians to buy back goods taken from them or their neighbours.

The evidence also evinces certain specific motivations and objectives behind the commission of rape. Indeed, some MLC soldiers considered victims to be "war booty" and/or sought to destabilise, humiliate, and punish suspected rebels and rebel sympathisers. Such objectives were often realised: rape victims experienced significant medical, psychiatric, psychological, and social consequences, including PTSD, HIV, social rejection, stigmatisation, and feelings of humiliation, anxiety, and guilt. Regarding the crime of murder, the evidence shows that, on some occasions, MLC soldiers killed or threatened to kill those who resisted acts of pillaging and rape.

A CRIME NOT PUNISHED

In 2003, Sinafesi Makelo, a Mbuti pygmy, told the UN Indigenous Peoples Forum that during the war Mbuti pygmies were "hunted down and eaten like game animals" by the militias and that none was more deadly than the group known as the Effaceurs (erasers). According to Minority Rights Group International, Les Effaceurs were soldiers in the MLC. Bemba's men used "mass killings, cannibalism, rape, and the threat of violence" to clear the Mbuti from the forests of North Kivu Province. According to testimony provided by Bantu farmers in the area, Bemba wanted the pygmies to leave the local forests where they had lived for generations so he could expand his illegal mining and logging operations without witnesses. UN officials in the capital, Kinshasa, and the eastern city of Goma said that widespread cannibalism had been established without question.

APPEALS CHAMBER DECISION

On June 8, 2018, the Appeals Chamber for the International Criminal Court reversed the decision of the Trial Chamber, finding Bemba innocent on all counts. In a majority opinion by three of the five judges, the ICC Appeals Chamber held that the trial court had erroneously convicted Bemba for specific criminal acts that were not sufficiently supported by the evidence. For comparison, review the Gotovina case (Chapter 27) in which the Appeals Chamber of the ICTY also reversed the verdicts of the Trial Chamber and acquitted the defendants. As pointed out in the discussion of the Gotovina acquittal, such reversals have been rare. The ICTY Appeals Chamber received a great deal of criticism from the legal community because many felt the judges who supported the majority opinion had exceeded their mandate. In the ICC appeal, the defense had raised the following issues:

> …Ground 1—the trial was unfair; Ground 2—the conviction exceeded the charges; Ground 3—Mr Bemba is not liable as a superior; Ground 4—the contextual elements were not established; Ground 5—the Trial Chamber erred in its approach to identification evidence; and Ground 6—other procedural errors invalidated the conviction. (Majority Decision—Appeal, 4–5).

Because, the original verdict in the Bema case was considered a legal landmark, the reversal raised a number of controversies. Previously, the ad hoc UN tribunals (ICTY, ICTR) had established the principle that a commander's responsibility extends to failures to take action to stop crimes he knows are being committed by subordinates. The Bemba trial verdicts denoted the first time that the ICC had used that rationale to convict a defendant of rape by interpreting command responsibility to include failure take appropriate action to stop the criminal actions of his troops.

To repeat an important point from the discussion of the Gotovina case, appeals in international courts (e.g., ICTY, ICTR, and ICC) should consider only two possibilities: (1) *errors of law* that involve violations/misinterpretations of either fundamental procedural rules or the interpretation/application of the appropriate substantive rule(s); or (2) on the absence of a reasoned opinion based on the facts. If any reasonable panel could have made the relevant finding on the strength of the record as presented, the Appeals Chamber normally will defer to the Trial Chamber. Hence, take particular note of the section on the standard of review articulated in the transcript by Presiding Judge Christine Van den Wyngaert, who delivered the majority verdict:

> Looking at the Trial Chamber's factual findings, the majority assessed whether or not the Trial Chamber applied the standard of proof correctly. The Appeals Chamber must be satisfied that the factual findings that are made beyond reasonable doubt are clear and unassailable, both in terms of evidence and rationale. Accordingly, when the Appeals Chamber is able to identify findings that can reasonably be called into doubt, it must overturn them. Furthermore, the Trial Chamber must accompany its finding with reasoning of sufficient clarity. This reasoning must unambiguously demonstrate the evidentiary basis upon which the finding is based as well as the Trial Chamber's analysis of this evidence. If the Trial Chamber fails to do so, the Appeals Chamber has no choice but to set aside the affected finding. It is also important that the duty of a convicted person to substantiate errors in the Conviction Decision should not lead to a reversal of the burden of proof ("Majority Decision—Appeal," 4–5).

The majority decision lists seven "serious" errors in the Trial Chamber's assessment of the factual foundation on which the decision for conviction rested ("Majority Decision, Appeal," 9–11). All seven errors reflected the conclusion that the Trial Chamber had used very vague standards of proof to link Bemba to the actual acts. Recall the earlier problems encountered by the ICTY and ICTR in finding an appropriate model and method that would adequately characterize the necessary links between superiors and subordinates to establishing complicity in the alleged crimes. Both the ICTY and ICTR had preferred "joint criminal enterprise" rather than "command responsibility."

> The Appeals Chamber notes that the Conviction Decision makes no reference to even an approximate number of the individual criminal acts of murder, rape and pillage that the Trial Chamber found established. Nor does it make any further demarcation of the scope of the conviction. The conviction would therefore appear to cover, potentially, all such crimes committed by MLC soldiers in a territory of more 10 than 600,000 square kilometres and over a period of more than four and a half months.

> The majority of the Appeals Chamber considers that the Conviction Decision must be understood as convicting Mr Bemba for the specific criminal acts of murder, rape and pillage that the Trial Chamber found to be established beyond a reasonable

doubt and which were recalled in the concluding sections of the Conviction Decision in relation to each crime. The broad disposition in the Conviction Decision and the only slightly less broad conclusions of the Trial Chamber in relation to the crimes charged do not in reality reflect what Mr Bemba was convicted for.... ("Majority Decision, Appeal," 6)

The Appeals Chamber thus find, by majority, Judge [Sanji Mmasenono] Monageng and Judge [Piotr] Hofmański dissenting, that the Trial Chamber's conclusion that Mr Bemba failed to take all necessary and reasonable measures in response to MLC crimes in the CAR, was materially affected by errors and Mr Bemba cannot be held criminally responsible under Article 28 for the crimes committed by MLC troops during the CAR operation. ("Majority Decision, Appeal," 11)

The Dissent

Judge Christine Van den Wyngaert summarized the views of the dissenting judges in the "Majority Decision" (12–19), but the two dissenting judges issued a separate minority opinion. They argued that the majority did not follow their own standards of review in reaching their conclusion:

While the Appeals Chamber in an appeal against a conviction has access to the trial record and can therefore consult the transcripts of the witnesses' testimony and documentary evidence and study the parties' and participants' submissions before a trial chamber, this does not replace the specific familiarity with the evidential record that the trial chamber enjoyed, resulting from its hearing of all witnesses and seeing the case unfold. The Appeals Chamber does not benefit from such extensive exposure to the evidence and the parties' and participants' arguments and it is unlikely that the Appeals Chamber, by merely reading the trial record, could ever attain the same level of familiarity with the case as the trial chamber. In our view, it is therefore natural for the Appeals Chamber to give a margin of deference to the findings of the trial chamber. If the Appeals Chamber were to assess all evidence de novo, according no deference to the first-instance findings, the appellate proceedings would necessarily turn into a second trial. That would pose the risk of inaccuracy, given the Appeals Chamber's above-mentioned limitations with respect to review of evidence. It could also lead to inordinate delays in the examination of appeals, contrary to the person's right to be tried without undue delay.

We therefore are unable to agree with the Majority's proposition that the margin of deference which the Appeals Chamber gives to factual findings of the trial chamber "must be approached with extreme caution". We also find it difficult to understand what this should mean in practice. The obvious alternative for giving deference to the trial chamber's factual findings is a de novo review of all evidence. It is not clear, however, whether the Majority's choice for "extreme caution" means that it is prepared to carry out such review. At least in the present case, it appears that the Majority's review of evidence was, in fact, very limited, as will be discussed in more detail below. ("Dissenting Opinion, Appeal," 5–6)

Final Note

The acquittal is another setback for the Office of the Prosecutor, which has had its share of recent failures. With Sudanese president Omar al-Bashir (indicted March 2009) still at large, and the unsuccessful prosecution of Kenya's president, Uhuru Kenyatta, and his deputy, William Ruto, Bemba was the highest profile politician to have been convicted by the Court. The trial of Ivory Coast president Laurent Gbagbo still continues but at a snail's pace (it began on January 18, 2016).

The final prosecution witness completed her testimony on January 29, 2018. Due to challenges to the accuracy of supporting documents, and the extent and nature of the evidence presented by the prosecutor, the trial had not resumed as of midsummer 2018. In early June 2018, the Trial Chamber had directed the two sides to remedy the gaps and errors accepted as necessary by the court ("Bemba Decision").

The ICC faces a major crisis. After Belgian authorities apprehended Bemba in 2008, Luis Moreno-Ocampo declared: "With the Rome Statute, nobody is beyond the reach of international justice. Nobody can side with the criminals and against the victims.... International human rights justice is in motion (quoted in Grono, 2008)." Ten years later, that hope and promise seem more than a little out of touch with contemporary reality. The Court has held very few trials given the wide range of its investigations. The recent trials clearly demonstrate the hazards and the deficiencies of trials as a method for dealing with incidents of mass atrocity.

Advocates argue that trials provide an important and historical function by investigating, examining, and illuminating the details of cases as well as dispensing a rough justice, particularly to the leaders, planners, and organizers regardless of their position. A byproduct would be the positive impact on advancing the cause of international human rights through the interpretation of substantive law as well as the development of appropriate process. But, trials by their nature seem an extraordinarily awkward, slow, and expensive way to deal with the types of problems presented by genocide and mass atrocity. Negatives flow from what critics perceive as the inherent limitations of the judicial process: inflexibility, cost, scope, and time necessary for trials. The "fairness" that underpins ideas of justice comes at a considerable cost in other values.

For the court truly to serve a deterrent effect for the future, it must expedite its procedures and accelerate the pace of investigations. Yet, to do so demands additional funding at a point where some may question the monies currently spent for the results achieved. The key to a more effective operation lies in overcoming the indifference of the many and the outright hostility of the few. Getting more vigorous support is difficult in a world where three of the five permanent members of the UN Security Council have not ratified the Rome Statute and seemingly have little interest in ever joining. This severely limits the possibility of garnering the political support to bring high-level individuals who abuse power to justice in a timely fashion.

References

"Bemba Decision Concerning the Prosecutor's Submission of Documentary Evidence on 28 April, 31 July, 15 and 22 December 2017, and 23 March and 21 May 2018." *The Prosecutor v. Laurent Gbagbo and Charles Blé Goudé*, ICC-02/11-01/15 (2 June 2018). https://www.icc-cpi.int/Pages/record.aspx?docNo=ICC-02/11-01/15-1172.

"Dissenting Opinion (Appeal)." *The Prosecutor v. Jean-Pierre Bemba Gombo* (Situation in the Central African Republic), Appeals Chamber, ICC-01/05-01/08-3636. https://www.icc-cpi.int/RelatedRecords/CR2018_02987.PDF.

Grono, Nick. 2008. "The International Criminal Court: Success or Failure?" Open Democracy (June 9, 2008). https://www.opendemocracy.net/article/the-international-criminal-court-success-or-failure.

Kisangani, Emizet François. 2012. *Civil Wars in the Democratic Republic of Congo, 1960–2010.* Boulder, CO: Lynne Rienner.

"Majority Opinion (Appeal)." *The Prosecutor v. Jean-Pierre Bemba Gombo* (Situation in the Central African Republic), Appeals Chamber, ICC-01/05-01/08-3636-Red. https://www.icc-cpi.int/Transcripts/CR2018_02994.PDF.

Mealor, Bryan. 2009. *All Things Must Fight to Live: Stories of War and Deliverance in Congo.* New York: Bloomsbury USA.

Prunier, Gérard. 2009. *Africa's World War: Congo, the Rwandan Genocide, and the Making of a Continental Catastrophe.* Oxford: Oxford University Press.

Stearns, Jason. 2011. *Dancing in the Glory of Monsters: The Collapse of the Congo and the Great War of Africa.* New York: Public Affairs Press.

"UN Condemns DR Congo Cannibalism." 2003. BBC News (January 15). http://news.bbc.co.uk/2/hi/africa/2661365.stm.

Index

Agius, Carmel, 269, 270, 271
Akayesu, Jean-Paul, 195, 257, 304; background, 289; trial, 290–295
Aktion Reinhard, 151
Aktion T-4, 109
Allied Control Council Law No. 10, 104–108
Almers, Kurt, 48
Ambros, Otto, 67
American Civil War, 5–8
American Colonization Society, 315
American Medical Association, 110–111
Amin, Idi, 201
Annan, Kofi, 317, 320, 332
Araki, Sadao, 126t
Arendt, Hannah, 158
Armée de Libération du Congo (LAC), 361, 363–364
Attritionists, 55
Auschwitz, 56, 64–66, 68, 73, 74–76, 100

Bagosora, Théoneste, 281–282; background, 296–297; sentencing, 302–303, 304; trial, 298–302
Bakic, Jovo, 264
Barahinura, Jean Shyirambere, 307
Barayagwiza, Jean-Bosco, 306; background, 307–308; trial, 309–314
Barker, Frank, 161, 162, 166
Bashir, Omar al-, 340, 370
Bataan Death March, 2, 38
Battle of Midway, 2
Battle of Solferino, 3
Battle of the Bulge, 85
Belligerents, 10–11
Bellinger, John, 339
Belsen trial, 68–77
Bemba Gombo, Jean-Pierre: Appeals Chamber decision, 368–371; Armée de Libération du Congo (LAC), 363–364; background, 360; Congo Wars, 360–361; indictment and arrest, 362–363; presidential election of 2006, 362; trial, 364–368
Bendel, Dr., 64
Bender, Omer, 246
Bergdahl, Bowe, 302
Bergen-Belsen. *See* Belsen trial
Bethmann-Hollweg, Theobald von, 20
Biagini, Erna, 63, 65
Bimko, Ada, 73
Bix, Herbert, 125, 133
Bizimana, Augustin, 281–282, 298, 301–302
Bizimungu, Augustin, 298
Blair, Tony, 204
Blaškić, Tihomir, 264–265, 267
Blome, Kurt, 111, 112, 113
Boban, Mate, 266
Bockarie, Samuel (Mosquito), 322, 323
Bokassa, Jean-Bédel, 201
Boldt, John, 20t, 23, 24, 27
Booh-Booh, Jacques-Roger, 282
Borger, Julian, 263
Bormann, Martin, 96t, 98
Bosnia, 227–228, 240
Bosnia and Herzegovina, 212
Bosnian Serb Army, 254
Bosnian Wars, 212–213
Bouhler, Philipp, 112–113
Boutros-Ghali, Boutros, 256
Bozizé, François, 362
Brandt, Karl, 109, 111, 112–113
Braun, Willie, 87
Broad, Perry, 64
Browning, Christopher, 55
Broz, Josip, 202
Buchenwald trial, 78–84

Bülow, Bernhard von, 20
Bursin, Valentin, 87–88
Burundi, 275, 276
Bush, George W., 338, 339

Calley, William Laws, Jr.: aftermath, 170–171; background, 161; My Lai Massacre and investigation, 162; trial, 165–170
Capture, 14
Central African Republic (CAR), 361, 362–363, 367
Čerkez, Mario, 264
Čermak, Ivan, 267, 268
Cesarani, David, 150, 158
Chamberlain, Neville, 39
Charlie Company, 161, 162
Charter of the United Nations. *See* United Nations charter
Chemical and biological weapons, 33–35
Chemical warfare, 58–59
China: bacteriological weapons program, 141–147; and Japan, 130
Chivalric code, 3
Chrétien, Jean-Pierre, 310
Christ, Friedrich, 88–89
Clausewitz, Carl von, 1–2, 6
Clay, Lucius, 84, 91
Clinton, Bill, 241, 338
CO Rocky, 324
Collective responsibility, 17
Commission on the Responsibility of the Authors of the War and on Enforcement of Penalties: World War I, 17–18
Concentration camps, 54–57, 78. *See also* Auschwitz; Belsen trial; Buchenwald trial; Ethnic cleansing; Final Solution; Zyklon B
Confiscation, 14
Congo Wars, 360–361
Conti, Leonardo, 111, 112, 113
Ćorić, Valentin, 266
Covenant of the League of Nations, 19, 28–32, 173
Croatia, 212–213, 227; Operation Storm, 263–273
Crucius, Benno, 20t

Dallaire, Roméo, 281, 282
Dayton Agreement, 228–229
Death camps, 78
Del Ponte, Carla, 265, 267

Demjanjuk, John, 148
Democratic Republic of the Congo, 360; background, 347–348
Des Forges, Alison, 275, 282
Diament, Gertrude, 74
Diels, Dr., 64
Dietrich, Josef, 89
Đinđić, Zoran, 231
Dithmar, Ludwig, 20t, 23, 24, 27
Doctor's Trial. *See* Medical Case (Doctor's Trial): *United States v. Karl Brandt, et al.*
Doe, Samuel, 315–316
Doihara, Kenji, 126t
Dönitz, Karl, 96t
Dostler, Anton, 44–53
Dover Castle trial, 21–23
Drina Corps of the Army of Republika Srpska, 254–255
Drosihn, Joachim, 62, 65
Dunant, Henry, 3, 4

Eden, Anthony, 40
Eichmann, Adolf, 97; background, 149–151; personality, 157–159; trial, 152–157
Einsatzgruppen Case: *United States of America v. Otto Ohlendorf, et al.*, 115–121
Elezovic, Hakija, 219–224
Elezovic, Salih, 220, 223
Elezovic, Samir, 220, 221
Ethnic cleansing, 213–214, 254, 263–264. *See also* Concentration camps; Final Solution
Euthanasia Program (Aktion T-4), 109
Everett, Willis M., 90–91
Extermination camps, 54–57

Filipovic, Esad, 246
Final Solution, 56–57, 60–61, 99, 149, 150–152. *See also* Concentration camps; Ethnic cleansing
Fisher, Shireen Avis, 325
Flomo, Boston, 324
Frank, Anne, 69
Frank, Hans, 96t
Frank, Margot, 69
Frankenstein problem, 58
Freyhofer, Horst, 114
Frick, Wilhelm, 96t
Fritzsche, Hans, 96t, 98
Führerbefehl, 44–46, 49, 50–51, 52–53

Funk, Walther, 96t
Furuichi (trial witness), 146
Futaki (research official), 144

Gahigi, Gaspard, 310, 312
Galang, Joaquin, 138
Gbagbo, Laurent, 340, 370
Gbao, Augustine, 324
Geffcken, Friedrich, 6
Geneva Conventions, 176–177, 193–194; Additional Protocols, 183–184; Common Articles, 182–183; Geneva Convention for the Amelioration of the Conditions of the Wounded and Sick in Armed Forces in the Field of August 12, 1949 (Geneva I), 177–178; Geneva Convention for the Amelioration of the Conditions of Wounded, Sick, and Shipwrecked Members of Armed Forces at Sea of August 12, 1949 (Geneva II), 178–179; Geneva Convention for the Protection of Civilian Persons in Time of War of August 12, 1949 (Geneva IV), 181–182; Geneva Convention Relative to the Treatment of Prisoners of War of August 12, 1949 (Geneva III), 179–181; Grave Breaches, 193; law and war, 3–5; prisoners of war (POWs), 35–38; Protocol Additional I, 184–187; Protocol Additional II, 187–191; Protocol Additional III, 191–192
Genocide, 261–262; Bagosora, Théoneste, 296–297; definition, 195; Rwanda, 287–289
Genocide Convention, 195–200
Germany: alliance with Japan, 123–124; Allied Control Council Law No. 10, 104–108; Belsen trial, 68–77; Buchenwald trial, 78–84; concentration and extermination camps, 54–57; Dostler, Anton, case, 44–53; *Dover Castle* trial, 21–23; Eichmann trial, 148–159; *Einsatzgruppen* Case: *United States of America v. Otto Ohlendorf, et al.*, 115–121; Holocaust, 40; Leipzig trials, 20–27; *Llandovery Castle* trial, 23–27; Malmedy massacre trial, 85–91; Medical Case (Doctor's Trial): *United States v. Karl Brandt, et al.*, 109–114; Nuremberg trial, 92–103; Treaty of Versailles, 19, 39; war crime trials, 40–41, 42; World War I, 17; Zyklon B trial, 58–67

Globke, Hans, 149
Goebbels, Joseph, 95
Gojovic, Radomir, 233–238
Göring, Hermann, 95, 96–97, 101; Medical Case, 109; Wannsee Conference, 151
Gotovina, Ante, 266–268, 269, 271
Gourevitch, Philip, 274
Grave Breaches, 193
Great Depression, 32, 39
Greiser, Governor, 112
Grese, Irma, 70, 72, 74
Güney, Mehmet, 269, 303
Guy, George, 135

Haber, Fritz, 58–59
Habimana, Kantano, 311
Habyarimana, Agathe, 296
Habyarimana, Juvénal, 276, 277, 280, 281, 282, 296, 297, 299, 306, 307, 308
Hadžić, Goran, 206
Hague Conventions, 8–13
Halleck, Henry, 5
Handloser, Siegfried, 111
Harris, Sheldon, 143
Hashimoto, Kingorō, 126t
Hassan, Omar, 339
Hata, Shunroku, 126t
Hatzfeld, Jean, 279, 312–313
Henderson, Oran, 162, 166, 170
Herzeg-Bosnia, 212–213
Heubeck, Second Lieutenant, 88
Heydrich, Reinhard, 57, 112; Eichmann trial, 149, 150, 156; Wannsee Conference, 151
Heynen, Karl, 20t
High Command case (*United States of America v. Wilhelm von Leeb et al.*), 139–140
Himmler, Heinrich, 41t, 56, 77, 86, 95, 97; Eichmann trial, 149, 150; *Einsatzgruppen* Case, 116, 118, 120; Medical Case, 111, 112
Hindenburg, Paul von, 20
Hiranuma, Kiichirō, 126t
Hirohito, 125–126
Hirota, Kōki, 126t
Hitler, Adolf: Brandt, Karl, 109, 112–113; early in Nazi Party, 39–40, 41; Eichmann, Adolf, 150; Final Solution, 60; Malmedy massacre, 85; Nazi oath, 72; suicide, 95; World War I, 19
Hofmański, Piotr, 370

Hollis, Brenda, 219, 224
Holocaust, 40
Homma, Masaharu, 134
Hoshino, Naoki, 126t
Höss, Rudolf: Auschwitz, 56, 75; Eichmann trial, 156; Nuremberg trial, 66, 68, 96t, 97, 98–101, 102
Hössler, Franz, 70, 73
Hostage case *(United States v. Wilhelm List)*, 139
Hoven, 113
Hughes, Glyn, 72
Hull, Cordell, 40
Human skins, 81–82
Hutu Ten Commandments, 277–279
Hutus, 275, 276; trial, 291–294

I.G. Farben, 66–67
Ikari, Lieutenant Colonel, 144–145
Interahamwe movement, 299–300
Internal armed conflicts, 187–191
International armed conflicts, 184–187
International Committee of the Red Cross, 3–5, 13
International Court of Justice (ICJ), 206
International Criminal Court (ICC), 206; Article 7 (Crimes against Humanity), 336–338; Article 9 (Elements of Crimes), 335–336; Article 16 (Deferral of Investigation or Prosecution), 334; background, 328–330; Bashir case, 340; crime of aggression, 340–346; Rome Statute, 330–332; structure and jurisdiction, 332–334; United States, 338–339
International criminal law (ICL), 102–103, 201
International Criminal Tribunal for Rwanda (ICTR), 195, 329, 332; Appeals Chamber, 207; Bagosora et al. trial, 297–304; establishment of, 283–284, 285–287; genocide, 287–289; mechanism for international tribunals, 208–209; Office of the Prosecutor, 208; problems, 209–211; structure, 206–207
International Military Tribunal (IMT), 92–94, 104
International Military Tribunal for the Far East (IMTFE), 94, 123–133
International Prize Court, 10
International Tribunal for the Prosecution of Persons Responsible for Serious Violations of International Humanitarian Law Committed in the Territory of the Former Yugoslavia since 1991 (ICTY), 241, 242, 329, 332; Appeals Chamber, 207; background, 201–204; guilty pleas, 209; mandate, 204–206; mechanism for international tribunals, 208–209; Office of the Prosecutor, 208; problems, 209–211; *Prosecutor v. Radovan Karadžić*, 243–249; rules of procedure and evidence, 214–217; structure, 206–207; Tadić trial, 218–226
Ishii, Shirō, 141, 142–143
Itagaki, Seishirō, 126t
Ivan the Terrible, 148
Ivy, Andrew C., 110–111, 113
Izbeca, 238
Izetbegović, Alija, 241

Jackson, Robert H., 92, 95, 101
Japan: alliance with Germany, 123–124; bacteriological weapons program, 141–147; Geneva Convention, 38; Khabarovsk war crime trial, 141–147; Tokyo war crimes trial, 123–133; *Yamashita* case, 134–140
Jaynes, L. C., 44
Jews. *See* Final Solution; Holocaust
Jodl, Alfred, 96t
Jungle, 324
Jus ad bellum, 1, 3, 32–33
Jus in bello, 1, 3

Kabbah, Ahmad Tejan, 317, 320
Kabila, Joseph, 348, 361–362
Kabila, Laurent-Désiré, 347, 348, 360, 361
Kabiligi, Gratien, 282, 297, 298, 299
Kagame, Paul, 276, 277, 280, 340
Kaltenbrunner, Ernst, 96t
Kangura, 305–307, 308
Kanneh, Eddie, 323
Kapos, 76–77
Karabasić, Emir, 213
Karadjić, Radovan, 264
Karađorđević, Peter, 202
Karadžić, Radovan, 210, 212, 228; appeal, 250–253; background, 240–242; conviction, 249–250; Serbian Democratic Party, 254; trial, 243–249
Karasawa (trial defendant), 146–147
Kaya, Okinori, 126t

Kayibanda, Grégoire, 275–276
Keenan, Joseph, 127
Keitel, Wilhelm, 96t
Kellogg, Frank, 33
Kellogg-Briand Pact, 32–33, 173
Kelsen, Hans, 132
Kenyatta, Uhuru, 340, 370
Kesselring, Field Marshall, 50
Khabarovsk war crime trial, 141–147
Kido, Kōichi, 126t
Kilolo Musamba, Aimée, 364
Kimura, Heitarō, 126t
Kingdom of Serbs, Croats, and Slovenes, 202
Kissinger, Henry, 338
Kiyoshi, Kawashima, 144, 146
Klein, Fritz, 70–71, 72, 73
Klement, Ricardo, 149
Koch, Ilse, 79–80, 81, 84
Koch, Karl-Otto, 79–80
Koiso, Kuniaki, 126t, 127
Konoe, Fumimaro, 127
Kordić, Dario, 263, 264; Lašva Valley Ten, 265–266
Kosovo, 229–231
Kosovo Liberation Army (KLA), 230
Koster, Samuel, 162, 170
Koštunica, Vojislav, 231
Kraft, George, 72
Kralj, Sinisa, 263
Kramer, Josef, 70, 71, 72, 73, 74
Krstić, Radislav, 228; appeal, 260–262; background, 254–255; Srebrenica Massacre, 255–256; trial, 256–260
Krupp von Bohlen und Halbach, Gustav, 96t, 98
Kruska, Benno, 20t
Kwon, O-Gon, 247–248

Lapus, Narciso, 138
Lašva Valley massacres, 263
Lašva Valley Ten, 265–266, 267
Laule, Adolph, 20t
Law and war, 2–3; Hague Conventions, 8–13; Lieber Code, 5–8
Law of war, 6–8
Lawrence, Geoffrey, 95
Laws of War, 136
Le Druillenec, Harold O., 73
League of Nations, Covenant of the, 19, 28–32, 173
Leipzig trials, 20–27

Lemarchand, René, 274
Lemkin, Raphael, 103, 195, 199
Lenin, Vladimir, 118
Ley, Robert, 95, 96t
Liberia: background, 315–317; Sierra Leone, 316–317; Taylor trial, 321–226
Lieber, Francis, 5–6
Lieber Code, 5–8
Lifton, Robert J., 109
Litwinska, Sophia, 73
Liu Daqun, 303
Llandovery Castle trial, 23–27
Lobowitz, Klara, 74
Lomé Peace Accord, 317, 320
London Charter, 92–94, 94–95, 101, 102–103
Lothe, Ilse, 72
Lubanga Dyilo, Thomas: background, 348; legal issues prior to trial, 352; referral and arrest, 348–352; trial, 355–359; trial proceeding stays, 353–355
Ludendorff, Erich, 20

MacArthur, Douglas, 94, 123, 125, 127, 134, 137, 141
Mafuta, Eloy, 357
Makelo, Sinafesi, 368
Malmedy massacre trial, 85–91
Manchester, William, 124
Manchuria, 33
Mandro, Yves Kahwa Panga, 357
Mandzic, Nesib, 257–260
Manhattan Project, 58
Maritime warfare, 12–13
Markać, Mladen, 267, 268, 269, 271
Marx, Dr., 63
Marzah, Joseph (Zigzag), 322–323
Matsui, Iwane, 126t
Matsuoka, Yōsuke, 126t, 128
McAuliffe, Anthony, 85
McCloy, John J., 105
McDonald, Gabrielle Kirk, 218
McNarney, Joseph T., 44
Meadlo, Paul, 166–167, 169, 170
Medical Case (Doctor's Trial): *United States v. Karl Brandt, et al.*, 109–114
Medical experiments, 81, 82; Medical Case, 109–114
Medical symbols, 191–192
Medina, Ernest, 161, 162, 166, 170
Mengele, Josef, 66, 74, 76, 111
Meron, Theodor, 269, 273, 303

Merton, Thomas, 157–158
Milanovic, Zoran, 263
Mildenstein, Leopold (Edler) von, 149
Mildner, Rudolf, 100
Military necessity, 6–7
Milošević, Slobodan, 202, 212; background, 227–228; Dayton Agreement, 228–229; indictment and transfer, 231; Izbeca, 238; Karadžić, Radovan, 240; Kosovo, 229–231; mixed legacy, 238–239; trial, 231–238
Minami, Jirō, 126t
Mladić, Ratko: arrest, 206, 242; Karadžić, Radovan, 241, 247; Krstić, Radislav, 256; Srebrenica, 243, 255; Vojska Republike Srpske (VRS), 228, 254
Mobutu, Joseph (Mobutu Sese Seko), 347, 360
Monageng, Sanji Mmasenono, 370
Mongor, Isaac, 323–324
Moreno-Ocampo, Luis, 371
Morgenthau, Henry, 40
Morris, Technician Fifth Grad, 89–90
Motlke, Helmuth von, 20
Mouvement de Liberation du Congo (MLC), 361, 362, 367–368
Mpiranya, Protais, 298
Mrugowsky, Joachim, 113
Mueller, Dr., 81, 118
Mukiza, Moustapha, 363, 365–366
Müller, Emil, 20t
Murphy, Frank, 139
Museveni, Yoweri, 276, 340
Mutō, Akira, 126t
My Lai Massacre, 160–172

Nagano, Osami, 126t, 128
Nahimana, Ferdinand, 306; background, 308–309; trial, 309–314
Nalic, Nafija, 245
Napoleon III, Emperor, 3
Nationalsozialistische Deutsche Arbeiterpartei (NSDAP). *See* Nazi Party
Naval warfare, 13–16
Nazi Party: Allied Control Council Law No. 10, 104–108; Belsen trial, 68–77; Buchenwald trial, 78–84; concentration and extermination camps, 54–57; Eichmann trial, 148–159; *Einsatzgruppen* Case: *United States of America v. Otto Ohlendorf, et al.,* 115–121; Final Solution, 60–61; Haber, Fritz, 59; Malmedy massacre trial, 85–91; Medical Case (Doctor's Trial): *United States v. Karl Brandt, et al.,* 109–114; Nuremberg trial, 92–103; organizations, 41t; origin, 39–40
Ndindiliyimana, Augustin, 298
Neumann, Karl, 20t, 21, 23–25, 26–27
Neumann, Robert, 20t
Neurath, Konstantin, 96t
Ngeze, Hassan, 277, 306, 307, 309; trial, 309–314
Nice, Geoffrey, 232, 238
Nicholas II, Tsar, 8
Nicholls, Julian, 246, 248
Nixon, Richard, 170
Nkurunziza, Pierre, 340
Norimitsu, Kikuchi, 147
Nsengiyumva, Anatole, 298, 299, 302–303
Ntabakuze, Aloys, 297, 298, 299
Ntaganda, Bosco, 357
Ntaryamira, Cyprien, 281
Ntiwiragabo, Aloys, 282, 298
Nuremberg Charter, 92–94
Nuremberg military tribunals, 107t
Nuremberg trial, 92–103
Nzuwonemeye, François-Xavier, 298

Obama, Barack, 339
Obote, Milton, 276
Ohlendorf, Otto, 116, 117–119, 120
Oka, Takazumi, 126t
Okawa, Shumei, 128
Operation Storm, 263–273
Oppenheimer, J. Robert, 58
Orentlicher, Diane, 313
Ōshima, Hiroshi, 126t
Oxford Handbook of International Law in Armed Conflict, 6, 27

Pal, Radhabinod, 130, 132, 133
Papen, Franz von, 96t, 98
Patassé, Ange-Félix, 362
Patriotic Force for the Liberation of the Congo (FPLC), 350–351, 348
Patterson, Robert P., 110
Patton, George, 85
Patzig, Helmut, 23–25, 26–27
Paybody, J. Douglas, 69
Pearl Harbor, 124
Peers, William, 162
Peiper, Joachim, 85, 86, 87, 89

Perišić, Momĉilo, 266
Petković, Milivoj, 266
Pflueger, Sergeant, 88
Philippines, 134, 136–138
Pinkville, 161
Pister, Hermann, 80, 81
Plavšić, Biljana, 241
Pocar, Fausto, 269, 270, 271, 303
Pokorny, Adolf, 111
Pol Pot, 201
Poland, invasion of, 54–55
Pook, Wilhelm, 63
Poppa Poppa, 290
Praljak, Slobodan, 266
Prisoners of war (POWs), 2; Geneva Conventions, 35–38, 179–181; Hague Conventions, 11–12; Japan, 125
Prizes of war, 10, 13–16
Prlić, Jadranko, 265–266
Productionists, 55
Prosecutor v. Jean-Bosco Barayagwiza, Ferdinand Nahimana, and Hassan Ngeze, 305–14
Prosecutor v. Théoneste Bagosora, Gratien Kabiligi, Aloys Ntabakuze, and Anatole Nsengiyumva (The Military Trial I), 297–304
Protection of civilian persons, 181–182
Prunier, Gérard, 274, 361
Public ships, 14
Pušić, Berislav, 266

Radakovic, Dragan, 222, 223
"Radio Machete" trial, 305
Radio Rwanda, 305–306
Raeder, Erich, 96t
Rambo, 324
Ramdohr, Max, 20t
Rascher, Sigmund, 111
Rashid, Rashid, 300
Ražnatović, Željko (Arkan), 264
Rees, Lawrence, 77
Renan, Ernest, 274
Renzaho, Tharcisse, 298
Resolution 96(1) (The Crime of Genocide), 195
Revolutionary United Front (RUF), 316–317
Ribbentrop, Joachim von, 96t
Ricarte, Artemio, 138
Rice, Condoleezza, 339
Richthofen, Manfred von, 96–97

Ridenhour, Ronald, 162
Robinson, Patrick, 232, 235, 236, 269, 303
Robinson, Peter, 249
Röling, Bert, 132
Rome Statute, International Criminal Court (ICC), 330–332
Roosevelt, Franklin, 124
Rosenberg, Alfred, 96t
Rostock, Paul, 111
RTLM (Radio-Télévision Libre des Mille Collines), 305–307, 308, 311–313
Ruehmling, Karl, 64
Rummel, R. J., 40
Rumsfeld, Donald, 338
Rutledge, Wiley, 139
Ruto, William, 370
Rwanda: genocide, 274–284, 287–289; Genocide Convention, 195–200; *Prosecutor v. Jean-Bosco Barayagwiza, Ferdinand Nahimana, and Hassan Ngeze,* 305–14. *See also* International Criminal Tribunal for Rwanda (ICTR)
Rwandan Patriotic Front (RPF), 276–277, 282–283, 290, 306, 307, 311
Rwigyema, Fred, 276, 277
Ryckmans, Pierre, 275

Saenger, General von, 50, 51
Sanišić, Jovica, 266
Sankoh, Foday, 317, 323
Satō, Kenryō, 126t
Saukel, Fritz, 96t
Schacht, Hjalmar, 96t, 98
Schack, Hans von, 20t
Scheer, Reinhold, 20
Schutzstaffel (SS), 41t
Security Section, 41t
Sehm, Emil, 63
Seizure, 14, 15
Semanza, Laurent, 304
Serbia, 227–228, 240
Serbian Democratic Party (Srpska Demokratska Stranka, SDS), 212, 240
Serbs: Operation Storm, 263–273
Sesay, Issa, 323, 324
Seyss-Inquart, Arthur, 96t
Shawcross, Hartley, 95
Shelley, Mary, 58
Shigemitsu, Mamoru, 126t
Shimada, Shigetarō, 126t
Shiratori, Toshio, 126t

Sicherheitsdienst (SD), 41t
Sierra Leone: diamonds, 316; Liberia, 316–317
Simatović, Franko, 266
Smith, Rupert, 241
Snyder, Timothy, 55, 69
Sonderbehandlung, 112
Sonderkommandos, SS, 56
Soviet Union: Geneva Convention, 38
Speer, Albert, 96t
Srebrenica Massacre, 255–256
Stabenow, Paul, 59
Stalin, Joseph, 40, 118, 119
Stenger, Karl, 20t
Stimson, Henry L., 40–41
Stojić, Bruno, 266
Stone, Harlan Fiske, 101, 139
Streckenbach, Lt. Col., 118
Streicher, Julius, 96t, 306
Sturmabteilung (SA), 41t
Suljagić, Emil, 232
Superior orders, 27, 160
Suzuki, Teiichi, 126t

Tadić, Duško, 210; background, 213–214; trial, 218–226
Tamba, Daniel, 324
Tarawalli, Mohamed, 324
Task Force Barker, 161
Taylor, Charles: appeal, 325–326; background, 315–317; trial, 321–226
Taylor, Telford, 95, 104, 110, 113, 114, 135
Tesch, Bruno, 59, 62, 63, 64–65
Tesch and Stabenow (Testa), 59, 62–63
Testa, 59
Thompson, Hugh, 162
Tirpitz, Alfred von, 20
Tito, Marshall, 202
Tōgō, Shigenori, 126t
Tōjō, Hideki, 125, 126t, 127
Tokyo war crimes trial, 123–133
Toshihide, Nishi, 144–145
Totenkopf verbände, 41t
Treaty of Versailles, 19, 31, 32, 39
Treblinka, 99–100
Truman, Harry, 95, 176
Trump, Donald, 339
Tuđman, Franjo, 212–213, 227, 241, 263, 264, 266, 268
Turk Bosniaks, 227

Tutsis, 274; genocide, 296–297; *Prosecutor v. Jean-Bosco Barayagwiza, Ferdinand Nahimana, and Hassan Ngeze,* 305–314; trial, 291–294
Twagiramungu, Faustin, 283

Uenzelmann, Anna, 63, 64
Uganda, 277
Umezu, Yoshijirō, 126t
UN Assistance Mission for Rwanda (UNAMIR), 281
UN Commission on Human Rights (UNCHR): Yugoslavia, 202–203
UN General Assembly (UNGA), 195
UN Security Council, 202–203
UN Special Court for Sierra Leone (SCSL) statute, 316, 317–321
Uniform Code of Military Justice, 160, 163–165
Union of Congolese Patriots (UPC), 348, 351
Unit 731 (Epidemic Prevention and Water Supply Unit 731), 142–143
United Nations charter, 173–176
United Nations Mission in Sierra Leone (UNAMISL), 317
United States and International Criminal Court (ICC), 338–339
United States of America v. Wilhelm von Leeb et al., 139–140
United States v. Karl Brandt, et al. See Medical Case (Doctor's Trial): *United States v. Karl Brandt, et al.*
United States v. Wilhelm List, 139
Ustaše Croats, 227
Uwilingiyimana, Agathe, 281
Uzar, Ivo, 245

Van den Wyngaert, Christine, 369, 370
Vandergrift, Alexander, 124
Vietnam War: My Lai Massacre, 160–172
Vojska Republike Srpske (VRS), 254
Volkenrath, Elisabeth, 70, 72
Vucic, Aleksandar, 263–264

Waffen SS, 41t
Waldeck-Pyrmont, Josias Prince zu, 79, 80, 81
Wannsee Conference, 151
Wantee, Tiagen, 323
War and armed conflict, 1

War and law. *See* Law and war
War crime, 1, 2
Webb, William, 127
Weinbacher, Karl, 62, 65
Weingartner, Peter, 70, 72, 76
White, Private, 89–90
Wiesel, Elie, 79
Wilhelm, Kaiser, 17, 18, 20, 102, 340
William II of Hohenzollern, 19
Williams, Emmanuel, 324
Wilson, Sergeant, 90
Wilson, Woodrow, 28, 29, 32
Winter, Renate, 325
Winwood, Major, 76
World War I: Germany, 17; Leipzig trials, 20–27; *Llandovery Castle* trial, 23–27; Treaty of Versailles, 19
World War II, 39; *Dover Castle* trial, 21–23; Nuremberg trial, 92–103
Wounded and sick: in field, 177–178; at sea, 178–179

Yamada, Otozō, 143–144
Yamashita, Tomoyuki, 134–140, 165
Yeaten, Benjamin, 323
Yugoslav Peoples' Army (JNA), 254
Yugoslavia, 201–211

Zangen, Gustav-Adolf von, 48, 49, 50, 51
Zaun, Alfred, 64
Zivanović, Milenko, 228
Zulić, Ahmit, 244–246
Zyklon B, 97
Zyklon B trial, 58–67

About the Author

James Larry Taulbee is professor emeritus of political science, Emory University. His previous written work has focused on international security issues, mercenaries and private military companies (PMCs), human rights and peacemaking, the ad hoc international criminal courts and the evolution of international criminal law, issues in American foreign policy, and the politics of international law. His recent books include *Norway's Peace Policy* (coauthor, 2014), *Law among Nations*, 11th ed. (coauthor, 2017), *International Crime and Punishment* (2009), and *Genocide, Mass Atrocity, and War Crimes: Blood and Conscience* (2 vols., 2017). He was awarded an Arthur S. Heilbrun Jr. Distinguished Emeritus Fellowship for the academic year 2017–2018 to continue his work on mercenaries and PMCs.

www.ingramcontent.com/pod-product-compliance
Lightning Source LLC
Chambersburg PA
CBHW060505300426
44112CB00017B/2554